Restoring the Balance

First Nations Women, Community, and Culture

Maria Hupfield, *An Indian Act*
(Moccasins), 1997

Restoring the Balance

First Nations Women, Community, and Culture

Gail Guthrie Valaskakis, Madeleine Dion Stout,
and Eric Guimond, editors

University of Manitoba Press

© University of Manitoba Press 2009

University of Manitoba Press
Winnipeg, Manitoba
Canada R3T 2M5
www.umanitoba.ca/uofmpress

Printed in Canada on acid-free paper.

Cover and interior design: Relish Design Studio

Cover image: Robert Houle, *MorningStar*. Collection of Indian and Northern Affairs Canada. Photo by Lawrence Cook. Reproduced by permission of Robert Houle.

Library and Archives Canada Cataloguing in Publication

Restoring the balance : First Nations women, community, and culture / edited by Gail Guthrie Valaskakis, Madeleine Dion Stout, Eric Guimond.

Includes bibliographical references.

ISBN 978-0-88755-186-4 (bound).--ISBN 978-0-88755-709-5 (pbk.)

1. Indian women—Canada—Social conditions. 2. Indian women—Canada—History. 3. Women in community development—Canada. I. Valaskakis, Gail Guthrie II. Stout, Madeleine Dion III. Guimond, Eric

E98.W8R48 2009   305.48'897071   C2008-907736-9

All author royalties are being donated to the National Aboriginal Achievement Awards of Canada.

The University of Manitoba Press gratefully acknowledges the financial support for its publication program provided by the Government of Canada through the Book Publishing Industry Development Program (BPIDP), the Canada Council for the Arts, the Manitoba Arts Council, and the Manitoba Department of Culture, Heritage, Tourism and Sport.

Contents

ix • **Dedication**

xi • **Acknowledgements**

xiii • **Notes on Co-editors**

xv • **Notes on Contributors**

1 • **Introduction**
by Gail Guthrie Valaskakis, Madeleine Dion Stout,
and, Eric Guimond

11 • **Theme 1: Historic Trauma**

13 • Trauma to Resilience: Notes on Decolonization
by Cynthia C. Wesley-Esquimaux

35 • Contributions That Count: First Nations Women and Demography
by Cleo Big Eagle and Eric Guimond

69 • First Nations Women's Contributions to Culture
and Community through Canadian Law
by Yvonne Boyer

97 • **Theme 2: Intellectual and Social Movements**

99 • Leading by Action: Female Chiefs and the Political Landscape
by Kim Anderson

125 • Creating an Indigenous Intellectual Movement at Canadian
Universities: The Stories of Five First Nations Female Academics
by Jo-ann Archibald

149 • Reflections on Cultural Continuity through
Aboriginal Women's Writings
by Emma LaRocque

175 • Sisters in Spirit
by Anita Olsen Harper

201• **Theme 3: Health and Healing**

203 • Heart of the Nations: Women's Contribution
to Community Healing
by Marlene Brant Castellano

237 • A Relational Approach to Cultural Competence
by Gaye Hanson

265 • **Theme 4: Arts, Culture, and Language**

267 • A Culture of Art: Profiles of Contemporary First Nations
Women Artists
by Viviane Gray

283 • Looking for Stories and Unbroken Threads: Museum Artifacts
as Women's History and Cultural Legacy
by Sherry Farrell Racette

313 • The Role of First Nations Women in Language
Continuity and Transition
by Mary Jane Norris

355 • Bibliography

List of Illustrations

Accompanying the essays in this volume is a selection of artwork by First Nations women artists from the collection of Indian and Northern Affairs Canada, Ottawa. The editors selected pieces that reflect the themes found in this volume and contribute to the dialogue about cultural continuity and community resilience. These appear on Plates 1 to 9 in the colour pages following Page 270; five of the images are also reproduced in the lead pages of the thematic sections and in the frontispiece. The images on Plates 10 to 14 are discussed in Viviane Gray's chapter, "A Culture of Art: Profiles of Contemporary First Nations Women Artists."

272 • Jane Ash Poitras

276 • Shirley Cheechoo

276 • Daphne Odjig

278 • Susan Point

Colour Plates Following Page 270

1. Susan Point, *Survivor*, 1992.

2. Alice Olsen Williams, *Midewiwin Women's Colours*, 1999.

3. Maria Hupfield, *An Indian Act* (Moccasins), 1997.

4. Zoey Wood-Salomon, *Meeting with the Chiefs*, 1993.

5. Joane Cardinal-Schubert, *My Mother's Vision*, 1983

6. Katia Kurtness, *Fragment of Textile*, 2004.

7. Teresa Marshall, *Mikmaq Worldview*, 2005.

8. Katia Kurtness, *Our Language on 3 Lines*, 2004.

9. Jane Ash Poitras, *Magenta Earth Manitou*, 1986.

10. Joane Cardinal-Schubert, *In the Garden, My Mother's Vision*, 1987.

11. Still from *Bearwalker*, 2000.

12. Daphne Odjig, *In the Bosom of the Earth*, 1969.

13. Susan Point, *Flight*, 1994. Commissioned
by Vancouver International Airport Authority.

14. Ann Smith displaying her traditional Ravenstail
woven dance robe with leggings and apron.

Credits and Permissions

Page 272, photo courtesy of Clint Buehler. Page 276, photo courtesy of Shirley Cheechoo. Page 276, photo by Fred Cattroll. Page 278, photo courtesy of Susan Point. Plate 1, collection of Indian and Northern Affairs Canada; photo by Lawrence Cook; reproduced by permission of Susan Point (image also appears on Page 11). Plate 2, collection of Indian and Northern Affairs Canada; photo by Lawrence Cook; reproduced by permission of Alice Olsen Williams (image also appears on Page 201). Plate 3, collection of Indian and Northern Affairs Canada; photo by Lawrence Cook; reproduced by permission of Maria Hupfield (image also appears on frontispiece). Plate 4, collection of Indian and Northern Affairs Canada; photo by Lawrence Cook; reproduced by permission of Zoey Wood-Salomon (image also appears on Page 97). Plate 5, collection of Indian and Northern Affairs Canada; photo by Lawrence Cook; reproduced by permission of Joane Cardinal-Schubert. Plate 6, collection of Indian and Northern Affairs Canada; photo by Lawrence Cook; reproduced by permission of Katia Kurtness. Plate 7, collection of Indian and Northern Affairs Canada; photo by Lawrence Cook; reproduced by permission of Teresa Marshall (image also appears on Page 265). Plate 8, collection of Indian and Northern Affairs Canada; photo by Lawrence Cook; reproduced by permission of Katia Kurtness. Plate 9, collection of Indian and Northern Affairs Canada; photo by Lawrence Cook; reproduced by permission of Jane Ash Poitras. Plate 10, collection of Indian and Northern Affairs Canada; photo by Lawrence Cook; reproduced by permission of Joane Cardinal-Schubert. Plate 11, photo by Sophie Geraud; © Girls from the Backroads, 2000. Plate 12, collection of Indian and Northern Affairs Canada; photo by Lawrence Cook; reproduced by permission of Daphne Odjig. Plate 13, photo courtesy of Susan Point. Plate 14, photo courtesy of Brian Walker.

Dedication

Dedicated to the memory of Gail Guthrie Valaskakis, who passed on to the spirit world on July 19, 2007. Your contributions will live on in the spirit of cultural continuity embodied in this work. Your dedication to sharing all knowledge, Western and traditional, for the betterment of all, is a guide to compassion and reconciliation. We are immensely grateful for your teachings throughout the journey of this project and we miss you.

Acknowledgements

WE WOULD LIKE TO THANK some of the many people who poured so much energy into this project. First, the book was shaped by the contributions of representatives of federal government departments and academic institutions who served on an advisory committee and provided many of the initial ideas on how to develop this project, as well as suggestions on the various topics. Among these individuals were Lila Duffy, Director of Women's Issues and Gender Equality, Indian and Northern Affairs Canada (INAC); Cleo Big Eagle, Senior Policy Officer at Aboriginal Affairs Directorate, Human Resources and Social Development Canada; Viviane Gray, Curator of the Indian and Inuit Art Centre, INAC; and David Newhouse, Chair of Indigenous Studies, Trent University. Second, staff within the Strategic Research and Analysis Directorate at INAC contributed substantial time and effort with respect to this project. These staff included Norma Chamberlain and Norma Lewis-Hartwick, who performed the myriad of administrative tasks necessary to get a manuscript ready; Stephanie Markovich, who contacted artists; and, most important, Beverlee Moore, who coordinated the call for papers and selection of authors and kept everyone on track. Third, senior bureaucrats at INAC—namely, Dan Beavon and Sandra Ginnish—supported the development of this book. We are indebted to all of the individuals mentioned above for their support and assistance. Above all, however, this book could not have been produced without all Aboriginal women who have worked tirelessly over the past seven generations to create better lives for the seven generations to come.

Notes on Co-editors

GAIL GUTHRIE VALASKAKIS

Gail Guthrie Valaskakis was a distinguished professor emeritus of Concordia University in Montreal, where she had served as dean, Faculty of Arts and Science; vice-dean, academic planning; chair of the Department of Communication Studies; and director of the MA program in media studies. In addition, Ms. Guthrie Valaskakis was a founding member of the boards of Waseskun Healing Lodge, the Montreal Native Friendship Centre (on which she served as secretary and president), the Native North American Studies Institute, and Manitou Community College. She served on the advisory boards of the National Film Board's New Initiatives in Film program for women of colour and women of the First Nations, and Studio One, the First Nations Studio. Ms. Guthrie Valaskakis personally researched the social and cultural change of Aboriginal peoples for three decades. Her writings on the development and impact of northern and Native communications, and on issues of Aboriginal cultural studies are widely published.

Gail Guthrie Valaskakis's background was Chippewa and she was raised on the Lac du Flambeau reservation in Wisconsin. She received a National Aboriginal Achievement Award in 2002 for her contributions to Aboriginal media and communications.

MADELEINE DION STOUT

Madeleine Dion Stout speaks Cree and was born and raised on the Kehewin First Nation in Alberta. She served as professor in Canadian studies and was the founding director of the Centre of Aboriginal Education, Research and Culture at Carleton University until 2001. Ms. Dion Stout also served as president of the Aboriginal Nurses Association of Canada. She earned a bachelor's degree in nursing from the University of Lethbridge, holds a master's degree in international affairs from Carleton University and received an honorary doctor of laws degree from the University of British Columbia in 2004. Madeleine has authored and co-authored several reports pertaining to Aboriginal health and gender. Ms. Dion Stout remains actively involved in Aboriginal health development and serves as an honorary professor at the School of Nursing at the University of British Columbia.

ERIC GUIMOND

Eric Guimond is of Mi'kmaq and French descent, born and raised in Montreal. He has earned both master's and PhD degrees in demography at the Université de Montréal. His educational background includes community health, physical education, and Aboriginal studies. Mr. Guimond is currently assistant-director at the Strategic Research and Analysis Directorate at Indian and Northern Affairs Canada. He also serves as adjunct research professor in the Department of Sociology at the University of Western Ontario and research associate at the Centre Interuniversitaire d'Études Démographiques in Montreal. Prior to joining these organizations, he collaborated on the development of electricity demand forecast models for Hydro-Québec International and served as a population projections expert at Statistics Canada. Mr. Guimond has published extensively in the areas of Aboriginal well-being, changes in self-reporting of Aboriginal identity, and Aboriginal youth.

Notes on Contributors

KIM ANDERSON

Kim Anderson (Cree/Métis) is the author of *A Recognition of Being: Reconstructing Native Womanhood* (Sumach Press, 2000) and the co-editor, with Bonita Lawrence, of *Strong Women Stories: Native Vision and Community Survival* (Sumach Press, 2003). Ms. Anderson has an MA from the Ontario Institute of Studies of Education and is currently completing her PhD studies in the Department of History at the University of Guelph.

JO-ANN ARCHIBALD

Jo-ann Archibald, Q'um Q'um xiiem, from the Sto:lo Nation, is an associate professor in the Faculty of Education at the University of British Columbia. Ms. Archibald received a bachelor of education degree from the University of British Columbia, and a master of education degree and PhD from Simon Fraser University. She is currently the associate dean of the newly established Indigenous Education Institute of Canada, which is sponsored by the Faculty of Education at the University of British Columbia. She received a National Aboriginal Achievement Award in 2000 for her work in education.

CLEO BIG EAGLE

Cleo Big Eagle is Nakoda (Assiniboine) from the Ocean Man First Nation in Saskatchewan. She is currently working as a senior policy advisor in the Aboriginal Affairs Directorate of Human Resources and Social Development Canada. She has over twenty-five years of work experience specializing in Aboriginal human resources, which include policy development and program delivery. Ms. Big Eagle has completed a degree in management development studies at the University of Manitoba, and is currently furthering her university education in community economic development.

YVONNE BOYER

Yvonne Boyer is a member of the Law Society of Saskatchewan and the Law Society of Upper Canada. She specializes in Aboriginal health law and policy. In 2002, she joined the National Aboriginal Health Organization, where she worked as the legal advisor/senior policy analyst and wrote the discussion paper series, *Aboriginal Health: Legal Issues*. Ms. Boyer currently practises law and is enrolled in the PhD program in law at the University of Ottawa.

MARLENE BRANT CASTELLANO

Marlene Brant Castellano, a member of the Mohawk Nation, Bay of Quinte Band, has pursued a number of careers: social worker in child and family services, a full-time wife and mother launching four sons into the world, professor and chair of Native studies at Trent University, and co-director of research for the Royal Commission on Aboriginal Peoples. She currently serves on the Interagency Advisory Panel on Research Ethics, which is charged with advising the presidents of the Canadian Institutes of Health Research, the National Sciences and Engineering Research Council, and the Social Sciences and Humanities Research Council on updating the Tri-Council Policy Statement on Research Ethics.

She holds a BA degree from Queen's University, a master's of social work degree from the University of Toronto, and has completed graduate study in the field of adult education at Ontario Institute for Studies in Education. Ms. Brant Castellano was awarded the title professor emerita on her retirement from Trent University in 1996. She received an honorary LLD from Queen's University in 1991, from St. Thomas University in 1992, and from Carleton University in 2004. She was inducted into the Order of Ontario in 1995 and in 1996 received a National Aboriginal Achievement Award for her contribution to education. In February 2005, the Governor General announced Ms. Brant Castellano's appointment as an officer of the Order of Canada.

VIVIANE GRAY

Viviane Gray is a member of the Mi'kmaq First Nation of Listuguj, Quebec. Viviane holds a bachelor of arts degree in anthropology and French from Carleton University and is a graduate of St. Francis Xavier University in community development and international relations. Ms. Gray has over forty years of experience in the field of contemporary Canadian Aboriginal art as a visual artist, including being Aboriginal arts coordinator for the Canada Council for the Arts and member of the Norval Morrisseau Heritage Society. She has occupied the position of curator of the Indian and Inuit Art Centre at the Department of Indian and Northern Affairs Canada since 1989.

P. GAYE HANSON

Gaye Hanson is an Aboriginal nurse consultant working with Aboriginal communities in Canada. As a former deputy minister of Health and Social Services in Yukon and former president of the Aboriginal Nurses Association of Canada, Ms. Hanson is well experienced in building relationships in a context of diversity. She demonstrates a passion for people in leading her consulting company with a focus on health and Aboriginal issues. Building on her Cree background and degrees in nursing and public administration, she is working in the areas of knowledge translation, palliative care, cultural competence, and quality of work life.

ANITA OLSEN HARPER

Anita Olsen Harper is Ojibwa from the Lac Seul First Nation, Ontario. Her undergraduate degree is in adult education from the University of Alberta, her graduate degree is in heritage conservation from Carleton University, and she is pursuing a PhD in education at the University of Ottawa. The focus of her doctoral studies is community-led anti-violence interventions in Aboriginal communities. Her research with the National Aboriginal Circle Against Family Violence over the past several years has focussed on violence against Aboriginal women.

EMMA LAROCQUE

Dr. Emma LaRocque is a scholar, author, professor, poet, and human rights advocate. She grew up in a Cree-speaking, hunting/trapping Métis culture in northeastern Alberta. Dr. LaRocque has written extensively in the areas of colonization, Canadian historiography, racism, identity, violence against women, and Aboriginal literatures. Dr. LaRocque is a leading figure in the growth and development of Native studies as a teaching discipline and intellectual field of study at the University of Manitoba, where she has been teaching for three decades.

MARY JANE NORRIS

Mary Jane Norris is a former senior research manager with the Strategic Research and Analysis Directorate of the Department of Indian and Northern Affairs Canada. She has specialized in Aboriginal studies and demography over the past twenty-five years and has published in the areas of Aboriginal languages, migration, and population projections. She is of mixed Aboriginal and non-Aboriginal ancestry, with family roots in the Algonquins of Pikwákanagán (Golden Lake) in the Ottawa Valley. Ms. Norris holds a master's degree in sociology and a BA (Honours) in sociology and economics from Carleton University.

SHERRY FARRELL RACETTE

Sherry Farrell Racette is an associate professor of art history at Concordia University, Montreal. She is a member of Timiskaming First Nation and has taught extensively in Aboriginal education, Native studies, and indigenous art. Ms. Farrell Racette received an interdisciplinary PhD (Native studies, history, and anthropology) from the University of Manitoba in 2004. As an interdisciplinary scholar with an active arts practice, she has illustrated seven children's books and contributed to a number of scholarly publications.

CYNTHIA C. WESLEY-ESQUIMAUX

Cynthia C. Wesley-Esquimaux has worked in the local, regional, and national Canadian Native political field as a treaty researcher, land claims coordinator, vice-chief, government and community advisor, and political advocate. Ms. Wesley-Esquimaux has written and co-negotiated several Ontario land claims, and has presented papers on historic trauma and Native health. In 2004, she completed her PhD dissertation at the University of Toronto in the Department of Anthropology. Over the past three decades, she has developed insight, compassion, an enduring optimism, and a genuine desire to work with Aboriginal people everywhere. Ms. Wesley-Esquimaux is currently assistant professor at the Factor-Inwentash Faculty of Social Work at the University of Toronto.

Introduction

Gail Guthrie Valaskakis, Madeleine Dion Stout,
and Eric Guimond

THERE IS AN UNPRECEDENTED LEVEL of interest in understanding how First
Nations individuals, families, and communities choose to locate themselves in
today's mainstream Canadian society. Drilling down into this locus exposes
power relations between First Nations and mainstream society, resistance to
assimilation, but, most importantly, it reveals a powerful commitment to self-
determination among First Nations peoples. As mainstream society and
scholars further recognize and explore this perspective, however, one critical
part is absent from the emerging discourse on self-determination, both in oral
and written forms: the contribution of First Nations women to their culture
and communities. This book attempts to address this absence by bringing
together the writings of Aboriginal women, both academics and activists,
from many different backgrounds and perspectives, presenting their views on
cultural continuity and community development.

First Nations women have long struggled for cultural continuity and
community development, trying to reconcile the numerous disconnects
between their holistic world view and the Western world view that is so often
atomistic, mechanistic, and antagonistic. Those disconnects have created for
First Nations an array of poverties. The "deficit analysis" genre of literature—
studies that focus on the disparities between First Nations and mainstream

Canadian society—has most often portrayed First Nations families and communities as becoming increasingly isolated from the mainstream as a result of their social dysfunctions and state of cultural turmoil—for example, lack of education, overcrowded and substandard housing, addictions, unplanned pregnancies, domestic violence—brought about by five centuries of colonization.

Contrary to the ever-expanding emphasis on studying the problems of First Nations, which inadvertently perpetuates the social stigmatization of First Nations, this book reflects a more positive perspective that directs energy, time, and resources to those areas most likely to support the tangible actions First Nations women have taken to protect their culture and promote their communities. In these actions, women are guardians of indigenous traditions, practices, and beliefs—and agents of change for their families and nations. Fittingly, the writings in this book by Canadian Aboriginal women emphasize the resilience and pragmatism First Nations women have demonstrated in response to their multiple burdens and challenges over time. These women are writing about a locally focussed and future-oriented cultural and community revival, characterized by a heavy lean against colonization and Eurocentric structures. This body of work portrays First Nations women in a novel and positive way while suggesting options for sustained improvement of their individual, family, and community well-being. The contributors present their material often through life histories and biographical accounts as well as in historical and balanced analyses, grounded, for the most part, in traditional thought and approaches.

RESILIENCE AND PRAGMATISM

In basic terms, "resilience" means getting along, getting through, and getting out of a difficult situation. In mainstream society, it is most easily understood as the "capacity to be bent without breaking and the capacity, once bent, to spring back."[1] A resilient person usually manages to have a good life outcome, often with a steady job, long-term relationships, and lack of mental illness despite exposure to situations with emotional, mental, or physical distress.[2] Recently, the term *indigenous resilience* has been applied to indigenous peoples, defined by Mason Durie, a Maori scholar from New Zealand, as follows: "Superimposed on adversity and historic marginalisation, indigenous resilience is a reflection of an innate determination by indigenous peoples to succeed. Resilience is the polar opposite of rigidity. It provides an alternate perspective to the more usual scenarios that emphasize indigenous disadvantage and allows the indigenous challenge to be reconfigured as a search for success rather than an explanation for failure."[3]

The contributors to this book raise the importance of the resilience and pragmatism of First Nations women: despite the challenges First Nations women encounter, they continue to strive for the good of their communities and culture. First Nations women from diverse backgrounds are driven by a common goal of bringing relief to their problems in order to improve their opportunities and outcomes for the betterment of their communities and culture. This book presents an array of voices, opportunities, and solutions to issues often considered too large and complex to be resolved by individual efforts.

The book's contributors address the complementary roles and responsibilities of First Nations women in the context of their cultural, socio-economic, and political realities. They sound out the root causes of cultural loss and community failures. Many of these women have successfully navigated beyond gender and racial discrimination, and are moving toward the reforms that will bring lasting changes. The contributors assert the influence First Nations women have in shaping their own lives and those of others through their particular accounts of the women's strengths and assets who, in the end, are their own best resource.

The editors have organized these essays according to the following four themes: (1) historic trauma; (2) intellectual and social movement; (3) health and healing; and (4) arts, culture, and language. Today, there is a hunger for evidence about the benefits of self-determination for the well-being of First Nations communities, especially as it relates to the "not-always-visible" participation of First Nations women. Individually speaking, First Nations women's actions would appear modest to many, even to those who directly benefit from them. We propose in this book that it is necessary to consider these actions for their collective, long-term benefits to cultural continuity and community development, two keys pillars of self-determination of First Nations people. This book, we hope, will be an important tool for policy makers, educators, and community people.

HISTORIC TRAUMA

The notion of "historic trauma" refers to the cumulative wounds inflicted on First Nations people over their lifetime and across generations, and which often resulted in debilitating social, psychological, and physical conditions. Until now, much of the literature on the consequences and treatment of traumatic events has assumed relative homogeneity in trauma experience. Little differentiation has been acknowledged on the basis of race, gender, or class, despite the well-known salience of these variables in the construction and interpretation of human experience, an omission addressed by the contributors in this theme area. In their writing about First Nations women who have survived traumatic experiences, the contributors argue for a deeper understanding of external contributing factors, such as colonization and its outcomes.

Cynthia Esquimaux-Wesley is a former vice-chief of the United Anishnaabeg Councils and the Chippewa Tri-Council in Ontario, and PhD in anthropology. She uses the metaphor "walk backwards to the future" to analyze the destructive effects of historic trauma. She draws on several disciplines—health, psychology, sociology, anthropology, and history—to propose a model in which constant social and cultural disruptions in communities cluster in traumatic events and into a disease. In her chapter, she portrays First Nations women as the "known, knowing and knowledgeable" and offers a discussion of cultural reclamation and resiliency and the cultural glorification of frailty as potential redemptive forces.

Cleo Big Eagle, Nakoda from Ocean Man First Nation in Saskatchewan, distinguished alumna of the management development program for women at the University of Manitoba, and Eric Guimond, of Mi'kmaq and French descent from Montreal, PhD in demography, provide an empirical assessment of the contributions of First Nations women to their culture and communities. The authors focus their attention on four fundamental demographic themes. They first describe and discuss the issue of *who is being counted* in current large-scale surveys such as the Census of Canada. With the second topic, First Nations population growth, the authors dispel a few misconceptions about demographic dynamics. The third theme of this chapter is well-being and gender equality in First Nations, which has become a very fertile area of social and demographic research over the last decade. Finally, the authors highlight the need for increased attention on the topic of reproductive health, which is especially relevant to achieving gender equality and empowerment of women.

Yvonne Boyer, member of the Law Society of Saskatchewan and of Upper Canada, writes her chapter in two complementary parts. The first part describes how customary law traditions have constituted a powerful discursive resource for First Nations women whenever they have had to deal with assimilationist laws and policies. The second part of her chapter focuses on the discrimination First Nations women have experienced due to past provisions of the *Indian Act*. Boyer describes the community confusion and chaos related to the promulgation of Bill C-31 in 1985, and she applauds the resilience of Sandra Lovelace, who fought against the application of European patrilineal norms for defining who is First Nations.

INTELLECTUAL AND SOCIAL MOVEMENTS

Social movements are a type of group action. They are large informal group-ings of individuals or formal organizations focussed on specific political or social issues; in other words, on carrying out, resisting, or undoing a social change. In this section, the authors provide case studies and life histories of social and intellectual movements First Nations women have cultivated in response to the harmful effects of colonization. These effects include the ethno-political actions of male-dominated non-First Nations and First Nations political structures and organizations. Among the issues examined are current tensions between the sexes and groups that have emerged within the First Nations' struggle for self-determination.

First Nations women often see their inclusion in communities and nations in biological and cultural terms, with the imposition of the *Indian Act* being a significant historical and discriminatory marker. According to the contributors in this section, essential elements of traditions, including the attainment of cultural and community goals, are the impetus for the intellectual and social movements First Nations women drive and experience. Future progress will require political will, support for capacity building, and recognition of violence against women.

Kim Anderson, a Cree/Métis educator, writer, and co-editor of *Strong Women Stories: Native Vision and Community Survival*, presents a contemporary study of female chiefs that explores their conditions and experiences. Her descriptions portray women who are socially conscious, accountable, coopera-tive and community-oriented. What stands out most from the chiefs' stories is their sense of accountability to their people. The women speak in holistic terms, both about the issues they wish to address and about their efforts to engage all community members in the movement forward. Theirs is a leadership style grounded in, and responsive to, community.

Jo-ann Archibald, Q'um Q'um xiiem, from the Sto:lo Nation in British Columbia, a PhD with a specialization in education, attempts to sort out the range of challenges and victories of five Aboriginal women who have been part of the first wave of Aboriginal academics in Canada. She emphasizes these women's accomplishments in research, teaching, and administration, but she also discusses the ways they came to public prominence inside and outside academia. Archibald suggests that by pursuing specific objectives in academia, like language retention and culturally appropriate research ethics, broader objectives of cultural continuity and community development have been successfully promoted by these female academics.

Emma LaRocque is a Cree-speaking Métis prairie writer and PhD in interdisciplinary studies in history and English. She argues that writing is a potentially transformative instrument for First Nations women and those who write about them. LaRocque dispels the view that writers have to adopt monolithic and totalizing reports of First Nations women. Instead, she makes unequivocal arguments for capturing more fully those specific relationships that bind the women to their cultures and communities, and for challenging the structures that have impeded their progress thus far.

Anita Olsen Harper, Ojibwa from the Lac Seul First Nation in Ontario, is an activist and scholar of community-led anti-violence interventions in Aboriginal communities. Her contribution to this book begins by articulating the sacred roles and responsibilities First Nations women hold in common, and ends it with an account of the Sisters in Spirit Campaign, which is focussed on bringing attention to the fate of missing and murdered Aboriginal women. She describes how the notions of male superiority and female inferiority are imbedded historically. But she also expresses hope for the future because she sees civil society, personal testimonies, and supportive government policies as engaged in ending violence against First Nations women.

HEALTH AND HEALING

Finding parallels between traditional and modern conceptualizations of health, First Nations women underscore the importance of combining traditional and mainstream medicine. First Nations women play important roles as practitioners and transmitters of such knowledge. The literature is filled with studies examining the social and economic factors that affect the health and well-being of First Nations women in Canada. What becomes evident to the contributors in this section from this existing knowledge is the need for balancing the Western and traditional perspectives of health, the latter involving a dimension of First Nations spirituality that is absent from the mainstream discourse on health issues and solutions. Questions relating to the health and healing of First Nations women therefore should include the following: How does their health and healing compare to that of other groups? What might explain the observed differences in health and healing? What are the implications for planning and delivering health and healing programs to them? What substantive role have First Nations women played in this process?

Marlene Brant Castellano, a member of the Mohawk Nation, Bay of Quinte Band in Ontario, professor emerita at Trent University and officer of the Order of Canada, highlights the agency of First Nations women at an everyday and at an institutional level through a thirty-year retrospective of health and healing initiatives. She documents health assessment, planning, implementation, and evaluation processes in First Nations communities by tracking national and regional policy decisions and community involvement. Castellano calls for the integration of indigenous values, spirituality, and traditions into a contemporary setting—"cultural renewal is not about going back"—and for paying attention to nation building, enhancing communal spirit, and developing ethical communities.

Gaye Hanson, of northern Manitoba Cree descent, former president of the Aboriginal Nurses Association of Canada and former deputy minister of health and social services in Yukon, relies on traditional principles of respect, harmony, and honesty to inform her interpretation of cultural competence, which she sees in terms of compassion and solidarity. According to the author, cultural competence is the human relational capacity to seek and find compassionate understanding within, between, and among people of differing cultural backgrounds and perspectives. She critiques existing theories of this concept using the sweet grass braid as metaphor, weaving together oral tradition, personal experience, and the teachings of others working in the field.

ARTS, CULTURE, AND LANGUAGE

Studying community development and cultural continuity through an examination of cultural products like beadwork and artwork not only highlights the significance of women's household work for the economic survival of their family, but also reveals an aesthetic unique to First Nations women. In their traditional gender role behaviour, women have been shown to serve as the chief providers for—and sustainers of—their families over time. First Nations women have certain rights and duties as heads of households and as keepers of cultures. When First Nations women are able to direct the affairs of their communities, they do so because they are mothers and grandmothers who have accepted traditional and modern responsibilities in the material world. In terms of artistic genius, First Nations women have attained a remarkable place in the art world. The visual arts provide new economic opportunities and avenues for expression of contemporary First Nations artists. Due consideration has to be given to fully integrating their cultural products in mainstream art and curatorial communities in order that their work is properly interpreted and marketed.

Sherry Farrell Racette, member of Timiskaming First Nation in Quebec, a PhD in interdisciplinary studies in Native studies, history, and anthropology, traces the evolution of museum artifact collections from treasure chests and material evidence of empires to ethnographic objects, market goods, and works of art produced with women's minds and hands. She notes that most artifacts are made by women for men's use, and also that oppressive government policies were instrumental in the confiscation of ceremonial objects. Her chronological view reveals the story of women who preserved traditional values, while struggling to provide for their families in a world of rapid change.

Viviane Gray, member of the Mi'kmaq First Nation of Listuguj in Quebec and curator of the Indian and Inuit Art Centre at Indian and Northern Affairs, profiles contemporary First Nations women artists with a sense of urgency because, as an experienced curator, she has observed the dearth of literature on First Nations female artists in contemporary Canadian art history texts. Despite this, she notes that socially minded Aboriginal female artists and their work have gained international status in the art world. The personal contributions of First Nations women artists have reinforced the identity and definition of contemporary Aboriginal art in Canada.

Mary Jane Norris, of Algonquian descent from Pikwákanagán (Golden Lake) in Ontario, MA in sociology and economics, examines the state and outlook for First Nation languages from the perspective of First Nations women. Women play a significant role in the development and transmission of the language and culture to children. As revealed by her analysis of census data, parenting patterns and place of residence of First Nations women are powerful determinants of intergenerational transmission of First Nations languages. Her essay concludes with a discussion on the outlook for Aboriginal women in their roles in the revitalization and maintenance of their languages and cultures. It considers the challenges of language maintenance confronting women today, especially those in child-bearing years—challenges exacerbated by intermarriage, family dissolution, migration from communities, and urbanization.

FINAL THOUGHTS: THE IMPORTANCE OF GENDER BALANCE

First Nations believe the eagle flies with a female wing and a male wing, showing the importance of balance between the feminine and the masculine in the human condition. Consideration of the feminine and masculine contributes to a more complete understanding of gender relations and reinforces relationships. When First Nations women are marginalized and dehumanized to the extent that they go "missing," gender imbalance prevails and self-actualization is not possible either for communities or cultures. Fortunately, First Nations women have been tenacious in pursuing their dual roles as nurturers of families and keepers of cultures, rejecting an overemphasis on individualism and Eurocentric values and, at the same time, working toward legal, economic, and political equality. The contributors to this collection of essays understand how the feminine, like the masculine, is a major and necessary resource in bringing about community cohesion and cultural continuity.

Notes

1   George Vaillant, *The Wisdom of the Ego* (Cambridge, MA: Harvard University Press, 1993), 284.

2   M. Rutter, "Psychosocial Adversity: Risk, Resilience and Recovery," in J. Richmond and M. Fraser, eds., *The Context of Youth Violence: Resilience, Risk, and Protection* (Westport, CT: Praeger Publishers, 2001), 13–43.

3   Mason Durie, "Indigenous Resilience: from disease to disadvantage to the realization of potential" (unpublished paper, Pacific Region Indigenous Doctors Congress, Rotorua, New Zealand, 7 December 2006).

Theme 1: Historic Trauma

Susan Point, *Survivor*, 1992

Trauma to Resilience:
Notes on Decolonization

Cynthia C. Wesley-Esquimaux

WITH THE COMING OF THE EUROPEANS and the advent of colonization in North America, First Nations' traditional belief systems came under assault[1] and Native people on this continent were confronted with increasing cultural and social fragmentation. Contact with Europeans imposed alien social structures and disrupted gender relations. The roles women played in their homes and communities were increasingly altered by external influences and demands. Contact and colonization had an equally destructive impact on men, but the most immediate and least discussed damage radiated from the heart and centre of the family—the women—and temporarily shattered the hoop that ensured balance in life. Separated from traditional social structures and First Nations' governance norms, stripped of defined roles and responsibilities, the people lost their inner balance as women struggled to maintain social equilibrium. In defeat of these efforts, the collective turned outward to the colonizer in an effort to survive.

This chapter is primarily an analysis of the "women's context," and is written foremost from a First Nations woman's perspective. I fully recognize that one cannot envisage a balanced, healthy community without giving equal attention to the men's historic and contemporary social sphere. I have decided, however, to focus on just one element of this healthy equilibrium: First Nations women, their experiences, their pasts, their evolving present, and their promising future. It is also my intention to speak in different voices. As an academic, I make reference to the past, paying attention to those aspects that more easily render themselves to a scholarly enquiry. As a First Nations woman, I speak about the potential future through our tradition of storytelling. By doing so, I am allowing all my various selves to speak as one. I am, in essence, decolonizing my own image; in the words of C.R. Rogers, "it is a movement from fixity towards changingness, from rigid structures towards flow, and from stasis to process."[2]

CONTACT AND DISEASE

Several studies of the indigenous population in the years immediately following contact in 1492 have emphasized the biological and cultural catastrophes that occurred. One study prepared Magdalena Smolewski and myself[3] for the Aboriginal Healing Foundation, *Historic Trauma and Aboriginal Healing*, has been liberally referenced for the foundations of this chapter. Far beyond simply annotating distant historical events, these studies can also speak to, and provide a greater understanding of, the psychological elements and impacts of encountering a once-isolated people[4] and of the far-reaching historical consequences of that encounter. In 1492, an estimated 90 million to 112 million indigenous people lived on the American continents. This would have included as many as 10 million people living on the Caribbean Islands, 25 million people living in what is now Mexico, 28 million in South America, and perhaps 15 million to 18 million living in what is now the United States and Canada.[5] Henry F. Dobyns[6] has provided the most generous estimates of total numbers, and Douglas Ubelaker[7] has provided the lowest population count at 1,894,350 for what is now the United States.[8]

Death and destruction came quickly, and, by 1493, in the southern hemisphere, the first point of contact, the Native population of San Salvador and its neighbouring island Hispaniola was completely devastated by the first influenza epidemic.[9] Within two generations, smallpox had completely destroyed one-third to one-half of the indigenous population of the American continents, and, until at least 1918, various epidemics devastated the lives of indigenous people across the continents, with some reaching as far north as Alaska and west to British Columbia. Dobyns[10] suggests that 90 to 95 percent of the indigenous population was wiped out by epidemic disease, warfare, and famine, with most people dying within 100 years of contact.[11] An anthropological viewpoint on the purported numbers of people who were lost and of the historical research on epidemics can clarify specific elements of the psychological, social, and cultural trauma that resulted. The intensive trauma from such massive death and destruction not only contributed a great deal to the inability of indigenous people to effectively protect their cosmological beliefs and social systems, it also rendered reconstruction of their devastated social and economic systems impossible. What followed, as the people turned their gaze away from their own powers, was what has been termed by anthropologists as "diffusion." This is the process in which people, often out of necessity, begin to integrate ideals and concepts from another people and begin to incorporate aspects of those ideals into their own way of life, as their former way of life becomes displaced. These concepts are not necessarily noble or just, they are simply prevailing, and, therefore, they can be overwhelming to those in a posture of defeat. They can create a process of internalized abuse, or what Antonio Gramsci has termed "self abuse" and "hegemony."[12] Hegemony has been described as a way of thinking as well as leadership: "It occurs when oppressed groups take on domi-nant group thinking and ideas uncritically and as 'common-sense', even though those ideas may in fact be contributing to forming their own oppression."[13] This process is ultimately followed by acculturation, especially when there is continuous and intense contact between two previously autonomous cultural traditions. This process of acculturation will then lead to extensive changes in one or both systems.[14] The entire process of acculturation is more than just the borrowing of material goods or the acceptance of certain ideals. It entails large-scale reorganization of a society to accommodate the presence of another cultural group. In every instance, one society is eventually, at least on the surface, subsumed by the other. In cultural terms, an acculturated group slowly loses its ability to remember its own cultural past. What was believed to have happened in the past now becomes a myth, and, according to Vecsey,[15] "the popular Western mind to this day equates myth with falsehood, stupidly believed and foolishly studied." Ultimately, the subsumed society comes to believe that its own reality is, in fact, mere allegory, and ceases to tell its own stories or relate its own history as being relevant and real. It becomes what the more dominant society says it is—idealized—and begins to see itself as a falsi-fied reflection of what the other society projects, ultimately losing its own ability to be self-reflexive and power-"full."

MISSIONIZATION

Almost immediately after the influx of explorers, Native women came under the gaze of missionaries, men who could not see women as equals, because these men were coming from a place where women were inferior to men. Native women were removed from their traditional roles and responsibilities and pushed to the margins of their own societies. The missionaries brought into the New World an old-European social hierarchy where "a woman's proper place was under the authority of her husband and that a man's proper place was under the authority of the priests."[16] Allen writes about Father Paul LeJeune, the Jesuit, and his quest to civilize the Montagnais-Naskapi of the St. Lawrence Valley in the mid-sixteenth century.[17] Father LeJeune wanted to introduce a new social structure in which Aboriginal people would adhere to the rules of patriarchal institutions of male dominance and female submission. Following the instructions of his church, Father LeJeune taught that a sacrament of marriage binds a man, who has all the authority, to his obedient wife for life. Further, divorce was not to be allowed under any circumstances. Birth control was forbidden and birth prevention was to be considered a grave sin.

Father LeJeune was not alone in his quest to civilize indigenous people. Many Aboriginal communities across the Americas and in the Pacific region met their own Father LeJeune at one point or another, each bringing the same message, which instructed these societies to replace "a peaceful, non-punitive, non-authoritarian social system wherein women wielded power by making social life easy and gentle with one based on child terrorization, male dominance, and the submission of women to male authority."[18] Far too often, the missionaries were successful in altering Aboriginal behavioural patterns. Bruce Trigger notes that, in 1648, "a Christian woman who lived in Ossossane is reported to have beaten her four-year-old son, a form of behaviour hitherto not reported among the Hurons and one that they would have regarded as disgusting and inhumane. The Jesuits, who believed that the Hurons had to acquire a new sense of discipline in order to be good Christians, heartily approved of her action."[19]

More significant, perhaps, was the process of repressing the natural expression of instinctual drives and impulses of First Nations peoples, including their beliefs in their own manitous, and converting them into a form seen as more socially and culturally acceptable by the missionaries. Those people not subscribing to church dogma were seen as savages in need of civilizing. As Attwood[20] notes, missionaries not only forcefully replaced the natural spiritual order of indigenous peoples they encountered, they emphasized and violated the moral boundaries between private and public space, and implanted into the First Nations belief system a duality of mind and body that forced a separation of self from spirit, a concept alien to the communal philosophy of Aboriginal people. As Allen[21] observes, the old social systems of Aboriginal people were cooperative and autonomous, peace-centred and ritual-oriented, and based on ideas of complementarity and interconnectedness. The new social ordering shattered the old and left indigenous peoples standing between two disconnected worlds.

All people, men as well as women, now had to learn how to behave differently so as to be acceptable to the missionaries. We understand today that a transformation of the social self effectively changes the underlying collective sense of "who" people are and how they act in what is perceived by the majority as a "normal" manner, in a socio-cultural sense. Over time, new or imposed moral norms can prompt a changing definition of what is accepted as the "appropriate gender behaviours" of men and women. Today, as Allen notes, "we [women] get placed in a 'bicultural bind': where we vacillate between being dependent and strong, self-reliant and powerless, strongly motivated and hopelessly insecure."[22]

It did not take long for the new religion to begin shaping societal and cultural expectations pertaining to sexual behaviours, and to influence standards of dress and even undress. As Erica Smith writes, "In Rupert's Land, this theme was echoed in the frequent refrain of fur traders who made pejorative associations between Indians' love of fine clothing and their low moral development."[23] The new religion also dictated physical activities, influenced entertainment, and, more importantly, had an impact on the performance of rituals, both social and religious. Women became increasingly removed from the ceremonial circle, pushed away from the drum and song, and relegated to the cooking fire and kitchen. The new religion ultimately legitimated gender distinction in work roles, home responsibilities, child care obligations, education, marriage commitments, political duties, and legal status.

In any stable society, social actions that people perform flow directly from what have become accepted and established norms or mores. Moral values develop from people's day-by-day experiences, from the teachings of religions, and from socially accepted ethical principles. Socio-cultural norms, therefore, develop from naturally evolving moral values. In the obverse, social confusion that results from too-rapid social changes can lead to questioning of values and mores, thereby creating even more confusion and doubt. Before first contact, indigenous societies had their own culturally prescribed norms of proper social conduct. These norms developed from generations of shared experiences, from contact with nature, which was seen as a spiritual domain, and from what had been worked out in their societies through consistent intragenerational relations. First Nations people's traditional morality placed exceptional value on ensuring that relationships between people (and people versus spirits) were maintained and on seeing that the needs of the vulnerable (elders, children, women) were met through communal caring. First Nations people saw morality in terms of protecting the integrity of relationships and minimizing pain. Their perception of what was appropriate and right was dramatically different from the values of non-Aboriginal people and missionaries.

Thus, through contact with missionaries and other colonizers, First Nations people were introduced not only to new beliefs, but also to a dramatically different canon of acceptable social and religious behaviour, particularly as it related to women.

THE EFFECTS OF COLONIZATION AND MARGINALIZATION

Many contemporary indigenous thinkers are convinced that, historically, the destruction of the First Nations social sphere began with the forced rearrangement of gender roles in First Nations societies and the religious and social devaluation of women. Traditionally, in many indigenous societies around the world, women, together with men, were the repositories of cultural knowledge, responsible for handing down tribal law and custom. Women were one of the primary forces that made possible the stability and continuity of life. First Nations women traditionally shared with men a common religious heritage based on their relationship with nature. Women and men were linked without discrimination to the same founding ancestors. Social benefits, as well as social responsibilities, were, in principle, also the same for both sexes. Those societies, in which the centrality of women to the social well-being of the entire community was never questioned, were also characterized by an equal distribution of goods, with the welfare of children and elders being of paramount importance.

In order to create and define clear models as well as best practices for First Nations women, and to continue strengthening and reinforcing First Nations women's capacity for social resolution and transformative social action, it is necessary first to understand the impact of mechanisms put in place by colo-nizers that led to the marginalization and devaluation of First Nations roles and lifeways. These mechanisms destroyed First Nations culture and social domains, restricted social mobility, disfavoured Native people generally in their access to resources, and created or accentuated inequities within and between First Nations communities and their members. Some of these mech-anisms were not entirely or consciously deliberate; nevertheless, they had a dire effect on the continuance of a healthy First Nations cultural identity and the strong social capacity of communities.

The persistent changes wrought through colonization on the social struc-tures of First Nations societies had profound psychological effects on the social psyche of the people over the course of time. These changes included the imbedding of social fatalism (they began to approach the world with distrust) and the impoverishment of communication (there was no healthy connection between First Nations people or with the world outside). The experience of being depersonalized as a social and cultural entity, and of losing social autonomy, the sense of social integrity, interdependence, and social control, is character-ized, according to Cattell and colleagues, by "feelings of unreality in reference to the self, the external world, or the passage of time; feelings of unreality or detachment, and a loss of affective response."[24] Eventually, First Nations people internalized constructions of themselves as "other," and buried or hid their own truths from themselves. As First Nations people became isolated from mean-ingful contacts with the externalized world, and increasingly cut off from inner traditional social meanings, their world views faltered and diminished. In effect, First Nations people began to walk backwards into the future, unarmed with the social and psychological strengths that would have been passed to their children if their societies had remained intact.

This First Nations discourse of loss has been treated as marginal, if consid-ered at all, within the narrowly defined Western historical memory. Non-Native researchers, anthropologists, social workers, and mental health practi-tioners working with Aboriginal people have failed to integrate Aboriginal people's narratives into the history of colonization that, for the invaders, most often included one-sided themes of power and hierarchy, rather than balanced or equitable relationships between them and the original owners of the lands they had come to occupy. Even when the history of oppression is critically analyzed, the analysis most often follows rules of linear causality and denies the importance of the myriad historical factors that have negatively influenced

First Nations people's lives. It is difficult to find anything positive in a narrative that ignores the values, voices, lives, and experiences of an entire people.

For generations, First Nations women's voices were silenced in historical narratives that sidestepped their influence and power. Today, First Nations women are increasingly using those voices to reclaim lost stories and narratives. Students of Aboriginal cultures have come to recognize and listen to the power underlying those hitherto silenced voices. First Nations women are beginning to understand that many of the social problems they deal with every day have roots in the extensive historic trauma that was experienced, but never properly voiced out and represented. The metanarrative of the Western world simply did not include the indigenous story of loss, impermanence, and socially debilitating marginalization.

However, because of this marginalization, recurrent recollections of trauma experienced by individual members of the society entered into social narratives of First Nations peoples and were transmitted to subsequent generations. Traumatic recollections, both historic and increasingly contemporary, entered into collections of cultural symbols and meanings, into rituals and ceremonies, into the group's shared cultural memory, and into behavioural patterns. Adults who were constantly reliving horrifying experiences in their minds and bodies, and in their social and interpersonal behaviours, were less able to cope with their parental and social obligations. Some were not able to cope at all. Over time, relations between people became increasingly dysfunctional. Families and relationships began to fall apart, and children were often psychologically damaged in the aftermath of parental breakups and violence. Many women, unable to speak or reclaim a sense of power, far too often found themselves equally unable to express love or tenderness. The combined effects of unexpressed historic trauma and the resulting emotional, psychological, and physical abuses have led to collective symptoms of repressed emotions, numbness, and the expected social and emotional depression that comes with unresolved issues and the loss of inherent identity.

Today, First Nations peoples are turning their gaze away from the colonizer and back to the hoop in an effort to reclaim their culture and free themselves from that which they could not control. As feelings have begun to surface, and the unspoken is spoken, some people have come to feel the intense alienation and the detachment, and are grappling with a sense of being profoundly alone and lonely. Some have passed their loneliness and sense of alienation on to their children. In some instances, their bodies have become things over which they have had little control, due to their own lifetime experiences of sexual and physical abuse. In their numbness, some have abused their own bodies by drinking themselves into oblivion or sniffing glue or gasoline. And now, far too many kill themselves. First Nations children do not have the conscious knowledge that they are reliving the past of their parents, grandparents, and great-grandparents. For many of them, the terror continues to happen here and now. Abandoned and neglected, some cannot see the future as anticipated opportunity; in fact, among many of today's First Nations children and their parents, there is no vision of the future at all.

Aboriginal researchers from the Lakota Takini Network Inc. explored this phenomenon of numbness and embedded cultural and social trauma, and have expressed it in contemporized physiological terms. According to the Historic Trauma Response (HTR) theory defined by Maria Yellow Horse Brave Heart,[25] a set of behavioural and psychological responses is formed in reaction to the trauma that a group of people has endured. It is comparable to the survivor syndrome manifested by Jewish Holocaust survivors and their descendants. The combination of symptoms may emerge differently in communities and individuals, but the roots are still the same, originating from cultural genocide. According to this theory, HTR symptoms include elevated suicide rates, depression, self-destructive behaviour, substance abuse, identification with the pain ancestors endured, fixation on trauma, somatic symptoms that do not have a medical reason, anxiety, guilt, and chronic grief. Yellow Horse Brave Heart states that the symptoms associated with social disorders related to historical trauma manifest themselves differently with respect to the genders:

> As the genocide began, men and women lost their traditional roles and experienced a sense of failure as protectors and providers. HTR theorizes that this sense of loss has been transmitted down through the generations, affecting many generations of Indian people with a deep sense of pain, anger and powerlessness. These destructive feelings manifest themselves as violence toward their loved ones, substance abuse, suicide, and an inability to communicate feelings and experiences. Many Native men adopted the oppressor's ways of operating: power through control, intimidation, manipulation, lack of respect for equality and nurturance of women, abandonment of family and responsibility, and a lack of honesty. For Native women, the traditional role of educator, healer, nurturer, head of the home, and sustainers of the family and Nation was gone. Faced with being victims of abuse and abandonment, women turned to substance abuse, suicide and hopelessness. In trying to provide for and protect children alone (as well as coping with traumatic events in their lifetime such as past sexual, physical

and emotional abuse), Native women found themselves and their children in poverty, and many times, unable to cope with all the stressors involved with going it alone.[26]

Yellow Horse Brave Heart proposes that an important element in HTR theory is that the trauma is transmitted through generations. Descendants of people who have suffered cultural genocide not only identify with the past, but also emotionally re-experience it in the present. Research has also shown that descendants can have a tremendous loyalty to their ancestors and relatives who suffered and died, and often find they perpetuate suffering in their own lives as a result. They continue to unconsciously recreate trauma experiences in an effort to connect with their feelings and with the past.[27]

More recently, Wesley-Esquimaux and Smolewski[28] have proposed another model, termed "historic trauma transmission" (HTT) in an effort to understand and track the various impacts of social and cultural diffusion that have devastated Aboriginal communities for so many years. In this model, historic trauma is understood as a cluster of traumatic events and as a causal factor operating in many different areas of impact; it is viewed as a disease itself. As in the Lakota Takini model, an underlying and almost fully unconscious or hidden collective of memories, as a result of historic trauma, or a collective non-remembering, is passed from generation to generation. This manifests as the maladaptive social and behavioural patterns symptomatic of many different social disorders caused by historic trauma. However, according to the proposed HTT model, there is no single historical trauma response, as proposed by Yellow Horse Brave Heart; rather, there are different social disorders with respective clusters of symptoms. In effect, then, social disorders can be understood as repetitive maladaptive social patterns that occur in a group of people and are associated with a significantly increased risk of suffering (for example, complex post-traumatic stress disorder, dissociative disorders, etc.).

Arthur G. Neal, in his book, *National Trauma and Collective Memory: Major Events in the American Century*, has also suggested that, with time, boundaries around traumatic events become blurred, stereotyped, and selectively distorted, and, as such, they enter the collective image of the past that people pass from generation to generation. Someone born in the twentieth century does not cognitively remember the suffering of his or her ancestors; what he or she carries forward are the "images of ourselves and of our external environment [that] are shaped by memories that are passed on by legions of men and women we have never known and never shall meet."[29] The oral transmission of information and memories is very pronounced in First Nations societies. Therefore, it is through this process that traumatic memory perpetuates itself and, in a sense, traumatic events then continue into the present. Neal agrees when he asks, "Who are the keepers of collective memories? In the final analysis, we all are. Therefore, the intersection of personal biography with historical events is crucial to unfolding the many aspects of knowing who we are and what we are to become."[30]

MOVING FROM NARRATIVES OF LOSS AND GRIEF

If one understands loss to mean being separated from a part of life to which one was emotionally attached, First Nations grief in the present can be understood as an attempt to restore equilibrium to contemporary social and cultural systems. This restoration, or cultural reclamation, that First Nations people are undertaking involves all the emotional, cognitive, and perceptual reactions that accompany loss, except that, in the present, a paradigm shift is occurring. Ideally, the experience of loss should be followed by an experience of recovery in which survivors restructure their lives. For First Nations people, loss of their cultural identity was not an abrupt event, but continued in one form or another through centuries of pain and suffering, and so they were never able to reach a full stage of recovery in the cycle of grieving. Therefore, in a very real sense, First Nations people are still grieving their earliest losses as well as those occurring in the last few centuries. According to Spikes,[31] grieving has three broad stages. In the first stages of denial and anger, the bereaved feel angry and frustrated by their losses. The second stage, depression, is characterized by apathy and disorganized behaviour. Finally, in the third stage, generally identified by the presence of acceptance and readjustment, the bereaved begin to reorganize their lives.[32] Many Aboriginal people have been stuck in the second stage and only more recently are finding the innate resiliency and inner fortitude that have begun to lift them out of social and cultural apathy and disorganization and into new stages of healing, a more healthy recognition and articulation of the stories of their past. They are, in effect, moving toward feeling, healing, and presence in the present moment and toward transformative change.

Alan Young[33] and Sidney Furst[34] each have identified how the present interpretation of past events can have an impact on lives, and how the conception of memories shapes one's sense of personhood and active or conscious memory. The way First Nations peoples, especially women, remember their past and interpret those events as individuals and as collectives contributes to contemporary social problems in First Nations communities. Research has demonstrated that we can extrapolate from the past an ongoing relationship between continuing First Nations cultural and social dysfunction and the psychogenic trauma generated by centuries of depopulation, cultural dislocation, and forced assimilation. New research supports the idea that psychological trauma does not result only from such events as combat and natural disasters, but also from everyday modern life and the experience of childhood abuse and spousal assault, family violence, abandonment, and neglect.

These psychological pressures have created emotional and spiritual barriers. Instead of working through their immediate and historic trauma, many Native women instead became caught up at the second stage of grieving, somewhere between anger and depression, apathy and disorganization. Many practised the social disengagement that, according to social theorists, can be a consequence of several factors, one of the most prominent being role loss as the individual's position in society changes. Without an awareness of the underlying damage, or possession of healthy, internalized representations of the dominant culture that could be manipulated to their benefit, women were left without a strong representation of their own self-identity and self-worth. Under these circumstances, Native women could not help but become "absent" from their own culture. However, as Kim Anderson writes, "With the foundations for resistance in place, Native women may strengthen their sense of identity through various acts of resistance. With each act of resistance, Native women can further define and confirm positive identity and challenge the oppression of Native people in general."[35]

Anderson emphasizes the need to recognize, engage, and challenge the negative representations and stereotypes that Native women have internalized. It means more frequently exposing themselves to the dominant culture as known, knowing, and knowledgeable subjects. As some anthropologists have suggested, extensive forced exposure of First Nations women to the dominant system may also strengthen and reinforce their capacity for social resolution and social action simply because it builds confidence and familiarity. According to Magdalena Smolewski, that very exposure can allow Native women to acquire more "tools" that potentially could further strengthen their determination to create social stability out of social chaos. She notes, "From all the conflicting cultural meanings that women were forced to internalize, they were able to create a new formula to resolve the tensions inherent in the task of formulating a new social and cultural identity during a time of change and possibility."[36]

Smolewski observed in northern Australia that many Aboriginal women, having this "piece of the oppressor" deeply planted in their lives, were able to free themselves from the constricting white sphere of influence by actively learning to understand the dominant culture, by accepting some of its elements, by twisting and turning them to create a new integration of the cultural and the social.[37] Having learned to participate in white social structures without subscribing to their values, and with this affirmation of difference, they are able now to retell and articulate their history. In this new (re)created history, they become reconstituted subjects and their future exists as an anticipated possibility. Currently, they are in the process of developing their own critique of the dominant culture, forging their individual strength and their collective unity, just as First Nations women are now beginning to undertake this process of cultural reclamation here on this continent.

Both Smolewski[38] and Wesley-Esquimaux and Smolewski[39] recognize through their research that prolonged subjugation by a foreign power creates a belief in an external locus of social control, which refers to the perception of events and experiences as being unrelated to one's own behaviour. Under those circumstances, the cultural and social gaze can turn outward, away from self-responsibility and self-awareness. Currently, First Nations women (and men) are on what has been termed in the United States and Canada "a healing journey," which can also be described as the process of discovering and escaping the temporality of traumatic life experiences and creating a new social reality out of unfavorable circumstances. Out of this newly constituted activity, the more recent social behaviour of First Nations people could be described as opportunistic and reactionary, deconstructive and reconstructive, but no longer passive. One may hypothesize, following Smolewski,[40] that they have been able to generate a higher than expected degree of resiliency and have started to reclaim their internal locus of social control (the perception that one can control events). This developing ability to cope from within may be having the effect of decreasing debilitating emotional responses to a variety of what have become "normalized," albeit unhealthy or negative, social stressors. What we do know is that Native women are finding their way home in more ways than one, and that there is a growing recognition of—or, perhaps more appropriately stated, a reclaiming and demonstration of—personal inner strength and resiliency.

RESILIENCY AND RECOVERY

In this chapter, I am suggesting that perhaps the most important factors that help First Nations women to rebound from negative experiences in life are in their awakening cultural and social resiliency. Researchers agree that one's ability to access and utilize the intuitive aspects of one's own life is the core of resiliency, and this ability can be understood both as a tangible factor and as a process in time. Resiliency is the ability to rebound from challenges one encounters in daily life. As a process, resilience allows for the integration of the teachings that those experiences present. According to James Neill,

> the central process involved in building resilience is the training and development of adaptive coping skills. Coping strategies are generally either outwardly focused on the problem (problem-solving), inwardly focused on emotions (emotion-focused) or socially focused, such as on emotional support from others. In humanistic psychology, resilience refers to an individual's capacity to thrive and fulfill potential despite or perhaps even because of stressors. Resilient individuals and communities are more inclined to see problems as opportunities for growth. In other words, resilient individuals seem not only to cope well with unusual strains and stressors but actually to experience such challenges as learning and development opportunities.[41]

As cited earlier, grieving proceeds in stages. So does healing: denial and anger are the first stages, often with self-blame, victimization, and indignation quickly following. With the knowledge we have today, we believe that each of us can eventually come to an expressed acknowledgement of oneself as victim and then survivor, recognizing our own compassion and strengths. But, surviving is not the end. Instead, it must become the precursor to the next step of integration and wholeness. Then a person can begin the process of reorganizing and celebrating new life and new insight. Our responsibility is to educate our minds and heal our spirits with understanding and knowledge at each grieving and healing stage so that at the next stage of life, what I term the "victorizing" stage, we will be able to reframe our life narratives and, to paraphrase Warren,[42] to situate them in ways that demonstrate how this narrative is culturally and socially contingent, and how it can be "reread" in different ways at different moments. To put it succinctly, it is our responsibility to become healed. "Victorizing" our lives, rather than focussing on being perpetually victimized (or perhaps being in a perpetual state of healing) is one way to do that. And, perhaps the most logical place to start is to celebrate our victory and our survival at home.

The fact that First Nations women possess the capacity to thrive and fulfill themselves is undisputable. They have clearly demonstrated an abundance of what has been called "social competency," endlessly flowing from their ability to laugh, express compassion, and feel empathy, to the extent that it has become a much commented upon "cultural" response pattern.[43] Native women are very present in First Nations communities, urban settings, academic institutions, and heading families, despite the colonizers' long-standing attempts at cultural and physical genocide. They play prominent roles in their communities, they teach, they heal, they tell stories, they set directions, and they develop social and economic frameworks. They indeed are here in the present and do amazing work towards self-(re)positioning as active and empowered (re)creators of Native traditions, spiritualities, and epistemologies; storytellers, healers, and teachers, whose voices are increasingly amplified by regained spiritual and cultural strengths, have come to recognize the need to speak in unison to produce an identity for Native women, finally uncontested and unsuppressed, and ultimately recognized and embodied as fully valid and autonomous. Even after what has been a long legacy of hurt and despair, they have found the room to solve problems for their families and nurture a sense of purpose and future orientation, all critical for a resilient and hopeful life.[44]

It is certain that, collectively, First Nations women need to reconstitute the value of domestic and professional spheres, and break out of the narrow confines that have been imposed on "who" Aboriginal women are and "how" they will live their lives. The most important part of this process will be the decolonization of our own minds and of our own beliefs at a very fundamental level. We need to reach down deep, so that we can reach up higher.

ARE WE THERE YET?

Perhaps we need to actively and collectively celebrate our victories and decolonize our "minds and spirits" on a very personal level so that First Nations women of all ages, particularly the very young, can claim or even regain personal power by being offered a clear and accessible demonstration of First Nations women's strengths. Steven Wolin, a Washington, DC, psychiatrist, stated: "The problem is, there are elements of our culture that glorify frailty.... In fact, you have considerable capacity for strength, although you might not be wholly aware of it."[45]

I propose three broad steps to decolonizing that can take us beyond perpetual healing and out of the state of our "glorified frailty." First, we need to deconstruct the historic and contemporary trauma we have all experienced by acknowledging its presence, speaking it, and then educating ourselves and our people about it. Then we must begin the decolonization process of the "marginalization" of our domestic spheres so our lives and experiences are not held at the edges of society any more, but are regarded as centralized, validated, and respected spheres of our influence. To do this, we have to regain control over our communities, our homes, and our children, even if our ambitions take us entirely outside the domestic or community sphere and into the structured world of formal mainstream schooling and regulated workplaces. We must take "affirmative action," clichéd or not. Being proactive and involved is the only way to direct the transition and ultimate transformation of our families and communities.

Secondly, we need to acknowledge and loudly proclaim our collective power as First Nations women, understanding the value of gender-specific transmissions of positive messages and success stories. G.M. White proposes: "Where dominant, patriarchal structures continually subvert the plans and desires of women ... lives tend to be recounted as more fragile, contingent, and inconsistent than they might be otherwise. In such conditions, the act of "telling one's story" may be an opportunity to imaginatively reform or transform the meanings of experience, even with therapeutic effects."[46]

We are storytellers. We have an obligation to tell our stories to each other and to other non-Native women. We may have to change the language of our stories and the focus of our discourse. Instead of telling only the stories about trauma and victimization and pain, let us talk about our survival and our undeniable strengths. It is essential for us to articulate the strengths that we have, not only in a way that validates our survival, but in a way that validates and "victorizes" our ability to take control of our lives and be, in spite of past pain and present dysfunction.

Thirdly, we need to reinforce our social action, inside and outside our communities, whether they are in urban centres or located in the more remote areas of central and northern Canada. First Nations women need to place greater emphasis on education of all kinds, not only for our children, but for ourselves. We need to "victorize" our academic and life education experiences as women—mothers, partners, and people of competence and professions—and stem the tide of dropping out of school and life, for all ages and both genders. Native people can reframe the past and learn to frame our present life stories as individuals who fulfill higher aspirations, both cultural and social, while, at the same time, realizing and validating our own smaller dreams and potentials. The women in our communities can remain true to First Nations social roots and cultural traditions and still pursue larger dreams in non-Native society, if that is what they choose. We can do our work at the community level and reach in and pull everyone up who can benefit from the boost, even if they are not yet conscious of their own need to free themselves from colonized thinking and stunted aspirations.

Having said that, is it possible we have spent too much time looking for a vision to guide us instead of learning how to live one? In our tradition, a vision quest is a journey of self-discovery that helps a person prepare for a significant life transition. It can "mark the change from childhood to adulthood, entrance into or out of an important relationship, a greater understanding of God or Mother Earth, or a celebration of positive change and growth in a person's life."[47]

ARRIVAL AT THE GATE

We can concentrate on identifying and promoting achievable goals and objectives and taking baby steps to create a decolonized Aboriginal world. We have already seen that we can identify smaller dreams, recognize concrete change, and promote tangible celebration, as well as realize grand visions. Each one of us can begin scaling the wall of personal, community, and national resistance, one step at a time, looking up from the ground, calling a friend or a possible mentor, allowing ourselves to seek and then hear the truth, applying for a better job, writing a letter of forgiveness, going outside to enjoy the day, taking a long walk: anything that moves from personal inertia and makes us do something other than contemplate, or, worse, unconsciously (re)live the trauma of our collective colonized past. According to Smolewski, "for Aboriginal women, being a fully functioning and fully realized Aboriginal social person, is not a 'developed' state—rather it is 'being-in-the-process', or as [C.R.] Rogers describes it, being in 'moments of movement'—'it is not a state at all.'"[50]

The major restriction that colonialism (in every form) imposed on Aboriginal women was on movement, in physical and metaphorical social senses. Moreover, as Rogers proposes, in the process of becoming a fully functioning person in any society, one learns how to open up to experience, how to live "existentially," and how to trust oneself.[51] Openness is a prerequisite to greater self-awareness and acceptance. With their social psyche under colonial threat, Aboriginal men and women became defensive instead of being open to experience.

Decolonization for First Nations women must mean opening up to experience. We cannot afford to encapsulate ourselves in the past, in silence and isolation. Instead, we must return to what Rogers terms "living in the moment"—existential living. This "existential living" means "a maximum of adaptability, a discovery of structure in experience, a flowing, changing organization of self."[52]

We must decolonize our homes, which simply means talking to our children, our partners, and our families, and connecting with them; telling them about historic and personal lies and about the beauty of our cultural and social truths. It means talking to our children as our ancestors used to do, before contact and the subjugation of women, before religious guilt and patriarchy took over, before the noisy, distracting inventions of the dominant culture took over everyone's freedom and minds.

We must acknowledge our collective power as women, which simply means talking to each other, learning from each other, sharing our accomplishments with other women. We must celebrate our achievements, rather than tearing them down. We need to learn how to hold up each other's daily victories as examples of what can be done, and encourage our children, our families, and our communities to do the same.

We need more women's stories "with women placing themselves as powerful agents within the social context. These very stories [would] also contain links between women's personal lives and the dominant socio-political structures in which they live."[53] These will be stories of power-"full"-ness and intention, stories that demonstrate the wisdom that comes from being present in each glorious moment and rappelling ourselves up and over challenging obstacles.

To regain our social agency, we need to take action and, to paraphrase Smolewski, actively resist the idea that we are "things" or "objects," knowing and expressing through our actions that there is something that can be done in our communities, and—more importantly—that we are the ones who have the power (both in a "traditional" and "modern" sense) to do it.[54] As Smolewski rightly says, our actions and our social involvement in communal life reconnect us to our own past (because, "traditionally," women were always considered healers, making their decisions from and within the narrative of responsibility and care) and to our recreated present (because, as "modern" women, we feel free to reclaim the domestic and communal spheres and make them again a source of social power): "[We have to] attend meetings, teachings, conferences and workshops, reestablishing cultural connections that were severed in the past.... [We have to] take part in social initiatives in and outside ... [our] communities which will regenerate ... [our] sense of leadership and social competence. ... [We have to] take upon ourselves the role of healers and educators, which will help rebuild ... [our] sense of responsibility and consequently infuse ... [our] sensed and exercised control over our own lives."[55] Furthermore, as Smolewski proposes, this newly reclaimed power will come from the realization that our experiences have value: "More and more Aboriginal women take part in projects that allow them to tell their individual stories embedded in the common Aboriginal past. By sharing their stories, they are able to identify with other women and overcome isolation and marginalization, while—at the same time— the 'affirmation of the individual' (followed by self-acceptance) helps overcome the negative messages still resonating in their past."[56]

These stories are about your life and mine, they are about the lives of our mothers and grandmothers, and they will be about the lives of our children, our daughters and our sons. They will be about success, as we define it for ourselves, about victories, both small ones and the ones that cannot be ignored by anyone, and they will be about the past, the present, and the future, but they will resonate with joy and the beauty of lives well lived, of enduring love, of the ability to overcome loss.

My story is very easily your story, an early narrative of trauma and grief that transformed into a story of healing and strength, a story about my arrival at the gate of "what is right for me" and learning to walk well in both worlds, a story of delving deep into the traditions of Aboriginal people and being able to clothe myself in courage and a past that has given me a reason to celebrate. My story includes walking with increasing confidence, deeper into the world of the colonizer, and then finding my way out with gifts that shine light in both worlds. This story is also your story, a story about survival, about an innate resiliency born of an historic adversary and grief, about climbing large mountains, about finding your own way, about learning how to "victorize" your journey, because, in the end, it is all about arriving home, wherever your heart belongs, strong and victorious.

I began writing this chapter as an academic, with an intention to conduct a sound, critical analysis of the factors involved in the long process of colonization of our hearts and minds. I ended up, as my editors pointed out to me, telling a story, albeit a personal one. Are these two voices irreconcilable, the academic and the First Nations woman? Did I produce a cacophony of voices, confusing the reader about who I am or who I became? Or is my voice throughout the chapter doing what Rogers,[57] whom I quoted in the beginning of this chapter, identified as creating "a movement from fixity towards changingness, from rigid structures towards flow and from stasis to process."

Notes

1   J.R. Miller, *Skyscrapers Hide the Heavens: A History of Indian-White Relations in Canada* (Toronto: University of Toronto Press, 2000); Olive Patricia Dickason, "The Many Faces of Canada's History as it Relates to Aboriginal People," in Ute Lischke, David T. McNab, eds., *Walking a Tightrope: Aboriginal Peoples and their Representations* (Waterloo: Wilfrid Laurier University Press, 2005); Ward Churchill, *Fantasies of the Master Race: Literature, Cinema, and the Colonization of American Indians* (San Francisco: City Light Books, 1998).

2   C.R. Rogers, *On Becoming a Person* (Boston: Houghton Mifflin, 1961), 189.

3   Cynthia Wesley-Esquimaux and Magdalena Smolewski, *Historic Trauma and Aboriginal Healing* (Ottawa: Aboriginal Healing Foundation, 2004).

4   Clark S. Larsen and George R. Milner, *In the Wake of Contact: Biological Responses to Conquest* (New York: John Wiley and Sons, 1994).

5   Christopher Vecsey, *On the Padres Trail. American Indian Catholics*, Vol. 1 (Indiana: University of Notre Dame Press, 1996).

6   Henry F. Dobyns, *Their Number Become Thinned: Native American Population Dynamics in Eastern North America* (Knoxville, TN: University of Tennessee Press, 1983).

7   Douglas Ubelaker, "North American Indian Population Size, A.D. 1500 to 1985," *American Journal of Physical Anthropology* 77 (1988): 289–294.

8   William H. MacLeish, *The Day Before America* (Boston: Houghton Mifflin Company, 1994).

9   Noble David Cook, *Born to Die: Disease and New World Conquest, 1492–1650* (London: Cambridge University Press, 1998).

10 Dobyns, *Their Number Become Thinned*.

11 Sherbourne F. Cook, "The Significance of Disease in the Extinction of the New England Indians," *Human Biology* 45, 3 (1973): 485–508.

12 Antonio Gramsci, *Selections from the Prison Notebooks* (London: Lawrence and Wishart, 1971).

13 Graham Hingangaroa Smith, "Transformative Praxis: Indigenous Reclaiming of the Academy and Higher Education" (paper delivered at the CINSA Annual Conference, 9 July 2005), 2–3.

14 Clyde M. Woods, *Culture Change* (Dubuque, IA: W.C. Brown Co., 1975).

15 Christopher Vecsey, *Imagine Ourselves Richly: Mythic Narratives of North American Indians* (New York: Crossroad/Herder and Herder, 1988).

16 Paula Gunn Allen, *The Sacred Hoop: Recovering the Feminine in American Indian Traditions* (Boston: Beacon Press, 1986), 38.

17 Ibid.

18 Ibid., 40–41.

19 Bruce G. Trigger, *Natives and Newcomers: Canada's "Heroic Age" Reconsidered* (Kingston and Montreal: McGill-Queen's University Press, 1985), 267.

20 B. Attwood, *The Making of the Aborigines* (Sydney: Allen and Unwin, 1989).

21 Allen, *Sacred Hoop*.

22 Allen, *Sacred Hoop*, 48.

23 Erica Smith, "'Gentlemen, This is no Ordinary Trial': Sexual Narratives in the Trial of the Reverend Corbett, Red River, 1863," in Jennifer S.H. Brown and Elizabeth Vibert, eds., *Reading Beyond Words: Contexts for Native History* (Ontario: Broadview Press, 1996), 368.

24 J.P. Cattell, R.A. MacKinnon, and E. Forster, "Limited Goal Therapy in a Psychiatric Clinic," *American Journal of Psychiatry* 120 (1963): 88–100.

25 Maria Yellow Horse Brave Heart, "Oyate Ptayela: Rebuilding the Lakota Nation through Addressing Historical Trauma among Lakota Parents," *Journal of Human Behavior and the Social Environment* 2, 1/2 (1999): 109–126.

26 Ibid.

27 Judith Herman, *Trauma and Recovery: The Aftermath of Violence, from Domestic Abuse to Political Terror* (New York: Basic Books, 1997).

28 Wesley-Esquimaux and Smolewski, *Historic Trauma*.

29 Arthur G. Neal, *National Trauma and Collective Memory: Major Events in the American Century* (New York: M.E. Sharpe Publishing, 1998), 202.

30 Ibid., 213.

31 J. Spikes, "Grief, Death and Dying," in E.W. Busse and D.G. Blazer, eds., *Handbook of Geriatric Psychiatry* (New York: Van Nostrand Reinhold Company, 1980).

32 Wesley-Esquimaux and Smolewski, *Historic Trauma*, 54.

33 Alan Young, *The Harmony of Illusions: Inventing Post-Traumatic Stress Disorder* (New Jersey: Princeton University Press, 1995).

34 Sidney S. Furst, ed., *Psychic Trauma* (New York: Basic Books, 1967).

35 Kim Anderson, *A Recognition of Being: Reconstructing Native Womanhood* (Vancouver: Second Story Press, 2000), 137.

36 Magdalena Smolewski, "Learning from the Known: Historical and Cultural Factors Influencing the Position of Women in Two Australian Aboriginal Societies" (PhD dissertation, University of Toronto, 2004), 5.

37 Ibid., 13.

38 Ibid.

39 Wesley-Esquimaux and Smolewski, *Historic Trauma*.

40   Smolewski, "Learning from the Known."

41   James Neill, http://www.wilderdom.com/psychology/resilience/PsychologicalResilience. html, accessed 30 May 2005.

42   K.B. Warren, ed., *The Violence Within: Cultural and Political Opposition in Divided Nations* (Boulder: Westview Press, 1993), 43.

43   Eduardo Duran and Bonnie Duran, *Native American Postcolonial Psychology* (Albany: State University of New York Press Press, 1995); Ute Lischke, "'Show me the money': Representation of Aboriginal People in East-German Indian Films," in Ute Lischke and David T. McNab, eds., *Walking a Tightrope: Aboriginal People and Their Representations*. Waterloo: Wilfrid Laurier University Press, 2005).

44   Bonnie Bernard, "Turning the Corner: From Risk to Resiliency, A Compilation of Articles from the *Western Center News*" (Portland, OR: Western Regional Center for Drug-Free Schools and Communities, 1993).

45   Hara Estroff Marano, "How to survive practically anything," http://www. psychologytoday.com/articles/pto-20030527-000005.html, accessed 30 May 2005.

46   G.M. White, "Afterword: Lives and Histories," in P.J. Stewart and A. Strathern, eds., *Identity Work: Constructing Pacific Lives* (Pittsburgh: University of Pittsburgh Press, 2000), 175.

47   See http://www.indianheadfirstnations.com/visionquest.htm.

50   Smolewski, "Learning from the Known," 158.

51   Rogers, *On Becoming a Person*.

52   Ibid., 189.

53   Smolewski, "Learning from the Known," 121.

54   Ibid., 149.

55   Ibid.

56   Ibid.

57   Rogers, *On Becoming a Person*, 189.

Contributions That Count: First Nations Women and Demography

Cleo Big Eagle and Eric Guimond

WHAT CAN THE SCIENCE of demography tell us about the contribution of First Nations women to their culture and communities? "Demography" is the statistical study of populations. It can be applied to any kind of dynamic population; that is, one that changes over time or space. Being at the crossroads of several disciplines such as sociology, anthropology, geography, economics, and epidemiology, demography offers analytical tools to approach a large range of population issues. It does so by combining a technical quantitative approach, which represents the core of the discipline, with many other methods borrowed from other perspectives, such as, in this case, a First Nations perspective. Demography brings an empirical component to the study of the contributions of First Nations women to their culture and communities.

The topic of First Nations women demographics is vast and the statistics available are inherently incomplete and fragmentary. The Census of Canada,[1] the First Nations Regional Health Survey,[2] or the Indian Register[3] do not seek information from First Nations on every demographic topic. In fact, such a feat is impossible to achieve. A detailed demographic analysis of First Nations women is much broader than what can be shared in this chapter. For this reason, we set our attention on the four following fundamental demographic themes: (1) Aboriginal identities and population definitions; (2) demographic growth and dynamics; (3) monitoring First Nations well-being and gender balance; and (4) reproductive health. The contribution of First Nations women to the preservation of their culture through language is carefully addressed later on in this book by Mary Jane Norris.

WHO IS BEING COUNTED?

Much confusion surrounds the use of the term "Aboriginal," especially within non-Aboriginal circles. Very often, expressions such as "Aboriginal," "Native," "Indian," "Registered Indian," "Treaty Indian," and "First Nations" are used interchangeably, irrespective of the specific history and meanings of these words. In Canada, the word "Aboriginal" includes many groups with unique heritages, languages, cultural practices, and spiritual beliefs, as well as distinct needs and aspirations. Section 35 of the 1982 *Constitution Act* of Canada recognizes three distinct groups of Aboriginal peoples: Indians (First Nations), Métis, and Inuit. Insofar as First Nations are concerned, the Canadian law further distinguishes between Status Indians,[4] who are registered as an Indian or are entitled to be registered as an Indian (also referred to as Registered Indians) according to the *Indian Act*, and non-status Indians, who self-identify as Indian but are not eligible to be registered under the *Indian Act*.[5] In this chapter, we prefer the use of the term "First Nations," recognizing that it might not always be possible because of the data sources and their respective terminology. For example, in the 2001 Census of Canada, the chosen expression to refer to First Nations was *North American Indians*. In such cases, the "source data expression" will be italicized in the text.

At first glance, coming up with a population count for First Nations would seem an easy task. Unfortunately, such is not the case. No statistical definition of First Nations affiliation or "Indianness" exists. The history of the Canadian census, for example, indicates that changes to the enumeration procedures of First Nations have been almost as regular as the census itself. Much of the time, these changes involved modifications to the terminology describing First Nations and/or to the criteria used for determining "Indianness."[6] With respect to terminology, the Census of Canada has used expressions such as *Indians, Native Indians, Status* or *non-status Indians*, and *North American Indians*. Since the first Census of Canada in 1871, skin colour, race, language, place of residence, ancestry of mother, ancestry of father, and ancestry of mother or father, are all criteria that have been used to define "Indianness" at one time or another.

In the 2006 census,[7] First Nations were enumerated through four separate concepts: (1) ethnic origin, (2) self-identification as an Aboriginal person, (3) Registered/Treaty Indian, and (4) membership to an Indian band or First Nation. For many years, *ethnic origin* was the ethnocultural characteristic most widely used in Canada to establish "Indianness." Since 1871, all Canadian censuses have enumerated First Nations by means of a question on ethnic origin. The concept of "origin" refers to the ethnocultural group to which a person's ancestors belonged. In theory, this concept could identify the descendants of populations who lived in America when Europeans arrived in the sixteenth and seventeenth centuries.[8] However, since very few people have thorough knowledge of their ethnocultural genealogy, only a fraction of true descendants from pre-colonial First Nations report a First Nations origin on a census form. In addition to genealogy, census data on ethnic origin varies according to societal concerns in general and the nature of the socio-political relations the Canadian mainstream society maintains (or not) with Aboriginal populations.[9] The Census of Canada reports that over 1.254 million individuals declared having *North American Indian* origin in 2006.[10]

The concept of "Aboriginal self-identity" is increasingly used to define affiliation to a *North American Indian*, Métis, or Inuit group. Ethnic identity is a subjective indicator of a person's affiliation to an ethnic group. Since objective indicators of ethnocultural affiliation (such as "real" ethnic origins and language) are increasingly ineffective for reasons of acculturation, urbanization, and intermarriage, ethnic identity is often considered the best ethnicity indicator available.[11] The concept of Aboriginal self-identity emerged in 1986[12] with the goal of improving the enumeration of Aboriginal populations.[13] According to the Census of Canada, 705,245 persons self-declared a *North American Indian* identity in 2006.[14]

In Canada, like in many other countries with an indigenous population, there are legal definitions of indigeneity.[15] As previously noted, the *Indian Act* is the key piece of Canadian law that explicitly attempts to define "Indianness" and, many would argue, artificially divides First Nations into two distinct subgroups: Status Indians and non-status Indians. The status/non-status distinction was initially established to determine the right of residency on Indian reserves, a right that is in itself a product of colonization.[16] The first version of the *Indian Act* in Canada's confederate era dates back to 1876[17] and has been amended several times since then. The latest amendments to the

Indian Act, which will be discussed in a following chapter by Yvonne Boyer, were made in 1985. According to the Census of Canada, in 2006 623,780 persons self-reported as a *Treaty* or a *Registered Indian*, as defined by the *Indian Act* of Canada.

The 1996 Census of Canada was the first survey of its kind to collect information about membership of an Indian band or First Nation (the question: "Is this person a member of an Indian band/First Nation?").[18] There are over 630 different Indian bands in Canada.[19] Since the 1985 amendments to the *Indian Act*, many Indian bands have exercised the right to establish their own membership codes, whereby it is no longer necessary for a First Nations or band member to be a *Registered Indian* according to the *Indian Act*. In 2006, 620,345 persons reported being a member of an Indian band or First Nation.

This discussion might imply a hierarchical structure to these dimensions of "Indianness." For example, the *Registered/Treaty Indian* population could be part of the population with *North American Indian* identity, which in turn could be part of the population with *North American Indian* origin. However practical or logical this view of "Indianness" may appear, the data show a much more complex reality. Indeed, the populations, as defined by these dimensions of "Indianness," only partly overlap (Figure 1). Together, the three dimensions of *North American Indian* origin, *North American Indian* self-identity, and *Registered/Treaty Indian* define seven groupings of varying sizes, the total of which is over 1.34 million individuals. The two largest groupings are composed of (1) people self-reporting origin, identity, and *Registered/Treaty Indian* status (538,235) and (2) people reporting *North American Indian* origin only (581,330). The other two "one-dimensional" groupings—*North American Indian* self-identity only and *Registered/Treaty Indian* only—respectively include 29,350 and 31,120 individuals.

FIGURE 1: Three Dimensions of "Indianness" in Canada, 2006

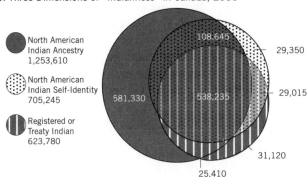

Source: Statistics Canada, 2006 Census of Canada, custom tabulation.

Who is being counted? From this analysis of concepts and definitions, it is clear that there is no simple and single answer to this question. The concept of First Nations affiliation, or "Indianness," in Canada is multidimensional, with each dimension yielding a different population count with its own level of complexity. The Royal Commission on Aboriginal Peoples recognized the multidimensional nature of the concept of Aboriginality, but leaned very clearly toward the subjective dimension:

> An Aboriginal nation cannot be identified in a mechanical fashion by reference to a detailed set of objective criteria. The concept has a strong psychosocial component, which consists of a people's own sense of itself, its origins and future development. While historical and cultural factors, such as a common language, customs and political consciousness, will play a strong role in most cases, they will not necessarily take precedence over a people's sense of where their future lies and the advantages of joining with others in a common enterprise. Aboriginal nations, like other nations, have evolved and changed in the past; they will continue to evolve in the future.[20]

Based on this diversity of ways individuals report their "Indianness" and the resulting "uncertainty" with respect to population counts, it can be argued that First Nations group boundaries are fuzzy in Canada. But this was not always the case. At the time of first contact between First Nations and European colonizers, these group boundaries were clearly defined.

FROM DEPOPULATION TO POPULATION REVIVAL

Estimates of the size of the First Nations and Inuit population in the year 1534 within current boundaries of Canada range from 300,000 to 2 million persons, with the most widely accepted figure reaching 500,000 persons.[21] Beyond the academic debate of which estimate is the most accurate, the disease-, war-, and famine-driven depopulation that followed the arrival of the European colonizers was brutal and even fatal for some communities (e.g., Beothuks, Hurons). The population size probably dropped to its lowest point at the start of the twentieth century while the European colonization of the West and North was entering its final stage (Figure 2).

FIGURE 2: North American Indian Origin Population in Canada, 1534–2006

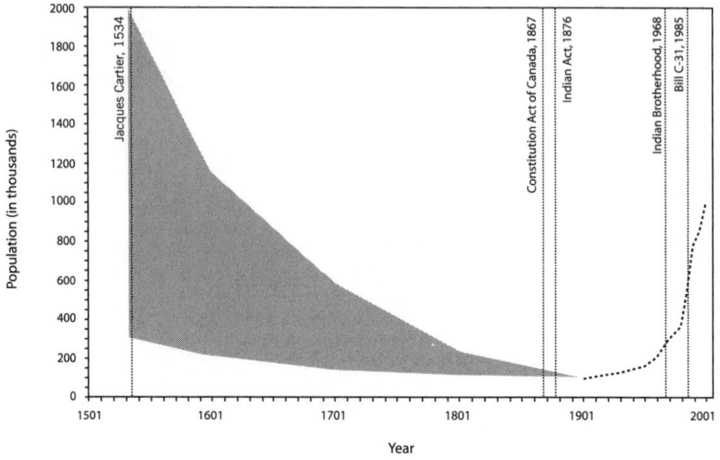

Sources: RCAP, 1996, Vol. 1, Chapter 2, Section 1; Goldmann, 1993; Statistics Canada, Census of Canada, 1901 to 2006.

The census figures for the *North American Indian* origin population have been on the rise since 1901. Growing slowly from the start to the middle of the twentieth century—from 93,000 to 156,000 people—this population began to exhibit very rapid growth from 1951 to 1971 and then skyrocketed from 1971 to 2006. Over the past thirty-five years, the size of the population has more than quadrupled (325 percent), from 295,000 to over 1.25 million people. For comparison's sake, the overall growth of the Canadian population was 47 percent over the same period. Regardless of how "Indianness" is defined, demographic growth during the last part of the twentieth century and beginning of the twenty-first was spectacular (Table 1).

The Natural Movement of Births and Deaths

The natural increase of the First Nations population at the start of the twentieth century, which corresponds to the excess of births over deaths (Figure 3), was relatively modest (about 1 percent annually), most likely similar to when the first Europeans arrived.[22] Because of harsh living conditions, the birth (about 40 births per 1000) and death (about 30 deaths per 1000) rates were very high by demographic standards.[23]

From a population standpoint, the period ranging from 1941 to 1971 was one of demographic transition for First Nations.[24] This transition began with a fall in mortality, with fertility remaining at a high level until the early 1960s.

TABLE 1: Growth of the North American Indian Origin Population, North American Indian Identity Population and Registered Indian Population, Canada, 1986-2006[1]

	Population Size					% Increase 1986-2006
	1986	1991	1996	2001	2006	
Census of Canada (Statistics Canada)[i]						
North American Indian Origin	548,955	783,980	867,210	1,000,905	1,253,610	128%
North American Indian Identity[2]	329,730	443,285	494,835	566,555	653,635	98%
Registered Indian	263,245	385,805	488,040	558,175	623,780	137%
Indian Register (Indian and Northern Affairs Canada)[ii]						
Registered Indian	387,829	511,791	610,874	690,101	754,700	95%

Notes: [1] The differences in the Registered Indian population counts are due to differences in data collection approaches between the Census and the Indian Register. For more information, see INAC, 2008, annex A.

[2] Excludes those individuals who do not have an Aboriginal origin.

Sources: [i] Statistics Canada, 1986 to 2006 Census of Canada, custom tabulations.
[ii] Indian and Northern Affairs Canada, 2005. Basic Departmental Data 2004, Table 1.1, p. 3.

The drop in mortality (from 26 to 8 deaths per 1000) was achieved through vaccination campaigns and access to basic health-care services in First Nations communities.[25] The combination of rising fertility[26] and declining mortality that followed resulted in a high rate of natural increase of the population (about 3 percent).

From 1971 to 2006, the demographic transition entered its third phase with a decline in fertility (from 36 to 25 births per 1000), which reduced the natural increase below 2 percent annually.[27] In the absence of any other factors, the overall growth of the First Nations population should have slowed down after 1971. Instead, the opposite occurred: the growth of First Nations accelerated, often exceeding the theoretical maximum natural increase of 5.5 percent per year[28] for a population that is subject only to the natural movement of births and deaths.[29] A population maintaining a growth rate of 5.5 percent per year doubles every thirteen years. After 100 years, that population would be more than 200 times larger than at the outset. Clearly, other factors contributed to the demographic growth of First Nations since 1971. If First Nations had grown at an annual rate of 2 percent between 1971 and 2006, as implied by natural increase (Figure 3), its population size in 2006 (based on origin counts) would have reached 600,000, not the 1.254 million recorded by the 2006 Census of Canada (Figure 1). In the following section, we describe how

First Nations women have contributed in a very specific manner to this population revival.

FIGURE 3: Crude Birth Rate and Crude Death Rate of the Registered Indian Population, Canada, 1901–2004

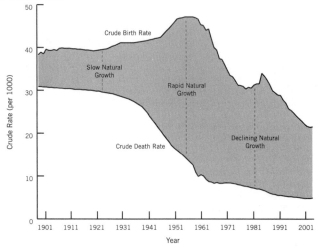

Sources: Romaniuc, 1981; Latulippe-Sakamoto, 1971; Piché and George, 1973; Loh et al, 1998; Clatworthy, 2006, unpublished data.

The Powerful Potential of Intermarriage

Population growth is not a closed process, such that a population reproduces itself through its members only. Applied to First Nations, this means that First Nations women would form couples and families with First Nations men only. It also means that the only way one could enter and exit a First Nations population is through birth and death. But population dynamics are far more complex. First Nations men and women do not always find a First Nations partner. Some First Nations individuals, of course, partner and have children with non-First Nations individuals. Intermarriage (legal or common-law) and "inter-parenting" are often perceived as having an adverse impact on the demographic viability of First Nations, but, again, this is a misconception.

Two hypothetical scenarios illustrate the potential positive impact intermarriage and "inter-parenting" can have on the First Nations population (Figure 4). First, if a population of 1000 persons marries only within (0 percent intermarriage), i.e., all its members find a partner within the population, then there are 500 couples in this population. If each couple has two children, then this population would generate 1000 births. Second, if a population of 1000

FIGURE 4: Potential Population Impacts of Intermarriage

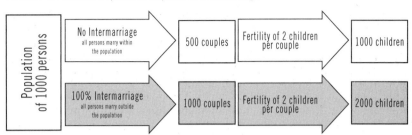

persons is fully intermarrying (100 percent), i.e., all its members find a partner outside the population, then there are 1000 mixed couples, twice as many as in the "marry within only" population. If each mixed couple also has two children, then this population would generate 2000 births, twice the number of the "marry within only" population. The point is that a population exhibiting a high rate of intermarriage has a higher potential for rapid population growth than a population with little or no intermarriage.

For most ethnocultural groups in Canada, the realization of this potential as demographic growth rests with the members of these groups currently in mixed couples: how do they identify themselves and their children? For First Nations, though, the government has defined inheritance rules regarding the legal recognition of "Indianness" through the *Indian Act*. Prior to 1985, specific provisions of the *Indian Act* wiped out any positive impact of intermarriage on the demographic growth by removing all *Registered Indian* women who outmarried, and their children, from the *Registered Indian* population. These women and their children have retained their cultural identity, despite not living in a First Nations community in most cases (82 percent in 1999.)[30] These people campaigned during the 1970s to pressure the government to eliminate these discriminatory provisions of the *Indian Act*. By the early 1980s, the discrimination against First Nations women was widely acknowledged in Canada.[31] The *Indian Act* was amended on 28 June 1985, when Parliament passed Bill C-31. Bill C-31 introduced three features: (1) new gender-neutral rules governing entitlement to Indian registration for all children born to a *Registered Indian* parent; (2) restored *Registered Indian* status and membership rights to those who had lost them because of inequalities in the Act; and (3) the opportunity for First Nations to establish their own rules governing membership.[32]

The legal battle fought and won by First Nations women in 1985, on behalf of their children and for recognition of their cultural identity, has resulted in significant demographic growth. Between 1985 and 2004, the total population impact of Bill C-31 on *Registered Indians* is estimated at 184,400 individuals.[33] As described in Figure 5, about 60 percent of this growth resulted from reinstatements and first-time registrations of children, while 37 percent were from births that would have been denied registration under the inheritance rules of the previous *Indian Act*. The remaining 2 percent, referred to in the figure as "net women retained," correspond to the difference between (a) the number of women who married a non-Indian after 1985 and retained their status and (b) the number of women who did not gain status through marriage to an Indian after 1985. Without the commitment of these women to their children and their culture, the *Registered Indian* population would not have enjoyed the observed demographic explosion. Instead, it would have been 35 percent smaller at the turn of the twenty-first century.[34]

FIGURE 5: Impact of Bill C-31 on the Registered Indian Population, Canada, 1985-2004

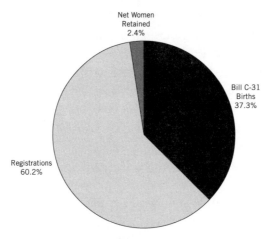

Source: Clatworthy, unpublished, in Guimond, 2006.

Looking at Future Demographic Growth

Despite eliminating provisions discriminatory to First Nations women, Bill C-31 still results in a growing number of individuals not entitled to Indian registration. According to section 6 of the *Indian Act*, which defines the status inheritance rules, two successive generations of inter-parenting between Status Indians and other non-entitled Canadians results in loss of entitlement to Indian registration for the children of the second generation.[35] As such, Bill

C-31 still limits the potential for population growth resulting from intermarriage and inter-parenting.

Clatworthy projects that the total population of survivors and descendants should increase throughout the next 100 years, most likely exceeding 2 million individuals (Figure 6).[36] The population entitled to Indian registration is projected to increase for about fifty years, the equivalent of two generations, peaking around 1 million individuals. The population of non-entitled descendants is projected to increase at an accelerating pace, reaching 1.3 million at the end of this century, which adds to more than 60 percent of all survivors and descendants. Off-reserve, where intermarriage and inter-parenting are more common, about nine out of ten (88 percent) survivors and descendants will not be entitled to registration. Loss of entitlement to Indian registration will occur much more quickly among descendant children (Figure 7). As noted by Clatworthy, three out of four children born on-reserve are expected to lack entitlement to registration at the end of the twenty-first century; in contrast, virtually no children born off-reserve will be entitled to Indian registration.

FIGURE 6: Projected Registered Indian Population, Canada, 1999-2099

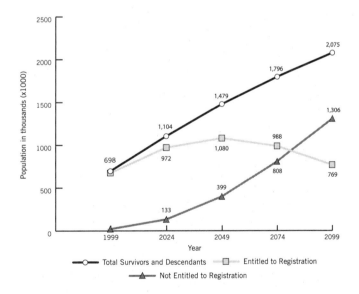

Source: Clatworthy, 2003a, Figure 3.4.

FIGURE 7: Projected Share of Births Entitled to Indian Registration, Canada, 1999–2099

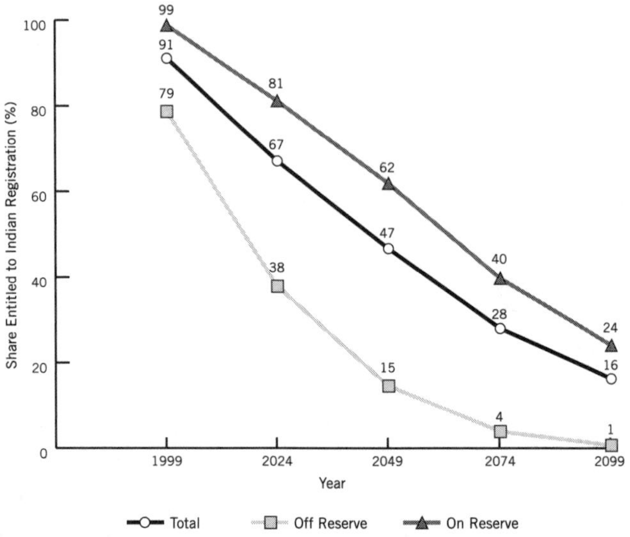

Source: Clatworthy, 2003a, Figure 3.7.

In light of current demographic trends and their implications for future population growth of First Nations, what will become increasingly salient is not entitlement to Indian registration. Rather, the issue will be how the non-entitled descendants of mixed parentage will self-identify. If a majority of these descendants (more than 50 percent) choose not to identify as First Nations, then the First Nations population is likely to start declining rapidly after two generations, as revealed by Clatworthy's analysis. If non-entitled descendants are raised with the knowledge of their cultural heritage and a majority of them choose to self-identify as First Nations, despite *Indian Act* rules, then the demographic future of First Nations communities is one of healthy growth. And what are statistics saying? According to current trends, inter-parenting patterns of First Nations, especially those of First Nations women,[37] will have a positive impact on future population growth of First Nations: a healthy majority of children (63 percent in 2001) under the age of fifteen raised in a family headed by a First Nations woman and non-Aboriginal man are reported as having a First Nations identity.

WELL-BEING AND GENDER EQUALITY IN FIRST NATIONS

The second theme of this demography chapter is well-being and gender equality in First Nations. There is an abundance of political and advocacy literature in this domain. Only recently, however, has solid scientific literature emerged. Cooke and Beavon[38] and Cooke, Beavon, and McHardy[39] have developed the Registered Indian Human Development Index (HDI) to compare the well-being of *Registered Indians* to other Canadians. Cooke and Beavon followed the methodology used by the United Nations Human Development Program to evaluate and monitor the quality of life of countries around the world. "Human development" is defined as an expansion of human choices, which requires *longer and healthier lives* (measured by life expectancy at birth),[40] acquisition of *knowledge* (measured by the proportion of the adult population with grade 9 and by the proportion with high school or higher),[41] as well as access to goods needed for a decent *standard of living* (measured by per capita income).[42] Data on life expectancy, educational attainment, and per capita income are combined to produce an HDI score, which ranges from 0 (lowest level of well-being) to 1. The HDI has received a great deal of attention in Canada because of Canada's consistent top-ten position in the HDI world ranking. Unfortunately, the 2006 HDI estimates were not yet available during the writing of this chapter. Also, there are no HDI estimates for non-status Indians due to the lack of information on their life expectancy at birth.

Overall, the HDI score for *Registered Indians* improved between 1981 and 2001, closing the gap with other Canadians (Figure 8). The HDI score for *Registered Indians* moved from 0.627 in 1981 to 0.765 in 2001, while the gap relative to other Canadians fell from 0.18 to 0.12. Over the course of these two decades, improvements to educational attainment have made the single greatest contribution (55 percent) toward closing the well-being gap, compared to life expectancy (29 percent) and per capita income (16 percent). In the 2001 international context, *Registered Indians* would have ranked forty-eighth, below Kuwait and Croatia, and above the United Arab Emirates and Bahamas.[43]

Although progress observed over the last two decades should be seen as a very positive outcome, First Nations youth still rank amongst the lowest group in Canada in terms of educational attainment in 2001 (Figure 9). The continued low educational achievement of First Nations relative to other Canadians remains a challenge. In the context of a highly competitive labour market, the lower educational attainment of First Nations youth suggests that, as these cohorts age, they will continue to lag behind other Canadians in employment and income, and will be at greater risk of dependency on income supplements.[44]

FIGURE 8: Human Development Index (HDI), Registered Indians and Other Canadians, Canada, 1981–2001

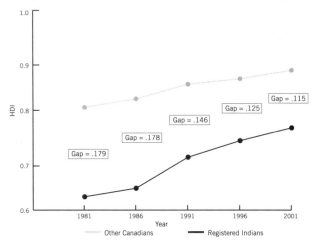

Source: Cooke and Beavon, 2007, Table 3.1, 53.

FIGURE 9: Proportion of Young Adults (20-29) with High School or Higher Education, Selected Ethnocultural and Aboriginal Groups, Canada, 2001

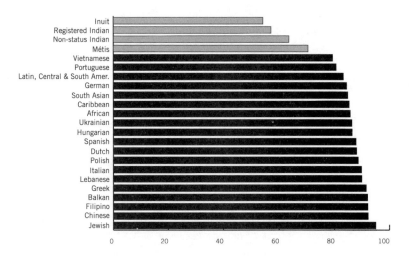

Note: Ethnocultural groups are defined on the basis of ethnic origin, single or multiple responses. Aboriginal groups are defined according to Aboriginal self-identification.

Source: Statistics Canada, 2001 Census of Canada, public use microdata file.

The HDI gender gap displayed by the *Registered Indians* is particularly wide by international standards (Figure 10).[45] In 2001, the HDI gender gap of *Registered Indians* (0.780–0.750=0.030) is almost eight times greater than the gap observed among other Canadians (0.004). Since 1986, other Canadian women and men have nearly identical HDI scores. Among *Registered Indians*, however, the HDI score of women has surpassed the HDI score of men. It should be noted, though, that the observed differences in well-being between women and men within the respective populations are generally small compared to the overall difference in well-being that exists between *Registered Indians* and other Canadians (0.115 in 2001; see Figure 8).

FIGURE 10: Human Development Index (HDI) by Gender, Registered Indians and Other Canadians, Canada, 1981-2001

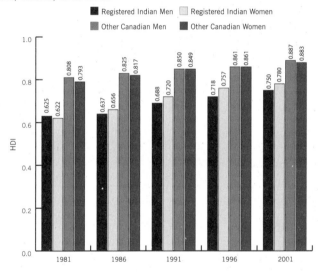

Sources: Cooke, 2007, Table 4.3; Cooke and Guimond, 2006, Table 1.

The quality of life of *Registered Indians* varies significantly from region to region, from on- to off-reserve (Figure 11). On-reserve *Registered Indians* living in the Prairies rank the lowest on the HDI scale. The HDI gap between *Registered Indians* and other Canadians is also the widest in these provinces. In 2006, about 46 percent of *Registered Indians* reside in the Prairies. In Manitoba and Saskatchewan, 9 percent of the total population is *Registered Indian*. The largest HDI gender gaps are observed in Manitoba and Saskatchewan; generally, in provinces where the *Registered Indian* HDI is the highest (e.g., Ontario), the gender gap is the smallest.

FIGURE 11: Human Development Index (HDI) by Gender, Registered Indians and Other Canadians, Canada, provinces and territories, 2001

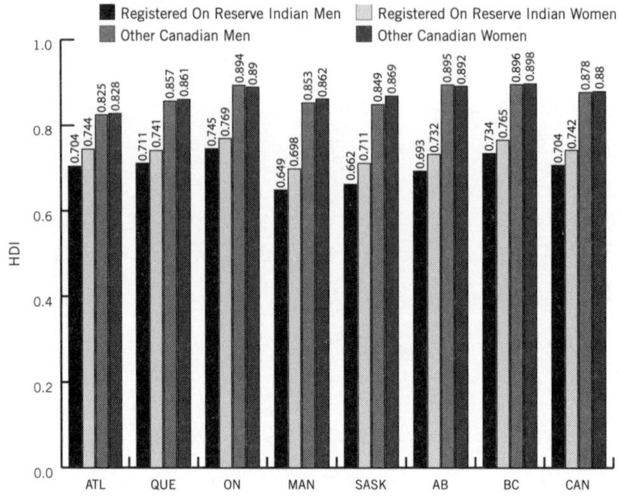

Source: Cooke and Beavon, unpublished, in Guimond, 2004.

Table 2 illustrates gender differences across the three components of the HDI. Along with benefitting from a higher overall HDI score, *Registered Indian* women hold advantages over men in both life expectancy and education. Since 1981, the advantage of women over men, in terms of life expectancy, declined markedly among *Registered Indians* and other Canadians. The small but increasing advantage in educational attainment of *Registered Indian* women over men contrasts with the slight disadvantage in education of other Canadian women. The gap in income between *Registered Indian* women and men decreased significantly between 1981 and 2001. Among other Canadians, however, the income gap between women and men is substantial and decreased by a smaller margin over the same period.[46]

TABLE 2: Gender Differences in Life Expectancy at Birth, Education and Income, Registered Indians and Other Canadians, Canada, 1981 and 2001

Indicator	Year	Registered Indian Women	Registered Indian Men	Gender Gap	Other Canadian Women	Other Canadian Men	Gender Gap
Life Expectancy	1981	68.9	62.4	6.5	79.1	72.0	7.1
at Birth (years)	2001	75.4	70.3	5.1	81.5	75.9	5.6
Proportion with	1981	60.0%	59.3%	0.7%	79.7%	80.6%	-0.9%
Grade 9 or Higher	2001	83.3%	81.6%	1.7%	90.0%	90.6%	-0.6%
Proportion with	1981	32.4%	33.7%	-1.3%	57.8%	61.6%	-3.8%
High School or Higher	2001	58.9%	54.2%	4.7%	75.2%	75.6%	-0.4%
Average Annual Income	1981	$4,248	$8,565	-$4,317	$9,164	$21,813	-$12,649
(Year 2000 Constant $)	2001	$8,766	$10,122	-$1,356	$16,071	$26,060	-$9,989

Source: Cooke and Guimond, 2006, table 1.

Cooke[47] and Guimond[48] assessed gender equality between *Registered Indian* women and men, again using a methodology developed by the United Nations Development Program: the Gender Empowerment Measure (GEM). This adaptation of the GEM incorporates: (1) women's participation in a population's political decision making, as measured by the percentage of administrative jobs in government held by women; (2) women's participation in a population's economic decision making, as reflected by the percentage of private-sector managerial, professional, and technical positions occupied by women; and (3) women's control over economic resources, as estimated by the percentage of total annual employment income earned by women. As with the HDI, these three indicators are combined to produce a GEM score, which ranges from 0 (lowest level of equality) to 1. High GEM scores indicate strong levels of equality between men and women, regardless of their actual well-being.

Figure 12 presents GEM scores for *Registered Indians* and other Canadians. GEM scores have been on the rise between 1991 and 2001 for both *Registered Indians* and other Canadians. *Registered Indians*' GEM score is higher than that of other Canadians but the difference is narrowing. In fact, GEM scores for *Registered Indians* in 2001 were higher than GEM scores of other Canadians in all provinces and regions, with the exception of Saskatchewan (Figure 13). The strongest levels of gender equality are observed among *Registered Indians* in the Atlantic region, British Columbia, and the territories. On all components of the GEM, *Registered Indian* women have a stronger score than other Canadian women, but remain mainly under-represented relative to *Registered Indian* men (Figure 14). *Registered Indian* women are over-represented in professional and technical occupations only.[49] Although the *Registered Indian* population has higher levels of gender equality than other Canadians, as Cooke points out, their well-being as measured by the HDI remains markedly lower than the well-being of other Canadians.

Analysis of the Human Development Index reveals that First Nations women's advancements over the course of the 1980s and 1990s, especially in the areas of education and health, had a remarkable outcome on the overall well-being of First Nations populations and communities. At the same time, analysis of the Gender Empowerment Measure provides evidence that a balance is being restored between men and women in First Nations communities.

FIGURE 12: Gender Empowerment Measure, Registered Indians and Other Canadians
Canada, 1991-2001

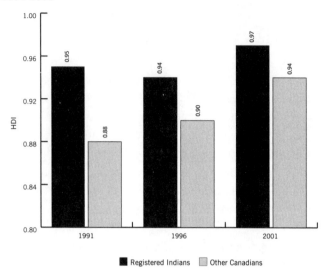

Source: Cooke and Guimond, 2006, Figure 3.

FIGURE 13: Gender Empowerment Measure, Registered Indians and Other Canadians
Canada, provinces and territories, 2001

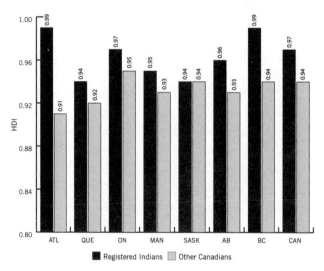

Source: Cooke and Guimond, 2006, Figure 4.

FIGURE 14: Gender Differences (Female minus Male) in Public Administration, Private Sector Managerial, Professional and Technical Positions, and Employment Income, Registered Indians and Other Canadians, Canada, 2001

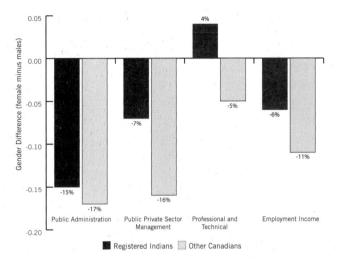

Source: Cooke and Guimond, 2006, Figure 5.

REPRODUCTIVE HEALTH OF OUR YOUNG WOMEN AND COMMUNITY DEVELOPMENT

In the context of sustainable development of First Nations communities, the broad human development goals of education, health, economic prosperity, and empowerment of women are all of considerable importance. International instances such as the 1994 International Conference on Population and Development held in Cairo and the 2000 Millennium Declaration agreed to by 189 nations have recognized that reproductive health is an integral part of this development package by ensuring (1) safe motherhood; (2) avoidance of sexually transmitted infections, including HIV/AIDS; and (3) enabling choices concerning whether, when, and how often to form sexual partnerships and to bear children. These three facets of reproductive health are especially relevant to achieving gender equality and empowerment of women, but also have been shown to play a much wider part in poverty reduction and in the broader sustainable development agenda.[50]

Little attention has been given in Canada to the situation of *Registered Indian* teenage girls (aged fifteen to nineteen) with respect to when and how

often to bear children, despite astoundingly high levels of fertility. At about
100 births per 1000 women since 1986 (Figure 15), the fertility of these teenage
girls is six times higher than that of other Canadian teens.[51] For First Nations
teenagers under the age of fifteen, the fertility rate is estimated to be as much
as eighteen times higher than that of other Canadians.[52] The rate among young
First Nations women is highest in the Prairie provinces (Figure 16). In Manitoba, one teenage *Registered Indian* girl in eight had a child during the 2000–
2004 period (125 births per 1000). The fertility of *Registered Indian* teenage
girls in Canada is more than twice the fertility of American teenagers, who
have the highest teen fertility of all industrialized nations. *Registered Indian*
teenage girls have a fertility level comparable to that of teenage girls in the
least developed countries such as Nepal (127 per 1000), Ethiopia (111), and
Somalia (75).[53] Between 1986 and 2004, almost 45,000 children entitled to
registration were born to a *Registered Indian* mother under the age of twenty.
This represents about 20 percent of all births to *Registered Indians* women.[54]
The Royal Commission on Aboriginal Peoples final report, which put forward
440 recommendations calling for sweeping changes to the relationship
between Aboriginal and non-Aboriginal people and governments in Canada,
is virtually silent on the issue of teen motherhood in First Nations communities. At the band level, there is great variation in teen fertility: the teen fertility
rate of the largest First Nations bands (i.e., with a female teen population of at
least fifty) varies from fifty-eight to 196 births per 1000 teenage girls.

FIGURE 15: Fertility Rate of Registered Indian and All Canadian Women Aged 15 to 19,
Canada, 1986-2004

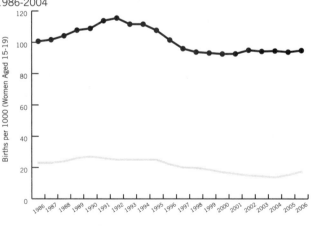

● Registered Indian Women (under section 6.1)   ——— All Canadian Women

Source: Guimond and Robitaille, 2007, Figure 1.

FIGURE 16: Fertility Rate of Registered Indian Women Aged 15 to 19, Canada, provinces and territories, 2000-2004

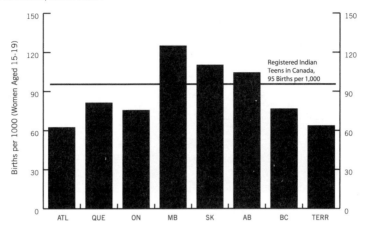

Note: ¹For only those women registered under section 6.1 of the *Indian Act*.
Source: Guimond and Robitaille, 2008, unpublished.

Early motherhood increases the vulnerability of a First Nations woman who is already disadvantaged socio-economically by reason of her cultural background and gender. She is at greater risk of academic underachievement, reduced employability, single parenthood, and an increased dependence on income assistance. The combined effect of early motherhood and cultural background is glaring in terms of educational attainment. According to the 2001 Census of Canada, First Nations women aged twenty-five to twenty-nine who had a child before the age of twenty are twice as likely (20 percent) not to have completed grade 9, than other First Nations mothers (10 percent) and other Canadian teenage mothers (8 percent).

From the moment of their birth, the future for many children of teenage mothers does not shine too brightly. Clatworthy[55] has shown that the rate of unstated paternity among children born to teenage mothers greatly exceeds that of older mothers (Figure 17). Between 1985 and 1999, about 30 percent of all children with unstated fathers were born to mothers under twenty years of age. Under the current registration rules of the *Indian Act*, "failure to report a registered Indian father results in either inappropriate registration of the child ... or denial of registration and loss of associated entitlements, benefits and privileges."[56]

FIGURE 17: Estimated Prevalence of Unstated Paternity of Children by Age of Mother[1] at Birth of Child, Canada, 1985–1999

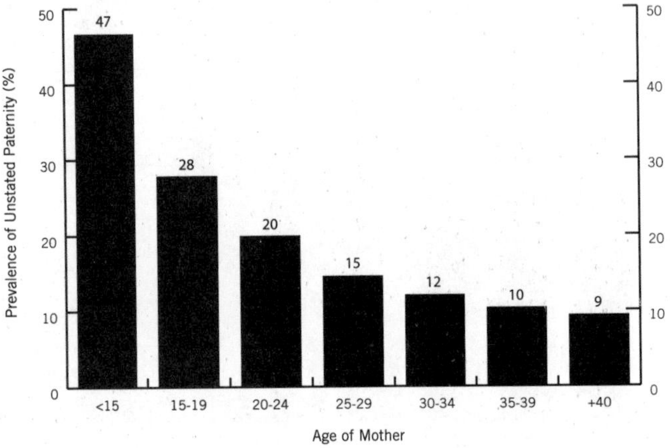

Note: [1]For only those women registered under section 6.1 of the *Indian Act*.
Source: Clatworthy, 2003b, Figure 2.

American statistics on early motherhood indicate that teenage mothers are at greater risk of not receiving proper prenatal care,[57] with the result that the frequency of fetal alcohol syndrome[58] is higher among children of teenage mothers. The children of teenage mothers are also more at risk of neglect and abuse, and therefore at greater risk of being uprooted from their families and placed in the custody of social services.[59] Owing to the economic situation of teenage mothers, their children grow up in conditions of poverty more often than children of older women. In 2001, 80 percent of First Nations teenage mothers lived in a family with a total income of less than $15,000 per year, compared to 25 percent of First Nations mothers aged twenty years or older.[60] According to an American study,[61] delaying childbearing from ages sixteen to seventeen until ages twenty to twenty-one would (1) increase the probability of graduating from high school; (2) decrease the probability of being economically inactive as a young adult; and (3) decrease the probability of daughters giving birth as a teen.

Teen fertility affects the well-being of an entire community, not just the individuals implicated and their families. Preliminary analysis of band-level data from the Indian register (1994 to 1998) and the Census of Canada (1996) reveals that teen fertility is negatively associated with the Community Well-Being (CWB) index (Figure 18).[62] In other words, the higher the fertility of First Nations teens in a community, the lower the well-being of that community.

The top twenty-five First Nations bands in terms of well-being (average CWB score of eighty-two) have a global teen fertility rate of seventy-five births per 1000 teen girls, compared to 158 births per 1000 for the twenty-five lowest ranking First Nations bands (average CWB score of forty-three).

FIGURE 18: Largest First Nations Bands by Community Well-Being Index (CWB) Score and Teen Fertility Rate, 1996

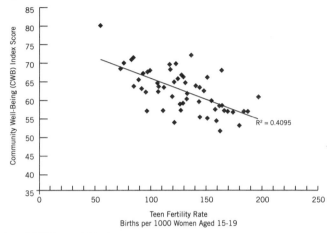

Source: Guimond, 2008, unpublished.

At the same time, while some people express concern about teen pregnancy in First Nations communities, others see it as traditional: First Nations teenage girls become mothers at an early age because that's the way it is in traditional First Nations culture. Guimond and Robitaille write that, given the consequences of early motherhood for the mother, child, family, and community, "the very idea of a teenage mother not being able to provide her child with a healthy environment conducive to physical, emotional, intellectual and spiritual development is diametrically opposed to the spirit of traditional culture, which places the child at the centre of family and community life. Debating the relevance of early motherhood solely from the perspective of culture is simplistic and indicative of a certain fatalism."[63] In the words of elder Maria Campbell, "The old women I have known said that we never had more children than we could grab and run away with if there was a battle. How many children can you grab? Probably no more than two. Today we are told that having babies is traditional. Catholic tradition maybe. I hardly believe it is traditional for us to have babies we cannot love, protect and provide for."[64]

At a time when the low fertility of Canadian families no longer ensures the replacement of generations, and in the context of a rapidly aging population, the high fertility of First Nations families is something to treasure. However, disregarding early (and too often lone) motherhood and its consequences certainly does not serve to leverage this richness. Rather, it perpetuates the welfare dependence of First Nations families and communities from generation to generation. Early motherhood in a healthy environment is the issue here, not motherhood in itself. Reflection and future actions must not focus on the number of children in First Nations families but, rather, on the timing and the conditions into which they are born.

Efforts are made by First Nations women to address the implications of teen fertility for the child, mother, family, and community. Most often, these efforts happen "below the radar," simply because of the extreme sensitivity of the topic in certain First Nations circles. Understandably, many people perceive any inquiry into family matters as an intrusion into privacy, or yet another attempt by government to "control" First Nations. This perception is especially strong if the inquiry originates from mainstream institutions.

In conclusion to this section on reproductive health, we highlight the outstanding contributions of two Aboriginal organizations. The Ontario Federation of Indian Friendship Centres (OFIFC), under the direction of Sylvia Maracle, released in 2002 a report on urban Aboriginal youth sexual health, with the intent "to motivate policy makers, community leaders, workers, parents, youth, and elders to take action and address the alarming health conditions of Aboriginal children and youth."[65] The research team, led by Kim Anderson, collected and analyzed data from 340 participants, including youth, youth parents, frontline workers, and elders. The findings of this study indicate that:

- more than 50 percent of the youth participating in the study reported little to no use of contraception;
- alcohol and drugs play an important role in the sexual practices of youth and in the high rate of teen pregnancy;
- 61 percent of the female participants in the study and 35 percent of the males reported having experienced some sort of sexual abuse. Sexually abused youth are more likely to have unprotected sex and more partners, and are also at greater risk of teen pregnancy;
- teens who become pregnant can feel stigmatized and isolated;

- despite self-declared allegiance to culture and spirituality, youth appear to lack the teachings or opportunities to access traditional knowledge; and
- most importantly, youth participants to this study agree that something should be done to offset the prevalence of teen pregnancy in their communities.

The OIFC report adds that, even though First Nations have been generally successful at avoiding the moral judgments that often characterize dialogue about teen pregnancy, perhaps the time has come to ask if "this acceptance has resulted in a complacency that has allowed Aboriginal communities, their leaders, and non-Native government leaders to renege on their responsibilities to Aboriginal children and youth."[66] The findings of this study are key to the development of culturally relevant policies and programs in the area of reproductive and sexual health of Aboriginal youth. Other First Nations organizations from across the country should replicate this remarkable study in order to further stimulate the dialogue on this issue, both locally and nationally.

In 2002, the Aboriginal Nurses Association of Canada (ANAC), under the leadership of Madeleine Dion Stout and Bernice Downey, and the sponsoring organization, Planned Parenthood Federation of Canada, released an educational guide, *Finding Our Way: A Sexual and Reproductive Health Sourcebook for Aboriginal Communities*. The guide was a result of concerns raised at the 1994 Cairo Conference on Population and Development about the reproductive health of Aboriginal people.[67] The direction for the preparation of this guide emerged from a national Aboriginal round table held in 1999 where participants identified gaps in culturally appropriate information and tools for programs and services in sexual and reproductive health.

This two-part sourcebook was designed for health and social service providers—nurses, community health representatives, teachers, public health workers, counsellors, and community developers—who work with First Nations, Inuit, or Métis people in northern, rural or urban settings. Part one of this sourcebook celebrates Aboriginal traditional ways and teachings about sexuality and reproduction. It also looks at the effects of European colonization, with a particular emphasis on the impact of residential schools. In the opinion of its authors, knowledge of the cultural and historical context is critical when involved in the delivery of health and social services to Aboriginal clients. The second part of this guide provides information on eighteen specific sexual and reproductive health topics covering all stages of life, including teen pregnancy, birth control options, and healthy pregnancies.

There has been tremendous demand for this ANAC publication ever since its release in 2002. Within the first year, more than 500 copies were distributed to ANAC members, Aboriginal Friendship Centres, health-care providers, practitioners, educators, academics, consultants, and many other groups in different health networks in Canada, but also in Australia and the United States.[68] This remarkable guide points to the need to educate young First Nations women about their gift of life, as well as their responsibilities as a mother. Appropriately, it also calls upon young First Nations men to respect women and to be responsible fathers. As observed by Newhouse, "Sexuality is a gift, a powerful gift that is to be respected ... it comes with a set of duties and obligations that govern its expression."[69] Achieving reproductive and sexual health in First Nations communities is fundamental to restoring balance between First Nations men and women and further improving the well-being of all.

FINAL THOUGHTS

From the brink of extinction at the start of the twentieth century, First Nations are rising again, in term of numbers, well-being, and gender balance. This chapter provided an opportunity to highlight some of the contributions of First Nations women to this rise.

First and foremost, First Nations women fought and won in 1985 the battle to eliminate the exclusionary rules of the *Indian Act* through which the First Nations identity of many women and their children was not recognized by the state. Without the commitment of these women to their children and culture, the *Registered Indian* population would have been 35 percent smaller at the turn of the twenty-first century. It is important to recognize the strength of these women who fought for the continuity of their cultural identity.

Second, in light of current demographic trends with respect to intermarriage and inter-parenting, self-identification will become increasingly important in the coming years, slowly but surely melting away the importance of entitlement to Indian legal registration. An analysis of statistics on identity of children in culturally mixed families reveals that a majority of children (63 percent) born to First Nations women in such families are raised as First Nations, thus resisting pressures to assimilate to the mainstream. The survival of First Nations culture rests on the shoulders of mothers and daughters and their ability to raise the next generation in First Nations traditional ways.

Third, according to the analysis of the Human Development Index (HDI), healthier and more educated First Nations women have contributed greatly to improvements in the overall well-being of First Nations populations and communities. Poverty is best fought by improving education, and First Nations women have clearly led the way over the course of the last two decades. The leadership of First Nations women in this realm of education has been and will continue to be crucial in this battle against poverty. Learning, both mainstream and traditional knowledge, is a key to self-reliance.

Fourth, balance between men and women is being restored in First Nations communities. Analysis of the Gender Empowerment Measure has shown that the *Registered Indian* population has higher levels of gender equality than other Canadians. But "higher" does not mean "ideal." Analysis of women's participation in political and economic decision making, and control over economic resources, still reveals significant inequality between First Nations men and women. To paraphrase the *End Poverty by 2015 Millennium Campaign*,[70] prosperity in First Nations communities can be achieved only once all First Nations men and women have equal opportunities to provide for themselves and their families. Societies where men and women do not stand equal can never achieve development in a sustainable manner.

Finally, enabling choices concerning whether, when, and how often to form sexual partnerships and to bear children is essential to gender equality and empowerment of women and, more broadly, to the eradication of poverty in First Nations communities. With teen fertility in First Nations communities showing no signs of decline, Aboriginal organizations, thanks to the contribution of dedicated First Nations women, are raising awareness and providing educational materials on issues related to the reproductive and sexual health of Aboriginal youth. Tackling these issues is tantamount to tackling child and youth poverty.

Notes

1   Every five years, Statistics Canada conducts a census. The census provides a statistical portrait of the country and its people. A vast majority of countries regularly carry out a census to collect important information about the social and economic situation of the people living in its various regions. In Canada, the census is the only reliable source of detailed data for all Aboriginal populations. Because the Canadian census is collected every five years and the questions are similar, it is possible to compare changes that have occurred in the makeup of Aboriginal populations over time.

2   The First Nations Regional Health Survey (commonly referred to RHS) is the only First Nations-governed national health survey in Canada. It collects information based on both Western and traditional understandings of health and well-being. See http://www.rhs-ers.ca/english/background-governance.asp.

3   In 1951, the government of Canada established the Indian Register and assigned responsibility for its maintenance to the department known today as Indian and Northern Affairs Canada. The register became operational in 1959. Only persons recognized as Indians pursuant to the *Indian Act* may be registered.

4   There is a subtle difference between Status Indians and Registered Indians. The first are eligible to be registered under the *Indian Act*, while the second are actually registered. Available statistics generally refer to the Registered Indians (INAC, 2004).

5   See E. Guimond, "Aboriginal Demographics: Population Size, Growth and Well-Being" (presentation to the Standing Committee on Aboriginal Affairs and Northern Development, Ottawa, 2006), 3.

6   See G. Goldmann, "The Aboriginal Population and the Census. 120 Years of Information—1871 to 1991" (paper presented at the Conference of the International Union for the Scientific Study of Population, Montreal, 1993) and E. Guimond, "L'explosion démographique des populations autochtones du Canada de 1986 à 2001" (PhD thesis, University of Montreal, 2009).

7   Also the case for the 1996 and 2001 censuses. See Statistics Canada, *2006 Census Dictionary* (Ottawa: Department of Industry, 2008), Catalogue No. 92-566-XWE, http://www12.statcan.ca/english/census06/reference/dictionary/index.cfm.

8   See N. Robitaille and R. Choinière, "L'accroissement démographique des groupes autochtones du Canada au XXe siècle," *Cahiers Québécois de démographie* 16, 1 (1987): 3–35.

9   As indicated for example by the absence of Métis in most censuses before 1981. G. Goldmann, "The Aboriginal Population and the Census," and E. Guimond, "L'explosion démographique."

10   Includes single (e.g., North American Indian only) and multiple responses (e.g., North American Indian and non-aboriginal, North American Indian and Métis). See Statistics Canada, *2001 Census Dictionary* (Ottawa: Department of Industry, 2003), Catalogue No. 92-378-XIE, 45–46.

11   See R. Alba, *Ethnic Identity: The Transformation of White America* (New Haven: Yale University Press, 1990), and F. Barth, *Ethnic Groups and Boundaries: The Social Organization of Cultural Difference* (Boston: Little Brown, 1969).

12   The 1986 Census data on Aboriginal identity were never officially disseminated, partly because of reporting errors detected within the non-Aboriginal population (see A. Crégheur, *Assessment of Data on Aboriginal Identity. 1986 Census of Canada* [Ottawa: Statistics Canada, Housing, Family and Social Statistics Division, 1988]). The data on the Aboriginal identity of populations of Aboriginal origin are considered reliable. See E. Guimond, "Ethnic Mobility and the Demographic Growth of Canada's Aboriginal Populations from 1986 to 1996," in A. Bélanger, ed., *Report on the Demographic Situation in Canada, 1998–1999* (Ottawa: Statistics Canada, 1999). Catalogue #91-209-XIE: 187–200.

13 See Statistics Canada, *General review of the 1986 Census* (Ottawa: Supply and Services Canada, 1989), Catalogue 99-137E.

14 Includes single (North American Indian) and multiple responses (North American Indian and Métis; North American Indian and Inuit; North American Indian, Métis and Inuit). See Statistics Canada, *2001 Census Dictionary* (Ottawa: Department of Industry, 2003), Catalogue No. 92-378-XIE, 43–44.

15 See T. Lee, *Definitions of Indigeneous Peoples in Selected Countries*, Quantitative Analysis and Socio-demographic Research, Working Paper Series 90-4 (Ottawa: Indian and Northern Affairs Canada, 1990).

16 This changed after the 1985 amendments to the *Indian Act* which now treats Indian status, band membership and residency as separate issues. See http://www. thecanadianencyclopedia.com/index.cfm?PgNm=TCE&Params=A1ARTA0003975.

17 See R. Savard and J.R. Proulx, *Canada. Derrière l'épopée, les autochtones* (Montreal: l'Hexagone, 1982).

18 See Statistics Canada, *2001 Census Directory*, 46–47.

19 See http://www.ainc-inac.gc.ca/ai/rs/pubs/sts/ni/rip/rip07/rip07-eng.pdf.

20 Royal Commission on Aboriginal Peoples, volume 2, part I, chapter 3, section 2.2.

21 See Olive Dickason, *Canada's First Nations: A History of Founding Peoples from Earliest Times* (Don Mills: Oxford University Press, 2001), chapter 4, 62.

22 See H. Charbonneau, "Trois siècles de dépopulation amérindienne," in L. Normandeau and V. Piché, eds., *Les populations amérindiennes et inuit du Canada* (Montreal: University of Montreal Press, 1984.)

23 See A. Romaniuc, "Increase in Natural Fertility During the Early Stages of Modernization: Canadian Indians Case Study," *Demography* 18, 2 (1981): 157–172; A. Romaniuc and V. Piché, "Natality Estimates for the Canadian Indians by Stable Population Models, 1900–1969," *Canadian Review of Sociology and Anthropology* 9, 1 (1972): 1–20; C. Latulippe-Sakamoto, *Estimation de la mortalité des Indiens du Canada, 1900–1968* (University of Ottawa, Department of Sociology, 1971).

24 [Translation] "The evolutionary process observed in many populations since the 18th century and characterized by a significant drop in mortality and fertility has been called demographic transition or demographic revolution. The process of transition from a situation in which both fertility and mortality were relatively high to one in which they are relatively low which has been observed in many countries, is called the demographic transition or population transition. Certain authors have [...] underlined the time-lag which usually separates a drop in mortality and a drop in fertility; as the latter generally precedes the former, we observe a phase of so-called demographic transition during which the population increases much more rapidly than during the preceding and following." L. Henry, *Dictionnaire démographique multilingue* (Liège, Belgium: Ordina Éditions, International Union for the Scientific Study in Population, 1981), 118.

25 See A.J. Siggner, *An Overview of Demographic, Social and Economic Conditions of Canada's Registered Indian Population* (Ottawa: Indian and Northern Affairs Canada, 1979); V. Piché and M.V. George, "Estimates of Vital Rates for the Canadian Indians, 1960–1970," *Demography* 10, 3 (1973): 367–382.

26 The main underlying cause of the rise in fertility between 1941 and 1961 is "found to be in the massive, almost abrupt shift from prolonged breastfeeding to bottle-feeding which took place prior to the onset of large-scale birth control practices." Romaniuc, "Increase in Natural Fertility," 157.

27 See S. Loh et al, *Population Projections of Registered Indians, 1996–2021*, prepared by the Population Projections Section, Demography Division, Statistics Canada, (Ottawa: Indian Affairs and Northern Development, 1998); F. Nault et al., *Population projections of registered Indians, 1991–2015* (report prepared for Indian and Northern Affairs Canada by the Population Projections Section, Demography Division, Statistics Canada, 1993).

28 This rate is obtained from the highest crude birth rate (60 per 1000 people; R. Pressat, *Dictionnaire de démographie* [Paris: Presses Universitaires de France, 1979], 246–247; G. Tapinos, *Éléments de démographie. Analyse, déterminants socioéconomiques et histoire des populations* [Paris: Armand Colin, 1985], 227) observable in exceptional conditions—young population, marrying young and using no form of contraception—from which the lowest crude mortality rate is subtracted (5 per 1000 people; United Nations, *Demographic Yearbook 1995* [New York: United Nations, 1997], table 4). Such a combination of high fertility and low mortality had probably never been observed.

29 In practical terms, the contribution of international migration may be considered to be nil. In the censuses of 1991, 1996, and 2001, about 5000 people of Aboriginal origin reported to be living outside the country five years before (Statistics Canada, custom tabulations).

30 See Stewart Clatworthy, *Re-assessing the Population Impacts of Bill C-31* (Ottawa: Indian and Northern Affairs Canada, 2001), 17.

31 See G. Hartley, "The Search for Consensus: A Legislative History of Bill C-31, 1969–1985," in J.P. White, E. Anderson, W. Cornet, and D. Beavon, eds., *Aboriginal Policy Research: Moving Forward, Making a Difference* (Toronto: Thompson Educational Publishing, 2007).

32 See Stewart Clatworthy, "Impacts of the 1985 Amendments to the Indian Act on First Nations Populations," in J.P. White, P.S. Maxim, and D. Beavon, eds., *Aboriginal Conditions: Research as a foundation for public policy* (Vancouver: University of British Columbia Press, 2003), 64.

33 Stewart Clatworthy, unpublished, in E. Guimond, "Aboriginal Demographics: Population Size, Growth and Well-Being" (presentation to the Standing Committee on Aboriginal Affairs and Northern Development, Ottawa, ON, 2006), 15.

34 According to the Indian Register, the Registered Indian population would have been just over 485,000 on 31 December 1999, instead of the 659,890 reported by INAC (2005).

35 Clatworthy, "Impacts of the 1985 Amendments," 64.

36 Ibid.

37 The contribution of First Nations women will be crucial, primarily because their "inter-parenting" rates (29 percent in 1999) are considerably higher than those of their male counterparts (11 percent). See Clatworthy, *Re-assessing the Population Impacts*, figure 14.

38 M. Cooke and D. Beavon, "The Registered Indian Human Development Index, 1981–2001," in J. White, D. Beavon, and N. Spence, eds., *Aboriginal Well-Being: Canada's Continuing Challenge* (Toronto: Thompson Educational Publishing, 2007), 51–68. D. Beavon and M. Cooke, "An Application of the United States Human Development Index to Registered Indians in Canada, 1996," in J. White, P. Maxim, and D. Beavon, eds., *Aboriginal Conditions: Research Foundations for Public Policy* (Vancouver: University of British Columbia Press, 2003), 201–221.

39 M. Cooke, D. Beavon, and M. McHardy. *Measuring the Well-Being of Aboriginal People: An Application of the United Nations' Human Development Index to Registered Indians in Canada, 1981–2001* (Ottawa: Indian and Northern Affairs Canada, 2004), http://www.ainc-inac.gc.ca/ai/rs/pubs/re/mwb/mwb-eng.asp.

40 Life expectancy at birth estimates are derived from the Indian Register. See R. Verma, M. Michalowski, and P.R. Gauvin, "Abridged Life Tables for Registered Indians in Canada, 1976–1980 to 1996–2000," *Canadian Studies in Population* 31, 2 (2004): 197–235.

41 Educational attainment estimates are derived from the 1981 to 2001 censuses of Canada.

42 Per capita income estimates are derived from the 1981 to 2001 censuses of Canada.

43 See Cooke and Beavon, "The Registered Indian Human Development Index, 1981–2001," 66, table 3.2.

44 See E. Guimond and M. Cooke, "The Current Well-Being of Registered Indians Youth: Concerns for the Future?" *Horizons* 10, 1 (2008): 29, table 4.

45 See Cooke and Beavon, "The Registered Indian Human Development Index, 1981–2001."

46 See M. Cooke and E. Guimond, *Gender Equality and Well-Being* (Ottawa: Indian and Northern Affairs Canada, 2006), http://www.ainc-inac.gc.ca/ai/rs/pubs/re/gewb/gewb-eng.pdf.

47 M. Cooke, "Using UNDP Indices to Examine Gender Equality and Well-being," in J. White, D. Beavon, and N. Spence, eds., *Aboriginal Well-Being: Canada's Continuing Challenge* (Toronto: Thompson Educational Publishing, 2007), 69–86.

48 Guimond, "Aboriginal Demographics."

49 It should be noted that this broad category of occupations includes jobs traditionally held by women, such as nursing and teaching.

50 For a discussion of a conceptual framework on population, reproductive health, gender, and poverty reduction, see J. Hobcraft, "Towards a Conceptual Framework on Population, Reproductive Health, Gender and Poverty Reduction," in *Population and Poverty: Achieving Equity, Equality and Sustainability*, Population and Development Strategies Series 8 (New York: United Nations Population Fund, 2003).

51 Teen fertility rate equals the sum of births to women aged fifteen to nineteen divided by female population aged fifteen to nineteen. Fertility rates can only be calculated for women registered under section 6(1) of the *Indian Act*. For more details about the source of data and the methodology, see N. Robitaille, A. Kouaouci, and E. Guimond, "La fécondité des Indiennes à 15-19 ans, de 1986 à 1997," in J.P. White, P. Maxim, and D. Beavon, eds., *Aboriginal Policy Research—Setting the Agenda for Change* (Toronto: Thompson Educational Publishing Inc., 2004), 201–224.

52   Standing Senate Committee on Aboriginal Peoples, *Urban Aboriginal Youth: An Action Plan for Change. Final Report* (Senate Committee Business, 37th Parliament, 2nd Session, 2003).

53   See E. Guimond and N. Robitaille, "When Teenage Girls Have Children: Trends and Consequences," *Horizons* 10, 1 (2008): 50, table 1.

54   Only for those women registered under section 6(1) of the *Indian Act*.

55   S. Clatworthy, *Factors Contributing to Unstated Paternity* (report prepared for the Strategic Research and Analysis Directorate at Indian and Northern Affairs Canada, 2003), http://www.ainc-inac.gc.ca/ai/rs/pubs/re/uncp/uncp-eng.asp.

56   Ibid., 2.

57   See Standing Senate Committee on Aboriginal Peoples, 2003. See also http://www.aecf.org/kidscount.

58   See Standing Senate Committee on Aboriginal Peoples, 2003.

59   See R. Maynard, "The Study, the Context, and the Findings in Brief," in R. Maynard, ed., *Kids Having Kids: Economic Costs and Social Consequences of Teen Pregnancy* (Washington, DC: Urban Institute Press, 1996), chapter 1.

60   Statistics Canada, 2001 Census of Canada, 2001 Census Public Use Microdata File (PUMF), individuals file.

61   See Maynard, chapter 1.

62   O'Sullivan and McHardy have developed the First Nations Community Well-Being Index (CWB) as a complement to the Registered Indian HDI. While the HDI measures average levels of well-being among Registered Indians at the national and regional levels, the CWB measures the well-being of individual First Nations communities.
E. O'Sullivan and M. McHardy, "The Community Well-being Index (CWB): Well-being in First Nations Communities, Present, Past, and Future," in J. White, D. Beavon and N. Spence, eds., *Aboriginal Well-Being: Canada's Continuing Challenge* (Toronto: Thompson Educational Publishing, 2007).

63   Guimond and Robitaille, "When Teenage Girls Have Children," 51.

64   Ontario Federation of Friendship Centres (OFIFC), *Tenuous Connections, Urban Aboriginal Youth Sexual Health and Pregnancy*, report prepared by the Write Circle (Kim Anderson, principal researcher) (Toronto: Ontario Federation of Friendship Centres, 2002), 51.

65   OFIFC, *Tenuous Connections*, 11.

66   OFIFC, *Tenuous Connections*, 59.

67   Aboriginal Nurses Association of Canada, *Finding Our Way: A Sexual and Reproductive Health Sourcebook for Aboriginal Communities* (Ottawa: Aboriginal Nurses Association of Canada, 2002), http://www.anac.on.ca/sourcebook/toc.htm.

68   See http://findarticles.com/p/articles/mi_qa3911/is_/ai_n9161463.

69 See D. Newhouse, "Magic and Joy: Traditional Aboriginal Views of Human Sexuality," Sex Information and Education Council of Canada newsletter in *Canadian Journal of Human Sexuality* 7, 2 (1998): 186.

70 See http://www.endpoverty2015.org/goals/gender-equity.

First Nations Women's Contributions to Culture and Community through Canadian Law

Yvonne Boyer

BEFORE COLONIZATION, First Nations women were revered for their capacity to produce new life. The respect accorded to women was an integral part of a balanced society that respected laws and relationships within the larger order of the universe. When the colonizers arrived, they imposed their system of values and laws upon the inhabitants. For First Nations women, this meant that their traditional roles were obliterated through tools such as the *Indian Act* and residential schools. This "old world" approach to colonization had devastating effects on the physical and social fibre of First Nations communities.

Today, there are many examples of the resilience, fortitude, and determination of First Nations women who have faced the harms resulting from colonization and attempts at forced assimilation. This chapter examines one such example: Sandra Lovelace's challenge of the state-imposed gender-discrimination through the *Indian Act*. The *Indian Act* provides the legal framework for the relationship between First Nations people and the Canadian government. Among other stipulations, the *Indian Act* determines how First Nations people must conduct themselves. Until Sandra Lovelace's challenge in the courts, women and their children lost their Indian status when they married non-Native men, while Native men kept theirs and transmitted it to their non-Native wives and children. In 1977, after losing her status and exhausting all her domestic remedies in the Canadian courts, Sandra Lovelace sought band membership through the international courts, and was successful in forcing Canada to amend the *Indian Act.*

Through efforts such as these, First Nations women are reshaping their relationships with the state, governments, each other, and with the communities of which they are a part.

FIRST NATIONS WOMEN'S ROLES IN TRADITIONAL SOCIETY

First Nations[1] law was given by the Creator through sacred ceremonies and is binding and unalterable. The promises and agreements encompass sacred principles, values, and laws that are to govern every relationship and interaction. The law not only informs relationships among humans but with all ecological orders.[2] It has accordingly been described as follows:

> Powerful laws were established to protect and to nurture the foundations of strong, vibrant nations. Foremost amongst these laws are those related to human bonds and relationships known as the laws relating to *miyo-wîcêhtowin*. The laws of *miyo-wîcêhtowin* include those laws encircling the bonds of human relationships in the ways in which they are created, nourished, reaffirmed, and recreated as a means of strengthening the unity among First Nations people and of the nation itself. For First Nations, these are integral and indispensable components of their way of life. These teachings constitute the essential elements underlying the First Nations notions of peace, harmony, and good relations, which must be maintained as required by the Creator. The teachings and ceremonies are the means given to First Nations to restore peace and harmony in times of personal and community conflict. These teachings also serve as the foundation upon which new relationships are to be created.[3]

First Nations women commanded the highest respect in their communities as the givers of life and, as such, were the keepers of the traditions, practices, and customs of the nation. It was well understood by all that women held a sacred status for their ability to bring new life to the world, and, by extension, new relationships with the Creator.[4] On the role of women, the Royal Commission on Aboriginal Peoples notes, "She did not have to compete with her partner in the running of the home and the caring of the family. She had her specific responsibilities to creation which were different, but certainly no less important, than his. In fact, if anything, with the gifts given her, woman was perhaps more important…."[5]

The newest members of the community were given the law of the Creator and were given responsibility to enter into new relationships in a "good way."[6] Women made integral decisions about family, property rights, and education.[7] Underlying principles of gender balance streamed through early society.[8] The issue of balance, however, is not to be construed or constructed as similar to the feminist or Western legal tradition understandings of "balance" as meaning "equality." First Nations law is not ordered around Eurocentric values or perceptions of equality. Rather, balance is understood as respecting the laws and relationships that women have as part of First Nations law and the ecological order of the universe. As Patricia Monture-Angus writes, "Aboriginal culture teaches connection and not separation. Our nations do not separate men from women, although we recognize that each has its own unique roles and responsibilities. *The teachings of creation require that only together will the two sexes provide a complete philosophical and spiritual balance. We are nations and that requires the equality of the sexes* [emphasis in original]."[9]

As a well-documented example, the Iroquoian culture is based on the principles of balance and equilibrium, gender being considered as only one component of balance. As Barbara Mann explains, "equilibrium was the animating purpose behind 'gendering,' or the interaction between male and female energies that dictated the separation of social functions by gender.... [T]he sexes functioned as cooperative halves. At once independent yet interdependent, they worked to create the perfect whole of society. In all the spheres—the social and the religious, the political and the economic—women did women's half and men did men's half, but it was only when the equal halves combined that community cohered into the functional whole of a healthy society."[10]

Unlike European culture, Iroquoian culture was not centred on conflict or subordination. Iroquoian culture required that each gender had a role and that each gender was superior in their sphere of responsibility. Both gender roles were viewed as equal and necessary for the health and survival of the community.[11] Barbara Mann writes of the important role of women in Iroquoian society: "The *gantowisas* enjoyed sweeping political powers, which ranged from the administrative and legislative to the judicial. The *gantowisas* ran the local clan councils. They held all the lineage wampum, nomination belts and titles. They ran funerals. They retained exclusive rights over naming.... They nominated all male sachems as well as all Clan Mothers to office and retained the power to impeach wrongdoers. They appointed warriors, declared war, negotiated peace and mediated disputes."[12] The women controlled the economy through the distribution of bounty and ruled the social sphere (including social practices such as inheritance through the female line, female-headed households, pre- and extramarital sexual relations for women, female-controlled fertility, permissive child rearing, adoptions, trial marriages, mother-dictated marriages, divorce on demand, maternal custody of children on divorce, and polyandry).[13]

The Royal Commission on Aboriginal Peoples reported of the traditional gender roles that "according to traditional teachings, the lodge is divided equally between women and men, and that every member has equal if different rights and responsibilities within the lodge.... The lodge governed our relationship with each other, with other nations, and with the Creator and all of Creation."[14]

The common thread running through all groups of Aboriginal society is that equality and gender balance was foremost: the men couldn't survive the harsh conditions without women and women could not survive without the male counterpart. Emma LaRocque notes, "Prior to colonization, Aboriginal women enjoyed comparative honour, equality and even political power in a way European woman did not at the same time in history. We can trace the diminishing status of Aboriginal women with the progression of colonialism. Many, if not the majority, of Aboriginal cultures were originally matriarchal or semi-matriarchal. European patriarchy was initially imposed upon Aboriginal societies in Canada through the fur trade, missionary Christianity and government policies."[15] Many scholars suggest that all First Nations traditions were marked by equality between men and women, with patriarchy and male dominance introduced only through the European missionaries[16] and institutionalized through the *Indian Act*.[17] These issues will be examined in the following section.

COLONIZATION OF FIRST NATIONS WOMEN

Unlike the laws of First Nations, based on respect and gender balance, the British common law developed through the legal traditions of the Romans, the Normans, church canon law, and Anglo-Saxon law, traditions whereby married women were generally considered to be under the protection and cover of their husbands.[18] The common law viewed women as having no social or legal status, but as chattels[19] and dependent first on their fathers and then their husbands:[20] "when a man and woman were married, that was just about the end of the wife (as a separate entity at least) for all practical and legal purposes.... For centuries the married woman was one with idiots and children; she was not thought competent to manage the wealth, the land."[21] British Jurist Sir William Blackstone described the coverture doctrine as follows:

> By marriage, the husband and wife are one person in law: that is, the very being or legal existence of the woman is suspended during the marriage, or at least is incorporated and consolidated into that of the husband; under whose wing, protection, and cover, she performs every thing; and is therefore called in our law-french a *feme-covert* ... under the protection and influence of her husband, her baron, or lord; and her condition during her marriage is called her *coverture*....
>
> For this reason, a man cannot grant anything to his wife, or enter into covenant with her: for the grant would be to suppose her separate existence; and to covenant with her, would only to be to covenant with himself....[22] (emphasis in the original)

Under coverture, a wife simply had no legal existence and was considered "civilly dead."[23] Claudia Zaher comments:

> Any income from property she brought into the marriage was controlled by her husband, and if she earned wages outside the home, those wages belonged to him. If he contracted debts, her property went to cover his expenses. *A man who killed his wife was guilty of murder and could be punished by death or imprisonment, but a woman who killed her husband was guilty of treason against her lord and could be punished by being drawn and burnt alive.* To put it most succinctly, upon marriage the husband and wife became one— him. Social norms, as reflected in the law, maintained that this was not only the natural way of things but also God's direct intent, quoting Genesis 3:16: "Your desire shall be for your husband, and he shall rule over you."[24] (emphasis added)

When North America was colonized, gender roles were redefined with the imposition of European laws. Some of the early impacts can be seen in the fur trade, where the European fur traders refused to deal with First Nations women.[25] The women's husband, father, or brother would make the sale or exchange of the fur, and, therefore, would receive the proceeds.[26]

Formal broad definitions of the term "Indian" came into effect in 1850 when the legislation governing Indians was created.[27] Section 3 of the *Indian Act* of 1876 states "the term 'Indian' means 'any male person of Indian blood reputed to belong to a particular band,' 'any child of such person,' 'any woman who is or was lawfully married to such person.'"[28] A First Nations woman's rights were now completely dependent on the rights of her father or husband.

In 1906, the *Indian Act* was amended to define a "person" as an individual *other* than an Indian.[29] An amendment to the *Indian Act*, redefining the term, was not made until 1951.[30] The restrictions that affected women as legal "non-persons" and denied their entry into medical schools and the legal professions would be applied to both Indian men and women from 1869 until voluntary and involuntary enfranchisement was repealed in the *Indian Act* in 1985.

Assimilation was the goal in attempting to colonize First Nations peoples, and the *Indian Act* proved to be a useful tool. Education played a large role in this assimilation project. It was also integral to annihilating the women's societal place as family anchor. Residential schools were a product of the *Indian Act* of 1876, which allowed the Minister of Indian Affairs to control education for Indians. The residential school experience entailed a separation of children from almost all family members. Parents were not allowed to visit their children in residential schools.[31] If children were allowed to return home at all, they were sent home for only two months out of the year.[32] Parents lost parenting skills and the children forgot how to live in a family. The insufficient health-care facilities, inadequate diets, and poor sanitation contributed to the spread of disease, suffering, near starvation, and death of students in residential schools.[33] One of the diseases that was largely spread in residential schools was tuberculosis, which ultimately reached epidemic levels.[34] The intergenerational effects of the loss of parenting skills (for both children and parents) and ill health resulting from residential schools[35] are evident in the current Aboriginal health statistics.[36]

In addition to the starvation and disease experienced in residential school systems, physical, mental, and sexual abuse were rampant.[37] The effect of the residential school experience on First Nations people has been devastating. First Nations peoples were severed from traditional practices, including medicinal practices. The residential schools forbade the use of First Nations languages, when much of the information relating to health could be communicated only through these languages. Traditional gender roles were obliterated as women lost their respected roles in the community, and patriarchy and paternalism became the dominant feature of First Nations society.[38] The traditional family unit was annihilated.

The *Indian Act*, residential schools, and other assimilation projects caused acute traumatization to the health and social fibre of Aboriginal people. Sakej

Youngblood Henderson describes a source of colonialism as Eurocentrism, being a "dominant intellectual and educational movement that postulates the superiority of Europeans over non-Europeans."[39] The intent behind colonization was to subjugate, by force if necessary, take possession of the land, assimilate the people through forced religious indoctrination, and promote adherence to Western society's norms, rules, organization, and ways of living and thinking.

There has been a denigration of First Nations women's roles in contemporary society due to the impact of colonization, and, as a result, "the cultural and social degradation of Aboriginal women has been devastating."[40] Several generations of *Indian Act* governance, and, in particular, the discriminatory provisions regarding intermarriage, have left many First Nations women without a voice.[41]

HARMS RESULTING FROM THE COLONIZATION OF FIRST NATIONS WOMEN

First Nations womanhood has been described as once being a sacred identity that was maintained through a knowledge system of balance and harmony. Women were politically, socially, and economically powerful, and held status in their communities and nations related to this power.[42] However, much harm against First Nations women resulted through discriminatory legislation, laws, and policies. State-imposed physical harms have affected all women, but, because of their disadvantaged place in Canadian society, in addition to the damages from the *Indian Act* and residential schools, First Nations women have been especially affected. Some of these issues will be examined in the subsequent section.

Forced Sterilizations

The eugenics movement can be traced back to nineteenth-century England, with the work of Sir Francis Galton (1822 to 1911), cousin to Charles Darwin. The term itself is derived from the Greek for "well born" or "good breeding." Eugenics policies spread to the United States, Canada, and several European countries, and later gained infamy in Germany.[43] Aboriginal women themselves were targets of a policy of involuntary surgical sterilization carried out in Canada and the United States, a blatant breach of the Genocide Convention.[44]

In the United States, a 1974 study of the Indian Health Services (IHS) by the Women of All Red Nations revealed "as many as 42 percent of all Indian women of childbearing age had by that point been sterilized without their consent."[45] These estimates were confirmed by a General Accounting Office investigation of four IHS facilities that examined records *only* for 1973 to 1976. The investigation concluded that "during this three-year sample period, 3406 involuntary sterilizations (the equivalent of over a half-million among the general population) had been performed in just these four hospitals."[46]

In Alberta, 2800 people were sterilized between 1929 and 1972 under the authority of the province's *Sexual Sterilization Act*.[47] Although many provinces considered the idea of eugenics, British Columbia and Alberta were the only provinces legislating in favour of eugenics.[48] Alberta sterilized ten times more people than did British Columbia.[49] Both provinces have historically had high Aboriginal populations.

The *Sexual Sterilization Act* was intended to stop "mental defectives" from having children. Instituted by the Act, the Eugenics Board was comprised of four people who were mandated to authorize sterilization in Alberta.[50] The Act initially required the consent of patients unless they were "mentally incapable," in which case "the consent of the next of kin had to be obtained."[51] In 1937, the Act was amended to ensure that consent was no longer required by patients or the next of kin if the patient was considered "mentally defective."[52] The 1937 amendment also targeted "individuals incapable of intelligent parenthood."[53] Aboriginal people were easy targets for the new amendment, especially with regard to being thought to be incapable of intelligent parenthood. In 1988, the Alberta government destroyed many of the 4785 files created by the Eugenics Board. The government of Alberta maintained 861 of those files. Professor Dr. Jana Grekul reviewed them and commented, "*most noticeably over-represented were Aboriginals* (identified as "Indian," "Métis", "half breeds", "treaty" and "Eskimo"). While the province's Aboriginal population hovered between 2% and 3% of the total over the decades in question, Aboriginals made up 6% of all cases represented [emphasis added]."[54] Furthermore, she concluded that with "few exceptions particularly in the 1930's (8%) more women than men appeared before the Board."[55] In addition, said Grekul, "We found that people were being referred to the board for reasons related to their social class, gender, and ethnicity, and there was no genetic condition for them to be considered for sterilization."[56]

In October 1989, Leilani Muir discovered that she had been sterilized and brought "legal action against the Government of Alberta for wrongful confinement and for wrongful sterilization" and won.[57] In Ms. Muir's case, "a single IQ test" had been enough to deem her mentally defective and therefore a candidate for sterilization.[58] Upon Ms. Muir's physical examination and discovery that she had been sterilized, her doctor reported that her insides "looked like she had been through a slaughterhouse."[59]

With the uncovering of the Muir case, the Government of Alberta's response was a proposition to override the Canadian Charter of Rights and Freedoms using section 33 to limit the compensation to victims; this was met with a massive public outcry.[60] The Government of Alberta finally apologized in 1999 and offered several individuals and groups the option to settle out of court.[61] For Aboriginal women, the impact on health and the stigma of having been wrongfully institutionalized and sterilized are insurmountable.[62] Further, First Nations women have been subjected to long-standing forms of abuse through government-imposed experiments in the corrections system and elsewhere.[63]

The First Nations Woman Is Legislated as "Prostitute"

Historians have established that prostitution occupied a central place in social reform initiatives during the late nineteenth and early twentieth centuries. Authors Carolyn Strange and Tina Loo question *why* prostitution became a social problem at this exact moment:[64] "Even though Scottish and French men started families with Aboriginal women during the fur trade, some Europeans began to propagate myths that such women were somehow more promiscuous in nature. These notions made it easier for all men to unfairly blame or victimize Aboriginal women for their problems."[65]

Anna Laura Stoler documents how and why specific sexual arrangements, like concubinage, were favoured by colonial elites over intraracial marriage and prostitution at various historical moments, but later were condemned and replaced by other conjugal relations. Colonial administrators deemed sexual relations between Native women and white men to be acceptable during the fur trade era, although these practices were to be censured and replaced by prostitution in later periods. Stoler further notes that the "regulation of sexual relations was central to the development of particular kinds of colonial settlements and to the allocation of economic activity within them."[66]

The first Canadian statute that dealt with prostitution was passed in Lower Canada in 1839.[67] In the late nineteenth century, prostitution was seen as a social evil and a racial problem. The "Native woman as prostitute" was identified as the new social problem and reported through sensational headlines such as "Indian Girl Sold for 1000 Blankets."[68] Government officials at the federal, provincial, and local levels implemented various legal and non-legal regulatory techniques to manage prostitution. Indian agents, missionaries, and local officials openly condemned both intra- and interracial prostitution, and many also emphasized the need for more "stringently applied laws."

By 1879, a series of provisions relating to prostitution was added to the *Indian Act*. These sections of the *Indian Act* underwent several revisions, each adding more force to the legislation. The *Indian Act* of 1879[69] focussed on punishing individuals who kept houses of prostitution. However, these sections were repealed and replaced in 1880 and again in 1884. The 1880 law prohibited the keeper of any house from allowing Indian women who were believed to be prostitutes on their premises. The 1884 Act extended the provisions of the earlier legislation from "keepers of houses of prostitution" to include any Indian woman or *man* keeping, frequenting, or found in a "disorderly house or wigwam."[70] The law was changed again in 1887 so that keepers and inmates of houses of prostitution would be equally liable to a fine of $100 or six months' imprisonment. These new provisions were aimed at eliminating intraracial prostitution only. The *Indian Act* criminalized Native women for practising prostitution and punished Aboriginal men for "pimping" and "purchasing" the services of prostitutes; however, few attempts were made to punish non-Aboriginal men. In 1892, with the enactment of the *Criminal Code of Canada*, the federal government removed all the prostitution sections from the *Indian Act* and inserted them into the *Criminal Code*. Consequently, many Aboriginal women who were arrested for prostitution-related offences were banished from cities and towns and were forced back to their reserves, if, indeed, their communities accepted them back.

Indian agents and missionaries emphasized that stronger marriage laws and the abolition of indigenous marriage customs[71] were necessary for the protection of Native women, the prevention of prostitution, and the preservation of white settlement. Traditional ceremonies, such as the potlatch,[72] were blamed for causing prostitution. As several historians have suggested, the potlatch was the ultimate sign of degradation, as it symbolized for them the depravity, savagery, and primitiveness of First Nations peoples.[73]

Aboriginal Women "Vanish"

In October 2004, Amnesty International released the *Stolen Sisters Report*.[74] This report was commissioned partly in response to the fact that over 500 Aboriginal women have been murdered or gone missing over the past twenty years, according to estimates by the Native Women's Association of Canada. The report highlights a 1996 Canadian government statistic that revealed that Aboriginal women between the ages of twenty-five and forty-four with status under the *Indian Act*[75] are five times more likely than all other women of the same age to die as the result of violence.[76]

Amnesty International's research posits that decades of government policies have been a major factor negatively affecting generations of Aboriginal women and children. Social strife, decades of involuntary uprooting of women and children, and lack of economic and educational opportunities within many Aboriginal communities have contributed to a steady growth in the number of Aboriginal people living in predominantly non-Aboriginal towns and cities. The report suggests that the same historical legacy has also contributed to a heightened risk of violence for Aboriginal women in urban centres in Canada. Many women now face desperate circumstances in Canadian towns and cities, a situation compounded by sexist stereotypes and racist attitudes towards Aboriginal women and girls and general indifference to their welfare and safety. The resulting vulnerability of Aboriginal women has been exploited by Aboriginal and non-Aboriginal men to carry out acts of extreme brutality against Aboriginal women.[77]

Despite the number of Aboriginal women who have been murdered or gone missing, their fate has not been adequately addressed by Canadian authorities, including the police and the public. Across the country, Aboriginal people face arrest and criminal prosecution in numbers that far outweigh the size of the Aboriginal population. The Manitoba Aboriginal Justice Inquiry suggested that many police have come to view Aboriginal people not as a community deserving protection, but as a community from which the rest of society must be protected.[78]

In conducting its research, Amnesty International interviewed a number of police officers, the majority of whom stated that they handle all cases the same and do not treat anyone differently because they are Aboriginal.[79] These statements, however, can be contrasted to the accounts of families. Many families reported that police did little when they reported a sister or daughter missing. Police response was that the majority of people who are reported missing have voluntarily "gone missing," that many choose to run away or have chosen to break off ties with their families.[80] Regardless of the circumstances, this does not justify incidents where, despite the serious concern of family members that a missing sister or daughter was in serious danger, police failed to take basic steps such as promptly interviewing family and friends or appealing to the public for information. Muriel Venne, founder of the Institute for the Advancement of Aboriginal Women, noted that hundreds of Aboriginal women have been killed or have gone missing across the country—"yet it has been largely met with indifference."[81]

According to Statistics Canada, 408,140 women self-identified as Aboriginal in the 1996 Canadian census.[82] The Amnesty International report confirms that 500 First Nations women went missing between 1995 and 2005. If Canadian women in general disappeared at that rate, 17,500[83] would have gone missing in the same period, a number equal to the population of a small city. A loss of that magnitude, about 875 women per year, would surely have triggered a massive response from the public, from police, and from all levels of government. How is it that so many Aboriginal women can disappear with hardly anyone taking notice?

The above section illustrates that the impacts of colonization have been great. However, in spite of the terrible circumstances that First Nations women have found themselves in, Sandra Lovelace tackled a most immediate and pressing problem: she had lost her Indian status and, in the process, an important part of her identity. The fact that the *Indian Act* had been in place for over 100 years did not daunt her. The following section briefly explains the structure of the United Nations and how Sandra Lovelace accessed the international law forum to challenge the discriminatory gender provisions in the *Indian Act*.

THE UNITED NATIONS FRAMEWORK

International law governs the relationships of nations or states who have agreed to be bound by various international agreements, covenants, and treaties. It recognizes the sovereignty of nations but also places limitations based on the consent of the nation that enters the international covenants. Therefore, human rights and the human rights of indigenous populations bind nations together to deal with such groups in a particular manner. Claims of Aboriginal peoples in Canada have been advanced internationally since the post-World War II era. The unique character of these claims challenges domestic and international legal regimes as Aboriginal peoples are caught in a dominant society with their own separate and distinct cultural, linguistic, and political groupings. The claims advanced are varied in that they dispute systemic discrimination in multiple sectors such as land rights, resources, sovereignty, self-government, territorial, and historical issues. The work of the United Nations in the post-war era has significantly improved and legitimized claims of indigenous people throughout the world. For instance, in 1982, a Working Group on Indigenous Issues was established, which drafted the United Nations Declaration of the Rights of Indigenous People. In 1993, the United Nations General Assembly proclaimed the year as the International Year of the World's Indigenous People and established a permanent forum for Indigenous Peoples with the United Nations. These efforts and many more have brought recognition to indigenous peoples and have fostered a growing international acceptance of the need to respond to Indigenous peoples' claims.

Canada has ratified a number of United Nations treaties that confirm the human rights of its citizens.[84] As to the position Canada globally takes on human rights, Canada has stated the following: "Canada does not expect other governments to respect standards which it does not apply itself. As a signatory of all the principal UN treaties on international human rights, Canada regularly submits its human rights record to review by UN monitoring bodies.... These undertakings strengthen Canada's reputation as a guarantor of its citizens' rights and enhance our credentials to urge other governments to respect international standards."[85]

The Government of Canada has stated that it sees itself as a leader in the area of human rights by setting an example through compliance with the two main instruments for dealing with human rights in Canada: the International Covenant on Civil and Political Rights (ICCPR), which includes the Optional Protocol to the International Covenant on Civil and Political Rights, and the International Covenant on Economic, Social and Cultural Rights (ICESCR).[86]

The ICCPR has a more direct impact on states who are parties to both the ICCPR and its companion, the Optional Protocol.[87] The ICCPR provides that individuals who claim that their rights have been violated and have exhausted all domestic remedies may petition the Human Rights Committee of the United Nations: "The Committee receives submissions from the petitioner and from the state against which the violation is alleged, and decide whether or not the state has violated the Covenant. The decision cannot be directly enforced, of course, but it is reported to the petitioner, the state and the General Assembly of the United Nations."[88]

These submissions are called "communications." Once admissibility and merits are determined, the onus is placed upon the state to provide the necessary information and explanations giving rise to the communication. The author of the communication is then provided an opportunity to refute or add to what the state has said. This is the route upon which Sandra Lovelace embarked.

STATE-IMPOSED DISCRIMINATION AND THE STORY OF SANDRA LOVELACE

Lovelace v. Canada

Sandra Lovelace is a Maliseet Indian woman who lost her Indian status, in accordance with the *Indian Act*, after marrying a non-Indian man. Also in accordance with the Act, an Indian man who married a non-Indian woman would not lose his Indian status. Sandra Lovelace brought her complaint against Canada under the International Covenant on Civil and Political Rights,[89] under the Optional Protocol,[90] and claimed that the *Indian Act* was discriminatory on the ground of gender and contrary to the Covenant. She further claimed that "all domestic remedies have been exhausted insofar as the jurisprudence rests on the decision of the Supreme Court of Canada."[91] In a communication dated August 1979, the Human Rights Committee reviewed the communication from Sandra Lovelace, which she submitted in April 1978. Meanwhile, the Supreme Court of Canada decided that the *Indian Act* provision that provided an Indian woman who married a non-Indian man loses her Indian status was valid, as it was not rendered inoperative by section 1(b) of the *Canadian Bill of Rights*.[92] Sandra Lovelace contended that, by this decision, all domestic remedies had been exhausted in Canada. In July 1979, the Human Rights Committee requested information from Canada to the issue of admissibility of the communication. The Human Rights Committee did not receive a response from Canada and, at the April 1979 meeting of the working group of the Human Rights Committee, a request was again sent to Canada. Finally, in August 1979, without response from Canada, the Human Rights Committee found Sandra Lovelace's communication admissible and again requested written explanations and the remedy, if any, taken by Canada, to rectify the situation.[93]

In September 1979, Canada responded that it had no comments on the admissibility of the communication, but requested that the Human Rights Committee not consider its response an admission of the merits of the author's allegations. Canada further stated that "many of the provisions of the *Indian Act*, including section 12(l)(b) require serious reconsideration and reform."[94] Canada stressed the necessity of maintaining the status quo of the *Indian Act* as an instrument to protect the Indian minority of Canada. They stated that Aboriginal peoples traditionally had patrilineal families, which determined legal claims to land. Further, they stated that the non-Indian men (as opposed to non-Indian women) were a threatening force to reserve land of the Indian and, for these reasons, legal enactments from 1869[95] provided that an Indian woman who married a non-Indian man would lose her status. In its tenth session in July 1980, the Human Rights Committee requested additional clarification from both parties on issues to help them form an opinion as to any breaches of articles 2, 3, 12(1), 17, 23, 23(l)(2) and 24 of the ICCPR.

The following year, in July 1981, the Human Rights Committee distinguished that Lovelace's marriage was prior to the date Canada entered into the Covenant, which would normally not allow the communication its admissibility, but recognized "that the situation may be different if the alleged, although relating to the events occurring before 19 August 1976, continue or have effects which themselves constitute violations, after that date." The committee found that the *Indian Act*'s denial of the right to live on reserve was unreasonable or unnecessary to preserve the identity of the tribe, and found it was an unjustifiable denial of her rights under article 27. They further found that the other rights[96] were only indirectly at stake and did not examine them. Accordingly, the Human Rights Committee, under article 5(4) of the *Optional Protocol to the International Covenant on Civil and Political Rights* found that the denial of Sandra Lovelace to live on her reserve was a breach under article 27 of the Covenant.

Canada's Response to Lovelace v. Canada

On 6 June 1983, Canada responded to the committee's views in regard to communication no. 24/1977 in which the committee held that Sandra Lovelace had been denied the right guaranteed by article 27 to enjoy her culture and use her own language in a community with other members of her group. Canada stated that although it was not found to be in contravention of article 26 of the Covenant, it appreciates the concern of Indian women that section 12(l)(b) of the *Indian Act* may constitute discrimination on the basis of gender. Canada further stated that the federal government is "anxious to amend the *Indian Act* so as to render itself in fuller compliance with its international obligations pursuant to Article 27 of the *International Covenant on Civil and Political Rights*." Subsequently, a parliamentary subcommittee on Indian women and the *Indian Act* was formed in August 1982. Five days of hearings were held and forty-one witnesses testified (Canada stated that most were "Indian persons"). Following, the Minister of Indian Affairs, John C. Munroe, announced that Canada was committed to amend the *Indian Act* to end the discrimination and was willing to draft amendments in consultation with Indian people. A report was tabled in September 1982 with a recommendation that Indian women would no longer lose their Indian status upon marrying non-Indians and that, on application, women who had previously lost it would be entitled to regain it. They also recommended that women be entitled to regain their band membership, which would entitle them to live on reserve and participate in community activities. The subcommittee also recommended that Parliament make funds available to make reinstatement possible.

In April 1982, the Canadian Charter of Rights and Freedoms[97] came into effect and the equality provisions of section 15(1)[98] were enacted. As of April 1985, domestic remedies became available for persons who claimed they had been discriminated against on the basis of gender. Canada further stated that section 27[99] and 28[100] of the Charter were also significant in relation to Indian women and the *Indian Act*, and that section 25 and 35(1) of the *Constitution Act, 1982*[101] provided for integrity of Aboriginal peoples. They further quoted part IV of the Act, entitled "Constitutional Conference," which requires Canada to conduct constitutional conferences on matters affecting Aboriginal peoples. A conference was held on 15 and 16 March 1983, where the Minister of Indian and Northern Affairs confirmed his intention to move forward on the *Indian Act* amendments. Following, a Constitutional Accord on Aboriginal Rights was signed by the federal and provincial governments with participation of Aboriginal groups. Canada also agreed to take the necessary steps to amend the *Constitution Act, 1982* to include the principle of equality between men and women in regard to Aboriginal and treaty rights.[102] Article 2(3) of the Covenant requires that state parties ensure that there are effective remedies for any persons whose rights have been violated, notwithstanding that the violation has been committed by persons acting in an official capacity, and sections 24(1) and 32(1) of the Charter brought Canada into compliance with this aspect of the Covenant.

The committee concluded that Canada responded in a constructive and responsible manner through taking substantial steps to amend the *Indian Act* and incorporate domestic remedies for anyone who alleged their rights to equality have been infringed.

CONCLUSION

Critical changes were made to the *Indian Act* on 28 June 1985, when Parliament passed *Bill C-31, an Act to Amend the Indian Act.* The bill was intended to bring the Act into line with the provisions of the Canadian Charter of Rights and Freedoms. Bill C-31 was introduced with the intention of eliminating gender-based discrimination, to restore status and membership rights to those who lost them because of inequalities in the Act, and to increase control of Indian bands over their own affairs.[103] On 31 December 2003 there were 113,354 individuals reinstated through Bill C-31.[104]

First Nations women are attempting to carve a relationship with Canada from an Aboriginal perspective as they push on for their rights, in light of the laws, legislation, and policies that have not only hindered them, but have caused serious harms. Their resilience and fortitude are evident through the study of one example of one individual—Sandra Lovelace—who challenged the gender discrimination in the *Indian Act*. First Nations women continue to push for the right to govern one's own people, end discrimination, and establish relationships of mutual respect with Canada. Canada speaks about its willingness to accept these new challenges; at the same time, a movement is emerging at the domestic level that may, in turn, influence international law forums for recognition of clearer and well-defined rights for First Nations women in Canada.[105]

REFERENCES

Treaties and Other International Agreements

Constitution of the World Health Organization, opened for signature 22 July 1946, 14, United Nations Treaty Series 185 (entered into force 7 April 1948).

Convention Against Torture and Other Cruel, Inhuman or Degrading Treatment or Punishment, GA Res. 39/46 Annex, 39 UN GAOR Supp. No. 51 at 197, UN Doc. A/3951 (1984), 1465, United Nations Treaty Series 85 (entered into force 26 June 1987).

Convention Concerning the Protection and Integration of Indigenous and Other Tribal and Semi-Tribal Populations in Independent Countries, adopted 26 June 1957, 328, United Nations Treaty Series 247 (entered into force 2 June 1959).

Convention on the Rights of the Child, UN Doc. A/RES/44/25 (entered into force 2 September 1990).

Convention on the Prevention and Punishment of the Crime of Genocide, 9 December 1948, article 2 text: United Nations Treaty Series No. 1021, vol. 78 (1951).

Communication No. 358/1989, UN Doc. CCPR/C143/D/35811989 (1991).

Communication No. 94/1981 (30 March 1984), UN Doc. CCPRJC/OP/2 (1990).

Concluding Observations of the Human Rights Committee, Sixty-Fifth Session, 7 April 1999, CCPRIC/79/Add.105.

International Convention for the Elimination of All Forms of Discrimination Against Women, GA Res. 34/ 180, 34 UN GAOR Supp. No. 46 at 193, UN Doc. A/34/46, 1249, United Nations Treaty Series 13 (entered into force 3 September 1981).

International Convention on the Elimination of All Forms of Racial Discrimination, GA Res. 2106 (XX), Annex, 20 UN GAOR Supp. No. 14 at 47, UN Doc. A/6014 (1966), 660, United Nations Treaty Series 195 (entered into force 4 January 1969).

International Covenant on Civil and Political Rights, 19 December 1966, 999, United Nations Treaty Series 171, arts. 9–14, Can. T.S. 1976 No. 47, 6 I.L.M. 368 (entered into force 23 March 1976).

International Covenant on Economic, Social and Cultural Rights, GA Res. 2200A (XXI), 21 UN GAOR Supp. No. 16 at 49, UN Doc. A/6316 (1966), 993, United Nations Treaty Series 3 (entered into force 3 January 1976).

Vienna Convention on the Law of Treaties, 23 May 1969, 1155, United Nations Treaty Series 331 (entered into force 27 January 1980).

Legislation

An Act for the Better Protection of the Lands and Property of the Indians in Lower Canada, S.C. 1850, c. 42, 13 and 14 Vic., s. 5.

Canadian Charter of Rights and Freedoms, Part I of the *Constitution Act, 1982*, being Schedule B to the *Canada Act 1982* (UK), 1982, c. 11.

Constitution Act, 1867 (UK), 30 and 31 Vict., c. 3, reprinted in R.S.C. 1985, App. II, No. 5.

Constitution Act, 1982, being Schedule B to the *Canada Act 1982* (UK), 1982, c. 11.

Indian Act, 1876, S.C. 1876, c. 18.

Indian Act, S.C. 1906, c. 81 am. S.C. 1924, c. 47.

Indian Act, R.S.C. 1985, c. I-5.

Sexual Sterilization Act, S.A. 1928, c. 37.

Case Law

Atkins v. Davis [1917] 38 O.L.R. 548 (Ont. SCAD).

Base v. Hadley [2006] N.W.T.J. No. 3, [2004] N.W.T.J. No. 23, [2001] N.W.T.J. No. 44.

Connolly v. Woolrich and Johnson (1867), 11 L.C. Jur. 197, 17 R.J.R.Q. 75, 1 C.N.L.C. 70 (QSC).

D.E. (Guardian ad item of) v. British Columbia, [2005] B.C.J. No. 1145, 2005 B.C.C.A. 289, [2005] B.C.J. No. 492, [2003] B.C.J. No. 1563.

Ex-Parte Cote (1971), 3 C.C.C. 2(d) 383 (Sask. QB).

Hearle and others v. Greenbank and others [1558–1774] All E.R. Rep. 190.

Lord Hastings v. Douglas [1558–1774] All E.R. Rep. 576.

Lovelace v. Canada [2000] 1 S.C.R. 950, [2000] 4 C.N.L.R. 145.

Manychief v. Poffenroth (1994), [1995] 3 W.W.R. 210, [1995] 2 C.N.L.R. 67 (Alta. QB).

R v. Bear's Shin Bone (1899), 4 Terr. L.R. 173 (NWTSC).

R. v. Edmondson [2005] Sask. D. Crim. 270.90.65.00-03, [2005] Sask. D. Crim. 250.90.65.00-03, [2005] Sask. D. Crim. 260.80.25.00-01, [2005] Sask. D. Crim. 260.30.32.80-01.

R. v. Kummerfield [1997] S.J. No. 149.

R. v. Nan-E-Quis-A-Ka (1889), 1 Terr. L.R. 211, 2 C.N.L.C. 368 (NWTSC).

R. v. Pickton [2002] B.C.J. No. 2830.

R. v. Point [1957] 22 W.W.R. 527.

Re: Noah Estate (1961), 32 D.L.R. 2(d) 185 (NWTTC).

The Attorney General of Canada v. Lavell [1974] S.C.R. 1349.

Notes

1 The term "Aboriginal peoples" is intended to encompass all original inhabitants of Canada as recognized by the *Constitution Act, 1982*, being Schedule B to the *Canada Act 1982* (UK), 1982, c.11 s.35 [*Constitution Act, 1982*] at s. 35(2), meaning Indian, Métis and Inuit peoples in Canada. The term "Native" is used where it is historically applicable. The most common term in international law, "indigenous peoples," will also be used and is intended to encompass these same groups. See United Nations Secretariat of the Permanent Forum on Indigenous Issues, *Study of the Problem of Discrimination Against Indigenous Populations*, http://www.un.org/esa/socdev/unpfii/en/spdaip.html. See p. 29, para. 379 for the definition of indigenous peoples.

2 H. Cardinal and W. Hildebrandt, *Treaty Elders of Saskatchewan* (Calgary: University of Calgary Press, 2001), 7.

3 Ibid., 15.

4 Aboriginal Midwifery Education Program (AMEP), "AMEP Elder Advisory Meeting Summary," 30 September and 1 October 2005), http://www.amep.ca/downloads/AMEP%20Elder%20Advisory%20Meeting%20Summary.pdf (accessed 5 March 2006).

5 Canada, Royal Commission on Aboriginal Peoples, *Report of the Royal Commission on Aboriginal Peoples: Gathering Strength* (Ottawa: Supply and Services Canada, 1996), vol. 4, *Historical Position and Role of Aboriginal Women: A Brief Overview*, quoting Osennontion (Marlyn Kane), http://www.ainc-inac.gc.ca/ap/pubs/sg/cg/cj2-eng.pdf (accessed March 5, 2006) [RCAP]. See also, Tsi Non:we Ionnakeratstha (the place they will be born) Ona: grahsta' (a Birthing Place) Six Nations Maternal and Child Centre, Brochure, "Six Nations Maternal Brochure" (2005): From Iroquois traditions, women were always regarded with special status and honor because of the ability to bring forth life to this

earth. In motherhood terms, she was an intricate part in the CIRCLE OF LIFE, since they are the source from whence a land is people. The circle has four main cycles; from baby to adolescent; from middle age to Elder, she is to bear the responsibility of upholding the cultural values and traditions from generation to generation.

6   AMEP, 2. The Aboriginal Midwifery Education Program Elders' Advisory Group created the vision statement for the newly formed Aboriginal Midwifery Education Program, "Through the Practice of Midwifery, we will again raise the sacredness of new life."

7   Canada, Indian and Northern Affairs, "Aboriginal Women: Meeting the Challenges," http://www.ainc-inac.gc.ca/ai/ss/pubs/wnm/wnm-eng.asp (accessed 5 March 2006).

8   Canada states that many First Nations were primarily matriarchal societies. Prior to European colonization efforts, many First Nation societies were matriarchal in nature. Missionaries and other Church officials discouraged matriarchal aspects of First Nation societies and encouraged the adoption of European norms of male dominance and control of women. According to the customary law of the Mohawk Nation, for example, the matrimonial home and the things in it belong to the wife and women traditionally have exercised prominent roles in decision-making within the community. (Martha Montour, "Iroquois Women's Rights with respect to matrimonial property on Indian Reserves," *Canadian Native Law Reporter* 4 [1987]: 1; Robert A. Williams, "Gendered Checks and Balances: Understanding the Legacy of White Patriarchy in an American Indian Cultural Context," *Georgia Law Review* 4 [1990]: 1019.) Quoted from Indian and Northern Affairs Canada, "The Historical Context," 23 April 2004, http://www.ainc-inac.gc.ca/pr/pub/matr/his_e.html> (accessed 5 March 2006).

9   Patricia Monture-Angus, "The Lived Experience of Discrimination: Aboriginal Women Who Are Federally Sentenced and The Law: Duties and Rights" (*Submission of the Canadian Association of Elizabeth Fry Societies to the Canadian Human Rights Commission for the Special Report on the Discrimination on the Basis of Sex, Race and Disability Faced by Federally Sentenced Women*, (2002), 6, http://www.elizabethfry.ca/submissn/aborigin/4.htm (accessed 5 March 2006).

10   Barbara A. Mann, *Iroquoian Women: The Gantowisas* (New York: Peter Lang, 2000), 60.

11   M. Annette Jaimes and Theresa Halsey, "American Indian Women: At the Centre of Indigenous Resistance in Contemporary North America," M. Annette Jaimes, ed., *The State of Native America: Genocide, Colonialization, and Resistance* (Boston: South End Press, 1992), 311–344.

12   Mann, *Iroquoian Women*, 117.

13   Ibid., 241.

14   RCAP, *Report*, quoting Marilyn Fontaine.

15   Emma D. LaRocque, *Violence in Aboriginal Communities* (Ottawa: National Clearinghouse on Family Violence, Health Canada, Ottawa, 1994), 73.

16   Liliane Ernestine Krosenbrink-Gelissen, *Sexual Equality as an Aboriginal Right: The Native Women's Association of Canada and the Constitutional Process on Aboriginal Matters 1982–1987* (Saarbrücken: Verlag Breitenbach Publishers, 1991).

17 Donna Greschner, "Aboriginal Women, the Constitution and Criminal Justice," *University of British Columbia Law Review*, special edition (1992): 338–359; P.A. Monture-Okanee and M.E. Turpel, "Aboriginal Peoples and Canadian Criminal Law: Rethinking Justice," *University of British Columbia Law Review*, special edition (1992): 239–277.

18 Claudia Zaher, "When a Woman's Marital Status Determined Her Legal Status: A Research Guide on the Common Law Doctrine of Coverture," *Law Library Journal* 94, 3 (2002): 460, http://www.aallnet.org/products/2002-28.pdf (accessed 5 March 2006).

19 *Black's Law Dictionary* defines "chattel" as "movable or transferable property; esp., personal property." *Blacks Law Dictionary*, 7th ed. (St. Paul, MN: West Group, 1999).

20 Zaher, "When a Woman's Marital Status."

21 A.M. Sinclair, *Introduction to Real Property Law*, 3rd ed. (Toronto: Butterworths, 1987), 21. There were exceptions to coverture. For instance, the Feme Sole Trader Laws enacted in the early eighteenth century allowed women who were abandoned or widowed the right to petition to transact business as a single women with the full protection of the law. See, for instance, *Hearle and others v. Greenbank and others* [1558–1774], All E.R. Rep. 190; *Magdalene College, Cambridge Case*, [1558–1774] All E.R. Rep. 236; *Lord Hastings v. Douglas* [1558–1774], All E.R. Rep. 576.

22 William Blackstone, *Commentaries on the Laws of England*, book 1, ch. 15.

23 1848 Seneca Falls Declaration of Sentiments, reprinted in Joan Hoff, *Law, Gender and Injustice: A Legal History of U.S. Women* (New York: New York University Press, 1991), 383, app. 2.

24 Zaher, "When a Woman's Marital Status."

25 Early Canadiana, "Aboriginal Women's Issues" (8 December 2003), http://www.canadiana.org/citm/specifique/abwomen_e.html (accessed 5 March 2006).

26 A telling painting by John Lambert created in 1810 during the British era of the fur trade, entitled *Indian and his Squaw*, depicts the status of Aboriginal women at that time. The painting is of a woman with a child on her back, standing near her husband, "an Indian," who is without pants, clearly drunk, and unwashed. See John Lambert, "An Indian and his Squaw," 1810, http://www.canadiana.org/citm/imagepopups/c014488_e.html (accessed 5 March 2006).

27 See the term "Indian" as defined in *An Act for the Better Protection of the Lands and Property of the Indians in Lower Canada*, S.C. 1850, c. 42, 13 and 14 Vic., s. 5.

28 *Indian Act, 1876*, S.C. 1876, c. 18.

29 *Indian Act 1906*, S.C. c. 81, s. 2(c). For a general discussion of the effect of this section, see *Atkins v. Davis* [1917] 38 O.L.R. 548 (Ont. SCAD).

30 See, for example, *R. v. Point*, [1957] 22 W.W.R. 527, in which the court held that "the accused, on the evidence, is an Indian within the meaning of the *Indian Act*, R.S.C. 1952, c. 149, and being an Indian is a person (definition *Indian Act*, s. 2 (1)(g)) and being a person is subject to the application of sec. 44 (2) of the *Income Tax Act*."

31 Canadian Broadcasting Corporation, "Abuse Affects the Next Generation," 2 April 1993, http://archives.cbc.ca/IDC-1-70-692-4008/disasters_tragedies/residential_schools/clip6 (accessed 5 March 2006).

32 Ibid. Officially, residential schools operated in Canada from 1892 until 1969. At one time, there were eighty-eight schools operating in Canada. Although the Government of Canada officially withdrew in 1969, a few of the schools continued operating throughout the 1960s, 1970s, and 1980s. Akaitcho Hall in Yellowknife did not close until the 1990s. These schools were run through a partnership between the federal government and the churches. An estimated 100,000 to 150,000 First Nation, Métis, and Inuit children attended residential schools. Thousands of former students have come forward to claim that physical, emotional, and sexual abuse were rampant in the school system and that little was ever done to stop it or to punish the abusers. Assembly of First Nations, *Residential School Update* (Ottawa: Assembly of First Nations, 1998).

33 M. Lux, *Medicine That Walks: Disease, Medicine, and Canadian Plains Native Peoples: 1880–1940* (Toronto: University of Toronto Press, 2001). See also Yvonne Boyer, "First Nation Métis and Inuit Health Care, The Crown's Fiduciary Obligation," Discussion Paper Series In Aboriginal Health No. 2. National Aboriginal Health Organization and the Native Law Centre of Canada (Saskatoon: Native Law Centre, 2004), 10.

34 R.G. Ferguson, *Studies in Tuberculosis* (Toronto: University of Toronto Press, 1955), 6, cited in G. Graham-Cumming, "Health of the Original Canadians, 1867–1967," *Medical Services Journal Canada* 23, 115–166. By 1929 the Indian death rate in this area was twenty times greater than for the non-Aboriginal population (p. 134).

35 Regarding the health of the pupils, the report states that 24 percent of all the pupils who had been in the schools were known to be dead, while, at one school on the File Hills reserve, which gave a complete return: "to date *seventy-five percent were dead at the end of the sixteen years since the school opened*" (emphasis added). P.H. Bryce, *The Story of a National Crime—Being a Record of the Health Conditions of the Indians of Canada from 1904–1921* (Ottawa: James Hope and Sons, 1922), cited in Lux, 192.

36 Health Canada, The Bureau of Women's Health and Gender Analysis: "The Health of Aboriginal Women" (1999), http://www.hc-sc.gc.ca/hl-vs/women-femmes/fi-if/index_e.html (accessed 5 March 2006).

37 "The first claim against the federal government and the churches for abuse in residential schools was filed in 1990. By 1996, 200 such claims had been received. In 2003 there were about 12,000." Canadian Broadcasting Corporation, "We Are Deeply Sorry," 7 January 1998, http://archives.cbc.ca/IDC-1-70-692-4011/disasters_tragedies/residential_schools/clip9 (accessed 5 March 2006). See also, Aboriginal Healing Foundation, http://www.ahf.ca (accessed 5 March 2006).

38 In addition to scores of litigation claims, on 23 November 2005 the Assembly of First Nations and the Government of Canada announced that an agreement in principle had been made toward a fair and lasting resolution of the legacy of Indian residential schools. The amount of $1.9 billion has been set aside for the direct benefit of former Indian residential school students. The government also announced that eligible former Indian residential school students sixty-five years of age and older would soon be able to apply for an advance payment of $8000. Canada, Indian Residential Schools Resolution Canada, News Release, 23 November 2005, http://www.irsr-rqpi.gc.ca/english/news_23_11_05.html (accessed 5 March 2006).

39   J. Sákéj Henderson, "Postcolonial Ghost Dancing: Diagnosing European Colonialism," in Marie Battiste, ed., *Reclaiming Indigenous Voice and Vision* (Vancouver: University of British Columbia Press, 2000), 57–58.

40   Status of Women Canada, "Traditional Roles of First Nations Women," Status of Women Canada (29 July 2003), http://www.swc-cfc.gc.ca/pubs/pubspr/066231140X/ 200111_066231140X_8_e.html.

41   T.S. Palys, "Prospects for Aboriginal Justice in Canada," draft paper, Simon Fraser University, 1993, http://www.johnco.com/nativel/abojust.htm (accessed 5 March 2006). See also "Aboriginal Women in Canada and the Law," http://www.usask.ca/nativelaw/ awomen.html (accessed 5 March 2006).

42   See, for example, Barbara A. Mann, *Iroquoian Women: The Gantowisas* (New York: Peter Lang, 2000).

43   Many countries enacted various eugenics policies and programs, including promoting differential birth rates, compulsory sterilization, marriage restrictions, genetic screening, birth control, immigration control, segregation, and extermination, http://en.wikipedia. org/wiki/Eugenics (accessed 5 March 2006).

44   *Convention on the Prevention and Punishment of the Crime of Genocide*, 9 December 1948, article 2. Text: United Nations Treaty Series 1021, vol. 78 (1951), 277. Canada signed the Genocide Convention on 28 November 1949 and ratified the convention on 3 September 1952.

45   M. Annette Jaimes and Theresa Halsey, "American Indian Women: At the Centre of Indigenous Resistance in Contemporary North America," in M. Annette Jaimes, ed., *The State of Native America: Genocide, Colonization, and Resistance* (Boston: South End Press, 1992), 311–344.

46   Ibid., 326.

47   *Sexual Sterilization Act*, S.A. 1928, c. 37. On 21 March 1928 the *Sexual Sterilization Act* became law in Alberta. Five years later Germany did the same.

48   Jana Grekul et al., "Sterilizing the 'Feeble-minded': Eugenics in Alberta, Canada, 1929– 1972," *Journal of Historical Sociology* 17, 4 (2004): 359.

49   Ibid.

50   Ibid., 363.

51   Ibid.

52   Ibid.

53   Ibid.

54   Ibid., 375.

55   Ibid., 371.

56   Wanda Vivequin, "Prof Reveals Eugenics Machine," *Express News* (University of Alberta), 18 July 2003, http://www.expressnews.ualberta.ca/article.cfm?id=4594 (accessed 5 March 2006).

57   James Horner, "The Sterilization of Leilani Muir," *Canadian Content*, February 1999, http://www.canadiancontent.ca/issues/0299sterilization.html (accessed 5 March 2006).

58   Ibid.

59   Ibid.

60   See Peter Hogg, *Constitutional Law of Canada, 4th ed.* (Toronto: Carswell, 1997), 36/3 and 36/8.

61   Canadian Broadcasting Corporation, "Alberta Apologizes for Forced Sterilization" (9 November 1999), http://www.cbc.ca/canada/story/1999/11/02/sterilize991102.html (accessed 5 March 2006).

62   For case in law in this area see, *Base v. Hadley* [2006] N.W.T.J. No. 3, [2004] N.W.T.J. No. 23, [2001] N.W.T.J. No. 44. See also, CBC North, "Sterilized Woman Sues Stanton Hospital," 2 August 2004, http://www.cbc.ca/canada/story/2004/05/19/unbornchild040519.html (accessed 5 March 2006). See also, *D.E. (Guardian ad litem of) v. British Columbia* [2005] B.C.J. No. 1145, [2005] B.C.C.A. 289, [2005] B.C.J. No. 492 , [2003] B.C.J. No. 1563, where eighteen people who were sterilized make an application that superintendents of the hospital abused their public office in recommending sterilizations. In Thunder Bay, Ontario, a First Nations woman miscarried her child and the hospital shipped it to her in a Purolator package. She received the decomposed fetus forty days later. See Canadian Broadcasting Corporation, "Family Wants Answers after Fetus Returned in Cardboard Box," 21 May 2004, http://www.cbc.ca/stories/print/2004/05/19/Canada/unbornchild040519 (accessed 5 March 2006).

63   For instance, in the 1960s, women imprisoned at the Kingston Prison for Women were subjected to LSD experiments. These experiments had devastating consequences and long-term effects on the generations of women to follow. See Elizabeth Fry Society, "'LSD Experiments at the Prison for Women.' A Letter to the Correctional Service Commissioner," Elizabeth Fry Society, 3 March 1998), http://www.elizabethfry.ca/eLSD.html (accessed 5 March 2006). See also Elizabeth Fry Society, "Another Bad Trip: CSC Malingering in LSD Compensation Case," 2000 Annual Report, http://www.elizabethfry.ca/areport/ar2000e/page20.htm (accessed 5 March 2006). In 1998, Solicitor General Andy Scott's incredulous response was, "How much informed consent in a circumstance like that can you really believe exists? Why women?" "Solicitor General's Response to LSD Experiments," *Ottawa Citizen*, 4 March 1998. Also, "LSD Tests Kingston Prison for Women 60's," *Ottawa Citizen*, 28 February 1998.

64   Carolyn Strange and Tina Loo, *Making Good: Law and Moral Regulation in Canada, 1867–1939* (Toronto: University of Toronto Press, 1997), 63–69.

65   Early Canadiana Online, "Aboriginal Women's Issues," http://www.canadiana.org/citm/specifique/abwomen_e.pdf, at para. 5 (accessed 5 March 2006). See also Early Canadiana Online, "Acts of the Parliament of the Dominion of Canada relating to criminal law and ... 1876 Indian Act," http://www.canadiana.org/ECO/PageView/9_02041/0056 (accessed 5 March 2006).

66   Ann Laura Stoler, "Making Empires Respectable: The Politics of Race and Sexual Morality in Twentieth-Century Colonial Cultures," in Anne McClintock, Aarnir Mufti, and Ella Shohat, eds., *Dangerous Liaisons: Gender, Nation, and Postcolonial Perspectives* (Minneapolis: University of Minnesota Press, 1997), 347. See also Renisa Mawani, "The 'Savage Indian' and the 'Foreign Plague': Mapping Racial Categories and Legal Geographies of Race in British Columbia, 1871–1925" (PhD thesis, University of Toronto, 2001), http://www.collectionscanada.ca/obj/s4/f2/dsk3/ftp04/NQ58938.pdf (accessed 5 March 2006).

67 See Constance Backhouse, "Nineteenth Century Prostitution Law: Reflection of a Discriminatory Society," *Social History/Histoire Sociale* 8, 35 (1985): 387–423, especially n. 4.

68 See National Archives of Canada, RG 10, reel 10 193c, vol. 3816, file 57,045, for a collection of newspapers detailing prostitution involving Aboriginal women.

69 For a clear discussion of these developments, see *The Historical Development of the Indian Act*, 2nd ed. (Treaties and Historical Research Centre, P.R.E. Group, Indian and Northern Affairs, August 1978), especially ch. 5.

70 This statement presumes that wigwams were "disorderly" by definition.

71 At the same time, the courts struggled with Aboriginal custom law. See, for instance, *Connolly v. Woolrich and Johnson* (1867), 11 L.C. Jur. 197, 17 R.J.R.Q. 75, 1 C.N.L.C. 70 (QSC); *R v. Nan-E-Quis-A-Ka* (1889), 1 Terr. L.R. 211, 2 C.N.L.C. 368 (NWTSC); *R v. Bear's Shin Bone* (1899), 4 Terr. L.R. 173 (NWTSC); *Re: Noah Estate* (1961), 32 D.L.R. 2(d) 185 (NWTTC); *Ex-Parte Cote* (1971), 3 C.C.C. 2(d) 383 (Sask. QB); *Manychief v. Poffenroth* (1994), [1995] 3 W.W.R. 210, [1995] 2 C.N.L.R. 67 (Alta. QB).

72 A potlatch is a ceremony or feast held by all Northwest Coast Native groups and was a very important part of their social life. It was usually a lavish celebration for a wedding or the birth of a son. The ceremonies kept the old ways alive and taught the young people the history of their family. Missionaries and government officials saw the potlatch as a heathen custom that encouraged waste, and it was banned from 1885 to 1951. When the ban was lifted in 1951, serious damage had been done to tribal identities. Today potlatches are still held, but they are not the large affairs they were in the past. http://www.thecanadianencyclopedia.com/index.cfm?PgNm=TCE&Params=J1ARTJ0006431, (accessed 28 July 2008).

73 Mawani, "The 'Savage' Indian," 167. Mawani also cites historian Tina Loo, "Dan Cranmer's Potlatch: Law as Coercion, Symbol, and Rhetoric in British Columbia, 1884–1951," *Canadian Historical Review* 73, 2 (1992): 125–165.

74 Amnesty International, "Stolen Sisters Discrimination and Violence Against Indigenous Women in Canada—A Summary of Amnesty International's Concerns," 4 October 2004, http://web.amnesty.org/library/Index/ENGAMR200012004 (accessed 5 March 2006).

75 *Indian Act*, R.S.C. 1985, c. I-5.

76 Canada, Indian and Northern Affairs, "Aboriginal Women: A Demographic, Social and Economic Profile," http://www.hc-sc.gc.ca/hl-vs/pubs/women-femmes/abor-auto_e.html (accessed 5 March 2006).

77 Amnesty International, "Stolen Sisters." See also *R. v. Kummerfield* [1997] S.J. No. 149, *R. v. Edmondson*, [2005] Sask. D. Crim. 270.90.65.00-03; [2005] Sask. D. Crim. 250.90.65.00-03; [2005] Sask. D. Crim. 260.80.25.00-01; [2005] Sask. D. Crim. 260.30.32.80-01. See also *R. v. Pickton* [2002] B.C.J. No. 2830.

78 Manitoba Aboriginal Justice Implementation Commission, *The Aboriginal Justice Implementation Commission Final Report* (Winnipeg: Government of Manitoba, 2001), http://www.ajic.mb.ca/reports/final_toc.html (accessed 5 March 2006).

79 Amnesty International, "Stolen Sisters."

80 Ibid.

81 *Edmonton Sun*, "Wake-up Needed Says Advocate," 21 November 2005, http://www.edmontonsun.com/News/Edmonton/2005/11/21/1316363-sun.html (accessed 5 March 2006).

82 Statistics Canada, "Population by Aboriginal Groups and Sex, Showing Age Groups for Canada, 1996 Census – 20% Sample Data" (18 December 2001), http://www.statcan.ca/english/census96/jan13/can.htm (accessed 5 March 2006). The statistics were collected only for Status Indians and have not been recorded for non-Status Indian, Métis, and Inuit women who have "disappeared." Considering this fact, the statistics will likely be much higher.

83 Ibid.

84 Canada, "Canada's International Human Rights Policy" (Ottawa: Department of Foreign Affairs and International Trade, 2004), http://www.dfait-maeci.gc.ca/foreign_policy/human-rights/hr1-rights-en.asp#1. Canada has ratified the following treaties: *Convention Against Torture and Other Cruel, Inhuman or Degrading Treatment or Punishment*, GA Res. 39/46 Annex, 39 UN GAOR Supp. No. 51 at 197, UN Doc. A/3951 (1984), 1465, United Nations Treaty Series 85 (entered into force 26 June 1987) [*CAT*]; *International Convention for the Elimination of All Forms of Discrimination Against Women*, GA Res. 34/180, 34 UN GAOR Supp. No. 46 at 193, UN Doc. A/34/46, 1249, United Nations Treaty Series 13 (entered into force 3 September 1981 [*CEDAW*]; *International Convention on the Elimination of All Forms of Racial Discrimination*, GA Res. 2106 (XX), Annex, 20 UN GAOR Supp. No. 14 at 47, UN Doc. A/6014 (1966), 660, United Nations Treaty Series 195 (entered into force 4 January 1969) [*CERD*]; *Convention on the Rights of the Child*, UN Doc. A/RES/44/25 (entered into force 2 September 1990); *International Covenant on Civil and Political Rights*, 19 December 1966, 999, United Nations Treaty Series 171, arts. 9–14, Can. T.S. 1976 No. 47, 6 I.L.M. 368 (entered into force 23 March 1976, accession by Canada 19 May 1976) [*ICCPR*]; *International Covenant on Economic, Social and Cultural Rights*, GA Res. 2200A (XXI), 21 UN GAOR Supp. No. 16 at 49, UN Doc. A/6316 (1966), 993, United Nations Treaty Series 3 (entered into force 3 January 1976) [*ICESCR*]. See also Hogg, *Constitutional Law*, 33–30.

85 Canada, Department of Foreign Affairs and International Trade, "Human Rights and Canadian Foreign Policy," http://www.dfait-maeci.gc.ca/human-rights/forpol-e.asp.

86 *ICCPR, ICESCR*, in ibid.

87 H. Kindred, *International Law Chiefly as Interpreted and Applied in Canada*, 5th ed. (Toronto: Edmond Montgomery, 1993), 597 and 598.

88 Ibid.

89 *ICCPR*, Art. 3 and 27.

90 *ICCPR*, Art. 5(2)(b).

91 *Sandra Lovelace v. Canada*, Communication No. 24/1977 (14 August 1979), UN Doc. CCPR/C/OP/1 at 10 (1984), *Sandra Lovelace v. Canada*, Communication No. 24/1977 (31 July 1980), UN Doc. CCPRIC/OP/1 at 37 (1984), *Sandra Lovelace v. Canada*, Communication No. 24/1977 (30 July 1981), UN Doc. CCPRIC.OP/1 at 83 (1984), *Sandra Lovelace v. Canada*, Communication No. R.6/24 (29 December 1977), UN Doc. Supp. No. 40 (A136/40) at 166 (1981), *Sandra Lovelace v. Canada*, Communication No. 24/1977 (6 June 1983), UN Doc. Supp. No. 40 (A/38/40) at 249 (1983) (information from Canada on measures taken) at 10.

92 *The Attorney General of Canada v. Lavell* [1974] SCR 1349.

93 The committee further requested that Sandra Lovelace provide information concerning her age and her date of marriage.

94 *Lovelace v. Canada*, (No. 24/77) Human Rights Committee Selected Decisions under the Optional Protocol, l0th Session, at 38.

95 The *Indian Act* S.C. 1876, c.18 defined "Band" to mean "any tribe, band or body of Indians" who have a reserve or annuity. As far back as the *Royal Proclamation of 1763*, legal enactments were created that recognized the Indian Nations of Canada. Similarly, legal enactments throughout the 1800s were created to govern the Indian's life.

96 Articles 12 (right to choose one's residence); Articles 17, 23, 24 (protection of the family and the children).

97 *Canadian Charter of Rights and Freedoms*, Part I of the *Constitution Act, 1982*, being Schedule B to the *Canada Act 1982* (UK), 1982, c. 11.

98 Section 15(1) states: "Every individual is equal before and under the law and has right to equal protection and equal benefit of the law without discrimination and in particular without discrimination based on race, nationality or ethnic origin, colour, religion, sex, age, or mental or physical disability."

99 Recognition of the value of cultural diversity.

100 The principle of equality between men and women.

101 *Constitution Act, 1982*.

102 Section 35(4) states: "Notwithstanding any other provisions of this Act, the aboriginal and treaty rights referred to in subsection (1) are guaranteed equally to male and female persons."

103 See Jim West, "Aboriginal Women at a Crossroads," *First Nations Drum*, Fall 2002, http://www.firstnationsdrum.com/Fall2002/PolWomen.htm (accessed 5 March 2006). The main focus of the bill was to make the *Indian Act* conform to s. 15 of the *Canadian Charter of Rights and Freedoms*. Since 1985, all Status Indians are registered under s. 6 of the *Indian Act*. A person must prove that he/she has two parents entitled to Indian status, and then he/she would be registered under s. 6(1). If a person has only one parent of Indian status, they are registered under s. 6(2). Those individuals registered under s. 6(2) must marry a Status Indian to pass the status on to their children. Section 6(2) thus creates a half Indian with its second-generation cut-off clause. They are the growing numbers of "Ghost People," wrote Pam Paul in her analysis of Bill C-31 entitled "The Politics of Legislated Identity," prepared for the Atlantic Policy Congress of First Nations Chiefs in September 1999. "Currently, the 'Ghost People' are children of the Bill C-31, 6(2) reinstates. However, in one or two years when the children born after 1985 who are registered under s. 6(2) reach childbearing age, and out-parent with a non-status person, the rise in the numbers of 'Ghost People' will grow." Unstated paternity is on the rise also, with implications that, on a national level, during the study period of this report, about 4480 children with unstated fathers have failed to "qualify" for Indian registration. This results in registration under s. 6(2) or a denial of registration and loss of associated entitlements, benefits, and privileges. See also Canada, Indian and Northern Affairs Canada, *Factors Contributing to Unstated Paternity* (20 January 2003), http://dsp-psd.pwgsc.gc.ca/Collection/R2-255-2003E.pdf (accessed 5 March 2006). Additionally, in April 1999, the Human Rights Committee

commented: "Following the adoption of the committee's views in the Lovelace case in July, 1981, amendments were introduced to the Indian Act in 1985. Although the Indian status of women who had lost status because of marriage was instituted, this amendment affects only the woman and her children, not subsequent generations, which still may be denied membership in the community. The Committee recommends that these issues be addressed by the State party." (Concluding Observations of the Human Rights Committee, 65th session, 7 April 1999, CCPRIC/79/Add.105, para. 19).

104 Canada, Indian and Northern Affairs Canada, *2004 Basic Departmental Data* (December 2005), http://www.ainc-inac.gc.ca/ai/rs/pubs/sts/bdd/bdd03/bdd03-eng.pdf (accessed 28 July 2008).

105 For instance, in 1998 the Minister of Indian Affairs and Northern Development created the Office of the Senior Advisor on Women's Issues and Gender Equality and produced the Gender Equality Analysis Policy. See Canada, Indian and Northern Affairs Canada, *Gender Equality Analysis Policy* (23 April 2004), http://www.ainc-inac.gc.ca/pr/pub/eql/eql_e.html (accessed 21 September 2006). Canada, as signatory to a number of international treaties and covenants, has also acknowledged the rights of indigenous peoples in international law. See for instance, Y.M. Boyer, "The International Right to Health for Indigenous Peoples in Canada," *Discussion Paper Series in Aboriginal Health*, No. 3 (Ottawa: National Aboriginal Health Organization and the Native Law Centre of Canada, October 2004).

Theme 2: Intellectual and Social Movements

Zoey Wood-Salomon, *Meeting with the Chiefs*, 1993

Leading by Action: Female Chiefs and the Political Landscape

Kim Anderson

The ultimate show of sovereignty is taking responsibility to make your own decisions. At the same time you also have to take responsibility for the consequences. I think that it is going to have to be the women that take that message forward. We have the role of keeping the communities together, keeping our communities healthy, and at the same time overseeing the leadership.

—Grand Chief Angie Barnes, Mohawks of Akwesasne

FOR OVER A CENTURY, First Nations politics have been "men's business." Although indigenous[1] women have always been active in their communities, chiefs within the *Indian Act* system have been predominantly male. This means that men have been charged with the official leadership, vision, voice, and direction of First Nations communities. What has this meant in terms of community development overall? Would it be different if there were more women in leadership positions? One way to address these questions is to look at the experiences and perspectives of current female leaders in First Nations communities. How is the current generation of female chiefs taking on the leadership role? This chapter explores these questions by drawing on interviews with twelve contemporary chiefs. Their stories allow us to examine how female First Nations leadership may be distinct from that of male leadership in terms of experiences, approaches, and goals. From there, we can consider what changes First Nations female leadership may bring to the larger political landscape.

In considering the roles and experiences of these contemporary chiefs, we need to look to the past and see how female political participation has been shaped. First Nations women have not always been excluded from the politics of their nations. Prior to the imposition of the *Indian Act*, women held political power as traditional or hereditary chiefs, as clan mothers, or through women's councils.[2] Indigenous women made decisions on key issues including land use, food allocation, and when to go to war.[3] Yet, colonial leaders, coming from patriarchal cultures where women held no political sway, did not recognize indigenous women in traditional leadership roles. From the time of earliest negotiations and trade, these colonial leaders chose to work exclusively with men.[4] Some scholars have argued that the colonizers realized that indigenous women's power would have to be displaced in order for conquest to succeed.[5] Women's power was not compatible with colonial rule, and, therefore, male-dominated systems of governance would have to be imposed.

The Canadian state formalized its patriarchal approach to governance with the introduction of the *Indian Act* in 1876. Overnight, this legislation shut First Nations women out of political leadership and influence. Traditional systems of governance that had previously provided women significant political authority were replaced with an electoral system that forbade First Nations women from seeking office, voting, or even speaking at public meetings. First Nations women were, therefore, officially politically silenced until the *Indian Act* changes of 1951, which finally allowed them to vote and run for office.

First Nations women continue to be under-represented in First Nations politics. At the time of writing this chapter, chiefs who were women comprised between 16 and 19 percent of the total number of chiefs in the over 600 bands across Canada.[6] While this number is on the rise,[7] it is still lower than the proportion of women who sit as members of the Canadian Parliament. Why are not more First Nations women holding political office, and what consequences does this bring? What are we missing and why?

WOMEN'S ISSUES AND CONCERNS

Aboriginal women's groups, as well as scholars, have pointed out that women's issues and concerns are often overlooked in a male-dominant political system. In their national study as part of a series on First Nations women, governance, and the *Indian Act*, Judith Sayers and Kelly McDonald conclude that "lack of women's representation in decision making has led to the perception that concerns articulated by First Nations women (accountable governing structures, gender equality and social issues) are not incorporated into the discourse on government and self-government."[8]

First Nations women have numerous concerns that they believe are not adequately addressed by their governing bodies. With relation to social welfare, Sayers and McDonald note that steps to deal with violence, for example, have been a "glaring omission" in recent treaty negotiations in British Columbia, in spite of the fact that First Nations women in British Columbia have advocated for equal power in treaty talks and measures to halt family violence. At the male-dominated tables, land and resource issues have taken precedence over social issues.[9]

For decades, Aboriginal women and their representative organizations have also spoken out on issues of gender equality and women's rights, and often in opposition to their male-dominated political organizations. First Nations women have called attention to flaws within the *Indian Act*, with issues of membership, women's rights, and matrimonial property at the forefront.[10] One of the most prominent struggles has been against *Indian Act* provisions that denied Indian status and rights to women who married non-Indians. These measures were repealed with the implementation of Bill C-31 in 1985, but the fight along the way pitted the Native Women's Association of Canada (NWAC) against the Assembly of First Nations, who opposed the bill.[11] Bill C-31 has also brought new problems related to membership and access to rights, and women continue to voice these concerns.[12]

First Nations women have been critical of the lack of their role in self-government, asking why they have been excluded from negotiations and treaty and constitutional talks. During the constitutional talks of 1992, NWAC mounted a court challenge to protest the exclusion of women from the discussions. At this time, they also argued for the application of the Canadian Charter of Rights and Freedoms to First Nations governments, demonstrating that First Nations women need systems of protection and redress from their own governments.[13]

After addressing the multiple ways in which women's concerns and issues are continually overlooked, Judith Sayers and Kelly McDonald conclude that First Nations women should be ensured the right to participate in self-government and treaty negotiations, and that they should have full and equal participation in governance. Sayers and McDonald examine models for equal representation, such as representation by the percentage of the female electorate, or by ensuring an equal number of men and women on council.[14]

Another paper in the same series on First Nations women, governance, and the *Indian Act* demonstrates that First Nations women face barriers to equality because a large body of *Indian Act* matters are exempt from the Canadian *Human Rights Act*.[15] The author of this paper, Wendy Cornet, concludes, "Participation in governance structure as leaders, councillors or representatives is an obvious way that First Nations women can influence the content of laws and decision making that affect their equality rights in all aspects."[16] A third paper in the series includes several recommendations related to enhancing First Nations women's capacity and opportunities for leadership.[17]

The assumption underlying all these recommendations is that leaders who are women would be more attentive than men to the issues and concerns that have historically been raised by women. This frames the question of what female leaders might address, as opposed to male leaders. How they would go about their work is another significant question. Do First Nations women have distinct leadership styles and approaches?

LEADERSHIP APPROACHES AND STYLES

There have been very few studies of First Nations women in leadership that might provide insight into whether female leaders take on different issues than do male leaders, and whether their leadership styles and approaches are distinct. Cora Voyageur is the only scholar who has written extensively about female chiefs. In a study published in 2003, Voyageur reported on her findings from conducting interviews and questionnaires with fifty-four contemporary female chiefs across Canada.[18] With regard to what the chiefs might address, Voyageur found that community members expected the female chiefs to take on social issues, including family violence, education, social services, and community healing. The chiefs themselves spoke of the need for community healing from the ill effects of residential schools and from addictions. Voyageur states, "The chiefs emphasized the need for a healthy community where children are well cared for by their parents and other social problems are under control. Although economic development is needed, it all depends on having healthy people to take on and maintain jobs."[19]

Voyageur's study also discussed leadership styles. The chiefs reported that they were expected to be "more motherly, gentler and more humanitarian in their polices and decision-making" because they are women.[20] Whether they adopt this approach is unclear, but the study does document a leadership style that is grounded in community. The chiefs stressed the need to have open dialogue with the community and to ensure transparency in governance.[21]

Voyageur's study offers insights into how women come into office and what might prevent more women from taking these leadership positions. Many of the chiefs in her study had been involved politically through band councils or in voluntary organizations prior to becoming chief, many were from political families, and many were asked by the community to run for office. Many came in with a sense that it was time for a change in leadership. The difficulties they experience as chiefs, including balancing the demands of family and work, dealing with sexism and disrespect in the workplace, and, remarkably, fearing for their physical safety, show the many challenges that women must overcome to fill these important roles.[22] In a study of women from Lake Babine First Nation, Jo-Anne Fiske, Melonie Newell, and Evelyn George also found that women became involved in governance because they wanted change, and often because they were asked to take on leadership positions.[23] They found the main barriers to female participation in governance were "sexism, bureaucracy, lack of support and not being heard."[24]

Sylvia Maracle has written about leadership among Aboriginal women in urban settings, demonstrating that, from a grassroots base, Aboriginal women have built organizations in response to healing needs. Maracle remarks on the accountability and action-oriented nature of this leadership.[25] Likewise, Fiske has written about how women on reserves have been politically active and have effected change through their voluntary associations and networks.[26] Community-based and action-oriented leadership is a theme in the many studies that document indigenous female resistance and activism.[27] In spite of the barriers to their participation in elected leadership roles, women continue to take responsibilities to effect community change.

Discussion of the leadership styles of Aboriginal women has often been framed within what Fiske has termed the "discourse around traditional motherhood."[28] Some Aboriginal women and women's organizations have called on traditional understandings of motherhood to position themselves as leaders of their communities. For example, during the 1980s, the Native Women's Association of Canada argued for the political authority of women by virtue of their traditional roles as teachers, nurturers, and mothers of the nation.[29]

In many indigenous societies, motherhood, or women's ability to create and nurture, has traditionally been linked to power, including political power.[30]

Fiske has written about the link between nurturing roles and political responsibility among Carrier women.[31] Mary-Ellen Turpel explains how this dynamic works among the Cree: "Traditional teachings by our Cree Elders instruct us that Cree women are at the centre of the Circle of Life. While you may think of this as a metaphor, it is in fact an important reality in terms of how one perceives the world and how authority is structured in our communities. It is women who give birth both in the physical and in the spiritual sense to the social, political and cultural life of the community."[32]

Mothers are seen as keepers of the culture, the nation, and the future.[33] Women are responsible for cultural and community continuity and they watch over present and future generations. There is an authority that comes with this role, which translates into political responsibility where women work in balance with men. This is exemplified in nations that have clan mothers[34] or in more informal governance structures where grandmothers are recognized as authority figures.[35]

With this background, we can move forward to introduce the chiefs interviewed for this study. Who are they, what are the issues that are important to them, and how have they enacted their leadership role?

WHO ARE THEY? THE CHIEFS AND THEIR FIRST NATIONS

Twelve chiefs were interviewed for this chapter, with interviews lasting from forty-five minutes to almost two hours. The chiefs were provided with the interview questions in advance, and then were interviewed, primarily over the telephone. The questions covered general information about the communities, biographical information about the chiefs, and their entry into politics, past accomplishments, current goals, reflections on their experiences as women in the job, reflections on male and female leadership, and expressions of sovereignty and nation building from a First Nations woman's perspective. All the interview material was transcribed, coded, and analyzed according to the themes that emerged.

The reader will note that the chiefs are identified by name in some quotes, while other quotes remain anonymous. This is an attempt to celebrate and honour these individuals, to give them a place in history, while at the same time preventing any repercussions from discussion regarding more sensitive topics. The chiefs who participated in this research are listed alphabetically, as follows:

Chief Kim Baird, Tsawassen First Nation (BC)

Grand Chief Angie Barnes, Mohawks of Akwesasne (ON, PQ, NY)

Chief Connie Big Eagle, Ocean Man First Nation (SK)

Chief Maureen Chapman, Skawlook First Nation (BC)

Chief Shirley Clarke, Gluscap First Nation (NS)

Chief Linda Jean, Gespeg First Nation (PQ)

Chief Tina Leveque, Brokenhead First Nation (MB)

Chief Susan McKamey, Leq'a:mel First Nation (BC)

Chief Alice McKay, Matsqui First Nation (BC)

Grand Chief Denise Stonefish, Association of Iroquois and Allied
     Indians (ON)

Chief Veronica Waboose, Long Lac #58 First Nation (ON)

Chief Shirley Wolfe-Keller, Muskowekwan First Nation (SK)

Participants were chosen according to recommendations provided by individuals in government, Aboriginal organizations, and the community. The only criterion was that participants be female chiefs in office at the time of the interview. Efforts were made to ensure geographic and national representation from across Canada.

The chiefs represent communities that vary in terms of population, land base, and remoteness. The smallest community, Matsqui First Nation, has a total population of about 190 people (on- and off-reserve), and the largest, Akwesasne, has an on-reserve population of 13,000. Two of the chiefs are grand chiefs. Angie Barnes leads twelve chiefs who represent the three districts that constitute the Mohawk Council of Akwesasne, and Denise Stonefish is the Grand Chief of the Association of Iroquois and Allied Indians, a political-territorial organization representing eight First Nations in south and central Ontario.

The majority of chiefs in this chapter are in their forties and fifties although one chief was in her mid-thirties and another in her early sixties. All had at least four years' experience as chief, and up to twelve years' experience in one case. Many of them had worked for twenty years or more in community/political areas, including work on council. Most had been active in their communities, through volunteer and committee work, prior to becoming chief. Many came from families where other members had been elected or were hereditary chiefs.

The chiefs brought a variety of experience to their jobs. Four had worked for their bands prior to becoming chief, in areas ranging from establishing a

Native language program, to driving a school bus, to working in health and social policy. One chief had worked in the private sector and two had worked in employment and training. Three had been teachers, two working with schoolchildren and one in adult education. Several chiefs had a background in social services, such as working in social housing, family support, and child welfare. Three of the chiefs have social work degrees.

The job of chief seemed to be part of a career in community service for most of these women. The majority did not seem to be "career politicians"; many spoke of wanting to go back to other aspects of community service after they had accomplished some of their goals as chiefs. Like the chiefs in Voyageur's study,[36] many of the chiefs had been encouraged to run for office. Some had specific issues they wanted to deal with, including improving general peace and community stability, building community infrastructure, working on the land base, and addressing treaty issues.

ISSUES OF CONCERN

Leadership is a lot more than fiery public speeches. It's leading by action.

—Chief Kim Baird

The chiefs were asked about their accomplishments to date, and about the areas on which they were currently focussed. They spoke about a broad range of accomplishments, including enhancing community infrastructure; improving the health, welfare, and safety for community members; and establishing better inter- and intracommunity relationships. Some of the chiefs have focussed on improving administration and governance policies, and three spoke about bringing down the debt in their communities.

After their responses about their current focus were coded, six major themes emerged: (1) self-determination and healing; (2) education, employment, and training; (3) economic development and community infrastructure; (4) membership, land claims, and treaty; (5) the inclusion of youth; and (6) return to (Native) culture.[37]

The theme of "self-determination"[38] came up repeatedly, both in terms of individual self-determination and self-determination as peoples. For these chiefs, fostering self-determination involves encouraging responsibility, accountability, strong work ethics, and self-reliance. A few of the chiefs noted that First Nations people had been utterly self-reliant in the past. Chief

Waboose brought this forward in a story about her upbringing: "I remember back when I lived with my aunt growing up. She was not married, but she did her own work. She made snowshoes, she made moccasins, she made moose hide, and she was a midwife. We didn't have any money, but we had lots to eat. She was able to clothe me and feed me. Even though we lived in a half tent and half house, we still lived! I never thought I was poor at that time because I had everything I needed." Chief Clarke also calls on the past to encourage self-determination in her people, by relating stories from her family history that demonstrate exemplary self-reliance and teamwork: "If you were in an Indian encampment—like my grandfather's camp, miles and miles away—everyone had their job. If you didn't do that, if you didn't pull the canoe or didn't want to paddle and just wanted to lay back and get a suntan, I think you would be in the river. If you were in a community and you had fire to make and cooking to do and you didn't pull your weight, you wouldn't be here."

Several of the chiefs talked about the steps they are taking with their people to inspire self-determination. Chief Big Eagle, for example, has encouraged youth to take responsibility for working with a drum and practising the protocols associated with it. She responded to a request from the youth for money to buy a drum by asking them to do some fundraising. In the end, the youth paid for their own sticks and drum cover, and the council presented them with a drum in a ceremony. In learning the protocols associated with the drum, the youth had the opportunity to learn about responsibility, community accountability, and teamwork.

An emphasis on healing is necessary for self-determination, and six of the twelve chiefs talked about how they are currently focussed on community healing. A few of the chiefs spoke about having their "eyes opened" to many pressing social issues in their communities as a result of their leadership positions. Understanding and giving priority to the healing needs of the community are vital to good leadership, as noted by Chief Wolfe-Keller: "The [people] do not only need someone with a political agenda. They also need someone who is healing and someone who can understand what really goes through some of the minds and the livelihood of these First Nations families, children, youth and elders."

Issues of substance abuse, child and family welfare, and violence came up in discussion as current priorities. Some of the chiefs live in communities with local or regional First Nations child-welfare authorities; others are working on establishing First Nations authorities or improving the systems that currently exist.

These self-determination and healing efforts are intended to increase individual and community well-being. At the same time, the chiefs recognize that community members must be provided with opportunities, including education, employment, and training. Chief Wolfe-Keller noted that First Nations students often graduate from high school and then are sent back from the post-secondary institutions because they are not prepared. She reflected on the demographic of the large number of Aboriginal youth in Saskatchewan, pointing out that these youth must be adequately prepared to take on their roles as the up-and-coming generation in the province. Chief Waboose has been working to expand and improve the buildings for both the elementary and the high school that her young students attend. Chief McKay's community now has a satellite adult education centre. Students who get their diplomas are then provided employment and training opportunities in the community. Chief Big Eagle talked about the adult employment and training opportunities she is working on so her community members can be employed in the nearby oil fields.

In terms of economic development and community infrastructure, three of the chiefs talked about current involvement in natural resource development, including developing a hydro site, logging and log salvaging, and developing oil fields on the reserve. Chief Leveque has focussed on establishing political stability in the community, the wisdom being that "if the political environment is unstable, the outside investor/entrepreneur will not see us as a safe place to invest in any kind of business venture."

A number of the chiefs talked about community infrastructure. The benefits of building are summed up by Chief Chapman, who foresees opportunity for the future generations in her community's new business facility: "I'm hoping our university students—if they want to hang a shingle—will come home and work and establish businesses from our community. Just because we're a small community doesn't mean that we have to do without. We're hoping that it plants a seed in our community, and opens another place for our surrounding communities." Among the chiefs, there was mention of building projects and plans for a community hall and gas station, administrative and recreation centre, traditional long house, powwow grounds, playground, recreation hall, cultural centre, and an eighty-house subdivision project.

The issue of membership is foremost in the minds of some chiefs, including dealing with the fallout of Bill C-31. A few of the chiefs talked about their struggle to get this issue on the table at the local and regional levels, as it is often dismissed as a "woman's issue." But, as Grand Chief Stonefish pointed out, "If we don't look at Bill C-31—if we don't have the ability to determine our membership and take it out of the hands of the federal government, we won't need sovereignty or nation building, because we won't have any members!" Five of the twelve chiefs talked about needing to address Bill C-31 issues. Chief Jean has experienced the stigma of being a "C-31 girl" and has now established rules defining membership with the community, working to ensure that members understand and participate in its development.

First Nations women have expressed concern about being left out of treaty or other negotiations in the past. Five of the chiefs mentioned their involvement with land claims, but most did not elaborate on the nature of this work. A few of the chiefs spoke about the significance of treaties. Chief Baird talked about how she came into her position as a negotiator, and why: "I don't think that any tinkering under the *Indian Act* can accomplish much. I'm a very strong believer of treaty negotiations, because I think we have to get to the bottom of the structural problems and barriers that our communities face. That's been my main goal, trying to promote big change." One chief told a story about how a women's council elder had once suggested that treaty negotiations should be left to the men:

> We were talking about portfolios. This Elder believed it should be left up to the men to do the natural resources, to do the fisheries, to do the governance, to do treaties, and those sorts of things. My question to her was "With all due respect, where, then, do our treaty issues get on the table? Who does that if we don't have men that are advocating for us? And I respectfully disagree with you, in that there's no one that's going to tell me I won't be at the negotiating table for my water rights; I won't be at the negotiating table for my treaties, and mining."

Others asserted that treaties are very much in the realm of "women's business."

The chiefs shared a common message about being inclusive of the youth. Several of the chiefs stressed the importance of involving the youth by providing opportunities and activities for them. Chief McKamey, for example, noted that a community goal was "to enhance our youth's health and lifestyle by implementing a strong sports and recreation program here in the community." Chief

Waboose stated "I always have youth on my mind. That's for them. I do this for my youth and my children." Because previous leaders had been accused of developing their own cadre of elders as advisors, Grand Chief Barnes has taken the approach of consulting with the youth: "If this means that I just go out one day, and say something to one of our youth in the corner store, ask him a few questions, I'll do that. I try to go to the two districts whenever I get that 'people intuition'—that this is what I should be doing. From there, I'll take back their comments to the council." Many of the chiefs talked about mentoring and engaging youth as leaders, and the importance of encouraging young women to become politically active.

Four of the chiefs referred to the importance of returning to their own cultural and traditional ways. Grand Chief Barnes discussed how community members are beginning to explore the true meaning of some of their traditional knowledge, such as the Thanksgiving address. Other chiefs talked about the resurgence of traditional Native spirituality. Chief Waboose is working on getting a powwow ground, which can also accommodate traditional spiritual gatherings and ceremonies. Grand Chief Barnes and Chief Waboose also pointed to the importance of retaining and regaining language. As a Native language teacher, Chief Waboose was very active in this regard in her community, prior to becoming chief.

ENACTING THE LEADERSHIP ROLE

> Serious women leaders are "doers." We do not sit around waiting to delegate the work to others. We roll up our sleeves and get at the task, while seeking out others to help.... Women will normally follow through with whatever it is they are attempting to achieve. Women will jump through hoops of fire, sift through the red tape, and keep searching until they find what they need to complete a project. Women are willing to do the work, write the reports, organize their time, dedicate the hours, communicate to the people, and seek out the resources.
>
> —Chief Susan McKamey

An analysis of the way the chiefs discussed their work illustrates that teamwork, accountability, and community involvement are prominent themes.

Six of the chiefs referred to the importance of team building as a component of their leadership style. Chief Chapman spoke about the way women have influenced the band work in her community, giving the example of how the collaborative work of a number of women in different roles was essential to getting funding for a recent project. Grand Chief Barnes emphasized how important it is to recognize and call upon the different skills and abilities of community members. When asked to speak of their accomplishments, many of the chiefs were quick to point out that their successes are also due to the hard work of the council.

The chiefs spoke often about accountability, highlighting work they have done to implement accountability mechanisms into their systems of governance. Transparency was a recurring theme. Chief Leveque explained why transparency is important to her: "What we want is good success in my community, and good success is based on integrity, accountability and transparency. All the words that are kicked around, they sound good in speeches, but people have no idea what they mean, to actually do them in their day-to-day life. Integrity is what you're doing when nobody is watching. Simply put, it's honesty all the time, even when it's not beneficial to you." Chief McKay pointed out that transparency is essential for good leadership: "Everything's open; if you want to come in here and see what we're doing, see every cheque we write, then you're more than welcome to come in and look at it. That way, you get people to support you."

The chiefs also encourage the community to be accountable. Chief Wolfe-Keller and Chief Waboose make it clear to band members that they expect them to take good care of new housing. These expectations can lead to conflict, but, as Chief Waboose pointed out, they are part of the growth process for a community, and a factor in accountable leadership: "You know that tough love they talk about? [I say] 'I'm not going to pay your hydro. You have to pay it yourself.' You've got to have that tough love because, the way I see it, I'm not here for myself, I'm here for the people." Chief Waboose notes that one of her councillors had warned her that they would lose votes by asking the community members to pay for their own hydro. Her response was: "We are going to do it, and I'm going to take the blame." She laughs, adding, "When the next election came on, I got the highest [number of] votes!"

Community involvement in decision making is part of accountability. Chief McKamey talked about the importance of "involving the community by seeking their input," and Chief Leveque noted, "All of [our new] policies are ratified at the community level, and changes have to be taken to the community. It can't be whoever is in chief and council." Chief Chapman indicated that her community has a monthly newsletter and Web pages so that people both on- and off-reserve have a chance to be involved. She notes, "Unless the people on the ground are involved, and own it, it's not going to succeed, no matter what you try to do."

REFLECTIONS ON GENDER AND LEADERSHIP

The chiefs were asked whether they thought female chiefs had different approaches and priorities from those of their male counterparts. There was relatively little discussion about whether female leaders had particular interests; most of the participants talked about leadership styles and approaches.

Ten of the twelve chiefs made comments related to communication, specifically on the strength of women as communicators and how this translates into the work of a chief. Chief McKay remarked:

> Women are talkers. One of the things that I really support is communication. I'm always reminding our governing body members that they have a job, and their job is to make sure that all of the information about what is going on gets to the family members. And if they are not doing that, then they are not doing their job. So I think that is something that [we do] as women. As talkers, we can sit in a room and brainstorm about the things that are really important and that we need to take care of.... As better communicators, we can open the door to people who want to come in.

One of the chiefs described the women's style of communication as being "less confrontational": "At other meetings, they're yelling and screaming and pounding on the table. That isn't occurring any longer [in my community]— with women in the room. The calming effect gets to the table. I think women negotiate; there's not that push and shove that there seems to be between men. With women, there's less of that 'This is my turf, my territory' thing."

A few of the chiefs mentioned being bothered by the swearing that sometimes happens in meetings. One chief pondered, "I don't think there is a need for any man to use it. I don't know why [they do]. Does it have extra clout or does it make them more macho? I don't know what it is." Some chiefs noted that there is less swearing when women are involved. Five chiefs commented on how women are less likely to engage in empty talk: "At provincial and national forums I very rarely speak. Usually the gamut of issues are covered and I don't feel like I need to have my thoughts out there ... eighteen different messages stated six times."

One chief commented, "A male counterpart, they talk the talk. I've found few, though, who walk the walk." Another chief pointed out how the women are used to organizing and doing community work. This, she said, translates into the work they do as leaders: "The women chiefs get right in there and they help with the work. The male chiefs still rely on the women in the background to do the research, the briefing, create analysis, and the secretarial work. Basically they do the work and the men stand up front and centre, taking in all the accolades." Like other chiefs who were careful about essentializing with their comments, this chief added, "But again, not all of them are like that."

Four of the chiefs commented on how ego can get in the way of doing the job right. Chief Baird said, "It's easy to get hung up on ego and personality and personal stuff if you take your eye off the ball. My biggest challenge is always trying to keep my eye on the big picture, and don't sweat the small stuff." Three of the chiefs remarked on how women are more likely to admit error. One reflected on how some male chiefs are threatened by female chiefs, as they fear a loss of power: "If the majority of male leaders would get rid of the fear that women leaders will outshine them, and instead accept them as their equals; agree to work together and realize they are all working toward the same goals for the people—they can spend more energy and time focussing on what is important, opposed to how to hold back the women leaders."

A few of the chiefs stated they were not afraid of losing power. Chief Waboose remarked, "I'm not afraid to make a decision before election, because that is the way we are as women. We're not afraid of losing votes, or anything—we view what is right. The decisions that we make."

The discourse of traditional motherhood came up in the interviews; half the chiefs equated women's leadership styles with motherhood. They spoke about leadership as a caretaking role, in which one assumes responsibility for the benefit of others. Chief Waboose and Chief McKay both related their leadership roles to motherhood. "As a woman, I looked after my family. I made sure they had enough to eat; I made sure that they were warm; had a nice place to live. A woman is a caretaker, and that is what we bring into being the chief. We want to take care of people. It doesn't mean that we want to make it easy for them. We want them to have a good life. That is what I want for my First Nation, for them to have a good life," related Chief Waboose. "I guess it's just the mother inside of us that makes us want to do what's best for everyone and not just us ourselves. It's like looking after your kids; you want them to be better and that's the way I think a lot of the women chiefs feel about the community members. Although they're not their kids, they're definitely looking to them for good leadership, to take them in a good direction," said Chief McKay.

Chief Jean commented that women are more likely to make decisions based on *potential* impact on the next generations, stating, "We never only think about us; we always think what the outcome would be to our children." Chief Leveque equated her goal of seeking community stability to managing a home: "If you have stability, then things continue and it's less likely [there will be] upheaval—because you have responsible people in place that have wisdom and implement practically. That is what women do in their home. They are the stabilizing force; the anchor." She noted, "Women in the home were the multi-taskers to begin with. Do the laundry, do the dishes, cook supper and just multi-task. We've done it for years. We're more results-oriented."

The chiefs remarked on women's ability to create relationships and how this is an important factor in their leadership. "A woman has heart," said one, while another commented: "I don't know if that sensitivity is why women chiefs are a bit stronger. They're more forgiving as well. [They] want to help, and not be quick to judge. [They] allow things to fall." Like mothers, many of these female chiefs can be simultaneously loving and firm. Chief Wolfe-Keller talked about how she can be "very caring and very sharing, but very stern as well." Chief Big Eagle remarked, "I'm not scared to say 'no' to people. I'll just say 'no' and if that makes them mad at me and they don't vote for me the next time, [that's okay]."

The chiefs were asked if First Nations communities would look different if there were more women as leaders. This led to discussion about whether women were more likely to pay attention to social issues. Some chiefs stated that men tend to be more interested in resource development, economic development, and treaties, and that social issues can fall off the table. As Chief Chapman pointed out,

> Women tend not to lose sight of the social issues in our community, where the male leaders are more focussed on logging and fishing, not realizing that the health of our young people is important in order for them to create a healthy community, and [to] be healthy leaders themselves. And a lot of lip service is given to, yes, I support the youth, and yes, I support the women, but the resources don't flow. If you look at any budget that's created by any band or tribal grouping in the country, look for a line item for youth and women, look for financial support, and it's rarely there.

Five of the chiefs thought women would pay more attention to health and social issues, three referenced family and children's issues, two talked about education, and two mentioned that dealing with violence would be a higher priority if there were more female leaders. One chief mentioned, "Not all men will tackle the family violence issues," adding, "there seems to be some sort of stigma attached to that." Another stated, "Women are still living with a high degree of violence in their lives, and children are still living in environments that aren't healthy. I think if the women could organize, they could mandate more of the funding to go towards these social ills." Chief Chapman emphasized how the women currently in power are working to ensure that social issues are addressed: "Social and health issues are getting to the table because the women are insisting they get to the table. When I go to the summit, I've said to the assembly, "We need to put health on the first or second day." I put the responsibility back on them, and say something like, "You claim that the children and the health are a priority, well, let's prioritize them and put them ahead so that we still have quorum." A lot of women are doing that. And so it's forcing the discussion to occur." Grand Chief Stonefish pointed out that many male chiefs are now responding to social issues because of the increasing influence of women on their councils.

Although the chiefs spoke generally about how women pay more attention to social concerns, at least five pointed out that all issues are of concern to both men and women. As Chief Big Eagle commented, "I think whether we're men or women or youth or elders, we're all after the same things, like self-sufficiency, self-government and so on." A few of the chiefs cautioned against ghettoizing "women's issues."

WHERE TO GO NEXT?

The findings of this study are consistent with much of the discourse regarding women and leadership that was raised in the introductory section. These twelve chiefs are concerned with issues that have been flagged by Aboriginal women as issues of concern, including social welfare and community health and healing, membership, transparency in government, and the women's role in treaty and self-government negotiations. At the same time, they also demonstrate commitment to a wider variety of issues that have been pegged as "men's business," such as land and resource management, treaty negotiations, and economic development. They are not, therefore, exclusively focussed on women's issues, but, rather, on the overall health and well-being of their communities, which, they recognize, must be addressed through multiple strategies and approaches.

The most notable distinctions about their leadership are not what they take on, but how they do it. The introductory section documented leadership styles for Aboriginal women as community-based, action-oriented, transparent and accountable, and often grounded in the discourse of traditional motherhood. All these elements came up in the interview with these chiefs. They talked about the need for open communication, being inclusive of the youth, and being understanding, as Chief Wolfe-Keller says, of "what goes on in the minds and livelihood" of all community members. A number of them make the link between the roles they play as leaders and how they would be as mothers.

It is not within the scope of this chapter to suggest how these women and their colleagues are shifting the political landscape, but it is possible to suggest that there is a need for more female leaders like them: leaders who pay attention to a range of issues—including violence, social welfare, and healing—as they work towards overall community well-being. The political landscape would certainly be richer with an infusion of the leadership styles and approaches that these leaders display. The question remains as to why more women are not involved and how more women might become involved.

The chiefs in this study had many stories that shed light on these lingering questions. Many talked of pressures and challenges that correlate to the findings of Voyageur,[39] Fiske, Newell, and George,[40] and others. They noted that the job can be all-consuming and talked about high expectations on the part of the community. As Chief Clarke pointed out, "Chiefs are not nine-to-five people. We're twenty-four hours. People phone you at all hours when anything happens." Many of the chiefs spoke about the pressures of being highly visible in the community, and some mentioned being uncomfortable with the way "people put you on a pedestal." Chiefs also have to deal with family and community politics, which can be very hurtful, and these chiefs talked about experiences of stress because of dynamics between or within families on a reserve.

These factors may be common among all chiefs, but sexism is something that is of particular concern for female chiefs. The chiefs in this study talked about the sexism they have experienced from other community members, councillors, mainstream government, and industry men. Most of the discussion centred on how the chiefs had experienced sexism among their counterparts in

First Nations politics. Nine of the twelve chiefs reported that they had encountered problems with their male counterparts, but they made sure to qualify these observations with statements such as "You can't paint all male chiefs with the same brush" and "I have met many male leaders over the years and some of them are wonderful, respectful, and show no sign of chauvinism."

Resistance to female chiefs because of their gender takes many forms, from subtle politicking to crass remarks. It is remarkable that four of the twelve chiefs discussed having to earn their respect as chiefs. A number of them talked about having to prove themselves before others would listen to them. Some of the chiefs talked about being ignored. Three chiefs talked about struggles with "the old boys' club" at tribal councils and in larger assemblies. Some reported on deliberate attempts to sabotage women's input, and several talked about male counterparts who had trouble with female chiefs who were "vocal," stating that "some feel threatened by a woman who speaks with authority."

In spite of these struggles, the chiefs believed that women should be in politics and they talked about ways in which this might occur. They noted that female chiefs need to be visible, as women often do not see politics as their arena. As one chief commented: "I think the lack of women's involvement has to do with the 'Euro' system of male dominance—I think a lot of women think, 'Oh I can't do that; I have to take care of my children.' I'm not saying that's not a priority, but I believe women have it in them to contribute. I don't think they know it just yet."

Chief Jean emphasized encouraging more female leaders by way of example, stating, "We bring the women the courage to present themselves as leaders in the community and not to be shy to go straight to the men and [share their] ideas." She encourages women to get involved in decision making by reminding them that "the leaders are talking about our children."

Many chiefs talked about how important it is to encourage young women to get into politics. Denise Stonefish is the first woman to be elected as grand chief of the Association of Iroquois and Allied Indians. From this position, she comments: "[We need] to be positive role models for the younger women coming up; tell them that, yes, they have every right and every ability to First Nations politics as a career." Grand Chief Barnes emphasizes the need to work closely with the younger generation of women so that there will be people to take over the current generation's work. Chief Chapman has been working directly to ensure that this happens, through conferences and workshops aimed at mentoring younger women in leadership.

The chiefs mentioned other avenues for women in which to be politically active. Many are involved in women's councils and are enthusiastic about the potential for these councils. Chief Baird pointed out that they give voice to women through formal structures of representation: "The women's council helps to legitimize women's voices. It's different to say, that you [as a woman] have the opportunity to step up to the microphone, like all of us do, versus 'These are the women's committee recommendations.'"

Many women's councils are in their early stages, still working through what issues they need to address and how they are going to be influential. A general assumption is that these councils will deal with social issues. In some cases, the initiative to deal with primarily social issues comes from the women. Other councils have been sensitive to the danger of having their work ghettoized as "women's issues" and, therefore, seen to be less significant than men's work. One chief noted that women's council leaders must be persistent so that women's councils will have significant authority. Others noted that chiefs and governing bodies can feel threatened that women's councils will take over their work. They said that resistance comes out of the fear that women's councils will tap into scarce community resources, adding that women's councils are often underfunded.

Some groups have taken the approach that women's voices must be structured into all aspects of governance. Chief Jean talked about the positive benefits of the Quebec Native Women's Association's having a seat at the Quebec chiefs' table. The women's council of the Assembly of First Nations (AFN) has proposed a portfolio system, where women's council members will sit with AFN vice-chiefs on their respective portfolios, such as housing, education, and so on.

Finally, in reflecting on how to increase women's influence and participation in politics, five of the chiefs spoke about traditional models of governance. Grand Chief Stonefish commented: "I think we have to go back—not to re-establish all traditions but to take from there. Everything that I've heard, from the different Nations, is that the women were first and foremost, right in front along with the men in making those decisions. They were truly their equals." Grand Chief Barnes pointed out that their spokespeople had traditionally been men, yet the women had been responsible for choosing them. Chief Big Eagle also talked about the traditional political influence of women: "We groomed our chiefs from birth: it was the women who taught them everything. Even in our language, our little boys spoke women's language until a certain age because that's who they were always with." The underlying message about traditional systems of governance was that there is a need for balance, equity, voice, and representation of all members of the community. The chiefs spoke about wanting to see more female political authority, as there had been in the past, but also about needing to include youth and elders in the renewal of our governance systems.

CONCLUSION

The First Nations political landscape is rich with development in the areas of self-determination, decolonization, sovereignty, and nation rebuilding. It will be all the richer if we can give serious consideration to gender. We need to give thoughtful attention to the impact of the patriarchal and hierarchical political systems implemented by the colonial state, and then think creatively towards a more balanced future. This could have a tremendous impact on the overall well-being of our peoples.

The profile of chiefs provided here demonstrates how important it is to encourage more female leadership as part of the equation. What stands out most from the chiefs' stories is their sense of accountability. The women speak in holistic terms, both about the issues they wish to address and about their efforts to engage all community members in the movement forward. Theirs is a leadership style grounded in, and responsive to, community. This may be reflective of their role as "doers" in their communities, or in indigenous frameworks of motherhood, which may, in turn, reflect larger roles of women in many First Nations communities. There are many commonly heard expressions that ring true here: "Women are the heart of the community"; "Women are the first teachers"; "Women have the responsibility to create and nurture"; "Women are the caretakers." In the context of this book, perhaps it is time to add: "Women are at the heart of community and cultural continuity," and to reflect on how this speaks to a need to have them in official leadership positions.

Ultimately, women as chiefs play a significant role in addressing the power imbalances that have had such devastating consequences on First Nations communities. Our healing as peoples will involve establishing both individual and collective self-determination, as these chiefs have so clearly expressed. It is to be hoped that their presence signals the end of an era where political power is concentrated among a handful of men, be it the village priest and Indian agent of the past, or the primarily male political tables of recent decades.

While we can celebrate the accomplishments of these female chiefs, we must also acknowledge the specific challenges that women face as they enter the still-male-dominated arena of First Nations politics. Whereas the chiefs here exemplify an admirable amount of courage and commitment, their experiences also demonstrate the need for systemic changes that will encourage female participation and validate women's voices. If we can implement systemic changes while continuing to encourage more female political participation and leadership, we will all benefit from a richer environment for growth as nations.

Notes

1   This article is about First Nations leadership, as it speaks exclusively to the experiences of chiefs, but I will occasionally use the term "indigenous" to indicate that the gender dynamics apply to other indigenous peoples and their leadership struggles, as well. As a Cree/Métis, I speak about the impact on "our communities" because all indigenous people—whether they fall under the *Indian Act* or not—have suffered the impact of Euro-Western patriarchal notions and systems of leadership.

   In summary, I use the terms "First Nations," "indigenous," "Native," and "Aboriginal" in this chapter. The term "First Nations," for the purpose of this chapter, refers to Status Indians; "Aboriginal" is used to refer to First Nations, Inuit, Métis, and non-Status people in Canada; "Native" is used when the term has been called up by others in quotes or in names of organizations or programs; and "indigenous" is used when I am referring more broadly to first peoples in Canada and the United States.

2   See "Women's Role in Politics," in Kim Anderson, *A Recognition of Being: Reconstructing Native Womanhood* (Toronto: Sumach Press, 2000), 65–71.

3   See ibid.; Kahente Horn-Miller, "Otiyaner: The 'Women's Path' Through Colonialism," *Atlantis* 29, 2 (2005); Klein and Ackerman, eds., *Women and Power in Native North America* (Norman: University of Oklahoma Press, 1995); Devon Mihesuah, "Colonialism and Disempowerment," in Devon Abbott Mihesuah, *Indigenous American Women: Decolonization, Empowerment, Activism* (Lincoln: University of Nebraska Press, 2003); and Nancy Shoemaker, ed. *Negotiators of Change: Historical Perspectives on Native American Women.*(New York: Routledge, 1995).

4   M. Annette Jaimes and Theresa Halsey have documented that "In not one of the more than 370 ratified and perhaps 300 unratified treaties negotiated by the United States with Indigenous nations was the federal government willing to allow participation by Native women." See Jaimes and Halsey, "American Indian Women at the Center of Indigenous Resistance in Contemporary North America," in M. Annette Jaimes, ed., *The State of Native America: Genocide: Colonization and Resistance* (Boston: South End Press, 1992), 322.

5   See Jeannette Armstrong, "Invocation: The Real Power of Aboriginal Women," in Christine Miller and Patricia Chuchryk, eds., *Women of the First Nations: Power, Wisdom, and Strength* (Winnipeg: University of Manitoba Press, 1996); and Paula Gunn Allen, *The Sacred Hoop: Recovering the Feminine in American Indian Traditions* (Boston: Beacon Press, 1986).

6   It is difficult to get precise numbers on the gap between male and female chiefs, and to track this historically. The Assembly of First Nations conducted a survey of the male/female ratio among chiefs in the summer of 2005, and found approximately 105 female chiefs of the approximate 633 First Nations. This is reportedly the highest number of female chiefs in at least eight years. Indian and Northern Affairs Canada (INAC) reported in January 2006 that there were seventy-eight female chiefs as of July 2005 out of 408 male chiefs from a total of 614 bands. INAC's report notes, "The discrepancy between the total number of bands and the total number of male and female chiefs (486) is due to a variety of factors. The latter numbers don't include Hereditary Chiefs or Grand Chiefs and in some cases bands without a Chief are represented by spokespersons or councillors. There are other variables as well which complicate the data such as bands in which all councillors are chiefs."

7   As noted above, neither the AFN or INAC has been tracking the rise of female chiefs, but the AFN has made an effort to do some recent study on this, noting the rise over the last decade or so. In one of her articles on women chiefs, Cora Voyageur has also marked the rise, stating, "Over the years there has been a steady increase in the number of women chiefs across the country, especially in the 1990s. Former Assembly of First Nations Grand Chief, Phil Fontaine, stated that there were 40 women chiefs in 1990.... According to the Assembly of First Nations ... there are currently 90 women chiefs, or about 15%." See Voyageur, "Keeping All the Balls in the Air: The Experiences of Canada's Women Chiefs" in Audrey MacNevin et al., eds., *Women and Leadership* (Ottawa: Canadian Institute for the Advancement of Women, 2002).

8   Judith F. Sayers and Kelly A. MacDonald, "A Strong and Meaningful Role for First Nations Women in Governance," in *First Nations Women, Governance and the Indian Act: A Collection of Policy Research Reports* (Ottawa: Status of Women Canada, 2001), 12.

9   Ibid.

10 See Sharon D. McIvor, "The Indian Act as Patriarchal Control of Women," *Aboriginal Women's Law Journal* 41, 1 (1994).

11 Katherine Beaty Chiste, "Aboriginal Women and Self-Government: Challenging Leviathan," *American Indian Culture and Research Journal* 18, 3/4 (1994).

12 See Fay Blaney, "Aboriginal Women's Action Network," in Kim Anderson and Bonita Lawrence, eds., *Strong Women Stories: Native Vision and Community Survival* (Toronto: Sumach Press, 2003); and Audra Simpson, "To the Reserve and Back Again: Kahnawake Mohawk Narratives of Self, Home and Nation" (PhD thesis, McGill University, 2003).

13 See Chiste, "Aboriginal Women"; Isaac Thomas and Mary Sue Maloughney, "Dually Disadvantaged and Historically Forgotten? Aboriginal Women and the Inherent Right to Self-Government," *Manitoba Law Journal* 21, 2 (1992); Joyce Green, "Constitutionalizing the Patriarchy: Aboriginal Women and Aboriginal Government" *Constitutional Forum* 4, 4 (1993).

14 Sayers and McDonald, "A Strong and Meaningful Role."

15 Wendy Cornet, "First Nations Governance, the Indian Act and Women's Equality Rights," in *First Nations Women, Governance and the Indian Act: A Collection of Policy Research Reports* (Ottawa: Status of Women Canada, 2001), 147.

16 Ibid.

17 Jo-Anne Fiske, Melonie Newell, and Evelyn George, "First Nations Women and Governance: A Study of Custom and Innovation among Lake Babine Nation Women," in *First Nations Women, Governance and the Indian Act: A Collection of Policy Research Reports* (Ottawa: Status of Women Canada, 2001).

18 Cora J. Voyageur, "The Community Owns You: Experiences of Female Chiefs in Canada," in Andrea Martinez and Meryn Stuart, eds., *Out of the Ivory Tower: Feminist Research for Social Change* (Toronto: Sumach Press, 2003). Cora J. Voyageur, *Firekeepers of the Twenty-First Century* (Montreal: McGill-Queen's University Press, 2008).

19 Ibid., 242.

20 Ibid., 241.

21 Ibid.

22 Ibid.

23 Fiske et al., "First Nations Women," 81–82.

24 Ibid., 86.

25 Sylvia Maracle, "The Eagle Has Landed: Native Women, Leadership and Community Development," in Kim Anderson and Bonita Lawrence, eds., *Strong Women Stories: Native Vision and Community Survival* (Toronto: Sumach Press, 2003).

26 Jo-Anne Fiske, "Political Status of Native Indian Women: Contradictory Implications of Canadian State Policy," *American Indian Culture and Research Journal* 19, 1/2 (1995): 1–30; Fiske, "Carrier Women and the Politics of Mothering," in Gillian Creese and Veronica Strong-Boag, eds., *B.C. Reconsidered: Essays on Women* (Vancouver: Press Gang, 1992); and Jo-Anne Fiske, "Native Women in Reserve Politics: Strategies and Struggles," *Journal of Legal Pluralism and Unofficial Law* 30 (1991): 121–137.

27 See Anderson and Lawrence, eds., *Strong Women Stories*; Jaimes and Halsey, "American Indian Women"; Horn-Miller, "Otiyaner"; Mihesuah, *Indigenous American Women*; Shoemaker, *Negotiators of Change*.

28 Jo-Anne Fiske, "Child of the State, Mother of the Nation: Aboriginal Women and the Ideology of Motherhood," *Culture* 12, 1 (1993): 17–35.

29 See ibid.; Native Women's Association of Canada, *Matriarchy and the Canadian Charter: A Discussion Paper* (Ottawa: Native Women's Association of Canada, 1991).

30 See Maracle, "Eagle Has Landed"; and Anderson, *Recognition of Being*, 168–173.

31 Fiske, "Carrier Women."

32 Mary-Ellen Turpel, "Patriarchy and Paternalism: The Legacy of the Canadian State for First Nations Women," *Canadian Journal of Women and the Law* 6 (1993): 174–192.

33 See Betty Bastien, "Voices Through Time," in Christine Miller and Patricia Chuchryk, eds., *Women of the First Nations: Power, Wisdom, and Strength* (Winnipeg: University of Manitoba Press, 1996).

34   See Tom Porter, "Traditions of the Constitution of the Six Nations," in Leroy Little Bear, Menno Boldt, J. Anthony Long, eds., *Pathways to Self-Determination* (Toronto: University of Toronto Press, 1984); and Theresa M. Jeffries, "Sechelt Women and Self-Government," in Gillian Creese and Veronica Strong-Boag, eds., *B.C. Reconsidered: Essays on Women* (Vancouver: Press Gang, 1992).

35   See Anderson, *Recognition of Being*, 67–68.

36   Voyageur, "Keeping All the Balls in the Air."

37   That is to say, what is understood to be the traditions and cultural practices and values of their own particular people.

38   I use "self-determination" broadly here to refer to the process of taking responsibility for one's destiny as well as the destiny of family, community, and nation.

39   Voyageur, "Keeping All the Balls in the Air."

40   Fiske et al., "First Nations Women."

Creating an Indigenous Intellectual Movement at Canadian Universities: The Stories of Five First Nations Female Academics

Jo-ann Archibald

ELDER VI HILBERT of the Upper Skagit Native American people of Washington State, US, told a story about Lady Louse, who lived in a longhouse. Along the west coast of British Columbia and Washington State the indigenous people traditionally lived in longhouses. Here is Vi Hilbert's story:

> Lady Louse walked into a longhouse that stood in her village. As she looked around the longhouse, she saw dust everywhere. No one had looked after it for many years. She remembered the days when the longhouse was full of family and community members. She remembered the potlatches and ceremonies where people feasted on food, stories, songs, and dances. Lady Louse decided that it was time to bring back the cultural ways of living in the longhouse. Cleaning the house was the first task she decided to do. She took her little cedar broom and started sweeping at one end of the longhouse. She went back and forth from one side of the longhouse to the other side. She swept vigorously, thinking about the good times ahead. As she swept, the dust started to rise. Lady Louse was deep in thought as she swept and swept. She did not notice that the dust was getting thicker and thicker the more she swept. When Lady Louse got to the middle of the longhouse, she got lost.[1]

The dust in the story is a metaphor for the imposition of Eurocentric or Western education that focussed first on Christianizing and civilizing and later

on assimilating generations of First Nations learners.[2] The Canadian educational experience for First Nations people has left an intergenerational legacy
where First Nations language, culture, and knowledge were denied during the
residential school era and omitted or marginalized from public school curriculum. The poor state of current-day Aboriginal education is one evident
outcome of this colonial legacy. The first national study that examined the
state of First Nations public education, *A Survey of the Contemporary Indians of
Canada: Economic, Political, Educational Needs and Policies*,[3] found the grade
twelve completion rate in 1962–63 for Registered Indian students was
4 percent, compared to 88 percent for non-Indian students.[4] Four decades
later, the 2004 Department of Indian Affairs and Northern Development
report, *Basic Departmental Data 2003*, notes a 30 percent high-school graduation rate for Registered Indian students. In comparison to 1962–63, the 2004
high-school completion rate looks like a substantial improvement. Yet, when
compared to the completion rate for non-Aboriginal people, it remains very
poor. The 2005 *Report of the Auditor General of Canada to the House of Commons*
estimates that it will take twenty-eight years to close the education gap between
First Nations people living on-reserve and the overall Canadian population.[5]
This same report cites a 2002 *Human Resources Development Canada* study,
which says that in the future "more than 70 percent of the new jobs created in
Canada will require some form of post-secondary education."[6] Low high-
school graduation rates result in lower attendance and completion rates at the
university level. The 2001 census data indicate that 5 percent of the Registered
Indian population aged twenty-five to forty-four had a university degree,
compared to 22 percent of the total Canadian population.[7] Overall, the crisis
of Aboriginal education is a long-standing phenomenon.

Many educators, both Aboriginal and non-Aboriginal, have worked vigorously, like Lady Louse, to improve educational attainment for Aboriginal
learners over the years. One area of education not often discussed is the
contribution of Aboriginal academics to the university education system. If
we stand aside and stop sweeping for a while to let the dust settle, we will
clearly see that a handful of First Nations female academics have made
substantial contributions to changing mainstream Canadian universities by
establishing innovative academic programs and units, increasing accessibility
and retention for Aboriginal learners, conducting meaningful research,
publishing widely, and creating an indigenous intellectual movement.[8] These
first-wave First Nations women include Freda Ahenakew, Marlene Brant

Castellano, Olive Dickason, Verna J. Kirkness, and Gail Guthrie Valaskakis. They were the first group of Aboriginal women to work at mainstream Canadian universities in tenure-track faculty positions.

This chapter emphasizes their scholarly leadership and contributions to creating transformative change in academe as First Nations public intellectuals. As public intellectuals, these five First Nations women influenced "social and political events and reality directly with their ideas."[9] Life-experience stories and discussion that pertain to the education and the educational influence of each woman are presented, followed by a concluding discussion that emphasizes their impact upon establishing an indigenous intellectual movement in Canada. In the Coast Salish oral tradition of the author and of many other First Nations cultures, when life-experience stories are used for educational purposes, the listener/reader is expected to make meaning with the story given.

What these wonderful women have in common is their community heart, tenacity, perseverance, depth of knowledge in their disciplines, vision, and commitment to work for the advancement of Aboriginal lifelong education. Each woman brought First Nations community needs and concerns into academe to challenge its existing institutional structures and values in order to create university educational opportunities to improve Aboriginal education. They also influenced provincial and national public policy through their work and position as academics. The life experiences of these five First Nations women are diverse and they show possibility, potential, perseverance, success, and many other lessons. This chapter will limit its discussion to their influence upon academe, even though they have had much wider impact upon Canadian society, and the term "First Nations" is understood as being inclusive of all persons of Aboriginal ancestry.

FREDA AHENAKEW: "TEACH THE CHILDREN"[10]

Freda Ahenakew, born in 1932, is from the Ahtahkakoop First Nation, Plains Cree, Sandy Lake, in central Saskatchewan. She completed her grade twelve education with her children. Each morning she and her nine children would board the school bus together. Freda said, "When the bus would come by, we would fill the bus."[11] Freda had twelve children before completing her bachelor of education degree at the University of Saskatchewan in 1979. She then taught at the elementary and secondary school levels at the Lac La Ronge

Band School (1979–80) and the Saskatoon Survival School (1980–81). Freda initiated the first Cree immersion classes in Saskatoon schools.[12] She also taught at the Saskatchewan Indian Cultural College (from 1976 to 1981) and later at the university level.

After completing her master of arts degree in Cree Linguistics at the University of Manitoba in 1984, Freda held various university positions. She began as an assistant professor of Native Studies at the University of Saskatchewan (from 1983 to 1985), and then became the director of the Saskatchewan Indian Languages Institute (from 1985 to 1989), before moving to the University of Manitoba to become an associate professor (from 1989 to 1996) and head of the Native Studies department (from 1990 to 1995). Freda retired from the University of Manitoba after she completed her term as department head and returned to her home province of Saskatchewan.

Freda is a prolific author of twenty-nine books and numerous articles and reports. One noteworthy area is in First Nations language. Her master's thesis *Cree Language Structures* was reprinted seventeen times for university courses. She has published children's storybooks and other Cree language-based curriculum for school use. Her publishing of Aboriginal stories as told by Aboriginal people had a humble beginning. Freda recalls, "When I was teaching in University, I had a class of fluent Cree speakers and their assignment was to do a story and I edited those stories. I published a cheap little booklet out of them. From those stories a publisher picked two of them and we made children's stories out of them.... I said I'd try and write a [children's] book every year but it is so hard to get an illustrator and then money for coloured books."[13] Adult learners who would not normally get to see their stories in print were given such an opportunity. Two of the stories were selected and later published as school storybooks.

An important project that occurred under Freda's tenure as director of the Saskatchewan Indian Language Institute was the recording of elders' speeches and stories. These recordings formed the basis of subsequent publications. Examples include *Ana kâ-pimwêwêhahk okakêskihkêmowina (The Counselling Speeches of Jim Kâ-Nîpitêhtêw)* (1998) and *Âh-âyîtaw isi ê-kî-kiskêyihtahkik maskihkiy (They Knew Both Sides of Medicine): Cree Tales of Curing and Cursing told by Alice Ahenakew* (2000). Freda worked with linguistics professor H.C. Wolfart to edit these and many other publications. Each book includes the Cree and English versions of the stories.

Her other important publication that has influenced narrative research includes *Kôhkominawak Otâcimowiniwâwa (Our Grandmothers' Lives, as Told in Their Own Words)* (1992, co-authored with H.C. Wolfart). Freda's scholarly work demonstrates careful, respectful documentation of elders' stories in both Cree and English. Freda explained to one of her research participants the documentation process she uses: "I try to write exactly what you are saying."[14] The elders, aged from sixty to ninety, recalled lived-experience stories that provide guidance to students studying First Nations language and literature, history, cultural studies, life writing, women's studies, feminist, anti-racist, and anti-colonial studies. A review by the *Resources for Feminist Research* journal states that "the book offers the possibility of learning one Cree word at a time and the context in which the word is used." The review then discusses the significance of the women's stories:

> The honesty displayed by these women encourages aspiring Aboriginal writers such as myself to continue to seek out our truths and givens. Each woman openly shares personal experiences, ranging from the spiritual to the gathering of food. Seldom has a book made me laugh and cry all within the same moment.... Elderly Indian women's lives have rarely been documented from their own perspective or received a just and accurate portrayal. Unfortunately, their voice was marginalized in print and often capitalized on by many non-Native writers who professed to speak for the grandmothers. Freda Ahenakew gives seven of those grandmothers an opportunity to share their experiences, to tell it in their own words, as the title of the book suggests.[15]

Freda Ahenakew's influence on academe is a result of placing two core aspects of indigenous knowledge into university programs and research: Cree language, and narrative research with elders from Cree perspectives. Her master's thesis became a useful text for learning Cree language at a time when few Aboriginal languages taught at mainstream universities used material developed by Aboriginal people. The First Nations language- and culture-suppression policies of missionary, boarding, and residential schools left generations of First Nations people without access to their language. Because of this colonial legacy, it is rare to find fluent First Nations language speakers who are university faculty. Freda is one of the few scholars who honours and promotes the First Nations language by including it in her publications.

There is much rhetoric about the importance of elders' knowledge, but there is very limited learning material available from the elders' voice and perspective. Freda's approach is simple but extremely effective: document the elders' words as they told them. Current and future Cree language learners are fortunate to have the Cree language documented in the way that elders speak it so that they can appreciate the quality of Cree language from fluent speakers. English speakers can appreciate the way that elders tell stories and about First Nations knowledge embedded in the way the story is told as well as in the story itself. English readers can also learn a great deal about First Nations' resilience in surviving colonization. The documentation of Cree elder women's lives and their stories will benefit their families, communities, and others interested in Cree life, stories, and knowledge. Freda once said that the purpose for her work was to "teach the children." Future generations of children will learn through the elders' stories because of Freda's scholarly work. Her belief that "Your language gives you an inner strength, a pride in your heritage, when able to speak it, even a little bit"[16] gives hope to adult First Nations learners who do not speak their language but want to, and to those who are at the beginning stages of learning their language.

Freda demonstrated excellence and steadfast persistence in pursing her scholarly passions and forming cooperative partnerships, such as the one with C.H. Wolfart, a linguist who has worked along with her on the Cree- and English-language publications.

In recognition of her work, Freda received many awards: Citizen of the Year by the Federation of Saskatchewan Indian Nations (FSIN), 1992; Mother of the Year Award, 1979, by FSIN; honorary doctor of laws degree in 1997 from the University of Saskatchewan; National Aboriginal Achievement Award for education in 2001; and the Order of Canada in 1999 for her work on Cree language preservation.

MARLENE BRANT CASTELLANO

My words represent Aboriginal knowledge only in the sense that they emerge from the consciousness of an Aboriginal woman fully engaged with the Aboriginal community as a family and clan member and as an educator. I acknowledge that my understanding has been shaped by inter-cultural experience, and my communication by the semantics of the English language. I have told my story with as much honesty as I can muster, but it represents only one view of reality, a perspective which needs to be evaluated in the context of other stories by other members of the community.[17]

Marlene Brant Castellano, born in 1935, is from the Tyendinaga Mohawk Territory near Kingston, Ontario. She completed her bachelor of arts degree at Queen's University in 1955, a bachelor of social work in 1956, and then a master of social work in 1959 at the University of Toronto. She began her professional career as a social worker in child and family services. In 1973, after a ten-year interval devoted to responsibilities as a full-time wife and mother of four sons, Marlene joined the ranks of faculty at Trent University, where the discipline of Native Studies was in its formative stage.[18] She taught Native Studies courses, served as department chair for three terms, and was promoted to the rank of full professor. Marlene was one of a handful of Aboriginal people who received full professorships at mainstream universities prior to 1996. Marlene is a significant leader in the development of Native Studies as a discipline at Canadian universities.[19] She helped to establish the PhD program in Native Studies at Trent University, which was also the first in a Canadian university. Marlene was at Trent University for twenty-three years, retiring in 1996. She continues with service on committees and occasional teaching and in her role as professor emerita.

As a co-director of research for the Royal Commission on Aboriginal Peoples (RCAP) from 1992 to 1996, Marlene continued to influence academe. She assumed major responsibility for developing the commission's research plan, overseeing social-cultural, historical, and community-based research, and writing and editing the RCAP report. The RCAP ethical guidelines for research, developed by an Aboriginal committee and facilitated by Marlene, have been widely used in universities across Canada and have become a catalyst for the development of community research protocols. Her research expertise and ability to engage both Aboriginal and non-Aboriginal people in the sensitive topic of research positively shaped the direction for RCAP research, for which academics and community-based scholars, both Aboriginal and non-Aboriginal, conducted over 200 studies on all facets of Aboriginal life. The RCAP study was one of the first opportunities given to Aboriginal communities to conduct research, reversing the trend where they have usually been the "subjects" of research. This research created an important information base for subsequent RCAP recommendations. A CD-ROM, *For Seven Generations*,[20] contains all the research studies, transcripts of over 100 community consultations, the five-volume report, and sample teaching units. This information is a very valuable resource for communities, governments, schools, colleges, and universities.

In Canada, the federal government funds research through three major research granting agencies: the Social Sciences and Humanities Research Council, Canadian Institutes of Health Research, and the Natural Sciences and Engineering Research Council. To receive funding, universities and research institutes, and scholars affiliated with them, are required to adhere to the Tri-Council Policy Statement: Ethical Conduct for Research Involving Humans (TCPS). An interagency advisory panel on research ethics was established in 2001 to revise and update the TCPS, including section 6, which is about research with Aboriginal people. Marlene serves on this panel. An article she published in the *Journal of Aboriginal Health* demonstrates her forward thinking about Aboriginal research ethics:

> Scientific research conflicts with Aboriginal sensibilities when it sets ethical guidelines for research involving human subjects, but assumes that the earth and the waters are inanimate or lifeless, and that mice, monkeys or fish can be treated as objects of research rather than co-inhabitants with humans of a living biosphere. Because many Aboriginal societies maintain primary dependence on a healthy natural environment to meet their needs, industrial development that sacrifices environmental values directly infringes on their well-being and human rights. Ethical regimes for Aboriginal research must therefore extend beyond current definitions of research involving human subjects to include research that affects Aboriginal well-being. This includes environmental research that will impact their physical environment or archival research that may perpetuate negative or inaccurate representations of Aboriginal Peoples.[21]

Other key boards that Marlene serves on include the institute advisory board of the Canadian Institutes of Health Research and Institute of Aboriginal Peoples' Health (IAPH), which is a national site of research excellence. The IAPH develops research-funding programs that address Aboriginal people's health, and is a major source of funding for Aboriginal and non-Aboriginal health researchers. Marlene also serves on the college of reviewers for the prestigious Canadian Research Chairs, which is another entity that provides significant funding for recruiting and retaining quality university faculty across Canada.

Marlene's knowledge in the fields of social work, Native studies, Aboriginal education, and Aboriginal health is impressive. Her publications tackle pressing issues in these important areas. In 2000, she edited and published, along with Lynne Davis and Louise Lahache, some of the research studies commissioned by the Royal Commission on Aboriginal Peoples: *Aboriginal Education: Fulfilling the Promise*. The articles in this book address key educational topics such as policy, curriculum, Aboriginal knowledge, learning, higher education, Aboriginal language, urban Aboriginal education, and communications. This book and Marlene's scholarly work in education give hope to the future role that education can play in improving Aboriginal people's lives.

Marlene has received the following awards: induction into the Order of Ontario (1995); National Aboriginal Achievement Award for education (1996); named an Officer of the Order of Canada (2005); and honorary doctor of laws degrees from Queen's University (1991), St. Thomas University (1992), and Carleton University (2004).

OLIVE DICKASON

> My goal has always been to present the situation as it actually was ... and to recognize the actual role of the Indians in our history—their fundamental role. The point is to try to make that [clear].[22]
>
> —Olive Dickason

Olive Dickason, Métis, was born in 1920 in Winnipeg, Manitoba. She grew up in northern Manitoba. Her Métis mother, who was a schoolteacher, taught the family how to live from the land. Olive said, "Living in the bush as I did during my adolescent years, I very soon learned that survival depended upon assessing each situation as it arose, which calls for common sense and realism. You neither give up nor play games."[23] Olive completed her high-school education through correspondence and supplemented it by reading classical books from a neighbour's library. She completed a bachelor of arts at Notre Dame College, a collegiate affiliate of the University of Ottawa, in philosophy and French, in 1943.

After completing a twenty-four-year career as a journalist for the *Regina Leader-Post, Winnipeg Free Press, Montreal Gazette*, and *Globe and Mail*, Olive returned to university to complete her master's and doctoral degrees. She was a single parent of three daughters during her journalism career. Olive received her master of arts degree in history at the University of Ottawa in 1972. When she began her master's, she was fifty years old, and she completed her doctorate in 1977, when she was fifty-seven. She recounts the difficulty she had convincing her faculty advisors that Aboriginal history existed. She wanted to write about the history of Canada's First Nations but faced opposition from the university faculty: "When I first approached the graduate-studies committee and said I wanted to study first contact between the French and the Indians, the reaction I got was, 'You can't do that, because Indians have no history' .... That was a generally held belief—in a society without writing, you can't have history."[24]

Olive's persuasive argument that there were oral and written records resulted in a faculty member's finally agreeing to supervise her dissertation research. It was subsequently published as *The Myth of the Savage and the Beginnings of French Colonialism in the Americas* (1984). Her third book, *Canada's First Nations: A History of Founding Peoples from Earliest Times* (1992), became a national best-seller. Numerous post-secondary history and Native studies courses across Canada use it as a course text. Both books document history from Aboriginal perspectives. Introducing and "embedding Amerindian perspectives," a term used by Olive, in scholarly disciplines has been a slow process, especially in history. It is evident in the following quote that Olive listens to and advocates for the concerns of First Nations: "Canada, it used to be said by non-Indians with more or less conviction, is a country of much geography and little history. The ethnocentricity of that position at first puzzled, and even confused, Amerindians, but it has lately begun to anger them. How could such a thing be said, much less believed, when their people have been living here for thousands of years? As they see it, Canada has fifty-five founding nations rather than just the two that have been officially acknowledged."[25]

Changing a Western paradigm of history is a daunting task. Olive acknowledges, "You can only go one step at a time.... For a totally native history, the material is there. But the perspective wouldn't be understood. It is too big a leap."[26] The approach used in *Canada's First Nations* is a chronological framework that most Europeans have used in describing history. However, Olive reversed "the perspective of the standard history." Christopher Moore explains this by using the following example:

> Pierre Radisson had gone unchallenged for three hundred years as the prime mover in the founding of the Hudson's Bay Company. Reversing the perspective, Dickason begins to examine how the destruction of the Huron confederacy in 1649 affected more northerly hunter-gatherers. They had long been used to trading with the corn-growing Hurons. With the Huron network shattered, Dickason argues, it was those nations, rather than a few enterprising coureurs de bois, who shifted the fur-for-provisions trade away from the Great Lakes. "It's much deeper and more profound than has been recognized. The Northern people turned the trade to Hudson Bay," says Dickason. In the reversed perspective she

offers, Radisson, King Charles, the Gentlemen Adventurers—and the whole courses of fur-driven colonial history—just responded.[27]

Olive was a professor of history at the University of Alberta from 1975 to 1992. She retired at age seventy-two instead of the mandatory age of sixty-five because she challenged mandatory retirement in the Alberta Human Rights Commission and the Court of Queen's Bench, where she won both cases. The University of Alberta won an appeal. Her case went to the Supreme Court of Canada, where she lost.[28] She said, "I had been encouraged to go and make this commitment of time and energy, at great expense to me and to the state as well, to earn my doctorate. Now I was just getting started—and in history you need years to let things simmer. Things were just starting to come together, and they wanted me to retire."[29] During the seven years that her case was in the various courts, Olive was allowed to keep her faculty position, which gave her time to complete more historical research and publications, and to receive promotion to full professor before she left the university, joining less than a handful of Aboriginal people at this top university rank. It was during those years that she was able to complete her research and writing for her seminal book, *Canada's First Nations: A History of Founding Peoples from Earliest Times.*

Olive fought "milestone battles" in academe, such as her historical research from the perspective of Aboriginal peoples, and then her challenge to mandatory retirement. Perhaps some of her resilience and persistent spirit stems from the influence of living off the land. As she said, "You know, when you grow up in the bush, if you allow yourself to get pushed around, you don't last very long."[30]

Olive Dickason refuted the common view that Canada's history began with European settlement. The difficulty and subsequent success of Olive's struggle, during the early to mid-1970s, to convince her university history professors that Indian people indeed had history is remarkable, considering that the discipline of history did not acknowledge or accept First Nations historical perspectives at that time. Today, her history books make a significant contribution to understanding a more complete picture of Canada's history. History that is told from the perspectives of Aboriginal peoples is now gaining more prominence in course material, even though these materials and perspectives are not yet integrated, or embedded, into core university and school curricula.[31]

Her achievement in completing advanced university study as an older learner, at a time when there were few Aboriginal people completing master's and doctoral degrees in Canadian universities, is remarkable. No national data exist about the numbers of Aboriginal people who have completed doctoral degrees and who have obtained tenure faculty positions at Canadian universities. When Olive assumed her faculty appointment at the University of Alberta in 1975, the only other First Nations woman who had a university tenure-track appointment at a mainstream university was Gail Guthrie Valaskakis.

Olive's feisty spirit is admirable, especially her battle with the University of Alberta regarding mandatory retirement. She continues to stay active in her scholarly endeavours of research, writing, and serving on various national education committees. Awards she received include being named Métis Woman of the Year by the Women of the Métis Nation of Alberta (1992); Sir John A. Macdonald Prize from the Canadian Historical Association (1992); Canada 125 Medal (1993); National Aboriginal Achievement Award for lifetime achievement (1997); Order of Canada for her work in Aboriginal history (1996); and numerous honorary degrees from Canadian universities.

VERNA J. KIRKNESS

> It is our responsibility to give voice to our ancestors, by learning from our Elders as they pass on to us the teachings of their ancestors. They are the keepers and teachers of our cultures. It is our responsibility in this generation to ensure that the ties between the Elders and the youth are firmly entrenched so that the youth of today can continue the process of mending the Scared Hoop for the benefit of future generations.[32]

—Verna J. Kirkness

Verna J. Kirkness, born in 1935, is Cree, from the Fisher River reserve in the Interlake area of Manitoba. She completed her bachelor of arts (1974), bachelor of education (1976), and master of education (1980) degrees from the University of Manitoba. She has held teaching positions and a principalship at public, residential, and Indian day schools in Manitoba. Verna was also a curriculum consultant in Indian education for the Manitoba Department of Education. She launched a number of Cree and Ojibwa language immersion initiatives in Manitoba schools.

A pivotal point in her educational career occurred when Verna was the education director for the Manitoba Indian Brotherhood (now Assembly of Manitoba Chiefs). She served as its representative on a national education committee that developed the landmark 1972 Indian Control of Indian Education Policy (ICIE) for the National Indian Brotherhood (now Assembly of First Nations). The federal government department of Indian Affairs and Northern Development accepted this policy document in 1973. The ICIE policy was the first attempt to declare First Nations jurisdiction of education through the principles of local community control and parental involvement. Increasing the numbers of First Nations teachers and counsellors, improving physical facilities, and developing culturally relevant curricula were critical components of the policy. The beginnings of band-operated schools, Native teacher education programs, and Aboriginal curricula were influenced by this national educational policy.[33] Verna promoted and implemented the foundational principles of local control of education, increasing the numbers of Aboriginal people becoming teachers, and ensuring cultural relevance to university education, particularly at the University of British Columbia.

In 1980, Verna moved to British Columbia to teach First Nations education courses and then became the supervisor of the Native Indian Teacher Education Program (NITEP), which is a bachelor of education degree program for Aboriginal people at the University of British Columbia created by a key group of Aboriginal educators and individuals in the Faculty of Education. Since its inception, a First Nations education council has continued to guide NITEP policy and programming. Before moving to British Columbia, Verna had been involved with creating similar Native teacher education programs in Manitoba. A strong advocate for First Nations teachers, she recalls that when she started teaching in 1954 there were fewer than fifty First Nations teachers across Canada.[34]

Major changes occurred to the NITEP program, such as increasing the number of First Nations education courses and ensuring that Aboriginal people taught these courses. Through Verna's fundraising efforts and leadership, NITEP greatly expanded its full- and part-time rural and urban community-based centres where Aboriginal students completed their first two years of the program, closer to home, before moving to the Vancouver campus to complete their degree program. Verna was the first First Nations person to assume a key leadership position within NITEP and later across the Faculty of Education.

In 1984, Verna became the director of Native education for the Faculty of Education and established the Ts`'kel graduate studies program in the educational administration and leadership area. "Ts`'kel" is a Halq'emeylem word that means "golden eagle." Ts`'kel students work to achieve their highest learning goals in order to improve Aboriginal education. Before Ts`'kel, many of the NITEP graduates assumed principalships and educational leadership positions, but felt they were not adequately prepared. Aboriginal students from across Canada enrolled in the Ts̕'kel program. It was the first of its kind at a mainstream university to offer a focus on First Nations education through a master's degree. Today, Ts̕'kel has expanded to serve the needs of indigenous doctoral students.

In 1997, Verna became the founding director of the First Nations House of Learning (FNHL) at University of British Columbia, which is a unit of the president's office with a mandate to work across the faculties and schools to make the university more accessible to First Nations people. The two founding co-chairs of the Native Indian Teacher Education Program, Joan Ryan and Bert McKay, suggested that the institute's name be the First Nations House of Learning because, in northwest coast First Nations languages there is a common concept of a house of learning. At the University of British Columbia, the inclusive term "First Nations" means any person of Aboriginal ancestry, despite the focussed political usage of the term in national contexts today.

One of the goals of the FNHL was to establish a longhouse as a student, faculty/staff, and program centre. In 1988, Dr. Jack Bell, a Vancouver philanthropist, donated $1 million to benefit First Nations people attending the University of British Columbia. This donation started a capital fundraising campaign, which Verna led. After five years of hard work, a Musqueam-style, 2322-square-metre longhouse was completed. It was the first building on a university campus in Canada, and probably North America, to reflect Aboriginal traditional architecture and to be for the primary use of Aboriginal students and communities.[35] During the ceremonial opening of the Longhouse in 1993, Verna received a Haida name from elder Minnie Croft, one of the founding elders' group: Ni-jing-jada, Longhouse Lady. Shortly after the official opening of the First Nations Longhouse, Verna retired from the university. Today, the First Nations Longhouse is a "home away from home" for indigenous students and others who study and visit the Vancouver campus.

Unlike the empty and neglected longhouse in the Lady Louse story, many diverse student groups, university units, and external community groups use the First Nations Longhouse. First Nations elders resumed an active decision-making role with the First Nations House of Learning. They serve on the president's advisory committee that guides the FNHL and on the longhouse building committee. The university students benefit from their teachings, which are practised in the daily activities and gatherings of the university's longhouse. After the First Nations Longhouse opened its doors, many other colleges and universities in Canada and the United States asked for information about the processes of fundraising and obtaining institutional support for such an entity. Evergreen State College in Washington State now has a longhouse, Trent University built a First Peoples House of Learning, and the University of Victoria has plans for building a First Peoples House.[36]

Verna had other impacts on the University of British Columbia. She made institutional changes to the hiring practices of the Faculty of Education so that First Nations people who had bachelor's or master's degrees along with substantial teaching experience could teach the First Nations courses and assume the roles of field centre coordinators. She ensured that the NITEP advisory committee (now First Nations Education Council) continued to provide an important decision-making role in program development and policy. The principles of the Indian Control of Indian Education Policy became practices in her NITEP leadership.

Verna's educational leadership and influence was and is national and international in scope. She has given numerous keynote talks at conferences, published widely, and participated in university reviews and new post-secondary educational development across Canada. Making educational change is a serious and intense endeavour. During her keynote speeches, Verna puts people at ease, but also challenges them to think deeply about what matters in education. In a 1985 conference presentation, she reflected on the previous twenty years of educational progress:

> I would like to begin by acknowledging the fact that we have made significant, though modest advances in education particularly in the last twenty years. I would like to suggest that we must become much more radical in our approach to education. It is necessary for us to put into practice our goals and objectives based on our reality. To do this, it is necessary for us, first to disestablish many of the current education practices that relate to centuries of colonial domination. We must see education for what it really is. If we are to have a future, we must look within ourselves, within our communities, our nations to determine the form our education must take. Today this is a process that requires total involvement.[37]

Today, her ideas about recognizing the impact of colonization and developing self-determination for educational jurisdiction are even more relevant and present in the current educational discourse.

A prolific writer, Verna has published numerous essays, speeches, journal articles, and books. She became one of the editors for the *Canadian Journal of Native Education*, which is the only peer-reviewed journal on Aboriginal education in Canada. The First Nations House of Learning began to publish one of the two annual issues. Verna worked with the prominent Coast Salish elder, Chief Simon Baker, to document his life story, *Khot-La-Cha: The Autobiography of Chief Simon Baker* (1994). Simon's autobiography, told in his words, is similar in intent to Freda Ahenakew's work with Cree women elders. A milestone article, "First Nations and Higher Education: The Four R's: Respect, Relevance, Reciprocity, and Responsibility" (1991), which Verna co-authored with Ray Barnhardt, is used by numerous indigenous graduate students and academics as a basis for an indigenous perspective for post-secondary education and research.

Verna received the following awards: Canadian Educator of the Year Award from the Canadian University Students' Association (1990); National Aboriginal Achievement Award for Education (1994); and the Order of Canada (1994). In addition, she received three honorary degrees from Mount St. Vincent (1990), University of Western Ontario (1992), and the University of British Columbia (1994). In 2000, Verna was among British Columbia's "top fifty living public intellectuals."[38]

GAIL GUTHRIE VALASKAKIS

> Research, too, hopes to contribute to greater understanding within not only the public, but among Aboriginal children and their parents and grandparents through the development of school curricula and other resources.[39]

Gail Guthrie Valaskakis was born and raised on the Lac du Flambeau reservation in Wisconsin, US. She was a tribal member of the Lake Superior Chippewa Indians. She completed a bachelor of science degree in 1961 at the University of Wisconsin-Madison, a master of arts degree in theatre and English in 1964 at Cornell University, and a PhD at McGill University in 1979. For her PhD research, she studied the impact of satellite communications on the people and their traditional way of life in Canada's north. Through her research, she became an advisor to many Native communities interested in establishing their own communications systems.

Concordia University benefitted from Gail's thirty-one-year academic career. In 1967, she began as a lecturer in the Department of Communications Arts, then known as Loyola College. In 1969, she moved to the assistant professor rank in communication arts, and, in 1979, became an associate professor. She was promoted to a full professor of communication studies in 1989. Gail served for seven years as the dean of the Faculty of Arts and Science, and was also vice-dean of academic planning. Gail was the first Aboriginal person in Canada to serve as a dean at a mainstream university.

After retiring from Concordia University in 1999, Gail became the director of research for the Aboriginal Healing Foundation (AHF), established by the federal government to fund community healing projects and research. The research conducted through the AHF has documented Aboriginal health knowledge and has created greater understanding of the residential school impact. The AHF 2004 Annual Report notes its research influence: "AHF research materials are now being widely used by funded projects, educational institutions (including public and private schools and universities), and health professionals for the purposes of education, training, improved service delivery, and increased public awareness of the Indian Residential School System and its legacy."[40]

In her role at the AHF, Gail helped establish university and community networking and research collaborations. Gail also served on the advisory board for the Institute of Aboriginal Peoples' Health, a centre of research excellence of the Canadian Institutes of Health Research. This board determines health research funding grant programs to which university faculty apply for their research, and disseminates research results. In addition, Gail was a member of the editorial board of the *Aboriginal Health Research Journal* of the National Aboriginal Health Organization.

Another of Gail's important academic contributions was her historical and critical analysis of the portrayal of Aboriginal women by American and Canadian society. Her publications about "Indian Princesses" address the stereotypes of Indian women prevalent in the early 1900s to the 1930s. Souvenir postcards, decorated calendars, beer trays, wall plaques, and even sheet music covers prominently displayed these stereotypic images. She said, "But what did these postcard representations mean in the lived experience of my great-grandmother, who was enrolled as a Band member when the reservation was established and who, at 90, bought a car and didn't speak to my father for two months because he didn't want her to get a driver's license?"[41]

In her most recent book, *Indian Country: Essays on Contemporary Native Culture* (2005), eight essays tackle issues of treaty rights, political struggles, stereotypical images of Native people, Indian identity, and research of indigenous people in the United States and Canada. In the first pages, she described the multiple contexts that shaped her Aboriginal identity and academic purpose:

> My voice is here, too, recalling the understandings and experiences of an Indian "insider-outsider," lived, remembered, and imagined. I am forever joined to Lac du Flambeau, where one of my paternal grandfathers signed the treaty that established this reservation that is my home; but I also live the heritage of a maternal grandfather, an East Coast sea captain and Dutch immigrant, who sailed commercial vessels along the colonial coast. I walk with a moccasin on one foot, a shoe on the other, allied to Indian Country and a mix of border zones, academic, urban, and social. My voice joins others that assert, contradict, and confront. Through a blend of conjoined voices, we can begin to unravel the meaning of Native experience and approach the points of connectedness between Natives and other North Americans.[42]

Indian Country contains examples of research methodology that graduate students can use and build upon to contribute to indigenous methodologies. As one example, Gail discussed the importance of personal location and testimony: "My search always begins with personal testimony, in part because the questions that drive the research arise in discourse, in the exchange circulating around contested practice or policy or objects; and in part because testimony is the most fragile, illusive, and uniquely informative evidence."[43]

Gail was a founding board member of Manitou College, the first post-secondary institution in eastern Canada for Aboriginal students. She helped create the Native Friendship Centre of Montreal and Waseskun Native Half-Way House in north Montreal for men, which is now a healing lodge for men in trouble with the law. Gail received the 2002 National Aboriginal Achievement Award for her exemplary work in communications. Her breadth of scholarly expertise and university experience regarding education, health, communications, women's studies, research, and university leadership is inspiring.

CONCLUDING COMMENTS: BUILDING A FIRST NATIONS INTELLECTUAL MOVEMENT

> If stories are to have any meaning, Indian intellectuals must ask what it means to be an Indian in tribal America. If we don't attempt to answer that question, nothing else will matter, and we won't have to ask ourselves whether there is such a thing as Native American intellectualism because there will no longer be evidence of it.[44]

In telling stories of what it means to be First Nations in our communities and in our country, we must acknowledge and understand the colonial legacy that all Canadians have inherited. First Nations have lived through legislation that banned cultural ceremonies and that enfranchised First Nations people who were literate in English and French and who completed a university education.[45] First Nations lived through a century of missionary and residential schooling that resulted in very few First Nations people graduating from high school and then continuing to university. Residential schools suppressed language and culture and their poor academic standards left First Nations people with poor self-identity and a minimum set of academic skills. Yet, a small set of First Nations people succeeded in completing high school and a post-secondary education. In telling the stories of what it means to be First Nations, we also need to move beyond the colonial legacy to acknowledge, understand, and celebrate the achievements of First Nations people who have succeeded in the Eurocentric education systems with their indigenous identity and knowledge intact, and who took on leadership roles to make the educational systems more responsive to First Nations learners.

The five First Nations women discussed here completed high school from the 1940s to the 1970s, a period when very few students graduated, and they completed their master's degrees from 1959 to 1984, when even fewer First Nations people enrolled in university studies. Olive and Gail completed their PhDs in 1977 and 1979, respectively, again at a time when doctoral studies were out of reach for the majority of First Nations learners. Being a university professor, department head, and dean were careers that were inconceivable to First Nations people during the late 1960s to early 1990s.

In the story that began this chapter, Lady Louse worked alone in her long-house, disconnected from her family and community. Each first-wave woman could have been like Lady Louse, consumed or changed by academe, and disconnected from her First Nations community values and knowledge. But, unlike Lady Louse, these five women did not get lost in the dust of their struggle. They kept their indigenous knowledge, values, and community connections alive, and they did not work alone. Throughout their university tenure, they formed coalitions and alliances, and mentored others to work beside them. Most importantly, they did not let their indigenous knowledge and values get lost in the dust of colonization. Instead, as public intellectuals, they began an indigenous intellectual movement in academe.

These first-wave female academics excelled in their university professor-ships and leadership positions. They taught, conducted research, published, and gave service to the university and external community. They fulfilled these academic expectations. But they did so much more. Each woman significantly changed the academic learning institution of which she was a part. Academic disciplines, accessibility and retention for Aboriginal learners, research ethics and methodology, Aboriginal faculty and staff, and policy were either increased or improved to address the learning needs and interests of Aboriginal commu-nities and their people. They wrote about what it means to be First Nations in Canada through tribally specific, regional, provincial, and national scholarship. They led an intellectual indigenous movement in mainstream universities that was non-existent before they joined the faculty ranks.

Freda Ahenakew and Marlene Brant Castellano developed and strength-ened the Native studies discipline through their positions as department heads. Freda ensured that the Cree language held a prominent place within her department. Marlene pushed to create a new doctoral program in Native studies. Olive Dickason changed the discipline of history to include Aboriginal perspectives. Her published work is widely used in university classrooms across Canada as well as being available to the public. Verna J. Kirkness created new institutional academic and student support units led by Aboriginal faculty, which are emulated in universities across the country. Gail Guthrie Valaskakis took on key university leadership positions and established new student support initiatives. All these women excelled in one or more disciplines and they created substantial and significant publication records. These five Aborig-inal women have created a similar corpus of Aboriginal-based scholarly litera-ture from their knowledge perspectives. Current and future students and academics have an excellent core collection of writings upon which to draw. They have a solid base of Aboriginal knowledge upon which to add pertinent Aboriginal research findings and methodology.

An often-stated criticism of the university is its "ivory tower" disconnec-tion from the real world and its touted elitism. The transformative work of these five women is in stark contrast to this criticism. Each woman spoke compassionately about the importance of addressing the learning needs of Aboriginal people, families, and communities. They recognized the impor-tance of a university education. More importantly, they realized the impor-tance of changing and transforming the university teaching, learning, and research functions to address the cultures and contexts of Aboriginal peoples.

Key issues that figure prominently in these women's scholarly work include community concerns about perpetuating First Nations languages, cultures, and Aboriginal knowledge; increasing the numbers of Aboriginal teachers; and improving research ethics and methodology.

Making institutional change, especially in a mainstream Canadian university, is a slow and difficult process. Each woman kept her university position(s) for a number of years until she had created the change she had set out to effect or until she had to leave. Personal characteristics, such as persistence, caring, commitment, resilience, high expectations, and determination form the basis of their academic leadership. Freda, Marlene, Verna, and Gail took on management roles to challenge and change university policy and practice. Olive challenged a key mandatory retirement policy that affects many universities across Canada. There is still much to learn about their university leadership style, challenges, and successes.

Second-wave Aboriginal academic women such as myself, and the upcoming third and subsequent waves, benefit from the indigenous intellectual movement and institutional changes that these five women fought for at mainstream Canadian universities. However, we who work in academe are fully aware that there is much more to do to make the university a respectful place of learning for and about Aboriginal peoples. Let us hope that we do not get lost in the dust like Lady Louse. In Coast Salish tradition, I raise my hands in thanks and respect to this first wave of Aboriginal academic women—Freda Ahenakew, Marlene Brant Castellano, Olive Dickason, Verna J. Kirkness, and Gail Guthrie Valaskakis—for starting an indigenous intellectual movement in the mainstream Canadian universities that is relevant to Aboriginal communities across this land.

Notes

1   A shorter published version of this story can be found in Vi Hilbert, compiler, *Lady Louse Lived There* (Seattle: Lushootseed Press, 1996).

2   Olive Dickason, *Canada's First Nations: A History of Founding Peoples from Earliest Times* (Toronto: McClelland and Stewart, 1992).

3   Harry B. Hawthorn, *A Survey of the Contemporary Indians of Canada: Economic, Political, Educational Needs and Policies*, vol. 2 (Ottawa: Indian Affairs Branch, 1967).

4   Ibid., 130.

5   Canada, Office of the Auditor General, *Report of the Auditor General of Canada to the House of Commons* (Ottawa: Office of the Auditor General, November 2004), 5.

6   Ibid., 3.

7   Annette Vermaeten, Mary Jane Norris, and Marion Buchmeier, "Educational Outcomes of Students Funded by the Department of Indian and Northern Affairs Canada: Illustration of a Longitudinal Assessment with Potential Application to Policy Research," in Jerry White, Paul Maxim, and Dan Beavon, eds., *Aboriginal Policy Research: Setting the Agenda for Change* (Toronto: Thompson Educational Publishing, 2004), 209.

8   There were a handful of First Nations men at mainstream universities, such as Carl Urion at the University of Alberta, LeRoy Little Bear at Lethbridge University, and Dave Courchene at Queen's University and later University of Saskatchewan. Since this book is about First Nations women's contributions, the academic contributions of these men are not included.

9   Jules Chametzky, "Public Intellectuals—Now and Then," *Melus* 29 (2004): 211.

10   National Aboriginal Achievement Foundation, "Dr. Freda Ahenakew (Hon.) Education," *National Aboriginal Achievement Award Recipients 2001*, http://www.naaf.ca/rec2001.html (accessed 4 July 2005).

11   Saskatchewan Indian Cultural Centre, "Freda Ahenakew," in *Our Elders: Interviews with Saskatchewan Elders*, digital archives, Saskatchewan Indian Cultural Centre, http://www.naaf.ca/html/f_ahenakew_e.html (accessed 26 April 2005).

12   Lorie-Ann LaRoque, "Citizen of the year: An inspiration to all," *Saskatchewan Indian*, May 1992.

13   Ibid., n. 11.

14   Freda Ahenakew and H. Christoph Wolfart, eds., *Kohkominawak otacimowiniwawa/Our Grandmothers' Lives as Told in Their Own Words* (Saskatoon: Fifth House, 1992), 303.

15   "Review of *Kohkominawak otacimowiniwawa/Our grandmothers' lives as told in their own words*, by Freda Ahenakew and H. Christoph Wolfart, eds.," *Resources for Feminist Research* 23, 1/2 (1994): 56–57.

16   Saskatchewan Indian Cultural Centre, "Freda Ahenakew," in *Aboriginal Faces of Saskatchewan: A Photo Gallery*, Saskatchewan Indian Cultural Centre, http://www.sicc.sk.ca/faces/wahenfr.htm (accessed 26 April 2005).

17   Marlene Brant Castellano, "Updating Aboriginal Traditions of Knowledge," in George Sefa Dei, Budd Hall, and Dorothy Rosenberg, eds., *Indigenous Knowledges in Global Contexts: Multiple Readings of Our World* (Toronto: University of Toronto Press, 2000), 32.

18   See David Newhouse, Don McCaskill, and John Milloy, "Culture, Tradition, and Evolution: The Department of Native Studies at Trent University," in Duane Champagne and Jay Strauss, eds., *Native American Studies in Higher Education: Models for Collaboration between Universities and Indigenous Nations* (New York: Altamira Press, 2002), 61–81.

19   *Trent University Daily News*, 27 April 2005.

20   Royal Commission on Aboriginal Peoples, *For Seven Generations: Report of the Royal Commission on Aboriginal Peoples* (Ottawa: Minister of Supply and Services Canada, 1996), CD-ROM.

21   Marlene Brant Castellano, "Ethics of Aboriginal Research," *Journal of Aboriginal Health* 1, 1 (2004): 103–104.

22 Brian Gorman, "Late Starter," *Canadian Geographic* 124, 5 (Sep/Oct 2004): 77.

23 See http://www.uwinnipeg.ca/index/cms-filesystem-action?file=pdfs/newsflash/olive_dickason.pdf.

24 Peter Nowak, "A Spiritual View of Indian History," *Globe and Mail*, 21 May 2003, p. R4.

25 Olive Patricia Dickason, *Canada's First Nations : A History of Founding Peoples from Earliest Times* (Toronto: McClelland and Stewart, 1992), 11.

26 Christopher Moore, "The First People of America," *Beaver*, Oct./Nov. 1992, 53.

27 Ibid.

28 Gorman, "Late Starter."

29 Moore, "The First People."

30 Gorman, "Late Starter."

31 RCAP, *Report of the Royal Commission on Aboriginal Peoples*.

32 Verna J. Kirkness, "Keynote: October 1, 1992," in Jo-ann Archibald, ed., *Selected Papers from the 1992 Mokakit Conference: Giving Voice to our Ancestors* (Vancouver: University of British Columbia, 1993), 15.

33 RCAP, *Report*.

34 Verna J. Kirkness, *Khot-La-Cha: The Autobiography of Chief Simon Baker* (Vancouver: Douglas and McIntyre, 1994), xiv.

35 Verna J. Kirkness and Jo-ann Archibald, *The First Nations Longhouse: Our Home Away from Home* (Vancouver: First Nations House of Learning, 2001).

36 University of Victoria, First Peoples' House, "Tsi Dza Watul: To Come Together and Work Together," http://web.uvic.ca/fphouse/ (accessed 20 April 2005).

37 Verna J. Kirkness, conference presentation, 1985. See also Verna J. Kirkness, "Aboriginal Education in Canada: A Retrospective and a Prospective," *Journal of American Indian Education* 39, 1, Special Issue–Part 2 (1999): 14–30.

38 Douglas Todd, "The Best B.C. Thinkers," *The Vancouver Sun*, 25 August 2000, p. A12.

39 Barbara Black, "Gail Valaskakis Wins Aboriginal Achievement Award," *Concordia's Thursday Report* (Concordia University, Montreal, QC), 14 March 2002, http://ctr.concordia.ca/2001-02/Mar_14/07-Valaskakis/index.shtml (accessed 30 May 2005).

40 Aboriginal Healing Foundation, Annual Report (Ottawa: Aboriginal Healing Foundation, 2004), 38, http://www.ahf.ca/pages/download/28_15 (accessed 18 April 2005).

41 Sheila Robertson, "Sexual and Racial Politics Underpin Collection of Indian, Cowgirl Images," *Saskatoon Star-Phoenix*, 12 August 2000, p. E17.

42 Gail Guthrie Valaskakis, *Indian Country: Essays on Contemporary Native Culture* (Waterloo: Wilfrid Laurier University Press, 2005), 6.

43 Ibid., 189.

44 Elizabeth Cook-Lynn, "American Indian Intellectualism and the New Indian Story," *American Indian Quarterly* 20 (1996), 214.

45 Dickason, *Canada's First Nations*, 225. According to the 1857 *Act to Encourage the Gradual Civilization of the Indian Tribes of Canada*, Indian males literate in English or French, of good moral character, and free from debt could enfranchise.

Reflections on Cultural Continuity through Aboriginal Women's Writings

Emma LaRocque

THIS CHAPTER PRESENTS A SELECTIVE survey of contemporary Indian and Métis women's writing and shows how these writers have translated the Aboriginal achievements, world views, and colonial challenges into meaningful and compelling art. This is not a literary or critical study of Aboriginal literatures; rather, it is a peek at cultural agency and accomplishments through literature. I will draw largely on autobiographical and creative works produced by Aboriginal women from different cultures and locations. Inevitably, I can only be selective: it is simply impossible to include all writers, or to discuss them in equal proportions, because it would take volumes to produce a thorough treatment of all literature by Native women. This, of course, points to the mass and the importance of Aboriginal literature, including that written by women.

I also want to deal with some troublesome issues concerning identity and terminology. As a writer and scholar of Métis Nation heritage, being invited to write a chapter focussing on the cultural contributions of First Nations women necessitates that I begin with a brief evaluative review of terms such as "Aboriginal," "Indian," "Métis," and "First Nations." These are all highly problematic terms, not only because they are, of course, colonial in origin, but also because they result in prejudicial treatment of many Aboriginal people, and so create, quite spuriously, political divisions. For example, who writes or speaks on behalf of, or about, Aboriginal and/or First Nations women? The relationship between identity and privilege is a discourse that yet needs to be opened up, but currently, it is virtually swollen shut with politics; here I can only offer some observations about the history and use of these terms.

Let's begin with the word "Métis," about which there is considerable misunderstanding or plain lack of knowledge. Some think being Métis is very much like being French. Or that simply having some Indian in one's background, however generationally or culturally remote, constitutes the full meaning of being Métis. Others assume being Métis is the same as being half-white, half-Native. Still others think being Métis is the same as "non-status." More recently, sociodemographic phenomena described as "hybridization" and "border crossing"—mostly by non-Aboriginal academics—further blurs the uniqueness of Métis Nation peoples. The usage, adoption, and even appropriation of the designation "métis" has become so broad and generalized that most Canadians are not familiar with the historical and ethnographic fact that vast numbers of Métis peoples, especially from western Canada, though a unique ethnocultural group, are also Aboriginal, whose connection to Aboriginal is genetic, familial, linguistic, epistemological, and ecological.[1] For example, the Prairies, perhaps especially the more central northern parts, are filled with Cree-Métis peoples who, of course, originate from both Europeans and Indians during the fur-trade era, but over time formed their own ethnicity (i.e., Métis marrying Métis) with a culture blended, yet distinct, from both groups.[2] Although these peoples were excluded from the *Indian Act* and treaties, they were and remain primarily connected to *Nehiyawewak* (Cree-speaking people), who themselves speak or grew up with *Nehiyawewin* (Cree language). Most were raised with parents, kin, and communities whose cultural lifestyles were intimately connected with the land and with other Aboriginal people. All these things are important to repeat because all the confusion, not to mention politics, surrounding the term "métis" can obscure the Aboriginal rights of those Métis Nation peoples whose cultures are centrally indigenous and whose lives contribute to the cultural continuity of all Aboriginal peoples.

As is well known, the term "Indian" is an imposed historical and legal designation first associated with Columbus's erroneous geography, and, in Canada, with the *Indian Act*, an Act quintessentially colonial in nature. The *Indian Act* and the treaties have defined a legally distinct identity and have, at least, offered a certain measure of rights and resources for those designated as

Status and/or Treaty Indians. Less well known is that the Métis Nation peoples, though connected to Indian peoples, as noted above, were excluded from the *Indian Act*. This exclusion has had numerous socio-political and economic consequences for the Métis in terms of identity, land, and resource rights.[3] And although the Métis were included as Aboriginal in the 1982 Canadian Constitution, they still struggle to have this put into practice.

Since the repatriation of the Constitution and the drive for self-government, Status Indian people have adopted the term "First Nations," a term now mostly understood as meaning exclusively those people who have historically had a "status" and "treaty" relationship with the Canadian government under the *Indian Act*. "First Nations" is in many ways an appropriate political self-designation for Aboriginal people. Unfortunately, "First Nations" has come to be used exclusively by and for Status and Treaty peoples, and with it the association of the term with Aboriginal rights. This, along with the unnecessary and often politicized confusion about the term "métis," has made it even more convenient for the Canadian governments to use the term "First Nations" in a way that especially excludes the Métis Nation, and perhaps those who are "non-Status Indian," of enfranchisement legacy. This has generally led to serious abrogation of rights for those Aboriginal people who are not "Status Indians" as per the *Indian Act*. By persisting in the association of Aboriginal rights almost exclusively with the phrase "First Nations," the Canadian government, whose constitutional mandate is to recognize equally the rights of all Aboriginal people, is in fact exercising inequality.

We should all be troubled by this, not only from the perspective of human rights and, in particular, Aboriginal rights, but also and certainly from a cultural perspective. In relation to this, and in every respect significant to indigenous culture building, western Métis Nation women, for example, are among Aboriginal women who should be included when considering cultural continuity and contemporary "contributions" to Aboriginal communities.

I begin here because I must locate myself in writing this paper. I am Métis and decidedly Aboriginal. The Cree-speaking, hunting/trapping and railroad-working community I come from is of the Métis Nation (Red River and far northwest) cultural group. In Cree we referred to ourselves as *Apeetowgusanuk*, or "half-sons"; other Cree peoples often referred to us also as *Otehpayimsuak*, "the people who own themselves."[4] In other words, Aboriginality is not exclusive to those people who have been defined by the *Indian Act* as "Indian" and who today generally refer to themselves as "First Nations."

Since culture is so much more than legal status, it is imperative that we include all Aboriginal people when considering something as vital as cultural continuity, especially on behalf of all those Aboriginal women who have kept their cultures alive despite all odds and despite colonial machinations of marginalization. This is in honour of my *Nokum*, my *Ama*, and *Nemis* (grandmother, mother, and older sister) as well as my aunts—all who have left this earth but all who have left me and this world with a rich Cree-Métis heritage and culture. Because they kept their *Nehiyowewin* (Plains Cree) and their *atowkehwin* (myths and legends) and their skills, among other things, they kept their cultures alive; because of that, I am alive. We are alive. By "alive" I mean literally and culturally.

When studying Aboriginal writing, it becomes quickly apparent that our sense of cultural knowledge, depth, and experience would be incomplete were we to exclude Métis Nation writers and scholars. Writers such as Jeannette Armstrong, Maria Campbell, Beatrice Culleton, Marilyn Dumont, Louise Halfe, Rita Joe, Lenore Keeshig-Tobias, Margo Kane, Lee Maracle, Eden Robinson, and Ruby Slipperjack, among others, are keepers of their cultures in contemporary modes. Not only have they confronted colonial history and misrepresentation, which I would argue is a "positive" response to colonial realities, they have drawn deeply from the well of their cultural memories, myths, and mother languages. And, as artists, Aboriginal writers form bridges in areas Western thinkers traditionally thought unbridgeable: many, perhaps especially poets, move easily from the oral to the written; all move from the ancient to the post-colonial and from historic trauma to contemporary vibrancy. Some form bridges from personal invasions to personal triumph. Native women have moved far beyond "survival"; they have moved with remarkable grace and accomplishments right onto the international stage. These writers not only retrieve our histories and experiences, a process that is both necessary and painful, but they also collect and thread together our scattered parts and so nurture our spirits and rebuild our cultures.

THE CIV/SAV DICHOTOMY

Generally, Western-biased historians have done a great disservice to knowledge and to Aboriginal peoples in their classically colonial renderings of Aboriginal peoples as stone-age primitives, with no significant cultural accomplishments or civilization. The ideological but systematized paradigm of cilivization versus the savage, what I have come to call the "CIV/SAV dichotomy," is still deeply entrenched in our educational and media institutions. But, in fact, indigenous cultures of the Americas have produced significant material and non-material aspects of culture. The most obvious examples of great material production come from central America, particularly from the Aztecs, Incas, and Mayans, who developed city states, built massive pyramids, along with other marvellous stone, adobe, and wooden structures, and developed mathematically precise calendars requiring knowledge of astronomy. Throughout the Americas, indigenous peoples developed a wealth of horticultural and agricultural skills (such as terracing and irrigation), foods, products, pharmaceutical and medicinal knowledge, and a fascinating array of techniques, tools, and textiles. Native peoples also invented unique dwellings, efficient means of transportation, precise tools, and numerous other land-based technologies suited to their cultural needs. For example, they practised perhaps the most effective resource-management systems anywhere in the world. The more northern peoples controlled the forest in such a way that both forest and humans thrived.

On non-material levels, indigenous peoples have invented thousands of wondrous and cultivated languages and literatures, and a great variety of political, economic, and religious systems. Such systems merit special attention because they were based on values that often continue to be relevant in today's society. Here, I want to caution that we avoid romanticizing or stereotyping by keeping in mind that cultural values are ideals we aspire to, not ones we always demonstrate. Human beings do not always live up to the best ideals within their communities. Nonetheless, it is important that we maintain values that enrich life. In Aboriginal societies, these values include the integration of the ecological system, which demands environmental sensibilities and ethics, and, with it, organization and standards for human dignity, egalitarianism, consensual decision making, and balance between humans and the earth, as well as between men and women. Some Native cultures were organized around matriarchal or semi-matriarchal systems, reflecting advanced understanding of the role of women in human and cultural development.

Native societies also developed exacting protocols for justice, ceremony, and art, with emphasis on the dignity and freedom of the human spirit. The notion of "human dignity," though, means different things to different peoples; in my culture, human dignity includes the valuation of personhood and individuality in the context of community and kinship responsibilities. And in these times of aggressive fundamentalism on one hand, and, yet, gross tolerance of mysogynistic behaviour on the other, we cannot emphasize enough the greatness and beauty of such values. These are often expressed in Native spirituality, a spirituality rooted deep into the soil and in the feminine, and which nourished the land, individual freedom for both genders, vision, and tolerance of difference. The achievements in the arts include sculptures, pottery, sand painting, rock painting, hieroglyphics, weaving, crafts, oral literatures, poetry, oratory, drama, music, and other fine creations of the heart and intellect.

This "quick list" overview is but a glimpse into the original accomplishments of our ancestors, the original peoples of the Americas.[5] This overview does not include the ingenious cultural adaptations after the arrivals of Columbus, the conquistadores, the Jesuits, the Daniel Boones, the cowboys, the fur traders, and Confederation. Such a quick view list is not complete without making the additional point that not only has the world borrowed (or appropriated) much from Aboriginal wealth, resources, and cultures but that modern North and South America is built on indigenous roots. As anthropologist Jack Weatherford has put it so precisely: "These ancient and often ignored roots still nourish our modern society, political life, economy, art, agriculture, language and distinctly American modes of thought."[6]

And what can we say of our achievements in cultural tenacity, spiritual integrity, and human endurance in the face of sustained cultural and legislated assaults? Europeans and their more modern descendants have indeed borrowed—or divested—much from indigenous peoples. In the last few decades, considerable scholarly attention has been given to colonization and its effects on Aboriginal peoples. Although this reading of history has been kind, it has recently evoked some interesting responses by some Native groups or individuals. Some feel that to explain everything about Aboriginal peoples in terms of colonization has a totalizing effect. They argue that they are more than the sum of colonization and that colonization does not define or even determine their existence in total. Such emphasis clearly calls for reflection on not only what has been lost, but also what has been kept, borrowed, adapted, or changed. For all the losses, Native peoples have shown remarkable elasticity, tenacity, and agency. This can be seen in the Aboriginal responses and transactions, from those with early Europeans right through to our contemporary times. We can trace women's cultural tenacity from the fur-trade era, even through the residential school era,[7] and on to the mid-1900s and now modern times.

When the European fur traders began to trade and form relationships with Aboriginal peoples, they were not dealing with peoples without culture. Women, in particular, were keepers of their cultures. Even though they were faced with new burdens and opportunities generated by the fur trade, Aboriginal women still acted as keepers of their families, languages, oral literatures, land-based technologies and skills, foods, clothing, art, music, and much more. They also served as cultural brokers between various Native peoples and cultures throughout the fur-trade era. Their roles, of course, were complicated and traumatized by the imperial mercantilist situation. The legacy of this historic trauma remains evident today, but, nevertheless, many of the skills and ways of life from the fur-trade era survived for many years, and were practised by my mother's generation among northern Alberta Native (many of whom are Métis) women. Because of that, such skills are still alive and well, especially in northern communities.

CONTEMPORARY ABORIGINAL WOMEN'S WRITINGS

In the tradition of our grandmothers and mothers, Aboriginal women have continued to work for the preservation of our families, communities, and cultures, and, in so doing, are keeping our peoples and cultures alive and current. Writing is one such expression of both creativity and continuity. Since the late 1960s, Aboriginal women have been creating a significant body of writing, which serves in many respects as a vehicle of cultural teaching and reinvention as well as cultural and political resistance to colonialism with its Western-defined impositions, requirements, and biases. But writing is also about the love of words, which at once expresses indigenous roots, social agency, and individual creativity.

A chronological, albeit incomplete and selective survey of this writing will serve to introduce a sense of the depth and scope of Native women's contributions to both Aboriginal and the larger Canadian cultures. Though the focus is on contemporary writing, any discussion on Aboriginal women writers must begin with Mohawk/Métis poet Pauline Johnson. Born in 1862 to an English mother and a Mohawk father on the Six Nations Indian Reserve, Johnson was to become the first Aboriginal poet, and the first Canadian woman, to be published. For all her firsts, and for her stature as a popular Canadian poet, Johnson was never free from the colonizer's language and imagery, as evidenced in some of her poetry in *Flint and Feather* (1917) as well as in the persona of

Indian princess she assumed during her recitations. Put in the difficult position of having to meet the demands set by the prejudices of a racially conscious Victorian-based Canadian society, she nonetheless vigorously championed Indian and Métis rights and humanity. Interestingly, my generation grew up reading her famous and delightful poem "The Song My Paddle Sings," but never read her resistance poems such as "The Cattle Thief" or "A Cry from an Indian Wife."

In Pauline Johnson's lifetime, the Canadian government shored up its urban and industrial encroachment on eastern Native peoples' lands, quashed western Métis Nation resistance, dispossessed Métis and Indian lands and resources through scrip and treaties, and then legislated the *Indian Act*, which gave the government control over "Status" Indian peoples while creating enfranchised "non-Status" Indians and bumping the Métis Nation peoples from their Aboriginal rights. In Johnson's lifetime, reserves, scrip, residential schools, Batoche, and "road allowance" were established. Canadian society enforced segregation, gender discrimination, and containment through local and social avenues. "Indians" became wards under the *Indian Act*, numerous Status Indian women lost their rights, and the Métis lost their Red River as well as their far northwestern lands under Confederation.

Once sidelined from mainstream Canada, Indian and Métis peoples were politically silenced for about a century. It was not until the late 1960s that the next (and now unstoppable) wave of Native writing was born. The next popular and socially revolutionary publication by an Aboriginal woman was produced by Métis author Maria Campbell. Her autobiography *Halfbreed* (1973) exploded Canada's naive notions of itself as a fair and caring country by situating her life of loss and abuse against the historical oppression of Métis Nation peoples. Her community and her family, rich in humour and Métis culture, was subjected to harsh poverty and racial discrimination in their town and public schools. Also published in the same year was Jane Willis's autobiography *Geneish: an Indian Girlhood*. Perhaps shadowed by the overwhelming reception of *Halfbreed*, this work remains less well known, but the story it tells is no less important. Jane Willis tells of her years in residential school in northern Quebec as a time of mental, intellectual, and corporal abuse. Routinely denounced as "savages" and stripped of all things Indian, Willis and fellow students were repeatedly subjected to hard labour and racist humiliations. Willis's book foreshadowed the stories to come about the Native experience in residential schools.

Racist humiliations were everywhere in these times. Salish/Métis writer Lee Maracle produced an autobiographical, edited account of largely urban-based life in *Bobbi Lee: Indian Rebel—Struggles of a Native Canadian Woman* (1975). This story showed that racism, sexism, and even cruel treatment of Native peoples was not confined to public or residential schools. Hot, harsh, poverty-ridden streets of Canada's cities exacted punishment on urban Native peoples, particularly in the era from the 1940s to the 1970s.

Not surprisingly, then, Native women were involved in a host of socio-economic issues, including legislated and social discrimination, poverty, violence, health, (in)justice, education, identity, and cultural renewal in the late 1960s on to the 1970s. Much of their writing from this period comes from Native newspapers, editorials, or essays in collections. The Native women, many of them educators, who wrote at this time include Victoria Callihoo, Ethel Brant Monture, Edith Josie, Verna Kirkness, Marlene Castellano, Gloria Bird, and Beverly Hungry Wolf, among others. Mi'kmaq poet Rita Joe, perhaps the most well-known Native woman poet of that era, wrote simply but movingly about the struggles and losses of her community and family, but also about the beauty of her people and culture.

The 1980s opened with a powerful, raw novel by Métis writer Beatrice Culleton. *In Search of April Raintree* (1983), a story of two adopted Métis sisters, is an unflinching exposé of the callous abuses of the 1960s' scoop of Indian and Métis children by the child and welfare system. It is equally an account of devastating violence and racism against Native women in urban centres. Several years later, Beatrice wrote *Spirit of the White Bison* (1985), an allegory of the wrenching consequences of separating child from parent. Though written softly, so softly it reduces one to tears, it is nevertheless a thunderous criticism of man's inhumanity to the great buffalo of the plains.

In the same year, Okanagan educator, activist, and writer Jeannette Armstrong published *Slash* (1985), a much-read historical novel set in the 1970s era of political resistance by Native peoples in both Canada and the United States. Jeannette chronicled the colonization of Native peoples in North America through her main character, Slash, a young Okanagan man who drifts from one political rally to another, but eventually finds his way back to home, to his traditions and to his homeland.

Ojibwa writer and educator from Sioux Lookout, Ruby Slipperjack, gently addresses community and family disintegration in *Honour the Sun* (1987). The story is told in the form of a diary written by Owl, who begins her diary as a carefree, funny, precocious, ten-year-old Ojibwa girl, but concludes it as a saddened teenager who must leave home as her life and the lives of her beloved family are disrupted by changes outside their control. The following year, Lee Maracle's *I Am Woman* (1988), although not a novel, became popular reading in Canadian literary and academic circles. Maracle's book roars against poverty, male violence, and Native organizational lethargy, but situates these problems in the context of colonialism and Canadian negligence.

During the 1990s, streams of Native-authored works were written in almost every genre. Often, Native authors cross genres, such as Shirley Sterling's *My Name Is Seepeetza* (1992). This has been classified as a children's book, but is also studied as adult-level fiction in literature courses. It is a semi-auto-biographical novel about a Native girl's experience in a residential school. Lee Maracle (*Sundogs*, 1992; *Ravensong*, 1993) and Ruby Slipperjack (*Silent Words*, 1992) published more novels, but the 1990s especially saw a growing list of anthologies with Native women's biographical and political essays, as well as creative writing, including short stories, plays, reinterpretation of legends, and, of course, poetry. Such anthologies include *All My Relations* (edited by Thomas King, 1990); *Seventh Generation* (edited by Heather Hodgson, 1989); *Native Writers and Canadian Literature* (edited by W.H. New, 1990); *Our Bit of Truth* (edited by Agnes Grant, 1990); *Voices: Being Native in Canada* (edited by Linda Jaine and Drew Hayden Taylor, 1992); and *An Anthology of Canadian Native Literature in English* (edited by Daniel David Moses and Terry Goldie, 1992). Two anthologies during that period featured exclusively writing by Native women: *Writing the Circle* (edited by Jeanne Perreault and Sylvia Vance, 1990) and *The Colour of Resistance: A Contemporary Collection of Writing by Aboriginal Women* (edited by Connie Fife, 1993). Also published in the 1990s was *Native Literature in Canada: From the Oral Tradition to the Present* (edited by Penny Petrone, 1990), the first critical study and survey of Native literature authored by a non-Native academic. And the first collection of critical essays on Native writing by Native academics, many women, and edited by Jeannette Armstrong, was also published as *Looking at the Words of My People: First Nations Analysis of Literature* (1993).

Of course, Native women writers have not stopped writing. The year 2000 opened with the publication of more novels: *Whispering in Shadows* by Jeannette Armstrong, *Monkey Beach* by Haisla sensation Eden Robinson, and *Weesquachak and the Lost Ones* by Ruby Slipperjack. These three novels have as their main character an Aboriginal female. Penny, in *Whispering in Shadows*, is a young, restless artist who breaks out of the apple orchards of the Okanagan, as well as a stifling relationship, in pursuit of her dreams to go to art school for a university education. She becomes an environmentalist who yearns to bring healing to the suffering indigenous humanity she encounters in her international travels. Penny is named after her grandmother, from whom she learns to see the extrasensory contours and colours of the land. Paced and quiet, yet seething with the spirituality of indigenous indignation, Armstrong lets the land do the speaking. Her book is a critique of globalization with its relentless and insatiable capitalist tentacles, drive, and greed.

In *Monkey Beach*, Lisa Marie, named after Elvis Presley's daughter, is a Haisla teenager haunted by ancestral and familial ghosts and half-hidden personal devastations. Set in both contemporary Kitimat and the Haisla ancestral beaches along Canada's Pacific coast, *Monkey Beach* features seaside and urban *b'gwuses*, monsters camouflaged as sometimes human and sometimes not.

Ruby Slipperjack's protagonist in *Weesquachak* is a young Ojibwa woman, Janine, who, after having gone to the city, comes back to her northern community. She gets involved with a trapper and both find themselves shadowed by something or someone. This "something" or "someone" provides a sense of menace and eeriness to this novel. In the bush Janine feels watched, even stalked, at times. Is it an ex-boyfriend? Is it just a clever raven? Surely, it is the Trickster. But what purpose does the Trickster serve in contemporary times?

Poetry is also a strong and active avenue of creative expression for Aboriginal women. Since the 1960s, thousands of published poems have been written by Aboriginal women. In the 1960s and 1970s, much of this poetry was found in Native newspapers and magazines, as well as in the earlier anthologies. Jeannette Armstrong remembers finding "small poems scattered like gems here and there in the pages of mimeographed Native flyers and bulletins which appeared at every Native political gathering."[8] Over time, Native poetry eventually appeared in some of Canada's leading literary journals and academic anthologies, such as *Ariel*, *Prairie Fire*, *Descant*, *Border Crossings*, and others. The growing list of books of poetry by Native women is an indication of the significance of poetry in our cultures.

Mi'kmaq poet Rita Joe (*Poems of Rita Joe*, 1978; *The Song of Eskasoni*; *More Poems of Rita Joe*, 1988) was among the first published poets. Other Native women who have published books of poetry include Jeannette Armstrong (*Breath Tracks*, 1991); Beth Cuthand (*Voices in the Waterfall*, 1989); Marie Annharte Baker (*Being on the Moon*, 1990; *Exercises in Lip Pointing*, 2003; *Coyote*

Columbus Café, 1994); Joan Crate (*Pale as Real Ladies: Poems for Pauline Johnson*, 1991; *Foreign Homes*, 2002), Joanne Arnott (*Wiles of Girlhood*, 1991; *Steepy Mountain*, 2004); Kateri Akiwenzie-Damm (*My Heart is a Stray Bullet*, 1993; and as editor, *Without Reservation: Indigenous Erotica*, 2003); Marilyn Dumont (*A Really Good Brown Girl*, 1996; *Green Girl Dreams Mountains*, 2001); Louise Halfe (*Bear Bones and Feathers*, 1994; *Blue Marrow*, 2004 rev); Lee Maracle (*Bent Box*, 2000); Sharron Proulx-Turner (*What the Auntys Say*, 2002).

Collaborative works that carry essays, poetry, or art by Aboriginal women include *My Home As I Remember*, edited by Lee Maracle and Sandra Laronde (2000); *Into the Moon*, edited by Lenore Keeshig-Tobias (1996); *Sweetgrass Grows All Around Her*, edited by Beth Brant and Sandra Laronde (1994); *Kelusultiek: Original Women's Voices Atlantic Canada*, edited by R. Ursmiant (1994); and *Indigena*, edited by Gerald McMaster and Lee-Ann Martin (1992).

There is more. In addition to poetry and novels, autobiographies and biographies, Native women also produce short stories, plays, children's books, ethnographic material, social and political commentaries, and contemporary retellings of legends. Aboriginal women academics are literally, in the words of Joyce Green, "transforming the academy" with their research and by the intellectual challenges they pose to old Western frameworks and biases. Those who have produced semi-biographical and semi-autobiographical works mixing analysis with voice and narrative include Janice Acoose (*Iskwewak*, 1995), Beth Brant (*Mohawk Trail*, 1985), and Patricia Monture-Angus (*Thunder in My Soul*, 1995). Gail Guthrie Valaskakis integrates personal Native narrative and socio-political experience with a critical and theoretical cultural studies approach in *Indian Country: Essays on Contemporary Native Culture* (2005).

To say that Native women's literary contributions are substantial is, obviously, to understate the volume and significance of what these women have produced. Indeed, their writing has evoked much intellectual excitement among literary critics and scholars from around the world. And, in time, as more Aboriginal people take to contemporary art and literature, Native writing will assume its high place within the Aboriginal community. Much has actually been written about Native women writers, particularly about Maria Campbell, Lee Maracle, Beatrice Culleton, and Jeannette Armstrong. Critics have generally focussed on their life stories, with an emphasis on the Native colonial experience. That is, much has been written about women's oppression and disempowerment. In effect, the emphasis has been on cultural discontinuity. For the most part, non-Native critics, particularly feminist-conscious men and women, have tried to be respectful and sensitive. This is especially noticeable since the 1990s. However, such critics have generally tended to look more for ancient cultural secrets or patterns[9] amid what I call "ethnographic tidbits" than for those crucial spaces of contemporaneity and agency that actually fill the pages of Native writing, as, of course, they fill the lives of Aboriginal people.

CULTURAL CONTINUITY THROUGH WRITING

Although I do often remark on cultural "tidbits" with some tongue-in-cheek, the question does arise: how do readers find cultural continuity in Aboriginal women's writings? One can ask such a question only if one views this writing as alien to Aboriginal peoples; and one can think this only if one believes in what J.M. Blaut calls "the colonizer's model of the world," which is the model that claims Europe is inherently progressive, in contrast to non-Europe, which is backward. Blaut challenges this presumed progressiveness, which he dubs the "European Miracle" that has been diffused throughout the globe through colonialism, enabling non-European peoples to finally evolve towards progress and modernization. In other words, the model claims that the colonized owe their lives to the colonizer; the non-European world owes its cultural life to Europe.

With respect to indigenous peoples of the Americas, the colonizer's model of the world has largely been translated and deduced into that "CIV/SAV" dichotomy mentioned earlier. That is, history of Native/white relations in the Americas has been presented as a moral "encounter" between civilization and savagism in which "savages" or "Indians" inevitably give way to civilized Euro-white North Americans.[10] In plain words, white North American history and school texts, as well as the media, have traditionally portrayed Aboriginal peoples as aimlessly wandering (read "nomadic"), uncultivated ("wild"), violent ("bloodthirsty") savages clearly inferior to Euro-white Americans or Canadians.[11] The legacy of such twisty and self-serving history and anthropology has classically cast Native peoples as unable to adapt to cultural change. Or, if they do adapt, they are, at best, borrowing, at worst, mimicking the colonizers' gifts flowing from the diffusion of the "European Miracle." Writing has been treated as one such gift. However, in historical and anthropological fact, Aboriginal peoples were not stone-age savages waiting for the European alphabet on the seashore. Aboriginal cultures were not in some frozen state of primitivity, unable to change or to adapt. Aboriginal peoples were and are uncongealed and dynamic. Writing is, in fact, an example of Native cultural fluidity.

That Aboriginal people are writing is in itself an act of cultural continuity. Any form of expression that is instrumental to our renewal is cultural continuity. Writing is really about "telling," and "telling" originates in orality. Whatever it is that we are telling, whether it is *atowkehwin* (myths and legends) or *achimoowin* (factual or non-fictional type of "stories") or *ehmamtowaytameh* (thinking, reflecting, analyzing), and however we do it, orally or in writing, as long as we are doing it, we are expressing a live and dynamic culture. Some indigenous peoples had their own writing systems and all had effective communication systems centuries prior to European incursion. It is not surprising that Native peoples did not greet the technique of writing as being alien to them. In Canada, for example, two Métis persons from northern Manitoba co-developed with a missionary the syllabic system that quickly spread throughout northern communities. It is not uncommon to find that there has been Native collaboration, input, or direction to creative works or socio-political systems that have been appropriated as originating solely from White authorship.[12] Writing is as much our culture as clay tablets used to be for Europeans.

Since this essay reflects on cultural continuity, let us look at how Aboriginal women writers are dealing with these issues of cultural discontinuity and continuity. It is, of course, relatively easy to find examples of discontinuity, given our colonial stories, but how does a reader find cultural continuity? What does cultural continuity look like, especially when, for example, the majority of my generation left home and built our lives around very different economic, material, and cultural environments? Most of us who left home, myself included, no longer know or no longer replicate the ways of our parents, much less the ways of our grandmothers. Nonetheless, there is evidence of cultural continuity being demonstrated by those of us who are in quite different locations from our original homes.

Cultural continuity is much more than about material or even linguistic replications that sociologists and anthropologists have traditionally identified as sustained "cultural markers" and by which they have judged cultural change among Aboriginal peoples. Indeed, and consistent with the CIV/SAV (or progress/primitive) view, both society and academia, including some Aboriginal people, have traditionally assumed any cultural change by Aboriginal peoples must ipso facto be viewed as assimilation. But Aboriginal peoples have long demonstrated that change, even under enforced circumstances, does not result in cultural amnesia. Culture shock or even catastrophic trauma are not the same as cultural amnesia. Obviously, cultural change for Aboriginal peoples has been complicated by colonization but it is equally true and still must be emphasized that cultural change is not alien to Aboriginal cultures. We must certainly shed the view that all things highly cultivated or "developed" and "modern" come from Europeans. We must also shed the notion that cultural change is foreign to indigenous cultures, whether in pre-contact times or now. We must rethink our own responses to all the twists and turns of colonial assumptions and stereotypes about us. We must assume our birthright to be whoever we are in today's world. For example, there is in this country an expectation that we be culturally different. The dialectics of cultural difference go squarely back to early colonial times in which it served and continues to serve colonizers to keep "natives" in their place, and one way to do that is to create a stereotype of difference. It is imperative we challenge the assumptions that attend these expectations. Further, notice that "difference" is almost always associated with traditionalism (which is itself stereotyped). This is consistent with the CIV/SAV view that Westerners, being inherently progressive, make history, but "natives," being statically primitive, can only maintain tradition.[13]

Clearly, the Native community faces many tough and interesting issues. The point here is that by taking our rightful place in our contemporary world, we are breathing cultural continuity. The act of writing is an act of agency, and agency is cultural continuity in its articulation of our histories, our invasions, and our cultural values. Aboriginal writers' cultural contributions to the Aboriginal (and wider) communities are profound. Among numerous other contributions, writers provide historical information and analysis of the Native colonial experience. Writers offer an inside perspective of ethnographic data. Interestingly, writers do say much about "difference," but in ways surprising and even unexpected. Writers certainly challenge both standard academic notions about cultural difference and change as well as political and societal demands that we stay different, that is, stereotyped.

EXPRESSING THE MATERIALITY OF ABORIGINAL CULTURE THROUGH WRITING

Not much is said about how Native writers express their cultures through their detailed descriptions of the materiality of their cultural backgrounds, particularly about their homes and the economic bases to their daily living. Undoubtedly, I am reflecting on my own generation, but I begin by pointing this out in a number of works written by Aboriginal women.

I turn again to Maria Campbell. For any Métis youth who wonders about his or her cultural heritage, that is, who asks the question of how Métis Nation people expressed their culture, say from the 1800s to the 1970s, reading Campbell would provide considerable cultural information. Campbell is of Cree/Scottish Métis Nation ancestry. Her parents raised her and her siblings with Métis material culture, as well as Métis values. It is of some interest that Maria Campbell begins her facts of biography with this: "I should tell you about our home now before I go any further."[14] She then gives minute details about their "two-roomed large hewed log house," telling us about their homemade tables and chairs, beds and hay-filled canvas mattresses, the hammock that babies swung from, the huge black wood stove in the kitchen, the medicines and herbs that hung on the walls, the wide planks of floors scoured evenly white with lye soap, and so forth. She reminisces, "The kitchen and living room were combined into one of the most beautiful rooms I have ever known."[15] Maria's parents were typically hard-working, resourceful Métis folks who lived well off the land but who also used as many modern conveniences as they were able to procure. In addition to store-bought goods, her parents relied on foods of the land, which meant they engaged in hunting/trapping, fishing, berry picking, and some gardening. They would have acquired and developed techniques and tools consistent with having to kill or harvest the resources. Skills such as hunting, trapping, snaring, shooting, fishing, boating, and building satellite camps and cabins were vital. Related skills in the butchering, dressing, and preserving of the foods were equally vital. Animals also offered shelter, clothing, accessories, and tools, as well as techniques of art. In this kind of setting, there was little demarcation between home and work.

As a rule, living from the land necessitates mutual respect between men and women, even though there were/are some gender divisions of labour. For example, men did big game hunting and trapping, so they left their homes during particular seasons. But this did not translate into the devaluation of women who stayed home to tend to their children and families. Nor were men and women confined to rigid gender-defined roles. Men could do housework and, indeed, were expected to assist, and women could go out hunting, and those who did were expected to carry their share of work out on the land. This theme is also evident in Maria's *Stories of the Road Allowance People* (1995).

An internationally respected environmentalist, intellectual, and activist, Okanagan author Jeannette Armstrong also turns to home and land as key themes in her first novel, *Slash*. Set in the heydays of the early 1970s American Indian Movement and confrontations with the FBI in the United States, *Slash* is an historical novel that recounts the historical and continuing impact of colonization as seen through the life of Slash, a young Okanagan man. The novel is rich with political commentary, but, for me, the most moving parts in the novel centre on Slash's relationship with his home and his land. His home is set on a ranch among the sage-brush hills of the Okanagan. His parents (and kin) are hard-working ranchers who tend to their homes and their children. Slash grows up with the Okanagan language and myths as well as strong family values and work ethic. Of course, the story is complicated by the legacy of colonization, and, all too soon, Slash finds himself adrift. For quite some time, he is lost between the safety and coherence of family traditions and the disruption of town and school, and then the post-colonial chaos of political rallies. Many times throughout the novel, the smells of home cooking and the texture of the Okanagan hills lead Slash back to his home. Finally, Slash grounds himself literally by coming home to stay. By this, he is reclaiming his home-land, his culture.

Land or the landscape (or sea and seascape, as in the case of Eden Robin-son's *Monkey Beach*) features significantly in women's writing. This is not surprising as land is the backbone to original cultures of the Americas. In *Honour the Sun*, Ojibwa novelist Ruby Slipperjack treats us to her character Owl's landscape. Owl, a carefree ten-year-old girl, enjoys her childhood by playing outside for much of the novel. Owl's summer playground is nestled in the heart of the Canadian Shield, home to bears and blueberries. Home also to the Ojibwa of northern Ontario, Owl's landscape is contoured with spruce trees, birch, poplars, craggy hills, rocks, sloping meadows, and lakes. And rail-road tracks. Owl's large family consists of her mother and numerous brothers and sisters. Owl's widowed mother, a strong, enduring matriarch of the family, keeps her many children fed and organized. Owl's "Mom" knows the ways of the land and lake. She routinely fills their canoe with her children and paddles them to a small island, where the family camps and relaxes. Many skills of the land are required for such an event. Making and cooking bannock, picking berries, fishing, filleting and frying fish, collecting and chopping firewood, usually birch, provide an oasis from the chaos of community. She feeds her kids with fish and berries, macaroni, potatoes, and bannock. Slipperjack's exquisite details of this land-based culture are lovely. One can almost hear the fire crackling and smell with Owl the·"birchbark and wood smoke drift into the tent."

Of course, having to make a living by using resources from the land (or waters), whether those resources are animals, fowl, fish, or gardening, or wood or plants, roots and berries, takes hard work and intimate knowledge of one's resources and ecological environment. Nor is the environment always gentle or non-violent, for being carnivores living off the land means killing animals for food. Living on the land can be difficult and harsh. We should be careful not to insult the hard work involved by romanticizing it inappropriately. Naturally, it has its beautiful, even "Hiawathian," aspects and moments, but this is a culture that entails much work, patience, knowledge, and expertise. It is not just camping: it is a whole way of life.

By providing us with such exquisite detail, these writers offer numerous teachings as well as anthropological and ecological data about our various cultures. There is much to learn from our writers. The data about Aboriginal use of both modern and natural resources, land or waters, tell us much about the intelligence, the planning, the organization, and, generally, the ingenuity and science of these cultures.

The academic community rather quickly cast such Aboriginal-derived knowledge as "traditional ecological knowledge" (now TK), different from Western science. Numerous studies—or, rather, typological charts—came out comparing presumed differences and similarities between Aboriginal (read traditional) and Western (read scientific) knowledge. While this discussion is ever changing, there remain stereotypes about indigenous knowledge.[16] However, even a quick overview of indigenous cultural developments immediately points to an Aboriginal-based science to not only the building of materially evident cultures, but to the collection and arrangement of data about the land and the animals, seasons, climate, geography, astronomy, and the environment. In other words, there is a science to knowing the nooks and crannies of land-based life, but much of this has gone unnoticed—or if noted, stereotyped—by both Aboriginal and non-Aboriginal readers and critics, especially by those who have grown up in cities and have no way to relate to rural or bush life. Such inability to fully appreciate this lifestyle is compounded by the Western bias for urbanization and industrialization.

But there is also much said, both explicitly and implicitly, about urbanization in Aboriginal writing. This is to be expected, not only because urbanization and industrialization has had an impact on Aboriginal cultures, but also because the Aboriginal population is increasingly urban. Since the 1950s, the numbers of Aboriginal people have been steadily growing in Canadian cities, and the 2006 census indicate that 53 percent of Aboriginal people reside in urban centres located outside reserve communities. And those who still live in rural areas, whether on reserves or in other settlements, have long been integrating urban and industrial aspects of Canadian life. Indigenous cultures built towns and cities long before Europeans arrived in the Americas. Also, particularly in northern Canada, as long as Native peoples have been engaged in the fur trade, they have been integrating metropolitan aspects of world culture. Perhaps globalization began with the fur trade. It is not surprising, then, that writers treat crackerjack popcorn, bubblegum, clocks, radios, railroads, boats, books, ranching, farming, flying, cars and trucks, or Elvis Presley, as being as commonplace as *Wisakehcha* or Seneca roots.

Writers treat urbanization as being both impositional and natural. What are considered impositional are governmental policies, interference, forced relocation, forced education, and other legal manoeuvres that threaten both the cultural and resource base of Aboriginal peoples. Material cultural change, on the other hand, is treated as part of the cultural landscape natural to Native peoples. Many policy analysts as well as academics have missed this Aboriginal approach to cultural change. To repeat a point made earlier, contemporary Aboriginal thinkers treating cultural change (when it is voluntary) as natural to Aboriginal peoples is consistent with all the archeological and anthropological evidence that indicates that our ancestors in the Americas were, under normal, that is, politically balanced, circumstances, dynamic peoples who engaged not only in material international trade but in the exchange of ideas, customs, and beliefs. Indigenous trade goes far back into indigenous history, much farther back than trade with Europeans. Again, it was the European colonizers who treated indigenous peoples as primitives afraid of change. It was colonizers who developed into an art form the various but well-known stereotypes of Aboriginal peoples as "traditional" peoples without history, that is, peoples stuck in ceremonial repetition (albeit "colourful") but peoples who cannot change without disintegrating or peoples who do not assume agency for their life. And, to the extent Native peoples have internalized these stereotypes, it has paralyzed our peoples, perhaps especially our youth, from assuming our/ their birthright as contemporary Canadians.

Yet, writers have long demonstrated the vibrancy of Aboriginal individuals and communities. Writers do not treat Native peoples as an amorphous collective. Rather, like all storytellers throughout the ages, writers present Native characters, whether fictional or non-fictional, as unique individuals who have names and personalities and the full range of humanity, that is, persons who are capable of the good and the bad. Some are very funny. Some are downright evil. Some are heroic. Most are ordinary, imperfect folks who laugh, cry, and work very hard to keep their families fed, well clothed, and safe. Colonial processes, such as land theft, forced relocation, residential schools, encroaching urbanization and industrialization, violence, and racial and cultural discrimination have certainly caused catastrophic trauma, as social conditions continue to indicate, but Native peoples have demonstrated personal and cultural strength, perseverance, and enormous creativity. They have continued to live their lives in inventive ways even throughout those moments in Canadian history when "out of sight, out of mind" was much in practice by most non-Native Canadians.

Aboriginal writing is, of course, infused with Aboriginal languages, ideals, values, norms, faiths, and belief systems. Many writers draw on myths and legends not only to keep the legends alive, but also often to make resistance statements about colonization. Lee Maracle opens her haunting novel, *Ravensong*, with the sound of Raven weeping. The novel tells the story about a deadly flu epidemic in the 1950s that claimed numerous lives of an urban Native family. Raven is a central mythological figure to cultures along the Pacific northwest coast, and it is Raven who sounds the cry from the bowels of the earth and sea in an effort to wake up the seemingly unconscious Native and white communities. Raven and Cedar work to get "white town" to notice the devastations and to guide Native women towards recovery.

Ojibwa writer Lenore Keeshig-Tobias uses the metaphor of Trickster to make multi-layered critical comments about the white man in her wonderfully sharp poem, "Trickster Beyond 1992: Our Relationship." But she also turns the critical knife towards Trickster, charging him with having disappeared at a crucial time in history. Ultimately, she is critical about herself and the newcomer: "He is like me, a Trickster, a liar ... a new kind of man is coming, a White Man."

Aboriginal languages are honoured in a great variety of ways in these writings. Eden Robinson opens her novel with six crows that speak to her in Haisla, "La'es, they say, la'es, la'es." Characters are given Aboriginal names or nicknames. Scholars use Native words to explain Native world views and philosophies. Or to correct misrepresentation. But perhaps no one writer has foregrounded a Native language like Cree poet Louise Halfe. The first time I came across Louise's poetry was when I was reading the manuscript for *Writing the Circle*. My heart sang when I read "Pahkakhos"—the flying skeleton of Cree legend, a legend my mother often cited to us. Of course, my mother had her own version, quite different from Louise's, but just to see it in print made me smile right out loud. From a cornucopia of Cree thought and grit of experience, the writer's love of words, Cree words, spill out, roar out onto the pages in all her publications. And into our own bones. Louise's poetry teases us to the edges of human encounters with bears, bones, rocks, ghosts, spirits, tricksters. She takes us even to the marrow of shadows and light that humans are—she lifts the rocks and makes us look at what is under there. For Louise Halfe, as it is for all great writers and thinkers, "healing" is no sweet, meditational journey; it is raw, terrible, and gutsy: "Flying Skeleton / I used to wonder / Where you kept yourself ... You lifted your boney hands / To greet me and I / Ran without a tongue."[17]

As colonized peoples, we all ran without our tongues in many phases or parts of our lives. In a previous era, Rita Joe wrote, "I lost my talk." But writing has served as the vehicle to recovering our tongues. By articulating our histories, our traumas, or our cultures, writing becomes the process, the result, and the expression of decolonization. Intellectual resistance in the form of writing opens possibilities for liberation. Louise Halfe, like most writers, has more than found her tongue. She has reinvented both Cree and English. Her "leddars" to the "Poop" are simply resistance par excellence. In her second collection of poetry, *Blue Marrow*, Louise takes us to places of terror and laughter. We hear voices of those who had the courage to test the edges of human senses. These courageous souls are our ancestors.

Writers serve our cultures by being reflective, often analytical. This work is known as criticism. But writers also mirror to us who we are. They deal with greatness as well as our smallnesses. They comment on our contemporary predicaments. For example, Lee Maracle lays open the cycle of abuse and neglect in Native families in her novel, *Daughters Are Forever*. Margo Kane's play, *Moonlodge*, confronts issues of identity wrapped up in stereotypes to which some Native characters succumb.

Writers serve our cultures by assuming the role of cultural critics. It is often assumed that criticism is only negative and that Aboriginal writers should just focus on what is positive. Or that we should just criticize white society and not Aboriginal actions, beliefs, proposals, communities, organizations, or leadership. In tandem with this, there is much anti-intellectualism in our society, both in the Native and larger communities. I believe such attitudes reflect a misunderstanding as to the nature of criticism and the social purpose of knowledge. When practised with social awareness, responsibility, and compassion, the critic's job is as positive as, say, a musician's job.

The need to be positive is understandable, given the magnitude of misrepresentation to which we have been subjected. It is a corrective response to the stereotyping of Native peoples as social problems. Further, there is no question that humans gravitate towards creativity and constructiveness. However, we do need to pay attention to R.D. Laing's meaning of "selective inattention," or false consciousness. We, as peoples in Canada, are not yet fully liberated or decolonized. We have not even begun to explore the seductive use of words often framed within positivism. For example, we now have "historic trauma" instead of colonization. We now pursue "healing" instead of decolonization. The two are not to be confused. The language of "healing" assumes woundedness and invites therapy; the language of decolonization assumes power politics and should invite exploration of political liberation (not to be confused with violence). The language of "healing" assumes personal responsibility; the language of decolonization assumes a confrontation with colonial forces and the rearrangement of the status quo. We must remain vigilant against being "psychologized" just as we must remain alert to being exclusively politicized (and culturalized, for that matter). We need to be clear that agency does not mean the abandonment of decolonization work. Of course, neither does it mean the shucking of our responsibilities as human beings. Accordingly, we should pay greater attention to our self-constructed mythical portraits of ourselves as well as to the vocation of being a critic. All this can be accomplished without neglecting to emphasize the much-needed corrective view of Native peoples, and certainly Native women, as peoples of persistence, adaptability, and regeneration.

CONCLUDING THOUGHTS

Women writers demonstrate great love and valuation of their people and many specifically honour their grandmothers, grandfathers, mothers, fathers, siblings, and other kin. I notice that many poems are dedicated to specific individuals. In several of my own poems, I recall the names of my *Ama*, *Bapa*, as well as the names of my sisters, aunts, and uncles, all people who have suffered enormously under the weight of colonial forces but people who also loved life and laughter. These were people who drummed along with my guitar, people who tickled and teased us and made us laugh. People who told us stories into the night. But they also sang haunting songs about loneliness, wanting to come home, about lost loves and times. They also wept for their fathers, mothers, and siblings. And many had to weep for their children lost to sickness. These were people who gave us language and culture. People who have left this earth, many in untimely, even jarring, fashion. And with their leaving, our families, our communities got so much smaller, numerically and, in some ways, culturally. Yet, despite these losses, rebirthing always takes place, whether with new generations or by creative processes. On these same lands or on new lands. Footpaths through ferns and spruce or sidewalk in the city—these are all our lands now. We all have the honour and the challenge of living our cultures for all generations, those of our ancestors and those for tomorrow.

Perhaps culture is ultimately about what people do together. It has been suggested that as long as Aboriginal people continue to do things together, there will be Aboriginal cultures alive. It is important, therefore, that we facilitate get-togethers—think tanks, conferences, potlatches, achievement celebrations, remembrances, sun dances, sweats, smudges, potluck dinners. And that we do this in our communities as well as on national levels.

As we all know, all sorts of conferences do go on all around us. Often, these conferences focus on socio-political and economic issues. All very important. But I notice there are not many conferences on Aboriginal writing or writers (or on other Aboriginal artists). It was with this in mind that I envisaged a conference on Native writers and writing, and, finally in 2004, with the assistance of a good friend and colleague, we organized a conference "For the Love of Words." It was truly a wonderful experience to read and listen to amazing, cultivated, indigenous-rooted, inspiring words of prose, poetry, plays, biography, and criticism, largely created by Aboriginal writers and scholars. Many writers expressed great appreciation for this rare opportunity to share creativity, one's inner being, and love of words with each other. This conference highlighted the great work of recovery and renaissance, not to mention the artistic and intellectual work that writers perform in our communities, in our country, and in our world. In this sense, doing things together, then, is decolonization. It is reconstructive. It confirmed to me the crying need for Native and white communities to celebrate artists, certainly writers.

Native women's writings have reached deep into the Canadian and Aboriginal intellectual culture. In very significant ways, Native women's writings have had a profound impact on both Native and non-Native communities. Aboriginal university students, for example, gain a greater understanding of cultural expression, critique, and political resistance; non-Native readers may gain a new appreciation of Aboriginal cultural and political locations in Canada with new commitments to supporting Aboriginal rights, lands, and resources. Today, Native women are not only cited by intellectuals on the international stage, they are among the sought-after intellectuals on the international stage.

When all the political wranglings have passed, what will stay will be the great thoughts, the great words. I find in Jeannette Armstrong's poetry of the soul a great call for human liberation:

> Wake up. All the shadows are gone. There is daylight even in the swamps. The bluejays are laughing.... Laughing at the humans who don't know the sun is up and it's a new day.... You are all turning yellow from too much sleep.[18]

Notes

1   My necessarily brief treatment here of the history, politics and identity of the Métis Nation peoples, particularly my argument that they, as Native-mated peoples, should be accorded the same rights and resources as other Aboriginal peoples, is based on my article, "Native Identity and the Metis: Otehpayimsuak Peoples," in David Taras and B. Rasporich, eds., *A Passion for Identity: Canadian Studies for the 21ˢᵗ Century* (Scarborough: Nelson Thomson Learning, 2001).

2   In an effort to show ethnic differences among the Métis/métis, some scholars have used small-m "métis" as opposed to the capitalized "Métis." Métis with a capital M generally refers to those peoples who became a distinct ethnic group by marrying within the group, that is, Métis marrying Métis. These peoples developed a distinct culture, especially around the Red River area. For an excellent exploration on the many origins of the Métis/métis, see Jacqueline Peterson and Jennifer Brown, eds., *The New Peoples: Being and Becoming Métis in North America* (Winnipeg: University of Manitoba Press, 1985).

3   See the Royal Commission on Aboriginal Peoples, volume 4, chapter 5, on the regional differences of Métis (or métis) identity, especially as these differences have been used to stall recognition of Aboriginal rights for the various Métis communities across Canada. The Royal Commission on Aboriginal Peoples provided many legal avenues by which the Canadian governments could and should recognize Métis peoples' rights.

4   See Emma LaRocque, "Native Identity and the Metis: Otehpayimsuak Peoples."

5   For a fascinating perspective on the cultural contributions of indigenous peoples of the Americas, see Jack Weatherford, *Indian Givers: How the Indians of the Americas Transformed The World* (New York: Fawcett Books, 1988) and *How The Indians Enriched America* (New York: Fawcett Books, 1991). For a sensitive anthropological overview of Aboriginal cultures in Canada, see R.B. Morrison and C.R. Wilson, eds., *Native Peoples: The Canadian Experience*, 3rd ed. (Oxford: Oxford University Press, 2004).

6   Jack Weatherford, *Native Roots: How the Indians Enriched America* (New York: Fawcett Columbine, 1991), 18.

7   See for example, Jo-Ann Fiske's study of Carrier women resistance responses to residential schooling, "Gender and the Paradox of Residential Education in Carrier Society," in Christine Miller and Patricia Chuchryk, eds., *Women of the First Nations: Power, Wisdom, and Strength* (Winnipeg: University of Manitoba Press, 1996).

8   Jeannette C. Armstrong and Lally Grauer, eds., *Native Poetry in Canada: A Contemporary Anthology* (Peterborough: Broadview Press, 2001), xviii.

9   See for instance, Beverly Rasporich, "Native Women Writing: Tracing The Patterns," *Canadian Ethnic Studies* 28, 1 (1996).

10 Classic studies on civilization/savagism include Roy Harvey Pearce, *Savagism and Civilization* (Baltimore: Johns Hopkins Press, 1967), and F. Jennings, *The Invasion of America: Indians, Colonialism, and the Cant of Conquest* (New York: W.W. Norton and Co., 1976). See also Olive P. Dickason, *The Myth of the Savage and the Beginnings of French Colonization in the Americas* (Edmonton: University of Alberta Press, 1984).

11 For a more thorough treatment of historical writing which assumes this "civ/sav" dichotomy, see Emma LaRocque, "Native Writers Resisting Colonizing Practices in Canadian Historiography and Literature" (PhD dissertation, University of Manitoba, 1999), in particular, ch. 2.

12 Weatherford, *How The Indians Enriched America*.

13 Deborah Doxtator, *Fluffs and Feathers: An Exhibit on the Symbols of Indianness* (Brantford: Woodland Cultural Centre, 1992), provides a perceptive analysis of how "Indians" are stereotyped as traditional in contrast to whites as makers of history. See my treatment of notions of progress in context of stereotypes in Emma LaRocque, *Defeathering The Indian* (Agincourt: The Book Society of Canada, 1975). See also Daniel Francis, *The Imaginary Indian* (Vancouver: Arsenal Pulp Press, 1992), 57–60.

14 Maria Campbell, *Halfbreed* (Toronto: McClelland and Stewart, 1973), 16.

15 Ibid., 17.

16 I pursue some of these issues in Emma LaRocque, "From the Land to the Classroom: Broadening Epistemology," in Jill Oakes, R. Riewe, M. Bennet, and B. Chisholm, eds., *Pushing The Margins: Native and Northern Studies* (Winnipeg: Native Studies Press, University of Manitoba, 2001).

17 Louise Halfe, *Bear Bones and Feathers* (Regina: Coteau Books, 1994), 8.

18 Jeannette Armstrong, *Whispering in Shadows* (Penticton: Theytus Books, 2000), 19.

Sisters in Spirit

Anita Olsen Harper

The traditional roles of women and men in pre-contact Aboriginal societies were balanced and stable; they allowed women safety and powerful places within those societies.[1] Within societies where men held political office, women were honoured and highly esteemed for their invaluable contribution to the survival of the whole nation, and for their places as mothers, grandmothers, wives, aunts, and sisters. The fact that many pre-contact Aboriginal societies were both matriarchal and matrilineal ensured women's authority and legitimate place.

In what is now southern Ontario, for example, Iroquoian clan mothers had a strong political voice; they were responsible for choosing and removing their leaders (*sachem*). They were autonomous and highly respected; while both women and men were considered equal, both exercised a great deal of personal autonomy within their societies. Other First Nations societies, even if they were patriarchal in structure, were similar to the Iroquoian in their recognition and placing of women in high standing. Hunting and gathering peoples considered their women essential and valued economic partners in the various work activities associated with each seasonal cycle. In these societies, women took on domestic roles that included food preparation, making of clothing, child care and socialization, as well as significant roles in essential livelihood activities such as tanning hides, winnowing rice, and preparing fish nets and weirs. It was common understanding that any harm suffered by women would have a negative impact on the whole nation.

Among the Ojibwa, women were given the responsibility of directly relating to the earth and keeping up the fires of creation. They maintained the fires that were used for cooking and heating. In servicing the community's fires for ceremonial purposes, they were vigilant about ensuring that their attitudes were spiritually pure and honourable to the Creator and Mother Earth. Both the physical and spiritual activities were recognized and esteemed by community members for it was recognized that not all members could serve in the same capacity. Like the Iroquois, Ojibwa women were personally autonomous, appreciated, and treated as valued members in all aspects of community life.

The foundation of education in Ojibwa and Cree societies were based on women. Creation history begins with a woman descending from a hole in the sky; she needs to care for the earth and become its steward. As part of her work, the woman, who is known as Grandmother or Nokomis, taught the original people about the ways of keeping Mother Earth alive and well; this included instruction about its healing ways. Grandfather, or *Mishomis*, is honoured for the four directions and the ways of the sky. This is why the Ojibwa still honour Mother Earth and use sweet grass, the hair of Mother Earth, in most types of ceremonies.

At the heart of all traditional Aboriginal teaching was the expectation that people would treat one another with honour and respect in all circumstances, including wife-husband relationships. Consequently, there was very little family breakdown in most indigenous societies.[2] Within societies as a whole, the First Peoples held strongly to their beliefs that the Creator gave women special and sacred gifts of life-givers and caretakers, as mothers and wives, and that everything, including gender gifts and roles, was bestowed by the Creator.

The equality of men and women in pre-contact times was accepted as the voice of creation. Although their roles and responsibilities were different, men were not considered "better" or "more important" than women, or vice versa. The fulfillment of both roles together held a balance that was necessary for meeting both the physical livelihood and spiritual needs of the entire nation. These understandings were a continuing source of strength and peace for Aboriginal societies.

CHANGING REALITIES FOR ABORIGINAL WOMEN IN CANADA

The Europeans who came into Aboriginal territories, lands they later called "Canada," originated from societies whose traditions, religions, and institutions were overwhelmingly in opposition to those of the First Peoples. Their societies, far from being egalitarian, were hierarchical in nature; Europeans embedded the concept of male superiority and female inferiority into the foundations of all their social, economic, and religious institutions. This was the beginning of a centuries-long imposition of Eurocentric values onto Aboriginal civilizations; altering the male-female balance was a significant part of their attempts to remake indigenous people and society into what was deemed acceptable by European standards. As well, European world views,[3] based on Christianity, identified indigenous peoples as pagan, although it was acknowledged that the Aboriginal peoples had the potential to become Christian, and, thereby, European. In response to what was interpreted as divine instruction, the newcomers saw themselves as the initiators and perpetrators of both religious change and the total reconstruction of the indigenous people.

In British society, where many newcomers had been socialized, women were relegated to property passed first from fathers and then to husbands. The idea of women as autonomous, contributing individuals was given no credence. And the Christian religion was integral to sustaining this viewpoint:

- marriage was called "taking a wife";
- wives were known as the "weaker vessel" (1 Peter 3:7); husbands were to help their wives "overcome sin" (Ephesians 5:26–27); wives were to submit to husbands (1 Peter 3:1); a woman was bound to her husband as long as she lived (1 Corinthians 7:39);
- widows and their daughters were excluded from land ownership; land was passed only to sons;
- women could not bear arms, enter into political office, or hold contracts.

During the colonial period, Native women took European men as husbands.[4] The clergy and others in high social standing, however, did not approve of intermarriage and, in retaliatory attempts, began to promulgate falsehoods about Native women being promiscuous and "easily available" in a sexual sense.[5] These myths provided a ready and convenient explanation for European men being willing participants in these relationships. There appears to have been little effort expended towards making European men accountable for their own behaviours and marriage choices. Mixed marriages, which almost never involved European women and Aboriginal men, were also frowned on because of the perceived disastrous consequences of "civilized" Christian men marrying "pagan" women, a "better" race marrying into a "lesser" race. However, Europeans ignored the motivation for these marriages, often initiated by the Aboriginal people themselves: they served to establish socio-economic ties with European men in order to increase the strength of their own kinship systems. The colonial regime was thus paving the way for the unfair victimization of Aboriginal women that has prevailed to this day.

Foreign settlement en masse, in particular the arrival of white women, further propelled the decreasing status of Aboriginal women. For example, it established the standard of white women as "the ideal wives and mothers"; because of her race, colour, and identity, an Aboriginal woman could not possibly become part of this elite.[6] Early on, the element of race played a role in establishing a class system in which white people were superior to Aboriginal people and white women were superior to Aboriginal women. Mixed marriages continued to be vilified and Aboriginal women blamed for being the cause. To reinforce these sentiments, conscious efforts were made to alienate Aboriginal women from "respectable" society. It was believed that white "ladies," being morally and racially superior, ought not to acquaint themselves with Aboriginal people, the women especially, lest they likewise became corrupt and tainted. Some historians note that the rise in the number of white women during these settlement years paralleled the increasing racism against First Nations women.

What became public opinion and common thought about Aboriginal people, and Aboriginal women in particular, was soon expressed in concrete action. The British colonial government mandated itself through legislation to administer what they called "Indian affairs," and later, in 1876, amalgamated several of these legislative pieces into the *Indian Act*.[7] Under this Act, both men and women were considered "minors" and "wards of the Crown," but the legislation was particularly harsh for Native women. Like European women of the time, they could not enter into contracts, vote, become professionals, or hold office. Men were allowed a few more rights: for example, male band members over the age of eighteen could make decisions about the land through surrenders. In 1906, the *Indian Act*, amended to state expressly that all Indians were "non-persons" under Canadian law,[8] marginalized First Nations people from general Canadian society and into its periphery.

The *Indian Act* also legislated a new system of governance for the reserves: the elected chief and council system could not include women, which was characterized as "democratic" by the government. Women were stripped of any formal involvement in the political processes of their nations. Further, the *Indian Act* imposed male lineage and formalized male-female inequality into law by defining an Indian as any "male person" of Indian blood. A woman could not be an Indian in her own right according to the law.[9] There were also inequalities with respect to the legislated registration: if an Indian woman married a non-Indian man, she and her children lost their place on the Indian Affairs registry. Conversely, when an Indian man married a non-Indian woman, his wife and children all became Status Indians. Up to 95 percent of all enfranchisements (i.e., those lost of Indian status)[10] were involuntary and resulted from these provisions of the Act.

The Department of Indian Affairs' Indian agents regularly reported on reserve activities. While their overall portrayal of Indians was derogatory,[11] those reports about Native women were particularly disparaging. For example, Aboriginal women were described as "poor housekeepers and bad mothers"— qualities contrary to ideal womanhood. As well, various churches were recruited to help implement the residential school system, which further eroded the image and traditional roles of Aboriginal women. This particular schooling experience was designed to make it difficult, if not impossible, for Aboriginal parents to raise their own children. Aboriginal mothers, suddenly finding themselves in a vacuum without their children, experienced deep spiritual desolation. More and more, they found themselves isolated, without legal protection, and, often, without their own community's support.

FROM THEN TO NOW: THE ROOTS OF SISTERS IN SPIRIT

It is indeed intriguing to view the status of Aboriginal women today, in the new millennium. Have life conditions and circumstances improved over the years, and, if not, is there an explanation? Might we find a correlation to the legacy enforced by the *Indian Act*?

First, in looking at the area of health, ample research uncovers hard evidence of the poor health status of Aboriginal women in Canada and of social disparities in their lives compared with other Canadian women. Data from the Canadian Population Health Initiative state that Aboriginal people are the unhealthiest group in Canada[12] and that Aboriginal women experience a disproportionate burden of ill-health compared to other Canadian women. Incidence of diabetes among First Nations women, for example, is five times greater than among other Canadian women.[13]

HIV/AIDS is another area of major concern to Aboriginal women. Aboriginal people are dramatically overrepresented in HIV/AIDS figures: the percentage of AIDS cases in Canada represented by Aboriginal women (23.1 percent) is almost three times that of their non-Aboriginal counterparts (8.2 percent). The Canadian Aboriginal AIDS Network states that "various social, economic and behavioural issues are believed to be influencing this health concern. In addition, Aboriginal women can experience a triple layer of marginalization, based on gender, race and HIV status." About 66 percent of new HIV cases result from injection drug use in the overall Aboriginal population; for Aboriginal women, this risk factor is six times greater than for non-Aboriginal women.[14]

Poor economic prospects for Aboriginal women in Canada contribute to their high rates of HIV/AIDS. Native communities, and particularly Aboriginal women living on-reserve, are notorious for their high rates of unemployment and lack of economic opportunity. Unemployment rates of the female Aboriginal labour force (17 percent) in 2001 are more than twice those of the female non-Aboriginal labour force (7 percent).[15] Many, driven from their communities by divorce, separation, or other family-related reasons, enter into the sex trade in urban centres because it is the only way they can see of providing for themselves and their children. Long-term conditions of poverty and racism leave many of them with little option but to work the streets to "make ends meet." A 2005 study of prostitution in Vancouver revealed that 52 percent of those prostitutes randomly interviewed were Aboriginal—a significant overrepresentation compared to the proportion of Aboriginal people (1.7 percent) within the general Vancouver population. Similar proportions were found in British Columbia's capital city, Victoria.[16]

The social circumstances and prospects of Aboriginal women, as well, are still far from ideal. The International Think Tank on Reducing Health Disparities and Promoting Equity for Vulnerable Populations report says that "the colonial legacy of subordination of Aboriginal people has resulted in a multiple jeopardy for Aboriginal women who face individual and institutional discrimination, and disadvantages on the basis of race, gender and class."[17]

Aboriginal women recognize that the racism of everyday Canadian society and government institutions must come to a full halt in order for them to reach economic, social, gender, and racial parity. For example, regarding the widespread incidence of family violence within Aboriginal communities, many women are emphatic that the broader context of institutionalized violence against all Aboriginal people, regardless of gender, must first be addressed. This would include addressing all the failings within the justice and police systems that appear to target specifically Aboriginal people, and, in particular, Aboriginal women.

Violence against Aboriginal women is a problem of overwhelming proportion in Canada that, for the most part, remains ignored. Amnesty International's 2006 annual report for Canada states that "high levels of discrimination and violence against Indigenous women continued. Federal and provincial governments announced initiatives to address these problems, but officials failed to advance a comprehensive national strategy. Crucially, police responses to threats against Indigenous women's lives were inconsistent and often inadequate."[18] Topping Amnesty International's list of Canada's violations is the disproportionately high incidence of violence against Aboriginal women.

Many people think that revealing these findings is long overdue and that the Canadian consciousness is still suffering from collective (and selective) amnesia regarding Aboriginal women being subjected to such violence. Educators, students, Aboriginal women themselves, social work and health-care professionals have, over the decades, begun to talk about these issues in both formal and informal discussions. They see it as one way of cultivating positive change. Many tenaciously refuse to let these issues continue to be swept under the carpet and insist that the causes be identified, examined, and addressed. They continue to work at building a collective voice that asks, "How can we advocate for changes within Canadian society so it can no longer glibly tolerate, even foster, violence against Aboriginal women?"

As shown in a previous chapter by Cleo Big Eagle and Eric Guimond, Aboriginal women show a sizeable lag behind non-Aboriginal women in all areas of well-being. Aboriginal women are in a constant struggle against factors of race, class, and gender that are systemic within mainstream society, and they most often bear the burden of social and economic dysfunctions within their own communities.

SISTERS IN SPIRIT: THE CAMPAIGN ARISES

The mid to late 1940s saw the rise of a new social consciousness within the Canadian public; finally, some changes regarding Aboriginal-related problems would be forthcoming. A joint Senate and House of Commons committee was established in 1946 through the efforts of Aboriginal advocates and their non-Native allies. The committee undertook an in-depth investigation of the *Indian Act*, a first since its inception, which led to a series of amendments starting in 1951. Some of the more notable changes were:

- all First Nations people became Canadian citizens;
- in 1960, Registered Indians were given the right to vote in federal elections;
- the Hawthorn Report of 1967 identified the First Peoples not only as Canadian citizens, but as *citizens plus*;
- the control of federal Indian agents on reserve communities was reduced following the 151 amendments to the *Indian Act*. Beginning in the 1960s, Indian agents were removed from all communities across Canada.

Unemployment on reserves had always been problematic, but the change from subsistence to wage-based economies encouraged women to leave their reserves to look for employment in urban centres. Because movement restrictions had been lifted, this was now easier to do. They also sought better life opportunities, through access to mainstream education. Communications were greatly improved, which led to the rise of public awareness on a number of issues. However, in spite of these legal and social changes, racism against Aboriginal women was not abating and, instead, continued to plague them, especially those arriving in the cities.

The number of Aboriginal women who met harm along their life journeys, those who may have gone missing or may have been murdered during these years, is not known. One woman stated, when she was asked about missing or murdered Aboriginal women: "Aboriginal women are constantly being victimized.... Very little attention from police is given to missing Aboriginal women. There is a mindset among many non-Native agencies that Aboriginal people are nomadic and they are somewhere visiting, and not missing. This is not, and has not always been true." [19]

One case in particular drew national attention to the extent of violence faced by Aboriginal women in Canada: this was the racialized, sexualized murder of Helen Betty Osborne in The Pas, Manitoba. The most appalling aspect about this murder was that while Osborne was killed in 1971, a full sixteen years passed before her murderers were brought to trial. Also shocking was the fact that, during those years, the townspeople knew who her murderers were and did nothing to inform the police. Further, the RCMP investigation of the murder was bungled to the extent that the province established the Aboriginal Justice Inquiry. Racism against Aboriginal people, and against women in particular, inherent within the justice system and the town of The Pas was liberally mentioned in the findings of the inquiry.[20]

The media flurry[21] associated with the Osborne case, late as it was by more than a decade and a half, served a constructive purpose in raising public awareness about what many Aboriginal community members had already known for a long time: that violence, even the murder, of Aboriginal women is readily ignored by Canada's police and public. Several other high-profile serial murder cases involving Aboriginal women were to surface over the next few years.

The first began in the early 1990s when sex-trade workers in Vancouver's notorious Downtown Eastside began noticing that, for at least the past decade, many of their peers were simply vanishing and not heard from again. Their queries to police were largely futile; they believed that police were reluctant to act because most of the missing women were prostitutes, drug addicts, and/or Aboriginal. As the numbers of missing women kept rising, however, the media itself began to hear rumours, and the curiosity of those further outside the neighbourhood was piqued. In September 1998, a group of women, mainly Aboriginal, confronted the Vancouver police and demanded that action be taken. Reporters began to ask questions, and soon the public was aware that there was indeed some truth about missing women. In response, the joint Vancouver City Police/RCMP task force was initiated, but by this time more than seventy women were officially missing.[22] In early 2002, nineteen years after the first woman was reported missing, Robert William Pickton was arrested and later charged with twenty-seven counts of murder. It is believed that at least one-third of Pickton's victims were Aboriginal. This is the largest serial-killer investigation in Canadian history.

Another area in British Columbia is known as the "Highway of Tears" because of the large number of Aboriginal women who have gone missing or have been found murdered along this nearly 800-kilometre stretch of northern highway between Prince George and Prince Rupert. Known suspicious activity began in the mid-1990s, when three fifteen-year-old Aboriginal girls were found murdered in three separate instances. As the years went on, more and more young women travelling on that highway were later reported missing. The official count is now eleven and the unofficial count is three times that number. Only one of these young women was non-Aboriginal. The only entire family to have ever disappeared in Canada—an Aboriginal family—fell victim in this area.

During the past fifteen years, the bodies or remains of nine women have been found in rural communities near Edmonton, Alberta. Most of the victims were involved in prostitution or drugs, or both; many were Aboriginal. Project KARE was established by the RCMP in response to these murders, with the main focus on the more recent deaths. Almost all sex-trade workers in the Edmonton area cooperate with police in this initiative.

While these are not, by far, the only cases in Canada regarding missing and/or murdered Aboriginal women, it is important to note that media involvement helps concerned Aboriginal groups and individuals mobilize police and other authorities into concrete action. Far too often, police simply view prostitutes as unstable and disconnected from societal norms. By extension, this becomes a reason for ignoring extremely violent crimes against sex-trade workers, most of whom are Aboriginal.[23] As well as media, non-Aboriginal women's groups have given their voices as a conduit for the concerns of Aboriginal women because the voices of Aboriginal women by themselves are obviously insufficient and inadequate to draw the attention required.

These are only a few examples of the severe discrimination against Aboriginal women. This is why Aboriginal women are coming together to lobby outside groups for needed action that will stop their loved ones from disappearing or being murdered. No longer will they tolerate being ignored by police and government authorities who should be helping them. No longer will they accept the ill-fated journey dictated by the colonial forces of century-old Canadian institutions.

SISTERS IN SPIRIT: FROM CAMPAIGN TO REALITY

Many non-Aboriginal organizations, particularly those involved in matters of social justice, are fully aware that Canada's justice system responds to violent crimes against Aboriginal women in a vastly different way than to crimes against non-Aboriginal women. The organizations that have helped the Native Women's Association of Canada (NWAC) in its push for the Sisters in Spirit campaign are mostly humanitarian, and include the Law Commission of Canada, Canadian Ecumenical Justice Initiatives (known as KAIROS),[24]

Amnesty International, the Canadian Association of Elizabeth Fry Societies, and various groups within major churches.[25]

One KAIROS spokesperson, Ed Bianchi, stated that it first became officially involved when it learned about the increasing numbers of Aboriginal women who were missing or had been murdered. He also knew that NWAC was very much involved in this specific area and that then-president Kukdookaa Terri Brown had suffered the loss of a close loved one to violent crime, one still unsolved. At KAIROS's next annual committee meeting, mutual networking began in this area, a relationship which is still ongoing.

Amnesty International was another organization that began working closely with NWAC. It, too, is fully aware that police respond with detailed and ongoing investigations of missing persons reports on non-Aboriginal women, in contrast to those for Aboriginal women, which are too often treated lightly and not given proper credibility. Amnesty International was approached by NWAC president Brown, who, at the time, was in the process of pulling together a church-group coalition to advocate and lobby for research funding regarding missing and murdered Aboriginal women in Canada. She invited Amnesty International to be a part of this coalition as NWAC needed as many independent and credible voices as possible for support. By coincidence, Amnesty International was then launching a Violence against Women campaign. To the advantage of both agencies, the objectives and the timing of those objectives were extremely closely related.

As well, Amnesty International had just hired two researchers for a project that would tell the stories of the victims, as related by their close family members, and articulate the extent and circumstances of the violence that resulted in Aboriginal women being missing or murdered. The researchers were Giselle LaVallee and Beverley Jacobs (in September 2004 the latter became NWAC's next president). The resulting document was called the "Stolen Sisters" report, released in October 2004, and the national awareness it raised within Canada and widespread international responses were very encouraging. Ms. Jacobs presented an overview of the findings in 2005 to the United Nations Permanent Forum on Indigenous Issues in New York. Many say that "Stolen Sisters" was the main reason for the federal government's approval of NWAC's funding request for the Sisters in Spirit initiative.

The Sisters in Spirit campaign was also supported, both financially and otherwise, by the United, Anglican, Catholic, and other smaller churches. The campaign ran from March 2004 to March 2005 and worked towards several distinct objectives:

- to estimate the number of Aboriginal women who had died from violence, or suspected violence, and the number of missing Aboriginal women in Canada;
- to put a face on every name that appeared on the lists of missing or murdered Aboriginal women in the country;
- to document the life histories of all these Aboriginal women;
- to draw more media attention and foster public concern regarding missing Aboriginal women;
- to procure $10 million aimed at stopping violence against Aboriginal women and to raise awareness of the specific issues faced by Aboriginal women within Canadian society;
- to foster constructive action from all those who could make a difference in lowering the numbers of missing or murdered Aboriginal women, including police, medical officials, courts, and Aboriginal leaders; and
- to provide public education that would increase awareness of the under-lying causes of violence against Aboriginal women.

Others working with NWAC, in the meantime, did not wait for government policy and legislative changes to address racialized, sexualized violence against Aboriginal women, but, instead, continued unceasing lobbying and advocacy efforts. Finally, in May 2005, the federal government announced that it would fund Sisters in Spirit in the amount of $5 million over five years. The contribution agreement between NWAC and the federal government, signed later that year on 15 November, enabled NWAC to start building its internal capacity, work in collaboration with other Aboriginal and non-Aboriginal women's organizations, and continue advocating for the human rights of Aboriginal women.

Sisters in Spirit supports initiatives that also work towards eradicating violence against Aboriginal women. NWAC representatives speak at various functions, articulating the integral connection of colonization to the displacement of Aboriginal women, and works to educate the public about the ways in which colonization has been the root cause of missing and murdered women in this country. The organization also strives for collaboration among all those who draw national, regional, and local attention to missing women and their grieving families, and discusses how awareness itself can help guard against further disappearances and murders.

SISTERS IN SPIRIT: CONDUCTING THE ACTIVITIES

Because the driving motivation behind the Sisters in Spirit initiative is the eradication of the specific type of violence directed at Aboriginal women that leads to their disappearance or murder, its overall goal is to reduce the related risks while increasing the safety of all Aboriginal women in Canada. An anticipated side benefit is that gender equality will be improved; as well, the initiative expects that Aboriginal women will be able to participate more fully in the various segments of Canadian society so their economic, social, cultural, and political aspirations can be realized.

The foundation for achieving this overall goal is research. In this context, the research entails the methodical and systematic collection and evaluation of information on the topic of racialized, sexualized violence against Aboriginal women in Canada. This type of research is extremely valuable in bringing about social change. Interested Aboriginal community members, individual families, and friends will be actively involved by providing useful first-hand information about the background and most recent activities of the victim. These individuals will be providing the Sisters in Spirit research team with a better understanding of the victim's real-life issues and experiences. The results of this research, once analyzed and placed, will be used to educate others, affect public policy, promote community involvement, and, most importantly, make meaningful social change that will alleviate violence against Aboriginal women. The process itself gives authority to Aboriginal women's voices—voices that benefit all Aboriginal people, women and men, by contributing to positive social changes in Canada. This type of problem solving is accomplished through what the Sisters in Spirit initiative calls its community-based research plan.

Because it is so important to preserve and maintain the various cultures of the Aboriginal women involved, the entire research process is driven within a cultural framework that amalgamates cultural and ethical values. The Sisters in Spirit initiative has captured these under the headings of caring, sharing, trust, and strength.

Qualitative information in the form of life histories, or case studies, shapes the main part of the data collection. This information is retrieved orally through a structured interview process with participating family members or friends. The goal of the process is to gain a better understanding of the circumstances, root causes, and emerging trends surrounding missing or murdered Aboriginal women. Quantitative information, including statistical data and the numbers of actual missing or murdered women in Canada, is also vitally important and is included in the Sisters in Spirit research program. From this information, community action kits are developed for use within the community agencies. These educational tools stress the importance of constantly keeping in touch with women who leave for any reason at all.

Regarding the policy agenda of the Sisters in Spirit initiative, the research team is working with participating families and the community to develop a strategy to initiate essential changes within various levels of government. A comprehensive strategic policy framework has been developed for use at both the national and international levels for discussion on indigenous women's human rights. The framework addresses the socio-economic, political, and legal status of indigenous women, and the underlying factors that contribute to racialized, sexualized violence against them.

There are several objectives in the Sisters in Spirit initiative. Primarily, the initiative aims to enhance public knowledge about the extent and global impacts of racialized, sexualized violence against Aboriginal women. In addition, it seeks to dispel popular myths and stereotypes about missing and murdered Aboriginal women by presenting the realities of racialized, sexualized violence, as derived from key informant interviews.[26] Also important to Sisters in Spirit is articulating the status of both Canadian and international laws as they relate to either supporting or suppressing the violation of indigenous women's human rights.

The following is a list of the benefits of the Sisters in Spirit initiative for Aboriginal families and communities:

- Sisters in Spirit will help mobilize the caring power of community;
- Sisters in Spirit will provide tools on its Web site to help all families of missing or murdered women navigate the justice and other systems effectively;
- The initiative's Web site will provide links to community organizations providing front-line service delivery in the area of violence against women, such as grieving support groups or victims' assistance;
- The Sisters in Spirit media strategy aims to reassure families that they are not forgotten and that their loved one is presented fairly, without stereotype or prejudice;
- Research will help to validate the experience of families of missing or murdered women, and help create much-needed networks that promote healing and wellness;

- The Sisters in Spirit initiative will target root causes, identify prevention strategies and risks, and assist in developing safety plans;
- In conjunction with other organizations, the Sisters in Spirit initiative will work to increase trust and inspire hope that violence against Aboriginal people, in particular, Aboriginal women, will end;
- The initiative will help families of missing and murdered women to have some peace of mind knowing that Sisters in Spirit is raising national awareness of their family member and the entire issue of racialized, sexualized violence against Aboriginal women;
- The Sisters in Spirit initiative will take into account the needs of the whole family and community, and friends.[27]

The Sisters in Spirit initiative is indebted to the participating families, for without their vision, strength, commitment, and efforts, it cannot move very far in achieving its stated objectives. Indeed, without them NWAC would not have been able to garner enough support to move the campaign into an actual initiative.

THE RESILIENCE OF WOMEN

Oriented towards the positive, not the negative, Sisters in Spirit acknowledges the resilience of many survivors and close friends of missing or murdered women. Their perceptions as survivors are valuable to all women, even to those who do not experience such trauma in their lives. The ways in which these women deal with grief and their motivation in moving forward in their lives are stories of personal power and immense courage.

A death by murder is extremely difficult to acknowledge and accept, and so is the situation of a close relative or friend who simply disappears, never to be heard from again. In a single moment, everything taken for granted about that person no longer exists, and, instead, feelings of complete emptiness, anguish, shock, vulnerability, helplessness, and sometimes guilt engulf and overwhelm the survivors.[28] The violence associated with most murders must surely be one of the worst feelings that survivors, especially parents, have to endure. Because the police and justice systems must be involved, the situation is exacerbated: the notorious relationship between Aboriginal people and police has well-entrenched roots in historical practices that compound and perpetuate the damaging experiences of Aboriginal people, including these kinds of experiences, within the Canadian justice system. Circumstances related to a death can further complicate matters for the family. For example, coroners decide when a body is released for burial—this may take weeks, or even longer. During this time, family and friends have to wait for closure regarding the earthly remains of their loved one. Also, because of the public nature of murder, media may be involved and its participation may be intrusive, inconsiderate, marred by inaccurate and irrelevant reporting, incomplete, and biased.

Family members and friends dealing with murder are at risk of post-traumatic stress disorder[29] and need coping strategies to deal with their grief. Some, particularly parents, question their spiritual beliefs because of being unable to adequately account for such extreme loss.[30] Survivors need support. Almost anyone can be involved by listening non-judgmentally and with companionship.[31] One survivor stated that what was not helpful was impatience and irritation about what was perceived as a "lengthy grieving process"; in reality, families and friends never get over the murder of a loved one. While each person grieves in different ways, almost all experience feelings of loneliness and isolation, and find that talking about their loved one in a caring and trusting environment is very helpful to them.

Some women talk about their realization that they are also the victims of murder, by "giving in" to grief and not progressing with their own lives. They come to understand that keeping an eye on the future is vitally important and that they have to take conscious action to reflect their determination of moving ahead. One woman stated that she keeps focussed by pursuing what she knows to be right, maintaining a positive attitude, having faith in God/the Creator, seeking and being sure to benefit from counselling, and fulfilling her own responsibility towards her other children and her friends.

There are elements in women's lives to describe the attributes of those who successfully cope with the stress and adversity that comes from the murder of a loved one. Some things to consider are[32]

- the family and community environments in which the survivor was raised, especially the extent to which significant nurturing and supportive qualities were present;
- the number, intensity, and duration of stressful or adverse circumstances that each woman faced, especially at an early age, and how she was able to deal with these; and
- each woman's internal characteristics, temperament, and internal locus of control or mastery.

"Locus of control" refers to a person's perception of what are the main causes of life events.[33] Simply, does a woman believe that she controls her own destiny, or that it is controlled by others, or by fate? There are two kinds of locus of control:

- *Internal*—an individual believes that her behaviour is guided by her personal decisions and efforts; outcomes are contingent on what the individual does; and
- *External*—the person believes that her behaviour is guided by fate, luck, or other external circumstances such as the actions and behaviours of others; outcomes are contingent on what others do and on events outside one's personal control.

These elements play a role in the extent of a person's resilience, adaptability, and ability to meet challenges.[34] One Aboriginal educator, Eber Hampton, says this about resilience:

> The Europeans took our land, our lives, and our children like the winter snow takes the grass. The loss is painful but the seed lives in spite of the snow. In the fall of the year, the grass dies and drops its seed to lie hidden under the snow. Perhaps the snow thinks the seed has vanished, but it lives on hidden, or blowing in the wind, or clinging to the plant's leg of progress. How does the acorn unfold into an oak? Deep inside itself it knows—and we are not different. We know deep inside ourselves the pattern of life.[35]

SISTERS IN SPIRIT: ONE WOMAN'S ACCOUNT

The following is a narrative[36] from one mother whose worst nightmares were confirmed—her daughter's DNA was found at the infamous pig farm in Port Coquitlam, British Columbia. This mother had last heard from her daughter through a Christmas card in 1998. Years later, on 17 May 2002, a policeman knocked on her door and told her that the search was over—the remains of one woman were positively identified as that belonging to her missing daughter. This mother was asked what kept up her strength, day by day, and what kept her from giving up on life:

> It is the spirit within that keeps me going. I myself did not grow up with my mother, and I know that my granddaughters have to grow up without theirs. I can relate to their pain at, say, Mother's Day—when I was in boarding school, making things for my mother such as a card with roses or other flowers on it, they were for my mom but she couldn't get them.... My

stepmother was cold towards me, and when I'd come home for summers and after my dad went to work in the mornings (he maintained the roads), I would go up and spend most of my days up in the hills. I knew which berries to eat, like cranberries, raspberries, chokecherries, and saskatoons. There was spring water there that I would drink. Back then you could drink this water.

My grandchildren were in foster care already, before their mom died. In 1998, November 18, the last time I spoke with her, she had put them into temporary care, but I told her to wait until the 20th when my practicum was over and I could take care of them. This was in Vancouver. When I did call her on the 20th, their dad had already taken them to another city on the other side of the country. My grandchildren are now in a good foster home, and once a month I talk to them. The foster mom is now OK with me having their phone number, but at first she wasn't because she was afraid that I would give it out to the dad, as she is afraid of his violence. There was a lot of trust that had to be built, and that is still going on.

That is what helps me, that they would know I love them. In spite of them not having a mother, the next step is to have a grandmother, and that is me. They are starting to build up trust with me.

When I first found out what happened to my daughter, I took time off work in 2002 and went to a psychologist. She did help me, but the greatest psychologist was my sister. I had gone, in January 2003, to visit her and she was crying. When I asked her what was wrong, she said something like, "that SOB[37] not only took my niece, but he's taking my sister, too." This is when I woke up. I realized that he was taking me as a victim, too, and that I was letting him still be a perpetrator to my family.

This really helped me on my healing journey; my sister is my psychologist. I had to realize that he was taking my life, as well. At first, there was a point that I didn't want to live, I wasn't suicidal, but I didn't want to ever wake up because at night, I was flying in spirit. I would get up and feed myself and do some other things, but I really wanted to go back to where I'd go at nights. I would go back to where I came from, my power place, back in the hills, where the spring was, and the fresh water was running, and where the berries were food for me.

My daughter was there, too. She was so healthy, so alive.

In the process of seeing the psychologist, I trusted her enough to tell her about where I'd fly to at nights. She said that I needed to be reprogrammed and helped me with that even though I didn't want to do that; it was my time of joy. Now I don't do that anymore as an escape. Now, it just happens and I don't always go back to those hills.

I go elsewhere, and every human being can do that, too. Going into a deep, deep meditation, I'd see my body lying there. I don't have to carry that body when I go away, but when you come back, you feel the heaviness, like a big thump. It's a beautiful light body when you go away like that, and my daughter was able to do that before she left. There were times when I used to feel her, and I would have to tell her to get back because of the "walk-in." Even though you are connected to your body with a long silver cord, another spirit can jump into your body if you stay away too long.

I had befriended a local city policeman who understood my flights, and he promised that he would find an answer to me about my daughter, as the Vancouver police weren't doing too much. He warned me that I may not get the answer I wanted, but that I would get an answer. It was a short time later, on May 17, 2002, that I heard the knock on my door from a New Westminster RCMP officer with very bad news.

I am not going to let Pickton take my life. The victimization stops here.

Through a journalist from this city, I found another lady who was in the same situation as I am—her daughter was found at the pig farm, too. We're in contact at least two or three times a week through e-mail; when I feel down, I write to her, and I feel better after I speak with her. We know we're there for each other, for support.

When that happened to my daughter, our family split up, and it's now all about my two granddaughters who are now eleven and thirteen years old. They will decide what they want to do with their mother's remains. By the time the trial is over, and after he decides to appeal, this can go on for another five years, and by then my older granddaughter will be an adult and she can make decisions.

This is really strange, something that happened to me recently. Where I work, a psychic came in who was really well-known at one time. He could tell that I had a deep pain I was carrying around with me, and I told him about it in confidence. "You're going to have to release that man," he said. "There's nothing you can do or say that can hurt him—and your thoughts are going to destroy you. Go out in the bush and the trees, walk in the water. God's punishment is a lot harsher than you can ever give." So about a week ago, I went with a friend to a nearby park and I found a place where there were trees surrounding me. There, I prayed and then went into the water to release this entity. I feel a lot better now, and when I got back to the car, my friend said that I looked so peaceful. Now I know that that man, the psychic, came into my life for a reason and that was to help me heal even more.

There is one big thing I need to say: When people and the press are so discriminating towards sex-trade workers, my thoughts and feelings are that they are women with a deep, deep, great inner strength. If I lived my life half as courageously as they do, only then can I consider myself a real woman. My daughter went to work to provide for her children but she got caught up in the drugs.

In 1995, my daughter gave me a portrait of herself when she lived in another city, and I see that she still smiles at me. She's my greatest support system and she's in spirit.

CONCLUSION

As Canada's most rapidly growing female population,[38]Aboriginal females are still experiencing the difficult social conditions and deprived economic reality that has plagued them over the past several centuries. This continuing historic marginalization results in a shocking statistic related by the Toronto Metropolitan Action Committee on Violence Against Women and Children: "Up to 75% of survivors of sexual assaults in Aboriginal communities are young women under 18 years old. Fifty percent of those are under 14 years old, and almost 25% are younger than 7 years old."[39] Violence against Aboriginal women only because they are Aboriginal (racialized violence) and because they are women (sexualized and/or genderized violence) has been ongoing in Canada for many generations. The *Indian Act* paved the way in formalizing the societal attitudes and behaviours that condone, accept, and perpetuate the marginalization of Aboriginal women and, ultimately, their victimization.

Many Aboriginal women become easy targets to dangerous, perverted, and violent men because their poverty forces them to live in unsafe situations with few viable options. These men, themselves products of Canadian society, are aware, whether on a conscious level or not, of Aboriginal women's vulnerability and of their lack of significant voice and value within society. They are also fully aware of the reticence of law enforcement agencies to take action when even very serious crimes are committed against Aboriginal women. Such violent men often vent against a specific social class or type, mostly on those they perceive to be the most defenceless.

It is in having to deal with adversity from the Canadian state and mainstream society, such as the unsolved murder of loved ones and the agonizingly slow draining of hope in cases of those missing, that Aboriginal women have come together. Their need for concrete answers and a strong desire for justice have resulted in common goals and understandings. They seek allies in the non-Aboriginal community who have already become aware that the type of thinking that normalizes violent activity against vulnerable populations, particularly against Aboriginal women, is still present in Canada. Recognizing that immediate action is needed, they also acknowledge that while attempts have been made through a myriad of policies and programs by various levels of government and different organizations, the actual outcomes for Aboriginal women are still vastly inadequate.

These are the circumstances into which Sisters in Spirit was born, originally as a campaign, then as a full initiative. Aboriginal people whose female family members went missing or were later found murdered began the process by networking and building camaraderie; others—most of whom did not share similar trauma in their lives—joined to show their support. Together, they built a collective resolve to take constructive and immediate action that would lessen future incidents and deal fairly, firmly, and absolutely with those found responsible. This group, perhaps loosely joined together in a formal sense, is woven together by a deep-seated understanding that effective strategies must target the cause of the problem, which is identified as really being the attitude of non-Aboriginal Canadians—a destructive and firmly entrenched attitude within mainstream Canada that allows and encourages the targeting of Aboriginal women for extreme violence and murder. Congruously, the same attitude permits Aboriginal women to drift away from society and its systems without notice—sometimes for great lengths of time, times in which despair and death may have actually overtaken them. Sisters in Spirit and its allies believe that the elimination of this condescending and pejorative attitude will eradicate sexualized, racialized violence, and indeed all types of violence against Aboriginal women.

Sisters in Spirit continues its work in helping to establish and maintain networks for surviving family members and friends. It has facilitated several circle-type gatherings in which participants meet and talk in a trusting and caring environment. Many family members and friends, once so isolated because of the racialized and sexualized violence that so deeply and permanently touched their lives, are finding ways to reach out to other survivors, to give and receive encouragement and hope. The network making up Sisters in Spirit, including those women who specifically work from NWAC, is finding creative ways and means of cultivating the internal resilience that rises above the suffering brought on by the murders and disappearances of their loved ones.

No doubt Sisters in Spirit will undergo transformations as it pursues its goals and as other groups or individuals become involved. Canada's Aboriginal community has been suffering from having its women go missing or found murdered for at least 180 years,[40] and those involved in Sisters in Spirit find that the time is ripe—indeed, long overdue—to rid the country of the bigotry and cultural bias that target Aboriginal people in general and Aboriginal women in particular.

Notes

1   Judge M. Sinclair, foreword, in Anne McGillivray and Brenda Comaskey, eds., *Black Eyes all of the Time* (Toronto: University of Toronto Press, 1999).

2   Aboriginal Justice Implementation Commission, *Final Report* (Winnipeg: Government of Manitoba, 2001), ch. 13, "Revenue Generation."

3   This concept consists of any number of suppositions about humankind's role within the universe and the resulting exchanges of humans with other living and non-living creation. As well, a world view holds a perception about how time passes and its bearing on all relationships. Another important element includes a concept of the essence of human nature; this assigns fundamental motives to the way humans should, and do, behave. These, in turn, shape and uphold a people's ideology, which is their belief in what constitutes perfect or ideal human interchanges with one another and with nature.

4   Sometimes men abandoned their "New World" families and returned home for good.

5   Sylvia Van Kirk, *Many Tender Ties: Women in Fur-Trade Society, 1670–1870* (Winnipeg: Watson and Dwyer Publishing Ltd., 1980).

6   Women in fur-trade society were considered the ideal wife. They provided an essential economic link with the Aboriginal tribes, they were skilled labourers in the construction of the supplies necessary for survival in the Canadian wilderness, and they were loving wives and mothers in a world that was characterized by its harshness and loneliness. However, changes in the nineteenth century reversed their role; sexual exploitation and racism served to increasingly alienate them from the new society that was developing in western Canada.

7   These were *The Act for Civilizing and Enfranchising Indians* (1859) and *An Act for the Gradual Civilization of the Indian Tribes of Canada* (1868). The very titles of these articulate their motivation and goals.

8   This was done by defining a "person" as an individual "other than an Indian."

9   "Women in First Nations politics," CBC News Online, 22 November 2005.

10   Indians could acquire full Canadian citizenship by severing their ties (culture, tradition, rights to land, etc.) to their home communities; the government used the *Indian Act* as a control while Indians were being assimilated through enfranchisement. The 1960 change to allow Indians the right to vote in federal elections was the first time that Canada acknowledged citizenship for Aboriginal people without the condition that they assimilate into mainstream society.

11 For example, Duncan Campbell Scott, deputy superintendent of the Indian department in 1920, stated that "I want to get rid of the Indian problem... Our objective is to continue until there is not a single Indian in Canada that has not been absorbed into the body politic, and there is no Indian question." D. Smith, *The Seventh Fire: The Struggle for Aboriginal Government* (Toronto: Key Porter Books, 1993), 38.

12 Canadian Population Health Initiative, "Improving the Health of Canadians" (Ottawa: Canadian Institute for Health Information, 2004), http://www.cihi.ca.

13 Health Canada, "Diabetes among Aboriginal People (First Nations, Inuit and Métis) in Canada: The Evidence" (Ottawa: Health Canada, First Nations and Inuit Health Branch, 2000).

14 The estimated increase of HIV infections is 91 percent (1430 to 2740) during the three years between 1996 and 1999 alone. On 5 March 2004, the Canadian Aboriginal AIDS Network issued a press release, "Aboriginal Women Continue to Face Major Challenges as International Women's Day Approaches," which included these figures.

15 Statistics Canada, *Women in Canada: A Gender-based Statistical Report*, 5th ed. Catalogue no. 89-503-XIE, p. 201.

16 Melissa Farley, Jacqueline Lynne, and Ann. J. Cotton, "Prostitution in Vancouver: Violence and the Colonization of First Nations Women," *Transcultural Psychiatry* 42, 2 (June 2005): 242–271.

17 Naomi Adelson, "Reducing Health Disparities And Promoting Equity For Vulnerable Populations" (paper presented at Reducing Health Disparities and Promoting Equity for Vulnerable Populations, International Think Tank, Ottawa, ON, September 2003).

18 Amnesty International Canada, 2006 Annual Report, http://www.amnesty.ca/resource_centre/annual_report/Canada.php.

19 Anonymous contribution, Nova Scotia Native Women's Association, *Sisters in Spirit* Promotion/Consultation Session, Millbrook, NS, 7 February 2006.

20 Aboriginal Justice Inquiry of Manitoba, *The Deaths of Helen Betty Osborne and John Joseph Harper*, Volume 2 of *Report of the Aboriginal Justice Inquiry of Manitoba* (Winnipeg: Aboriginal Justice Inquiry of Manitoba, 1991).

21 These include Lisa Priest, *Conspiracy of Silence* (Toronto: McClelland and Stewart, 1989); Aboriginal Justice Inquiry of Manitoba, *Report of the Aboriginal Justice Inquiry of Manitoba* (Winnipeg: Government of Manitoba, 1991); *Conspiracy of Silence*, TV mini-series (Toronto: Canadian Broadcasting Corporation, 1991).

22 Officially, the issue of a large number of prostitutes missing from Vancouver's Downtown Eastside came to public attention in July 1999. This came in the form of a poster offering $100,000 from the Vancouver Police Department and the Attorney General of British Columbia for information leading to those person(s) involved. The American television program *America's Most Wanted* aired a segment on this shortly afterwards, but without results.

23 Farley, Lynne, and Cotton, "Prostitution in Vancouver," 256. In the city of Vancouver, the Aboriginal population is only 7 percent of the overall population but 75 percent of the prostitutes in the Downtown Eastside are Aboriginal.

24   KAIROS is a faith-based ecumenical movement for justice and peace; it consists of 100 communities spread across the country. Its Aboriginal component began in August 2001. See http://www.kairoscanada.org/e/index.asp.

25   These include eleven churches and church organizations, but is not limited to the Anglican, Catholic, United, Christian Reformed, Mennonite, Presbyterian, and the Religious Society of Friends (Quakers) Churches.

26   A "key informant" is anyone who is in a position to know the community as a whole or the specific portion that relates to this issue. This may be someone in a position of authority in government, justice, health care, and so on. The best way to derive information from these key informants is through a face-to-face interview.

27   These objectives are taken directly from the contribution agreement signed between Status of Women Canada and the Native Women's Association of Canada.

28   Amick Resnick Kirkpatrick, Fact Sheet (Medical University of South Carolina, National Crime Victims Research and Treatment Center).

29   Martie P. Thompson and Paula J. Vardaman, "The Role of Religion in Coping with the Loss of a Family Member to Homicide," *Journal for the Scientific Study of Religion* 36, 1 (1997): 50.

30   Ibid., 45.

31   Jennifer Clegg, "Death, Disability, and Dogma," *Philosophy, Psychiatry, and Psychology* 10, 1 (2003): 69.

32   Ester R. Shapiro, "Family Bereavement and Cultural Diversity: A Social Developmental Perspective," *Family Process* 35, 3 (September 1996): 317–322.

33   Theodore D. Graves, "Urban Indian Personality and the 'Culture of Poverty,'" *American Ethnologist* 1, 1 (1974): 72–73.

34   See D. Brown and J. Kulig, "The Concept of Resilience: Theoretical Lessons from Community Research," *Health and Canadian Society* 4, 1 (1996): 29–50. Also, Beverly D. Leipert and Linda Reutter, "Developing Resilience: How Women Maintain Their Health in Northern Geographically Isolated Settings," *Qualitative Health Research* 15, 1 (2005): 49–65.

35   Eber Hampton, "Towards a Redefinition of Indian Education," in Marie Battiste, Marie and Jean Barman, eds., *First Nations Education in Canada: The Circle Unfolds* (Vancouver: University of British Columbia Press, 1995), 31–32.

36   Telephone conversation, 14 June 2006. Name of interviewee withheld by request.

37   She is referring to Robert William Pickton, the accused in this case.

38   "From 1996 to 2001, the number of Aboriginal females rose by 22% compared to the 4% growth rate among non-Aboriginal females. The female Aboriginal population is growing much more rapidly than the rest of the female population in Canada." Statistics Canada, *Women in Canada*, 183.

39   METRAC (Metropolitan Action Committee on Violence Against Women and Children). Statistics Sheet: Sexual Assault, http://www.metrac.org/programs/info/prevent/stat_sex.htm (accessed 25 June 2006).

40   An Algonquin artist, Janet Kaponoichin, depicts the true story of an Algonquin girl who was raped and murdered by British soldiers during the building of the Rideau Canal in 1827. This painting hangs in the Maniwaki Cultural Centre in Maniwaki, QC.

Theme 3: Health and Healing

Alice Olsen Williams, *Midewiwin Women's Colours, 1999*

Heart of the Nations: Women's Contribution to Community Healing

Marlene Brant Castellano

A nation is not conquered until the hearts of its women are on the ground. Then it is finished, no matter how brave its warriors or how strong their weapons.

—Tsistsistas, Cheyenne[1]

TRADITIONAL WISDOM about the centrality of women to the strength and survival of nations is often quoted in Aboriginal circles, yet women struggle to have their voices heard in public discourse. This essay highlights the contributions of women to the renewal of their communities and collective well-being over the past thirty years.

The last quarter of the twentieth century was marked by the emergence of First Nations, Inuit, and Métis peoples from virtual invisibility in Canadian cities and relative isolation on reserves, in northern hamlets, and rural settlements into the forefront of national affairs. Encounters that drew media attention were typically political and often confrontational as land claims and assertions of nationhood and self-determination were put forward. The voices of women were heard occasionally in political forums, but their work more often was carried out on a different stage. Their concerns centred around the family and quality of community life, hearkening back to their understanding of values and knowledge passed on by the grandmothers. With increasing frequency, they were stepping outside the private domain of family to lead initiatives in their communities and to network with women across the country who shared their concerns.

Women often describe their work as healing, in the Aboriginal sense of restoring physical, emotional, mental, and spiritual balance to the lives of individuals, families, and communities. As their work reverberates beyond their communities, they can be seen also as healing their nations, bringing a distinct approach to renewal that asserts the authority of experience and the wisdom of the heart.

My account of how Aboriginal women are affirming traditional agency, the power to act and cause things to happen, is likewise rooted in experience, although placed in the frame of larger events. I draw on reports of projects with which I have been associated over the past thirty years, some of them focussed on First Nations in the province of Ontario, others having Canada-wide scope. I use the terms "Native" and "Aboriginal" as inclusive of women's diverse backgrounds and identities in the groups I have known and from whom I have learned. The term "Indian" is used in place of First Nations as appropriate to the historical context.

The examples presented to illustrate women's agency suggest progressively broader involvement, from individual service to committee work to regional and national initiatives and impacts. That progression reflects my own optimistic view of the gains made in recognizing women's influence. Of course, the work continues at all levels and women continue to confront challenges to their full, effective, and gendered contribution to well-being.

This story begins with my own socialization into a gendered world, where women and men held differently defined responsibilities, while retaining flexibility and mutual support in the business of daily living. In the 1975 book, *Speaking Together: Canada's Native Women*, Aboriginal women describe how they were responding to a changing environment, working primarily from a family base but increasingly engaged with the non-Aboriginal world and gaining recognition for their contributions on the local, regional, and national scene.[2]

In the 1980s, Ontario provincial government support for local involvement in health development opened the door for First Nations communities to engage in planning, bringing women from reserves in Ontario into political forums to lobby for their priorities through a health steering committee. In 1991, Ontario Aboriginal women took a leading role in developing a coordinated provincial response to family violence, which was subsequently transformed into a holistic approach to health and healing in First Nations, Métis, and urban communities through the Aboriginal Healing and Wellness Strategy.

Women and their organizations had an unmistakable voice in the hearings of the Royal Commission on Aboriginal Peoples (RCAP), which were held from 1991 to 1996. They argued that nation building can succeed only if healing of relationships and spirit at the community level is accorded equal priority with political and structural change, and that women's full, partnered participation is essential to both tasks. Community initiatives responding to the legacy of residential schools and helping to articulate a new paradigm of healing constitute the final illustration of women's contributions in this chapter. The theme running through the actions and events reported is the distinct agency of Aboriginal women who speak and act from their place at the heart of their families and communities. They insist that initiatives to cope with a changing world, to promote health and healing, to rebuild nations, must engage both men and women in mutually respectful collaboration. Where respect has been trampled underfoot by external or internal forces, it is women's responsibility to stand tall, to resist, to educate, to heal their communities and nations.

A GENDERED WORLD

I find it difficult to focus exclusively on women's contributions, perhaps because I was raised in a subsistence farming community where the rhythm of work swung smoothly from women's domain inside the home to men's domain in the barn and fields, with alternating responsibilities depending on the season. In the summer when seasonal wage employment was available, Mother and the children took charge of the animals and the garden. In the winter, it was Dad who rose early to coax fire from the embers in the woodstove and cook porridge for the children, advising them to let Mother rest for a while. Her skills in managing scarce resources and her microenterprises to supplement the family income were as essential to survival as the heavy labour and protective stance that Dad and the boys assumed. Her voice in family decisions was strong and her counsel among the relatives who came to visit was influential.[3] Honour to women was a way of life, and to emphasize it was unnecessary, perhaps even disruptive, to the balance that existed.

The Tyendinaga Mohawk community where I grew up had abandoned the longhouse as an extended-family dwelling and ceremonial centre generations earlier. The English language was progressively replacing Mohawk as the mode of public communication. The use of oral history to pass on knowledge of our Mohawk past was fragmented and challenged by school texts that painted Mohawks as savages threatening the colonists from beyond the pale of civilization. What a surprise it was, then, to hear traditional teachings from Chief Jacob Thomas, an Iroquois ceremonialist, linguist, and historian, that awakened in me awareness of how very traditional my upbringing had been.

In a lecture at Trent University, Chief Thomas spoke in metaphoric language about male and female and the relationship that prevailed between them in traditional Iroquois society. He described the protocol for gathering medicine in these words: "When you go out to gather medicine you must prepare yourself with prayer and cleansing, otherwise the medicine will hide from you. When you find the medicine it will be growing in families and you must leave the babies because they are the next generation. You must be careful to gather both the male and the female, otherwise your medicine will have no power."[4]

The truth of Jake's words resounded deep within me. What I heard was not just a recipe for preparing herbal remedies. I heard a profound statement about the nature of the universe and the ordering of relationships in alignment with natural forces. As with many of Jake's teachings that followed, the richness of that particular lesson has unfolded in varied contexts over the years. My early experience prepared me to believe that men and women have distinct, gendered characteristics and that they share responsibility to make medicine with power to heal. My observations and experience as a social worker, researcher, and policy analyst have revealed the extent to which the capacity to fulfill that responsibility has been disrupted in First Nations, Inuit, and Métis families and communities.[5]

In diverse communities and successive projects over the years, I have had the privilege of working with First Nations, Métis, and occasionally Inuit women who were deprived of resources, disempowered, and even brutalized in relations with settler society and in their own communities and households. Many of these women and others with more affirming life experience carried a strong sense of their identity as Aboriginal women. Regardless of their background, they shared the vision and purpose of restoring safe, respectful, collaborative, and gendered relationships in their communities and in the Aboriginal world, often calling their work "healing." I see them regaining *agency* in their lives, reclaiming the power, traditional to their cultures, to act and to cause things to happen.

TRADITIONAL ROLES IN CONTEMPORARY SETTINGS

In a 1975 essay on women's roles in contemporary society, I wrote:

> Native women of today are breaking their silence to lobby for improved
> social conditions, to protest the injustice of white man's law, to practice and
> teach Native arts, and even to run for public office. They are not breaking
> from traditions, as some have suggested. They are women who share the
> same concerns as their mothers and grandmothers before them. They are
> actively engaged in the protection of the quality of family life, in wresting
> necessities from a harsh environment, and infusing beauty into daily expe-
> rience. Contemporary Native women have simply accepted the reality that
> achieving these traditional goals in modern society requires that they put
> aside their reticence and work out their destiny in public as well as private
> endeavour.[6]

That statement was a reflection of the process that I was going through in
1975, integrating multiple identities as a Mohawk woman valuing my heritage,
a wife and mother making the transition from a full-time homemaker role, and
a university professor assuming responsibilities in the discipline of Native
studies, then in its formative stage.

Many other Native women across Canada were making the transition
from private to public life. As a project of International Women's Year 1975,
the Department of the Secretary of State sponsored the publication of fifty
profiles of Native women, including me, in *Speaking Together*. Preparation of
the volume was coordinated by Jean Goodwill, a Cree from Saskatchewan,
with the assistance of a Native women's advisory board, which selected a cross-
section of women recognized for their community service locally, regionally,
or nationally. The women selected included First Nations, Inuit, and Métis
individuals. They were drawn from every region of Canada and included
elders, adult, and younger women. Many of them were active in reserve and
rural environments; others lived and worked in cities; still others were already
making their mark on the national scene.

The biographical sketches drew on the women's own narratives of their
lives, presenting a mosaic of the places and spaces where women were acting
on their concern for community well-being. The women selected for profiling
in *Speaking Together* were not held out as being representative of Native women
across Canada, but their diverse experiences provide an authentic snapshot of
women's initiatives as they moved from the private world of family to the
public world of community service.

Women of older generations spoke of learning values and skills in the family and putting them to use in community service, sometimes jarred into awareness of community needs by personal crisis. Pitseolalak Kelly, an Inuk, was interviewed in Frobisher Bay (now Iqaluit), where she was president of the senior citizens' group. She did not know her age but remembered living in igloos and sealskin tents, moving from camp to camp when her father was hunting. She recalled, "I used to wonder why mother was giving away our clothing but found out that she was helping the people who didn't have too much…. [T]he Inuit never stayed in settlements all the time. They would spend summers there but would rather live in their camps in winter. I helped many women who had to give birth and I did many things whenever I was asked. Even now I am getting old, others ask me to do something and I am willing to help. That's the way I am brought up. If I can do it, I never refuse."[7]

Eva McKay, Dakota, was living on the Sioux Valley reserve in southern Manitoba at the time of the interview. She related,

> I stayed home and raised my 12 children. Life was hard…. Then our house burned down. That was the turning point. I couldn't get any help. Government wouldn't listen. Suddenly I realized life had to change. Indian people have to help themselves. I didn't want the same thing to happen to anyone else. That was in 1959. The next year I became a band councillor, went to all sorts of meetings and did lots of volunteer jobs. Then I took leadership and sensitivity training and did some speaking at Brandon University about Indian religion…. Most of my work has been voluntary. In 1970, when I was 50, I got my first pay cheque from the Manitoba Indian Brotherhood and I didn't know what to do with it.[8]

Almost without exception, the women were motivated by a desire to maintain their own and their peoples' culture, language, and identity. Most acknowledged the importance of support from their husbands and parents in taking on new challenges, balancing their responsibilities to home and children with involvement in the community. Their interests spanned a broad range of issues, with the needs of children and youth especially prominent.

Education was the arena where almost half the women became engaged, although only three of them were professional teachers. They organized daycare, taught languages, came together to raise money, and "do something for the kids."[9] Their ingenuity in finding ways to support education is illustrated in the story of Elsie Knott, Mississauga, of Curve Lake, Ontario, who was the first female chief to be elected in Canada:

When I went to school there was no mention of high school. We stopped after grade eight. The first year I became chief, five students wanted to go to high school real bad but the reserve was six or seven miles from the highway and there was a problem over transportation.... I said I would drive them until they got somebody else if it was important to them. I guess they never found anyone else because that was 22 years ago and I'm still driving them. When others saw those children going to school, they wanted to go too. The next year I had 29 and now there are 130.... All I had at first was an old van with no seats so we put car seats on the floor. I really wanted those children to get a better education."[10]

Verna Kirkness, Cree from Manitoba, was challenging stereotypes and inappropriate pedagogies through curriculum work and leadership in writing the National Indian Brotherhood document *Indian Control of Indian Education*.[11] Said Kirkness, "I am very concerned about the exaggerations and injustices done to the Indian people in history books written by white people. All too often the Indian is seen as the bad guy ... he is a loser. I worry about what these pictures do to the white youngsters who have no personal contact with Indians and what they do to Indian self-esteem.[12]

Health services were a second strong focus of activity, with one woman attaining registered nursing credentials, another working her way from secretary to administrator of an on-reserve hospital centre, and others taking up such roles as nursing aide, practical nurse, interpreter, hospital worker, or volunteer visitor.

Crafts instruction, production, and marketing often provided a venue for women to come together, combine their traditional skills, reinforce their cultural identity, and create employment. Frances Woolsey described her work with the Yukon Arts and Crafts Society as "promoting Indian handcrafts and reviving old traditions and skills that are on the verge of being forgotten. We find outside markets and supply raw materials to the crafts people. By selling their handcrafts and supplementing their incomes, people are helping themselves and taking pride in their work and their race. The main crafts are slippers, jackets, vests, etc. They are all heavily beaded on native tanned and smoked moose or caribou hide. I find this work very rewarding and satisfying."[13]

Women were involved in court work (one of them as a magistrate), housing projects, land reclamation, sports and recreation, and employment development. Perhaps because of their public profile, seven women from arts and communications were interviewed. Alanis Obomsawin had begun her career as a storyteller in song and film, grounding her work in the voices of the old ones and children: "I grew up with old people. They were very strong, beautiful people and had a way of thinking, of living and of being which was very good.... What I brought [to audiences] was a present from our people of long ago.... Since my main interest is children, I have tried to concentrate in touring schools, summer camps and generally places where children go.... I have found a new way to communicate with children and people all over the world."[14]

Maria Campbell, Métis from Saskatchewan, had published her autobiographical book *Halfbreed*. In *Speaking Together*, she reflected on her own experience to expose the victimization of Native women: "Society is much harsher on women than it is on men. Native women have always been portrayed as unfeeling, wild and dirty by historians and later by movies and television. This, coupled with the traditions of white society which regard women as inferior, made the realities for a native woman on the street pretty hopeless. Perhaps that attitude of native men towards their women was the most painful because, along with the white man's stereotypes, there is the ancient Indian belief that women have special powers."[15]

Margaret White, Cree from Alberta, brought deep compassion to helping women cope with life in the city: "When people from home knew I had moved to Vancouver, they said, 'Would you please, if you have time, look for our girl. We know she's there somewhere.' My goodness, I didn't find one, I found many—in horrible conditions too.... I'd lived on skid row for practically two years, lived down there and knew the girls. So many of them have died and it's so sad."[16]

Millie Redmond, as director of Anduhyan, a home for Native girls in Toronto, described her philosophy of community living: "The whole thing about living here is that the girls realize it is a home where they can get involved in helping each other and where they can know there is pleasure in giving, and pleasure in living.... People used to say you mustn't mingle the good girls with the bad girls, but who knows who is a good girl. Tell me who knows? As far as I'm concerned they are all good."[17]

Native organizations played an important role in facilitating the engagement of women in community activities. Almost one-third of the women were members of Native women's organizations—homemakers clubs in the case of some older women, Indian Rights for Indian Women, which had come together to press for changes to the discriminatory provisions of the *Indian Act*, Voice of Alberta Native Women, among other regional groups, and the Native Women's

Association of Canada, which was formed in 1974. Another third were associated with band councils and provincial and national Indian organizations such as the National Indian Brotherhood. Women in urban locations were active in the formation of friendship centres to support the adjustment of increasing numbers of Native people living in cities.

While the ultimately unsuccessful court challenge to section 12(1)(b) of the *Indian Act* had received much media attention in the early 1970s, discussion of Indian status received relatively little attention in *Speaking Together.* The women framed their comments on discrimination more in terms of social justice, economic opportunity, and relations with white society. On-reserve, urban, and non-Status women decried the artificial divisions created by legal status and urged more unity of purpose. Jeannette Corbiere-Lavell had recently been through a bruising legal battle over discrimination in the *Indian Act* in which both the government and Indian political organizations had opposed her suit. She said, "Not only was this a legal loss but I felt it was also contrary to our traditional values of recognition and respect for each other. Thinking about it now, I still feel it was a victory and worth all the worry and anxiety it produced because now native people as well as our political native organizations are looking at the whole question of Indian status and membership."[18] Seven years later her stance would be vindicated with inclusion of gender equality in the Canadian Constitution and the consequent revision to registration and membership provisions of the *Indian Act.*

The personal transformation that women were experiencing and the social transformation they were leading in this decade were described by Helen Martin, Mi'kmaq of Sydney, Nova Scotia. Helen had spent her childhood in hospital, never learning to read and write, and suffering humiliation and discouragement. As an adult, she found someone to help her become literate. After being widowed, she seized an opportunity to try something new and became an organizer of Native women's groups throughout the province: "When I lost my husband I just didn't know what to do and was really depressed. I had no income, living in an old abandoned place with no lights or water. Then one day someone was going around talking about an election that night to select someone to go to Alberta on meetings. I got elected, then nearly backed down as I'd never been on an airplane, but I said to myself, 'I'm only going to die once.'"[19] On her return Helen found a responsive audience for her report of what women elsewhere were doing: "I began to organize eight reserves and they are still developing and doing things on their own....

Now we have the Micmac Cultural Institute and our children will be learning the language in schools.... After this experience, I feel that if a woman wants to do something it is not necessary to have a high education, just plain common sense."[20]

Confidence in the "plain common sense" of Native people, including women, was being asserted vigorously by women engaged in the political arena. Gloria George, president of the Native Council of Canada, declared, "We are going through a developmental stage with long-term objectives, economically, socially and culturally. Native people were always intelligent but this talent bank has been dormant too long. Part of our transition is to use these human resources."[21]

In 1975, in a period when land claims and Aboriginal rights were being contested in legal and public discourse, women were exercising agency in every aspect of community affairs, affirming the importance of culture and tradition in daily life, and addressing practical questions of education, health, housing, employment, and racist barriers to participation in Canadian society. Their perspectives and actions would be mirrored in succeeding decades as Native women adopted new roles in pursuit of well-being for their families, communities, and nations.

ASSERTING COMMUNITY PRIORITIES IN HEALTH

The path marked out by individuals in the 1970s was followed by many more women in the 1980s. Education and health continued to be primary concerns, as was the necessity of bringing their issues to the attention of political leaders.

I had the opportunity of working with an initiative focussed on health, sponsored by the Union of Ontario Indians (UOI), representing forty-six bands in central and southern Ontario.[22] The health steering committee (HSC) was convened in 1980 with funding from the federal Department of Health and Welfare (now Health Canada) in support of Indian community involvement in health planning. It was not specifically a women's initiative, although nine of the twelve members were women who brought a distinctive approach to policy formation.

The policy initiative flowed from forward-looking statements in Marc Lalonde's report, *A New Perspective on the Health of Canadians* (1974) and the *Indian Health Policy* announced in 1979, as well as international advocacy of primary health care pursuant to the Declaration of Alma-Ata in 1978.[23] The definition of primary health care adopted in the Alma-Ata declaration affirmed that health is "a state of complete physical, mental and social wellbeing, and not merely the absence of disease or infirmity," and that health for all could be attained, among other means, by relying "at local and referral levels on health workers, including physicians, nurses, midwives, auxiliaries and community workers as applicable, as well as traditional practitioners as needed, suitably trained socially and technically to work as a health team and to respond to the expressed health needs of the community."[24]

The board of the UOI selected ten reserves that would reflect variations in size, location within the UOI territory, distance from urban medical services, and level of development of community health structures such as health committees. Band councils chose their representatives, and two members of the board, both elected male chiefs, were appointed to provide liaison with the UOI leadership. On the HSC, in addition to the two chiefs, were three community health representatives (CHR), three band employees in other social programs, one member of a local band council, and three band members without formal positions. Formal education ranged from elementary to secondary levels, with one member, a registered nurse working as a CHR, having post-secondary education. Ages of members ranged from thirty-five to sixty-five years. Nine of the ten community appointees were women. An elder was invited to each meeting from the local community where meetings were variously held. The UOI provided staff support. I was engaged as an adult educator to help plan and facilitate workshops where the HSC came together for what the UOI perceived as the committee's primary task: to act as a planning body supporting the UOI in developing health policy. The way in which the HSC went about its work turned out to be more dynamic than anyone expected.

I was excited about the fit between primary health care and what I knew of traditional understandings of health. At my first meeting with the HSC, I eagerly spoke of the opportunity open to us to propose health policies that addressed physical, mental, and social well-being, not just symptoms of disease. The elder present, a woman from a local community, acknowledged that the World Health Organization was taking a good approach, but she noted that they had left out the spiritual aspect of health. Her gentle but firm advice, orienting the HSC, was a signal that the work ahead would not be limited by external definitions of health and policy requirements.

In accord with adult education principles, HSC members themselves determined what they needed to know to proceed with their work. Since only the three CHRs had previous exposure to health education, increasing their own awareness of health was the HSC's first priority. All the members identified a need to understand the government system that controlled resources for health services and most of them were uninformed about the Indian political system that represented their communities in relations with government.

In 1980 and 1981, a total of seven workshops were held, focussing on developing a work plan, strategies to raise awareness of health in members' communities, practise in making presentations to band councils and public meetings, the government budget cycle, survey planning, data collection and analysis, and preparing funding proposals. In each workshop, members reported to the group on activities in their communities in the months between meetings. Sharing successes in promoting health motivated their peers to try new strategies; identifying stubborn obstacles helped to set the learning agenda for subsequent workshops.

Initially, members encountered resistance to addressing health issues. They received comments such as "Our band council just doesn't care about health. We (health committee) could not get on the agenda to go to a band council meeting" and "We started a health committee but we had to cancel meetings because no one showed up." As heard in other comments, participation in the HSC reinforced members in being persistent and taking a gradual approach in promoting awareness of health: "They have started a trappers course and that comes under health, if you get caught in a trap because you don't know how to set it properly"; "I am talking to people more. I go to them and talk about health and how we need to learn about it because of what is happening to us with pollution from the mines and a nuclear plant being built nearby"; and "I proposed to Council to have a babysitting course on the reserve. We ended up having 47 teen-agers take the course."

At a UOI chiefs' meeting, members conducted a lobby to have their work plan discussed and endorsed. Their assessment afterwards was very positive, and included these comments: "Chiefs and delegates were supportive after the project was explained to them"; "We found out that a lot of the delegates were more interested in health than we gave them credit for"; and "It would be good if all HSC members could attend chiefs' meetings in their district because that's where you find out what is happening not only in health but in other areas."

Information about government budget cycles and decision making was provided by Health and Welfare officials invited for the purpose. Peer support in the HSC encouraged members to exercise patience and persistence in refining and resubmitting proposals, finding interim resources to move ahead with community priorities, and maintaining commitment to health initiatives in their communities.

Individual and community empowerment generated by HSC involvement can perhaps best be illustrated in the experience of Arnelda Jacobs, Anishinabe from Serpent River. Arnelda was forty-seven years old and had grade eight formal education. Prior to joining the committee as a volunteer, she was at home, doing handcrafts to supplement the family income. After an initial period of quiet observation and unobtrusive participation, she began reporting on activities she was engaged in between meetings:

> I reported on the Health Steering Committee workshop to the band council. We had a discussion in the community on setting up committees and learning how to work together. We invited UOI staff to come in and hold workshops on setting up committees in recreation, education, health and socio-economic development.... [March 1981]

> I was nervous about doing the [survey] research project because I have mostly been at home. I got encouragement from the HSC to go out and do something. I ended up visiting for hours and was only able to complete five interviews. It was a chance to get to know others on the reserve. Chief and council are very interested.... [June 1981]

> We did a health profile on the community, door to door, assisted by an outside resource person. I was appointed to do the questionnaire because of past experience on the HSC. The results will be kept on file because there are problems with the water caused by tailings from the uranium mines.... Because of our small population [300] we cannot hire a nurse, so we are trying to get together with two neighbouring reserves to obtain nursing service on our reserves. We started having meetings to orient ourselves and get to know each other. It is a challenge to get together as three reserves and work together. [October 1981]

> We set up a board to hire a nurse and it turned into a permanent district health board. I went to X reserve and met with their health committee and explained to them about what we are doing on the Health Steering Committee. We got the three councils to pass resolutions in support of the health board and each one of the Council members signed the resolution. We sent the council resolutions to Medical Services Branch with a request for funds but we received a letter saying they couldn't give us anything for the Board although they are providing for the nurse and medical supplies. We just can't operate without funds because it costs money for gas and things....

> In the last couple of months, I have been very busy with the Board and I couldn't really be involved with our local committee. We put up posters for more volunteers and at the last meeting I told them about what is happening with the district health Board and the Health Steering Committee.... I wasn't interested in health myself until I came to this Health Steering Committee. I never realized how much work needed to be done.... This is for our people. It's something we never worked on before. [February 1982][25]

In the original work plan, the procedure envisaged for developing a database for policy formulations was the standard method of gathering information through a survey and drawing principles from a summary of advice received. Plans never came to fruition to initiate such a survey that would include reserves other than those represented on the HSC. In the summer of 1981, when the HSC had been in existence for over a year, the UOI staff team recognized that members were not proceeding with asking people what they *thought* were priorities in Indian health promotion because they were too involved in *acting* on those priorities. Further, the priorities that were being actively asserted were not based on individual perceptions of HSC members but were a reflection of the collective judgement of the communities that were becoming mobilized.

The method of carrying out the work plan then shifted from attempts to define what Indians in the forty-six bands said they wanted to establish as health priorities to analysis of what the people actually were doing, given the knowledge, skills, and opportunity to act. In two subsequent workshops, October 1981 and February 1982, the HSC worked on analyzing their community experience and abstracting principles for inclusion in a policy statement to be reviewed by bands in the region.

The HSC also sought to gain a better understanding of the role of traditional medicine in contemporary communities. Staff commissioned a First Nations researcher to study traditional health practices as they were reported in HSC transcripts and as they were understood by elders and practitioners in regional communities. The report subsequently became influential in UOI health policy. It concluded that there is room for mutually respectful cooperation and coexistence between distinct health systems, and, "in conjunction with the medical profession, Indian people must determine ways of making the Western medical system more responsive to Indian values and more supportive of traditional Indian medicine."[26]

The work of the HSC was interrupted in 1982 when the complex arrangement for distributing federal funds for health consultation to regional groups via the Assembly of First Nations broke down. One further workshop was held in 1983. Actualization of the ideals of primary health care on a systemic basis was put on hold. However, the community mobilization that was stimulated by the HSC continued to have impacts in improved access to health services in the communities represented on the committee, in the priority assigned to health in UOI policy and planning, in the methods of research and development applied in many sectors, and in the affirmation and recognition of traditional understandings of holistic health.

The community representatives on the HSC, predominantly women, joined the project with a basic awareness of the importance of health to their families and communities. They were encouraged by the example of elders who gently but firmly asserted the authority of traditional knowledge and they embraced adult education and participatory research approaches to expand their knowledge. They declined to take on the role of experts making choices on behalf of the people, but became skilled at identifying priorities back home and sharing the strategies they were learning to act on those priorities.

The HSC adopted an organic approach to community development and policy formation. They built on existing strengths and took advantage of diverse opportunities to introduce new information and choices in informal meetings around the kitchen table and more publicly in chiefs' meetings. Was their way of operating particularly feminine? Or was it an expression of the traditional Anishinabe ethic of not interfering forcefully in others' lives? In any case, the HSC succeeded in placing health issues squarely on the agenda of their regional organization at a time when predominantly male leaders were preoccupied with protection of Aboriginal rights in the Constitution. The HSC promoted an essential balance between the practical requirements of improving life at home and the political work of negotiating space for First Nations self-determination in the world at large.

A JOINT VENTURE IN POLICY DEVELOPMENT

By the 1990s, Aboriginal women had become more prominent in positions with Aboriginal political organizations, in urban friendship centres, and in their own organizations representing women's concerns. The Aboriginal Healing and Wellness Strategy (AHWS), launched in 1994, is a policy initiative that has brought together representatives of First Nations and Métis people on-reserve and in rural and urban communities across the province with multiple ministries of the Ontario government in a unique partnership. I have been marginally involved as a workshop facilitator, occasional advisor, and writer from the early beginnings of AHWS. The following commentary draws on program documents and research conducted by Suzanne Dudziak.[27]

Like other initiatives described in this chapter, AHWS is not specifically a women's initiative, although women have had a predominant role in its formation and ongoing management. A government participant in the planning process commented, "The day [AHWS] was approved I sat in the legislature looking out at the row of women—all of these incredibly powerful women from the organizations sat in the front row watching the MPPS. That to me was a real high point, because so many of the women … traditionally had been excluded from decision making power period, vis-à-vis non-Aboriginal government, and in many cases, to be honest, vis-à-vis Aboriginal government."[28]

The first planning meeting took place in July 1991, but the beginnings of AHWS went back to 1986 when the Ontario government approved a five-year strategy for education and prevention programs related to wife abuse and sexual assault. The multi-ministerial effort was led by the Ontario Women's Directorate, which funded, among others, the Ontario Native Women's Association (ONWA) to explore the issue. ONWA released its report, *Breaking Free*, in 1990, documenting that 80 percent of Aboriginal women and 40 percent of Aboriginal children in Ontario were victims of family violence. ONWA received much criticism and also many thanks for opening the door on what had been a dark secret.

The Ontario Women's Directorate was mandated to form an Aboriginal subcommittee to consult with Aboriginal groups and communities and develop a culturally appropriate response. In the meantime, an NDP government was elected to replace the Liberals, and within months the new provincial government signed a Statement of Political Relationship with First Nation leaders, making Ontario the first government in Canada to formally recognize the inherent right of First Nations to self-government. The statement signalled openness on the part of government to new modes of interaction with First Nations and Aboriginal people.

Seven Aboriginal organizations representing First Nations, Métis, and non-Status Indians, women, and urban Aboriginal people, along with seven ministries, attended the first meeting; they would be joined by others in the course of the planning phase. Conditions of engagement were laid out by the Aboriginal caucus and included these terms: that the initiative be Aboriginal-focussed and -directed; that it be action-oriented, long-term, and broad enough to address root causes of violence; that that there be an Aboriginal co-chair and resources for an Aboriginal caucus meeting prior to joint meetings; and that responsiveness to immediate needs in communities would be enhanced, not jeopardized, during the joint process. The requirement of funding for community consultation on a strategy was also discussed at the first meeting.

The initiative moved forward under the leadership of a joint steering committee and with a commitment to consensus decision making. Consensus decision making stretched the capacity of government participants in particular; it meant they had to take responsibility for decisions reached in the steering committee and take these to their hierarchy for endorsement, rather than making a passive response—a process that often allows government to make pre-emptive decisions.

The influence of Aboriginal philosophy and world views was clearly reflected in the approach adopted in community consultation, the transformation of the strategy's focus from family violence to family healing, and the conceptual framework underpinning the strategy that emerged. The limitations of joint decision making with government partners also became evident in the final phase of policy formation.

All parties agreed that broad community consultation was necessary in formulating policy on addressing family violence. Government preference was to design a survey instrument and ensure consistency in its administration and interpretation. Aboriginal participants insisted that their organizations had to have the flexibility to conduct the consultation in a manner adapted to the diversity of their constituencies, and that they had to be able to respond in culturally appropriate ways to the intensity of responses that would arise from opening up issues laden with strong emotions. In the end, the organizations were funded to gather input from 6000 persons, representing 250 communities, within a framework of goals rather than a template of required responses. As one participant responded, "This process was different as it was not merely 'consultation' as is used in many policy development practices, where government produces a consultation document, formulates and implements its recommendations; this was a 'joint process' where government and the stakeholder group representatives worked together at the same table to develop by consensus both the process and product, and where the stakeholders were resourced to do their own consultations. It was not organized by government."[29]

Transforming the diverse reports into a coherent document was also a joint process, in which a three-day residential retreat for the full membership of the joint steering committee was pivotal. These meetings led to several breakthroughs that defined the philosophy and shape of the strategy.

A shift from defining the issues in terms of family violence to a focus on family healing occurred and began to give a positive direction to the whole exercise. Said a participant, "The other thing that did occur in terms of shaping of the strategy was that mid way through the consultations some of the elders said, 'This should not be about family violence, we're not here to talk about violence in our communities, we're here to talk about family healing, so that's what we really want the strategy to address, we want it to talk about our healing.' And that was a major transformation in the entire strategy which required us to re-configure what we were doing."[30]

Another pivotal shift emerging from the retreat was the definition of family violence and a statement of the comprehensive approach required to deal with it. The statement read as follows:

> The Aboriginal People in Ontario define family violence as consequent to colonization, forced assimilation, and cultural genocide, the learned negative, cumulative, multi-generational actions, values, beliefs, attitudes and behavioural patterns practiced by one or more people that weaken or destroy the harmony and well-being of an Aboriginal family, extended family, community, or nationhood.... This would include understanding the holistic implication of the issue that Aboriginal family violence refers not to isolated, specific incidents of abuse, but rather to the physical, mental, emotional and spiritual welfare of Aboriginal individuals, families, extended families, communities, and nations.[31]

The scope of the strategy was conceptualized within the framework of the medicine wheel or, rather, a series of medicine wheels representing (1) the life cycle articulated in eight stages: infant, toddler, child, youth, young adult, parent, grandparent, and elder; (2) the four domains of holistic health: physical, emotional, mental, and spiritual; and (3) the healing continuum, likewise framed in eight phases: promotion, prevention, crisis intervention, curative, rehabilitative care, promotion of stability, training, and supportive resources.

The high expectations generated by Aboriginal participants in the planning and consultation phase up to 1993 had to be significantly modified on the road to adoption and implementation. A parallel process of consultation on an Aboriginal health policy had been in progress to fill gaps in delivery of provincial services to First Nations. The Aboriginal health policy process borrowed concepts from the family healing strategy and joined forces for consultation in some quarters, but basically followed a more conventional path of policy development. In January 1994, with the NDP government approaching the end of its mandate and facing almost certain defeat in an election, Cabinet designated both Aboriginal health initiatives as a priority, with conditions: integration of the family healing strategy and the Aboriginal health policy, reduction of projected costs, securing of resources, and engagement of federal involvement (specific to the Aboriginal health policy). The Aboriginal organizations participating in both initiatives, with substantial overlap, were faced with the prospect of losing both unless they accepted the conditions. While merging the two initiatives made sense in the context of holistic health, the breakdown in joint decision making created a sense of betrayal among Aboriginal members of the joint steering committee and distrust that would reverberate throughout the implementation phase. Nevertheless, consent was obtained, and on 15 June 1994 the Ontario Cabinet approved the Aboriginal Healing and Wellness Strategy with $49.5 million to be spent over a five-year period. The strategy was announced in the Ontario legislature on 20 June, the eve of Aboriginal Solidarity Day.

The broad scope of AHWS and the philosophical framework supporting flexibility in local implementation were retained. Eligible programs and projects include health access centres on-reserve and in urban centres, shelters for women and children in crisis, healing lodges for treatment of sexual violence and addictions, a maternal and child centre supporting midwifery training, and hostels and translators for patients who must travel to receive health care. Community prevention and promotion workers and crisis intervention teams serve multiple communities and friendship centre clientele. By 2004, when AHWS was renewed for a third five-year cycle, the budget had grown to over $42 million annually. The program continues to be guided by a joint management committee as a partnership between fifteen Aboriginal entities and four Ontario ministries.

While AHWS was developed through a partnership among many players and reflected the wisdom of countless supporters, two women's contributions deserve special mention. ONWA was a catalyst at the outset with its courageous naming of the problem of family violence within Aboriginal families and communities in Ontario, and Sylvia Maracle, the Aboriginal co-chair of the joint management committee, played a pivotal role. Sylvia, the executive director of the Ontario Federation of Indian Friendship Centres, provided inspired leadership, analyzing, arguing, and cajoling diverse participants toward the vision of an Aboriginal policy framework and a commitment to consensual decision making that have stood the test of time. Again, a government participant commented on the process:

> I think the Aboriginal co-chair just made us feel so guilty that we would go around again to do something about it…. She really was great that way especially when you had sat in a [government] caucus meeting an hour before, "We can't give in this way, and we don't have that money and there's no way [senior officials] are even going to consider doing that." And then you come out of the joint meeting, yes, in fact you were now going back and doing a briefing note saying, "We need to do such and such and so and so." But I think we learned to do more, we wouldn't have stretched that far had we not had to reach consensus.[32]

Involvement of women in the forefront of the AHWS initiative demonstrated again their commitment to the well-being of their families and communities, their respect for the authority of elders, and their creativity in adapting traditional understandings of health and leadership to the realities of policy making. They were successful in holding together a coalition of First Nation, Métis, and non-Status Aboriginal people from reserve, rural, and urban communities to transform a conventional response to family violence into a multi-dimensional program to enhance wellness.

CHALLENGING PATRIARCHY: ABORIGINAL WOMEN SPEAK TO RCAP

The Royal Commission on Aboriginal Peoples, established in 1991, was directed, as part of its mandate, to examine the position and role of Aboriginal women at present and in the future. The Royal Commission paid particular attention to the voices of Aboriginal women in all aspects of its work and, in addition, gathered together recurring statements of women's concerns in a chapter devoted to women's perspectives in volume 4 of its report, *Perspectives and Realities.*[33] Women's submissions also figured prominently in the RCAP's discussion of family and family violence.[34]

Commentary on the expansive interests of women was presented by Merle Beedie, an elder who quoted her own elders at a commission hearing in 1993:

> One elder, an Anishnawbe-kwe [Ojibwa woman], said, "The next 500 years are for Native people." That is so encouraging. And they say, "Promote talking circles, teaching circles, healing circles to the Native and the Non-Native communities. Promote healing lodges in our territories, develop all forms of teaching materials for the schools, TV programs, plays for the theatres, movies, et cetera, et cetera. Educate all the community about our history, what our history was and is. Invite non-Native people to add to this history because some non-Native people out there know about our history and the part they played in this and they have to match roles, and we did survive together. Get our women into politics of our communities and nations and support women's groups whenever and wherever in our communities because they are our life givers, they are our peace keepers, they are our faith keepers."[35]

The avenues for women to exercise agency in all these areas are often blocked. Submissions to the RCAP from women's organizations focussed particularly on the legacy of discrimination under the *Indian Act*, the need to develop culturally appropriate health and social services under Aboriginal control, the extent and consequences of violence in families and communities, and the exclusion of women from decision making, especially in the context of self-government.

Discrimination against women under the *Indian Act* historically deprived them and their children of Indian status, band membership, and residency on-reserve if they married men who were not Registered Indians. Revisions to the *Indian Act* in 1985, necessary to conform to equality rights enshrined in the Canadian Constitution in 1982, allowed women who were involuntarily enfranchised to regain status, along with their first-generation children. However, the conditions of reinstatement under Bill C-31 still leave them at a disadvantage, even in comparison to men who married outside their bands before 1985.

Another carry-over from patriarchal traditions that women contested is the bias toward awarding certificates of possession for on-reserve property to male family members. In the case of marriage breakdown, a woman cannot apply for possession of the matrimonial home unless the certificate of possession is solely in her name. The most she can hope for is an award of compensation to replace her half-interest in the house, which would be very difficult to enforce. In an abusive situation, this could mean that a woman would be forced to leave her community and support system.[36]

Women expressed an overriding concern with social conditions that placed the heaviest burden on women and children and health and social services that were often inadequate and culturally inappropriate. Jeri Von Ramin of Aboriginal Women's Canadian Labour Force said, "Despite their many contributions and developing roles as leaders, Aboriginal women continue to face special challenges ... high unemployment, very low income, high rates of conflict with the law, poor health and a high incidence of suicide and teenage pregnancies.... Aboriginal women also have to deal with issues such as abuse, negative stereotyping and limited participation in decision-making positions."[37] Shirley Gamble, of Brandon, Manitoba, said,

> For some women, the circumstances precipitating a move to an urban area mean that they arrive seeking healing. But they usually find that the kind of support they need is not available. Rarely do urban support services offer traditional spiritual practices, healing medicines or women's teachings that reflect Aboriginal values. Access to elders is limited, if available at all. Aboriginal women also find, when dealing with non-Aboriginal agencies and institutions, that the staff is untrained to deal with issues critical to Aboriginal women such as cultural expectations with regard to family roles and the effects of long-term colonization on individuals and families.[38]

Aboriginal people responding to the 1991 Aboriginal Peoples Survey conducted by Statistics Canada identified family violence as the third most prevalent problem, after unemployment and substance abuse, in their communities: 44 percent of Indians on-reserve, 36 percent of Indians off-reserve, 39 percent of Métis, and 43 percent of Inuit respondents expressed this concern.[39] Women speaking at commission hearings called family violence "the most rampant social problem of our time," affecting not only women but children, elders, and disabled persons, as well. Studies carried out by Native women's associations in Ontario and Alberta reported that as many as 80 to 90 percent of Aboriginal women surveyed had experienced some form of violence to their persons.

First Nations, Inuit, and Métis women told the RCAP that if they spoke out against abuse, they had good reason to fear retaliation, even from those charged with public trust to lead and protect Aboriginal citizens: "If we go out and speak publicly, we are threatened over the telephone.... Our president in the Indigenous Women's Collective had threatening telephone calls. There are all kinds of ways of trying to silence us."[40]

The genesis of family violence was often attributed to inequality of opportunity, affecting whole communities and creating high levels of frustration. The impact of residential schooling on family life and the erosion of traditional values further undermined the social supports to deal constructively with despair.

Women's organizations, formed to support their members in contesting discrimination and violence, often became targets of hostility, since they were perceived as pitting women's rights against Aboriginal rights. Opposition to the Lavell-Bedard action before the Supreme Court to overturn section 12(1)(b) of the *Indian Act* was framed in this way. Action by the Native Women's Association of Canada to gain a designated seat and funding for participation at constitutional talks also failed when it reached the Supreme Court in 1994, deepening the protagonist lines between predominantly male organization leadership and women's groups.

In the RCAP hearings and submissions, women's organizations made eloquent pleas for imbedding measures to ensure accountability to all Aboriginal citizens and recognition of women's voice in recommendations for self-government that the RCAP was considering. Joyce Courchene of the Indigenous Women's Collective of Manitoba said, "Presently the women in our communities are suffering from dictatorship governments that have been imposed on us by the *Indian Act*. We are oppressed in our communities. Our women have no voice, nowhere to go for appeal processes. If we are being discriminated against within our community, or when we are being abused in our communities, where do the women go?"[41] In her comments to the commission, Madeleine Parent said,

> Unless Aboriginal women are guaranteed the right to share equally with men the powers to develop the forms of self-government and the instruments required for dealing with poverty, conjugal violence, incest, the consequences of unemployment, the exclusion of C-31 women and their children from their communities, there will be no significant improvement in living and social conditions. Since women are the main caregivers for the children, the ailing, the disabled and the very old, the organization of educational, health and other social and community services can only be successful where women share in powers of planning and carrying out those services.[42]

Aboriginal people—particularly women—accorded enormous significance to the commission's work on health and healing. Many named "healing" as a first priority among the touchstones for change put forward by the RCAP in discussion papers. Many more identified healing as a prerequisite for progress toward self-government and economic self-reliance.

Recognizing the justice of their cause, the RCAP made two sweeping recommendations on women's participation in decision making. The first recommended the provision of funding to Aboriginal women's organizations, including urban-based groups, to enable their full participation in all aspects of nation building and the design and development of self-government. The second recommended provision for full and fair participation of Aboriginal women in the governing bodies of all Aboriginal health and healing institutions.[43]

First Nations, Inuit, and Métis women were unanimous in their assertion that they had in the past, and would have in the future, a central role in securing the health and well-being of their families and communities. The women who came together in women-specific organizations and made representations to the RCAP were often those who had suffered exclusion in their communities or rejection for seeking an autonomous voice in political forums. The turbulence in relations with predominantly male-led organizations would subside, but women's determination to have a voice in securing the health of their nations would not be silenced.

TOWARD A NEW PARADIGM OF HEALING

In my concluding example of women's agency, the lens shifts from the national scene back to actions within particular geographic communities and communities of interest, suggesting that women are leading the way in reconceptualizing healing processes and how they can be facilitated. A new paradigm of healing has the potential for impact well beyond the local situations in which it is being explored.

In May 2006, an historic agreement to deliver redress and healing to thousands of survivors of the Indian residential schools system was announced by the federal government in accord with recommendations of the government's appointee, the Honourable Frank Iacobucci, and following discussions with the Assembly of First Nations and legal representatives of survivors engaged in class-action lawsuits. The agreement includes a lump-sum payment for former students, a process to compensate victims of physical and sexual abuse, and a Truth and Reconciliation Commission. As well, the Aboriginal Healing Foundation (AHF) is to receive funding to support community healing initiatives until March 2012. On 11 June 2008, from the House of Commons in Ottawa, the Prime Minister of Canada, the Right Honourable Stephen Harper, offered an historic formal apology to survivors of Indian residential schools. On behalf of the Government of Canada and all Canadians, the prime minister apologized and sought forgiveness for the students' suffering and for the damaging impact the schools had on Aboriginal culture, heritage, and language. This was a momentous occasion that will represent an important milestone in the healing and reconciliation process for survivors, their families, and Canadian society at large.

Like other initiatives described in this essay, healing from residential school trauma is not exclusively a women's project. Securing public acknowledgement of injuries inflicted by residential schools and achieving financial redress for survivors have been the mission of churches, community groups, and all the national Aboriginal organizations, spearheaded by Phil Fontaine, national chief of the Assembly of First Nations, and himself a survivor of residential school abuse. However, reports of AHF-supported initiatives to promote community healing document the predominant role of women in conceptualizing, proposing, implementing, and evaluating projects. In 2006, the AHF published a three-volume report on its work over the initial seven years of its mandate. The following account draws substantially on Volume 1 of the report, *A Healing Journey, Reclaiming Wellness.*[44]

The Aboriginal Healing Foundation was created in 1998 with a one-time grant of $350 million from the federal government to support healing of physical and sexual abuse in residential schools, including intergenerational impacts. The AHF was required by its funding agreement to allocate the entire fund within a five-year time frame, although actual disbursement of the allocations could extend for an additional five years. In fact, the original grant was allocated by October 2003 with termination of all project funding scheduled for 2007 and closure in 2008. The federal government announced an interim grant of $40 million in 2005, which allowed for extension of a number of projects but did not alter the closure date. In November 2005, as part of the agreement for redress to come in May 2006, a further $125 million endowment and a five-year renewal of the AHF were announced.

Over seven years, from its inception in 1998 to 2005, the AHF received close to 4600 proposals, of which about 40 percent, or 1775, fell within the mandate and funding criteria relating to physical and sexual abuse and intergenerational impacts. A total of 1346 projects were funded in 725 distinct organizations and communities. The AHF did not prescribe the nature of healing activities that could be funded. Beyond the basic criterion of relating to residential school abuse or its intergenerational impacts, projects were required to demonstrate community support and reasonable prospects of achieving their goals through a project work plan and the use of appropriate personnel.

Evaluation of project impacts was based on three cycles of evaluation surveys and statistical analysis of regular monitoring reports. Best practices were explored in a separate survey in 2002. Based on these survey responses, an estimated 111,000 persons participated in 394 healing projects over a five-year period to 2004, and 28,000 persons participated in 246 training projects during the same period.

While gender breakdown of project personnel did not form part of the evaluation data, surveys did attempt to identify the proportions of men and women participating in healing and training activities. In projects involving individual therapy, healing circles, and cultural events reaching out and creating safety for survivors, 38 percent of participants were women and 25 percent were men. Elders and youth participants were identified separately, without specifying gender. Training for project personnel and community members enhanced understanding of residential school experiences and intergenerational impacts. Women made up 53 percent of training participants and men made up 27 percent.[45] The boundary between healing and training participants was fluid, with participants in healing projects becoming motivated to take training and assist others, and trainees uncovering their own needs and seeking healing.

If the numbers of participants reported in surveys were extrapolated to estimate participation in all funded projects, the number of participants engaged in healing would rise to more than 200,000. Projects reported that half to two-thirds of their communities had not previously engaged in residential school healing initiatives.

Projects set a priority on involving survivors and employing Aboriginal persons, with the result that 90 percent of project staff were Aboriginal and, of these, 30 percent were survivors. Staff effort was supplemented by volunteers who were contributing an estimated 13,000 service hours per month in 2001, effort that would add value of $1.5 million per year if it were compensated at the rate of ten dollars per hour. The data indicate a huge pent-up demand for healing involvement that is driven by community priorities, and a great, previously untapped capacity of community members to lead their own healing.

A survey and analysis of best practices presented in the AHF report identified the conditions that were typically put in place to initiate healing and the healing approaches that were most valued and considered most effective.[46] Conditions important to initiate healing were identified as follows:

- Working from a base consistent with Aboriginal values and world view, including values of wholeness, balance, harmony, relationship, connection to the land and environment, and a view of healing as a process and a lifelong journey.
- Creating personal and cultural safety. A safe setting in which victims of trauma can explore painful memories is a recognized component of healing. Projects identified an additional requirement, that of creating cultural safety, reinforcing expressions of First Nations, Inuit, or Métis identity that were suppressed and punished in residential schools.
- Establishing skilled healing teams that included elders, residential school Survivors, and volunteers as well as culturally competent Western-trained therapists.

Three approaches were perceived as most effective:

- *Reclaiming history.* Learning about the residential school system and its impacts allowed personal trauma to be understood within a social and historical context, reducing self-blame, denial, guilt, and isolation.
- *Cultural interventions.* Group activities that encouraged reconnection with culture, language, history, spirituality, traditions, and ceremonies reinforced self-esteem and a positive identity. Cultural activities promoted a sense of belonging that supported individuals on their healing journey.
- *Therapeutic healing.* Projects employed a wide variety of therapies. Healing circles, counselling by elders, and ceremonies drew on traditional practices. They were often used in combination with counselling and treatment by medical doctors, psychologists, psychiatrists, educators, and social workers. There was a strong ethic among survivors who had made progress on their healing journey of wanting to help others, constituting a resource that is missing in most Western therapeutic models.

The evidence shows that healing the trauma from the legacy of residential schools is an enterprise community members care about intensely and about which they feel they can do something. They assumed ownership of healing projects and worked with staff and board of the AHF to shape the foundation to better fit their needs. Building on local strengths, they applied their skills of sharing and caring, and sought out training to become more effective. As deep-seated wounds of survivors, their families, and subsequent generations were uncovered, community members drew on the expertise of professionals and services outside their circle.

The judgement of those closely associated with the work of the AHF, further endorsed in the settlement agreement of 2005 that extended the life of the foundation, is that the AHF has been a resounding success in fostering effective, community-led healing at hundreds of sites across Canada. The way in which Aboriginal people have undertaken their own healing is leading toward a new paradigm of healing that draws on ancient wisdom in concert with contemporary knowledge.

For at least a quarter of a century, intercultural discourse has acknowledged that education, health, and other human services should respect Aboriginal cultures and adopt holistic approaches. Achieving wellness in body, mind, emotions, and spirit has become a mantra even though spiritual dimensions of healing are ignored in policy, programs, and research. Documentation of AHF projects has begun to clarify what Aboriginal people mean by spiritual healing as an essential component of holistic healing.

Spiritual healing is often assumed to be a mystical awakening that happens in the sweat lodge, and it is that—sometimes, for some people. But spiritual healing is broader than enlightenment mediated by ceremony. It happens in many more ordinary ways. For residential school survivors who were forcibly divested of their language, recovering their language was a profoundly healing experience. One participant exclaimed, "In residential school we were punished for speaking our language; now we are rewarded for it. It's like residential school backwards!" For Inuit, going out on the land and engaging in traditional survival and harvesting activities was often key to healing. In Métis projects, people researched their history and found that making contact with their relations was transforming. Women who had been isolated sat in a quilting circle and shared stories that opened up new awareness of themselves, their past, and their common experiences. Fathers came reluctantly to parenting workshops and discovered how awesome it can be to look at the world through the eyes of a child. Sharing circles and healing circles facilitated by elders and residential school survivors created bonds of trust and mutual care.

My role in reporting was to assist the AHF in synthesizing learning accumulated over seven years and to weave the insights from multiple reports into a narrative of the healing journey. In looking for common threads in the healing that people described, it seemed that they were talking in different ways of making a connection to something bigger than themselves and their individual grief. The experience that "I am a part of it"—whether of nature, or the stream of history that they came from, or family or community, or a non-material world, or in some cases a connection with a spiritual being that was friendly—all those experiences awakened an internal awareness of being that was liberating, that made people feel, "I am alive and I can do something with this life."

Spiritual healing, like knitting together a broken bone, is not instantaneous, although in a moment of encounter it may seem so. The late Anishinabe elder, Art Solomon, used the metaphor of fire. He said that *Ishkote*, the sacred fire of traditional teachings, almost went out, and we need to brush away the ashes and fan the embers into life again. Our relations, whose spirit has been covered over and dimmed with deprivation and abuse, are discovering the embers of spiritual life within themselves and they need plenty of oxygen and fuel and protection from harsh winds if they are to burn brightly.

For some years, therapists have been making connections between post-traumatic stress disorder and what was labelled "residential school syndrome"— nightmarish memories, numbing of feelings, difficulty maintaining positive relationships, avoidance behaviour, and substance abuse. Native American therapists have brought new insights to the field. Bonnie and Eduardo Duran in California wrote about the soul wound of Native American patients that had to be treated in concert with individual symptoms, a wound that was more than an individual trauma, that was rooted in dislocation that affected the entire tribe and the community's collective sense of order and meaning.[47]

Maria Yellow Horse Brave Heart developed a theory of historic trauma as it applies to Native Americans of Dakota background. Historic trauma refers to responses to stress that are transmitted from one generation to another. The responses may be adaptive or maladaptive. The Aboriginal Healing Foundation commissioned a study, published in 2004, titled *Historic Trauma and Aboriginal Healing*,[48] which reviews the literature around this topic. Following Yellow Horse Brave Heart, the report argues that Aboriginal communities have suffered successive traumatic events of huge proportion—epidemics, starvation as a result of destruction or depletion of food sources, confinement on tiny reserves, relocations to make way for development projects, removal of children to residential schools and child welfare placements, and stereotyping and racism when they stepped outside their reserves.

Television has given us some inkling of what large-scale disasters do to people around the world, and, for Aboriginal people, what they have experienced is akin to a hurricane followed by a flu epidemic followed by occupying forces followed by disappearance of half the children in the community. According to the theory of historic trauma, these experiences have become imbedded and unspoken in the memories of Aboriginal people and are major contributors to normalizing dysfunctional behaviours including lateral violence and direct and indirect suicide.

I believe that in initiatives supported by the AHF we are witnessing healing of historic trauma, creating in contemporary form the sacred fire around which people gather in community to help one another. The insights into healing being generated by residential school initiatives are particularly an expression of women's knowledge. In self-directed community projects, women are taking the lead in honouring their traditions and finding paths through trauma into health. As the means of facilitating this kind of healing are further documented and refined, I believe, the emerging therapeutic paradigm will have broad relevance for Aboriginal people and for non-Aboriginal people who are likewise wounded in spirit.

REBUILDING ETHICAL COMMUNITIES

This chapter has been about women's contributions to healing, drawing connections from intervention at an individual level to the larger work of healing communities and nations. I have been involved professionally for close to half a century in family and children's services, education, health, and cultural renewal, and it is clear to me that on all these fronts, we are doing the same thing. Whether we call it healing or education or justice or economic development or nation building, the goal is the same—to uncover those deep, life-affirming values that are part of our heritage and to reconstruct in contemporary form the ethical rules that give expression to values.

Confidence in the ethical order of the universe is instilled by experience in the family and reinforced by the larger community, by ceremonies that generate shared awareness, and by language, the signs and symbols by which we define and share our perceptions of reality. This concept of an ethical universe stabilized by family, community, ceremony, and language is not unique to Aboriginal society. What is distinctive about our experience as Aboriginal peoples is the history of having each of those stabilizers systematically undermined by the colonial experience, leaving individuals isolated and vulnerable in a universe that appears chaotic and is definitely threatening.

Cultural renewal is not about going back to live in tipis and longhouses, although periodic retreat to such highly symbolic space may be very valuable. Daily usage of Mohawk language is not likely to be restored in communities like my own in southern Ontario, but conservation of the language is essential to maintaining our capacity to probe the philosophical depths of Iroquoian ethics of peace. Securing lands and resources will provide home and livelihood to some Aboriginal people. To many others, homelands will serve as assurance of continuity, symbolizing a physical and spiritual place of origin.

The political work of securing Aboriginal rights—that is, the legitimacy of our survival as peoples—is essential because the survival of First Nations, Inuit, and Métis identities have been put at risk by public policy. This work, which looks outward to external structures and powers, is predominantly led by men.

Equally essential is the contribution of Aboriginal women in asserting what survival of identity and culture means in personal and family terms. This is not to say that women cannot be chiefs or warriors. That has been an option open to them in most of our traditional societies. Neither does it mean that men are locked into a protector role, strangers to their own need and capacity for nurturance. The promise of the future lies in restoring the balance, continuing to dismantle the barriers to full and equitable participation of women in community life, and creating the conditions where male and female gifts can come together to make powerful medicine and heal individuals, families, communities, and nations.

Notes

1 Turtle Island Native Network News, http://www.turtleisland.org/news/news-women. htm (accessed 31 March 2005).

2 Canada, Secretary of State, *Speaking Together: Canada's Native Women* (Ottawa: Secretary of State, 1975).

3 "Pearl Antoinette Hill Brant, 1898–1979, Mohawk Matriarch," in *Quinte Women of Distinction* (Belleville, ON: Canadian Federation of University Women, Belleville and District, 2002).

4   Jacob E. Thomas, *Teachings from the Longhouse* (Don Mills, ON: Stoddart, 1994).

5   For additional commentary on male and female roles in Iroquois and Ojibwa societies see Marlyn Kane and Sylvia Maracle, "Our World According to Osennontion and Skonaganleh:ra," *Canadian Woman Studies* 10, 2/3 (1989): 7–19, and Marlene Brant Castellano and Janice Hill, "First Nations Women: Reclaiming Our Responsibilities," in Joy Parr, ed., *A Diversity of Women, Ontario, 1945–1980* (Toronto: University of Toronto Press, 1995), 232–251.

6   Marlene Brant Castellano, "Native Women—Past," in *Portraits: Peterborough Area Women Past and Present* (Portraits Group, 1975), 27; reprinted in part as "Women in Huron and Ojibwa Societies," in Nuzhat Amin, et al., eds., *Canadian Woman Studies: An Introductory Reader* (Toronto: Inanna Publications and Education Inc., 1999), 101–106.

7   Pitseolalak Kelly, *Speaking Together*, 124–125.

8   Eva McKay, *Speaking Together*, 74–75.

9   Rose Charlie, *Speaking Together*, 14.

10   Elsie Knott, *Speaking Together*, 100–101.

11   National Indian Brotherhood, *Indian Control of Indian Education* (Ottawa: National Indian Brotherhood, 1972).

12   Verna Kirkness, *Speaking Together*, 50.

13   Frances Woolsey, *Speaking Together*, 26–27.

14   Alanis Obomsawin, *Speaking Together*, 104–105.

15   Maria Campbell, *Speaking Together*, 60–61.

16   Margaret White, *Speaking Together*, 54–55.

17   Millie Redmond, *Speaking Together*, 108–109.

18   Jeannete Corbiere-Lavell, *Speaking Together*, 94.

19   Helen Martin, *Speaking Together*, 102.

20   Ibid., 103.

21   Gloria George, *Speaking Together*, 67.

22   The following account draws substantially on Marlene Brant Castellano, "Canadian Case Study—The Role of Adult Education Promoting Community Involvement in Primary Health Care," *Saskatchewan Indian Federated College Journal* 4, 1 (1988): 23–54.

23   Health Canada, *A New Perspective on the Health of Canadians* (Ottawa: Health Canada, 1974); Health Canada, *Indian Health Policy 1979* (Ottawa: Health Canada, 1979); International Conference on Primary Health, *Declaration of Alma-Ata*, Alma-Ata, USSR, 6–12 September 1978.

24   Ibid.

25   Arnelda Jacobs, Health Steering Committee transcripts, quoted with permission. In 2006, Arnelda continued to serve her community on local committees and as a member of the elected band council.

26 Lesley Malloch, "Indian Medicine, Indian Health: Study Between Red and White Medicine," Health Steering Committee, 1982, subsequently published in *Canadian Woman Studies* 10, 2/3 (1989): 105–112.

27 Suzanne Dudziak, "The Politics and Process of Partnership: A Case Study of the Aboriginal Healing and Wellness Strategy," PhD thesis, University of Toronto, 2000.

28 Ibid., 211.

29 Quoted in ibid., 173–174

30 Quoted in ibid., 179.

31 Aboriginal Family Healing Joint Steering Committee, *For Generations to Come: The Time is Now*, final report of the Aboriginal Family Healing Joint Steering Committee (Toronto: Aboriginal Family Healing Joint Steering Committee, 1993), 10.

32 Government participant, quoted in Dudziak, "Politics and Process," 173.

33 Royal Commission on Aboriginal Peoples, Report, volume 4, *Perspectives and Realities* (Ottawa: Royal Commission on Aboriginal Peoples, Canada Communications Group, 1996). The full report available at http://www.ainc-inac.gc.ca/ap/pubs/sg/sg-eng.asp.

34 Royal Commission on Aboriginal Peoples, Report, volume 3, *Gathering Strength* (Ottawa: Royal Commission on Aboriginal Peoples, Canada Communications Group, 1996), chapter 2 ff. The full report available at http://www.ainc-inac.gc.ca/ap/pubs/sg/sg-eng.asp.

35 *Gathering Strength*, 21.

36 *Perspectives and Realities*, 52.

37 Jeri Von Ramin, Aboriginal Women's Canadian Labour Force, *Perspectives and Realities*, 55.

38 Shirley Gamble, *Perspectives and Realities*, 578.

39 *Gathering Strength*, 58.

40 Joyce Courchene, Indigenous Women's Collective, Manitoba, in *Gathering Strength*, 66.

41 Joyce Courchene, quoted in *Gathering Strength*, 77.

42 Madeleine Parent, quoted in *Gathering Strength*, 79.

43 *Perspectives and Realities*, 53 and 60.

44 Aboriginal Healing Foundation, *A Healing Journey, Reclaiming Wellness* (Ottawa: Aboriginal Healing Foundation, 2006).

45 Aboriginal Healing Foundation, *Healing Journey*, 64 and 66.

46 Aboriginal Healing Foundation, *Healing Journey*, Chapter 5. The concepts are developed fully in the report of the Aboriginal Healing Foundation, Volume 3, *Promising Healing Practices in Aboriginal Communities* (Ottawa: Aboriginal Healing Foundation, 2006).

47 Eduardo Duran and Bonnie Duran, *Native American Postcolonial Psychology* (Albany, NY: State University of New York Press, 1995), 195.

48 Cynthia C. Wesley-Esquimaux and Magdalena Smolewski, *Historic Trauma and Aboriginal Healing* (Ottawa: Aboriginal Healing Foundation, 2004).

A Relational Approach to Cultural Competence

Gaye Hanson

CULTURAL COMPETENCE IS an area of study and dialogue that is gaining prominence as we encounter more human diversity in our work and our lives. Organizational leaders and human resources specialists are making contributions to the field along with educators and researchers from an array of academic traditions. Learning how to respond to cultural diversity and build effective individual and group relationships that harness unique contributions and create new synergistic solutions is a central challenge of our increasingly global societies. Of all those leaders in cultural competence who have established the foundational understanding upon which we will build future knowledge, the teachings of Canadian indigenous women are the focus of this chapter.

In remaining true to the intent of demonstrating cultural competence in the preparation of this chapter, I found it necessary to explore my personal understanding of newly emerging patterns of indigenous scholarship and its unique features. The central characteristics are based on our collective and historical understanding of how human development is supported by teaching and learning. As I have been taught, when we are asked to become a teacher, we must first honour our ancestors, our family, and guidance provided from spiritual sources. With humility, we take on the role of teacher, knowing that the more generous we are with what we give, the more the spirit world will bless us with the wisdom that comes with deeper understanding. The most important part of what we have to offer are our stories, our personal experience, and our insights, which carry our unique contribution to the collective "story" and community learning.

In building on the work of others, which is a long-standing academic practice, I use the traditional principles of respect, harmony, and honesty. In expressing my respect for the work of others, I take what fits for me and leave the rest. In the spirit of harmony, I engage the work of others with a peaceful heart. The honesty rests in choosing what to take and what to leave with no specific requirement for critical analysis or academic argument countering the work of others. The intent in sharing what others know is taking on the role of "carrying their story" and must be done with the spirit of "coming together" of conscious shared understanding, not "tearing apart" others' ideas and contributions, which is typical of some mainstream academic practices. I have struggled throughout my career in coming to a personal understanding of how to bring to others what I have learned from my infinite teachers, while honouring what I understand to be our family traditions. I have shared my insights with other indigenous scholars and have found that my thoughts are in resonance with theirs. As this is a relatively new area of thought, this is the approach I take in this chapter and do not intend that it be generalized to other writers.

I define "cultural competence," the central concept around which this chapter is developed, as a human relational capacity to seek and find compassionate understanding within, between, and among people of differing cultural backgrounds and perspectives. This chapter explains the elements of this definition and how it arose from the experience that I have shared with First Nations women as we work together toward a shared understanding of the process of building healthier relationships that engage and transcend culture. The chapter will be like a braid of sweet grass with one strand being that of oral tradition informed by my Cree ancestry, another that brings in written documents informed by experience and academic research, and the third representing my personal journey of understanding. The next two sections demonstrate the practice and provide information to assist the reader to understand cultural competence in context.

KNOW WHERE YOU COME FROM AS A WOMAN

Looking back at the family and cultural influences that have contributed to current perspectives is foundational to my personal journey of understanding. Part of being culturally competent is to know one's own heritage. I can develop compassion for the experience of others to the extent that I have developed compassion for myself and my personal journey. As the elders say, you can take someone only as far as you have gone yourself. Compassion and respect for self provides a foundation for relating with others and is at the core of personal integrity. Also, the elders always say that we don't know who we are unless we know where we come from. A good friend of mine often said as we facilitated cross-cultural workshops, "Always look back to see what kind of a path you are leaving. If it is crooked and confused, that is the trail you are breaking for your children to follow." So, I will follow that advice. My grandmother and her mother were keepers of cultural continuity for me and my family. My great-grandmother was a Cree woman who married a Scottish Hudson's Bay man. As was the tradition of the day, he brought her into his household, and she was taught to run the affairs of the home in line with his traditions and rules. Despite the limitations, she maintained her connection with her culture and taught her children the Cree language.

My grandmother Sally identified my interest and willingness to learn at a young age. She taught me what she knew from her experience as a community midwife who delivered more than 200 babies in her lifetime. Married to a Norwegian fisherman, she still managed to maintain her connection to community and culture. Sally worked with healing plants and knew what to do in case of an emergency. One of the memories shared with me by her children was that she always had a fresh linen delivery pack to go out to deliver babies, by dogsled or often on foot in winter, or by canoe in the summer. She also had a new infant gown or two to give as gifts to the newborns, an expense that her family could not afford with five children to feed. Sally felt it was important for a new baby to come into this world to new clothes, even if it was the only new clothing the child ever had as the infant grew to adulthood in financial poverty.

Sally's commitment to community development also included her passion for berry picking, gathering of plants, and gardening, interests that were shared by others in the community. She was also the community "values keeper" and was often called to assist in resolving conflicts. Her five sons, including my father, were active in the community, trapping and fishing with their father, assisting the missionaries with wood and water, and delivering groceries throughout the community. My mother was adopted and raised in a Métis household. Her cultural identity is clouded and confused, as she knows little of her birth parents. In her own family, my mother has created a culture of closeness and comfort marked by security, a culture that fills the void in her past. The honouring of culture and the preservation of identity remain with me as a gift passed on through oral tradition, which I in turn pass on to my daughter. Ours is a tradition of strong women with an ability to hold the community in our hearts as we contribute to the people. Our voice is to speak for the people who cannot speak for themselves, and to do that we must develop the cultural competence to be true advocates and responsive leaders.

I have struggled with my cultural identity throughout my life, as many of us with mixed blood do. A wise old Yukon Tlingit elder put my confusion to rest with a few simple words one day. In response to my expressed confusion, she stated, "There is no such thing as a little bit Indian. If you are willing to claim us and all the pain of our past and hope for our future, we claim you."

KNOW WHERE YOU COME FROM AS A LEARNER-TEACHER

My intention in bringing this work forward is to be a spirit-led scholar and scribe in the indigenous tradition as I understand it. There are many challenges in bringing a cultural and traditional approach to an academic task. The first is the problem of attribution or naming the source of all the ideas that form the substance of this chapter. How does an indigenous woman attribute what she knows at more than fifty years old? There have been so many teachers in both this "ordinary" world and that of the spiritual domains. My Cree grandmother taught me on this physical plane until I was sixteen years old. Since her death, she has been my teacher from the other side—from the realms of the spirit.

My current understanding of cultural competence is an expression of the sum total of all I have been taught and continue to be taught from an infinite number of sources with an infinite scope of wisdom. The work is built on the contributions made to my understanding by the human teachers I have had so far in this lifetime: my family, my formal educational teachers, my friends and colleagues, my many patients and clients and the steady stream of "strangers" who bring snapshots of understanding into my life as our lives mesh in a series of brief encounters. All these wonderful teachers have shared who they are in their pain, their joy, and other expressions of their humanity.

The teachings of nature are profound for me. The plants, animals, birds, and fish know how to live in community. The elements of the natural world do not always live in harmony, but they live in community. The wisdom of the rocks—known as ancient ones—and the other elements of water, fire, earth, and wind, all have teachings for us when we know how to listen and learn. The gifts given to me by spiritual teachers have opened me up to the immeasurable teachings from spirit realms.

With an important topic, elders ask us to think about it for a long time, talk about it for a long time, try it out, and then when provided with the inspiration, we are asked to move beyond our oral traditions and write it down. The reason for this, I believe, is that in the intrapersonal space (thinking) and the interpersonal space (talking and doing), the emerging knowledge remains in a fluid state, easily guided by the heart and spirit. Once it is "written," the process is frozen. Thinkers and writers who come later review the ideas that are frozen in written form, interpret the writing through their own filters, and piece it together to support their own work. True spirit-led scholars allow the knowledge to thaw and be fed from the oceans of the collective conscious and unconscious wisdom of the ages, add their drop of unique understanding, and find the courage to bring it forward when the time is right. I will do my best to walk the path of a spirit-led scholar. I see this role as one powerfully rooted in one's own personal and cultural values and ethical principles, connected to a source of spiritual guidance and guided by a personal commitment to honesty and respect for nature and all living things. Characteristics of deeply reflective practice leading to increasing self-knowledge, gentleness, and a sense of wonder are also aspects of my approach to work and life that I am committed to nurturing.

As a woman of mixed blood and a ceremonialist who connects both worlds, maybe my unique gift is in translating and connecting. I have had the amazing opportunity to be placed in the company of teachers from many parts of the world and from a multiplicity of backgrounds. In order to understand what I have to share, I ask that you seek to understand where I come from and the background and perspective that I bring.

MOVING TO CULTURAL COMPETENCE THROUGH LIFE EXPERIENCE

One of the principles of knowledge management is that you know what you need to know only when you need to know it. When I ask myself about where and how I learned about cultural competence, memories and ideas flood my mind. I am often amazed at how an experience can become imbedded in the mind and how the lessons can stay fresh in the heart even after two decades have passed. I remember being on the road to Broome in northwestern Australia. I was on an outback tour after a year of studying midwifery in Melbourne. In that year, I had not met one Australian Aborigine.

We stopped for a break in a small town. It was hot and dry. I walked into a small low building, which turned out to be the bar. I was confronted by a group of smiling black faces. I smiled back and stopped walking. Somehow, in those two actions, I conveyed my interest, curiosity, and openness without speaking a single word. They spoke their language within the group and then offered up an English speaker from their midst. I had a brief exchange about who I was and where I was from. I told them that the beauty of their land fed my soul.

A few minutes later, I walked out of the building into the hot sun, to be attacked by the driver of the four-wheel-drive bus. He physically and forcibly pushed me up against the bus and put his face close to mine as he spat out the words "you could have gotten yourself killed talking to those drunk Abos—don't do it again." I was speechless in the face of his rage. Later, as I thought about the incident and talked it over with my tent mate, who was a wonderful female physician from England, I realized that underlying his anger was fear—fear of the indigenous people whom he had been taught to fear and fear of not being able to predict their behaviour. He was also afraid for me and afraid for what his role as my "driver and guide" might ask of him if he was called on to protect me.

I wonder, as I think of that life event: How do we teach people not to be afraid? I believe we do that by helping them to open up to compassion and mutual understanding. Self-reflection is also fundamental to increasing the capacity for culturally competent relationships. Knowing ourselves and loving who we are as human beings help us to develop compassionate understanding of others. As human beings, we increase our ability to understand human behaviour as we become more aware of our own behaviour as it conveys our thoughts, feelings, personal history, and stereotypes. Our behaviour affects others and triggers their response.

We learn new ways of deepening our understanding of what in us is expressed in an effort to connect with the other. Cultural competence is not only a learned set of skills, although it helps to have a broad range of communication skills in the areas of listening, talking, assessing, responding, and writing. Cultural competence is not only a unique body of knowledge, although knowledge contributes to awareness and capacity to understand. It is important to have knowledge of your own background and socialization process, knowledge of the other, in both personal and specific terms, as well as knowledge about history, the traditions, and other aspects of their cultural context that may influence the individual and how they relate to others. Cultural competence requires a compassionate presence that provides fertile ground with which to engage the other person in an effective relationship.

ELEMENTS OF CULTURAL COMPETENCE

Cultural competence is the human relational capacity to seek and find compassionate understanding within, between, and among people of differing cultural backgrounds and perspectives. Successful cultural competence is created through a combination of the following elements:

Human. The common ground of our shared membership in the human race is the foundation of engaging in effective communication and building a relationship, no matter how brief it might be. On the other side, we know that problems between cultural groups worsen when one group sees the other as less than a full and equal member of the human race.

Relational. Cultural competence is demonstrated in the ability to use human relationships to seek and find compassionate connection and engagement. The ability to turn inward and seek an honest and authentic connection through which the "inner work" of cultural competence occurs is fundamental. Coming to terms with your own culture and the multiple cultural lenses through which you relate to others is essential to building cultural competence. Culture is like a fish living in water: when you live there all the time, it is invisible to you but it is still the medium through which you see everything. That relational interface, which has its first interface directed toward self, has a second interface that is directed toward the individuals and groups to which you intend to relate.

Seek and find. Successful relationships are about the willingness to seek, and the capacity to actually find, a connection that is more than purely instrumental.

Compassionate understanding. The experience of human compassion is founded on human beings coming together in a relational space that provides for respect and dignity. Compassion combined with understanding ensures a willingness to connect and respond to the dynamics of a relationship. Even with profound differences in culture, compassionate understanding provides the connectivity to make relationships work.

Within, between, and among. The reference to "within" refers to the compassionate understanding of self—we need to compassionately understand ourselves to honour who we are and learn what we need to know. "Between" references a relationship with one other and "among" with more than one other human being. Virginia Satir, the renowned family therapist, spoke of the goal of therapy as being peace within, between, and among people. Similarly, I believe that these three dimensions of human relationship are also part of cultural competence, as peace is predicated on compassionate understanding, even in the absence of acceptance or forgiveness.

People of differing cultural backgrounds and perspectives. Differing cultural backgrounds create the situation in which cultural competence becomes important. In some cases, individuals may have a similar cultural background but very different perspectives.

MY PALLIUM EXPERIENCE

Professional experience also contributes to our learning of cultural competence and the multiple layers at which it can be applied. Michael Aherne and Dr. Jose Pereira approached me at a national conference on palliative and end-of-life care and asked me to become an Aboriginal relations advisor for the Pallium Project, an initiative based in Alberta with an agenda to build capacity in palliative care across the country. One of the many Pallium subprojects was the development of a curriculum to increase cultural competence in the system as it relates to Aboriginal people. We began planning for the curriculum from a perspective of how quality of care for dying Aboriginal people and their families could be improved by providing educational experiences for busy health-care professionals. We questioned how to increase the cultural competence of care-giving behaviours through conveying information and providing access to educational experiences that provide opportunities to engage knowledge and wisdom to deepen understanding of Aboriginal people, their community context, and the diversity of ways that they live and die. We began down the path of cross-cultural awareness, thinking that if people know enough about the history, traditions, and cultures of various groups of Aboriginal people, that might change behaviour.

The challenge of building such a curriculum that would be accurate, appropriate, and relevant in each region and traditional territory across Canada became obvious very quickly. Not only did we have the problem of speaking to the realities of the various First Nations cultural and linguistic groups across the country, but we also needed to speak to the issues related to the Métis and Inuit peoples. In addition, the differences related to residency—whether people lived on reserves or in rural, remote, or urban communities—were very significant. The degree of exposure to traditional teachings and lifestyles ranged widely, as did the effects of acculturation over time and differences in lifestyle characteristics across these diverse populations.

We were concerned about creating stereotypes of Aboriginal people, which would result in less effective relationships. The comparative Aboriginal–non-Aboriginal information used in many cross-cultural courses, taken out of context, may foster assumptions and generalizations that may not be true for a specific Aboriginal individual or family.

After much discussion and self-reflection, we decided on a relational approach to building cultural competence. We believed that knowledge and skills related to reflective practice and respectful communication would be foundational to the development of cultural competence. The capacity to ask about and understand individual preferences and underlying values and beliefs is important, and even more important is to find ways to enhance responsiveness in the care relationship. The focus of the culturally competent relationship for the purpose of providing palliative care is to ensure that everything possible is done to meet the needs of the dying person and those friends and family providing support.

The Pallium Project provided an opportunity for me to apply what I had come to know to a specific group of palliative-care providers responding to the needs of individuals and families through the dying process. Through that experience I came to a profound recognition that no matter what an individual knows about the history and cultural practices of a specific indigenous group, it is behaviour and compassion on the part of the provider that contribute to the possibility of successful engagement with a person or group from a different culture. The recipient of care also has to take a step into the relationship to be able to see cultural competence at play. Through that relationship, specific cultural information can be shared. Knowing what to ask about and how to ask, including protocols related to sacred and traditional knowledge, add depth to what can be shared.

BEING AND DOING IN FOUR ASPECTS

Cultural competence is a human relational capacity. It is "human" because the foundation of intercultural understanding is in honouring our common bond of humanity. It is in our sameness that we experience safety and security in exploring our differences. Cultural competence is "relational" because as we come together, we become co-keepers of a shared relational space in which people come together from differing cultural backgrounds and in which cultural competence can be experienced.

I believe that the responsibility for the creation of an acceptable "space for relating" is shared. On an interpersonal level of cultural competence, the idea that both parties have a responsibility for creating a relationship is not a commonly held concept. The responsibilities are not often equal as one person may hold unique or additional roles or responsibilities, such as the case of a service provider or spiritual helper. However, both or all those occupying a "shared relational space" must be willing to wade into the river of human experience that flows between them to connect with each other. We often get caught in the trap of thinking that cultural competence is about "doing" some-thing differently. The doing is important, as we can certainly demonstrate a lack of cultural competence by doing the wrong things. More importantly, cultural competence is about cultivating a state of being that is non-judge-mental, compassionate, accepting, and welcoming. Optimally, true compe-tence is demonstrated when the "state of being" meets the "action of doing," meaning the actions reflect and demonstrate cultural competence and are effective in building mutual trust and connection.

The First Nations concept of the medicine wheel or "four aspects of self" is important to understanding culturally competent relationships. The four aspects—physical, emotional, mental (or intellectual), and spiritual—are equally important to our development as human beings. Similarly, a relation-ship must be congruent in these four aspects. A culturally competent relation-ship will ensure that the messages being communicated from the mind through the physical action of communication are in harmony with the emotional state and spiritual intent. Trust is compromised when the spiritual or emotional aspect of self is communicating non-verbally something that is at odds with words or actions. In order to express this dynamic state of congruence, a degree of self-awareness and self-efficacy must be developed to ensure blocks and personal issues do not cloud the relational space any more than necessary.

CULTURAL COMPETENCE AS UNDERSTOOD BY OTHER CONTRIBUTORS

The roots of the concept of cultural competence date back to the 1960s and further as the human rights movements began to urge greater cultural awareness, sensitivity, and appropriateness in policy and programs. In particular, First Nations and other Aboriginal nurses, who are mostly female, have made a significant contribution to the development of the current understanding of cultural competence in Canada.

Lisa Dutcher, then president of Aboriginal Nurses Association of Canada (ANAC) made a presentation entitled "ANAC's Efforts Relative to Cultural Competency" to the thirtieth-anniversary conference of ANAC in 2005. She defined "cultural competence" as the knowledge, skill, attitudes, and personal attributes required by caregivers to provide appropriate care and services in keeping with the unique cultural characteristics of their clients. Cultural competence includes valuing diversity, knowing about culture and traditions in the populations one works with, and incorporating this knowledge, with respect, into care that is delivered. Cultural competence is important, as culture affects our perceptions of wellness and illness; attitudes towards health services and health care; help-seeking behaviours; and decisions about the type of care and our use of alternative care or traditional medicine. It increases knowledge, skills, and patient safety, while increasing understanding and decreasing judgement. In moving towards cultural competency or awareness of self and others, the caregiver explores his or her own culture and traditions to understand self, personal values, assumptions, and beliefs. Cultural competencies consider historical and political events, demographics of the particular community, determinants of health, prevalence of disease, and resilience factors. To complete her presentation, Dutcher quoted Laurie M. Anderson et al. in stating that "the goal of culturally competent care is to ensure the provision of appropriate services and reduce the incidence of medical errors resulting from misunderstandings caused by differences in language or culture."[1]

In 2006, the Aboriginal Nurses Association of Canada published a report entitled *Aboriginal Health Nursing Project: Initiating Dialogue*. The work was authored by Roberta Stout, a young First Nations woman, and directed by a committee led by Lisa Dutcher, then the president of the ANAC. Cultural competence is a component of Aboriginal health nursing (AHN) and also spans a universe of relationships beyond the AHN concept.[2]

The Maori nurses of New Zealand have been pioneers in the development of the related concept of "cultural safety." In their view, health professionals lacking sensitivity, knowledge, and awareness of the social and historical context of health and health care, and who practise culturally incompetent and unsafe care, often confuse Aboriginal culture with the culture of poverty.[3] The ANAC board of directors, in a meeting in November 2000, identified five categories of *kitimakisowin* (a term that refers to a Cree concept of poverty).[4] This discussion was based on the work of Madeleine Dion Stout, who has identified the following categories of poverty:

1. the poverty of participation due to marginalization;
2. the poverty of understanding due to poor education;
3. the poverty of affection due to lack of support and recognition;
4. the poverty of subsistence due to lack of resources; and
5. the poverty of identity due to the imposition of alien values, beliefs, and systems on local and regional cultures.

This describes the socio-political context within which the most vulnerable First Nations people live and within which cultural competence is essential.

The idea of "cultural safety" has generated much debate in New Zealand and beyond. The premise is that by operating in a culturally safe way, health practitioners improve the health of Aboriginal people because issues such as access and communication are better addressed. "One of the major difficulties with this term [cultural safety] is there is no fixed definition of what culturally safe care constitutes," said Sunita Kosaraju of the National Aboriginal Health Organization. "Rather cultural safety is defined by what it is not. For example, culturally unsafe care has been defined as any action that might demean or disempower the cultural identity and well-being of an individual." Kosaraju continued, "Cultural safety is about attitude change, it deals with educating health practitioners about historical processes of colonization; the current social, economic, and political climate; and the impact this has on the health of Aboriginal Peoples.[5] In the same article, the cultural safety approach was differentiated from cultural competence. The article described cultural competence as "the current focus of cultural competence education in nursing and medical schools where the focus is on teaching students about the specific cultural practices of various minority groups."

One paper authored by the National Aboriginal Health Organization suggests that "although distinct by nature, cultural competency and cultural safety are mutually interdependent. Whereas cultural competency is the application of skills that ensure the delivery of safe care to the client, cultural safety is how the client will perceive and feel safe within the health care encounter."[6] Cultural safety seeks to analyze existing power imbalances, institutional discrimination, and how colonization and post-colonial policies continue to apply to health care interactions.

The late Dr. Irihapeti Ramsden, a Maori nurse, is recognized as a leader of this movement. To quote her: "Cultural safety is the effective nursing of a person/family from another culture by a nurse who had undertaken a process of reflection on his/her own cultural identity and recognizes the impact of the nurse's culture on nursing practice. Unsafe cultural practice is any action which diminishes, demeans or disempowers the cultural identity and wellbeing of an individual."[7] She further refined the definition to include the idea that "cultural safety is the effective nursing or midwifery practice of a person or family from another culture, and is determined by that person or family. Culture includes, but is not restricted to age or generation; gender; sexual orientation; occupation and socioeconomic status; ethnic origin or migrant experience; religious or spiritual belief; and disability."[8]

The above noted definition and distinction are based on the care provider being the active participant in the health care relationship and the client being the passive recipient. I believe that in order to create a relational space, there needs to be a mutual commitment to a degree of communication and work to establish the foundation of a relationship. To view the Aboriginal person as a passive recipient of care is to take away the power held by every human being to relate or not. Rather, the experience of the relationship is created by two or more people, with the care provider holding additional responsibility for using culturally competent methods of communication and relationship building. The most skilled care provider may not be "enough" to provide an experience of safety for a deeply wounded individual or family.

Taking this view, cultural competency is defined as relational space for which both the provider and recipient have some degree of responsibility for creating. The construct provides room for both a "culturally competent" care provider and a client who also has some ability to communicate their needs and preferences to the provider, assuming a common language or available interpreter services. In addition, within the relational construct, the entire responsibility for the nature of the interchange and "making the client feel safe" is not held by the provider. Providers may demonstrate cultural competence and still not be able to control or change the many perceptions influenced by a personal history of bad experiences, which may cause a recipient to feel unsafe. Relationships require mutual engagement and the effective playing out of roles and responsibilities. A health care provider is unable to respond to needs and preferences that are not communicated and communication is compromised by a lack of trust, which may be a common legacy of colonization.

Cultural safety, in the way it has been described to date, is a minimum requirement of a care system and health care provider, and puts the onus for a safe relationship on the care provider. A relational approach recognizes the additional burden of responsibility held by the care provider or person entrusted with additional responsibilities, but also acknowledges the importance of at least some willingness by the recipient to engage and communicate.

Purnell and Paulanka suggest that the defining characteristics of cultural competence are

1. developing awareness of one's own experience, sensation, thoughts, and environment without letting it have an undue influence on those from other backgrounds;
2. demonstrating knowledge and understanding of the client's culture;
3. accepting and respecting cultural differences; and
4. adapting care to be congruent with the client's culture. Cultural competence is a conscious process and not necessarily linear.[9]

In addition to these fundamental building blocks, cultural competency is the ability of the health professional to understand the mainstream biomedical establishment, while at the same time understanding his or her own personal beliefs, values, and assumptions, as well as those of the patient. In order to be considered culturally competent care, health care must be provided within the framework of the clients' expectations and preferences.[10] Cultural competence is not to be confused with cultural awareness, cultural knowledge and understanding, and sensitivity, although these areas contribute to cultural competence.

In an article entitled "Cultural Competence for the Registered Nurse," Laurie Dokis, an Aboriginal nurse practising on Vancouver Island, writes that "cultural competence is important for the registered nurses working in culturally diverse populations. Awareness and understanding of cultural differences strengthens the measurable outcomes of nursing services, contributes to cost-effective programming and enhances the best practices of the profession." The need for culturally competent care has been described in many national publications, including the Inuit Regional Health Survey, the Royal Commission on Aboriginal Peoples, the Canadian Medical Association's *Bridging the Gap*, and the Aboriginal Women's Health Report. Dokis states that "increasing the cultural competence of registered nurses is a priority for Aboriginal organizations, practicing nurses, nursing organizations and health authorities." She recommends mandatory cultural training; the provision of a cultural advisor and the development of an Aboriginal cultural advisory council.[11]

Dr. Cornelia Wieman is Canada's first female Aboriginal psychiatrist and she has worked to further cultural competence in the field of mental health. Her work establishes important linkages among poverty, stress, depression, and diabetes. Her stories demonstrate traditional ways of knowing, important to a deeper understanding of the experience of Aboriginal people, and how to take a holistic approach to providing care. She is an advocate for health professionals using "your heart and your mind." Cornelia's work demonstrates cultural competence in program design and development.[12]

Dr. Marlene Brant Castellano is a former professor and chair of Native studies at Trent University with many honours to her credit, including an appointment as Officer of the Order of Canada. She has also contributed to the development of the concept of cultural competence and the importance of Native studies as a distinct academic discipline. The book *Aboriginal Education*, which she co-edited, is an excellent example illustrating the importance of Aboriginal philosophies and priorities in teaching methods, program design, and institutional development.[13]

Dr. Janet Smylie, an indigenous physician, makes an important contribution to the field as the principal author of "A Guide for Health Professionals Working with Aboriginal Peoples." The paper includes recommendations related to clinical relationships as well as program- and policy-related advice on support for creation of community-directed health programs and community-directed participatory health research with Aboriginal people.[14]

Dr. Judith Bartlett, Métis physician, currently co-director at the Centre for Aboriginal Health Research of the Department of Community Health Sciences, Faculty of Medicine at the University of Manitoba, was a second author with Dr. John O'Neil and Dr. Javier Mignone on a paper on best practices in intercultural health. Intercultural health in this study is understood essentially as practices in health and health care that bridge indigenous medicine and Western medicine, where both are considered complementary. The basic premises are those of mutual respect, equal recognition of knowledge, willingness to interact, and flexibility to change as a result of these interactions. Intercultural health takes place at different levels, including the level of the family, practitioner, health centre, hospital, and health system. This study was an international research project, and we can learn a great deal about cultural competence in looking to relationships with international indigenous peoples. The multilevel concept of intercultural health is parallel to the way in which I define relational cultural competence.[15]

CULTURAL COMPETENCE AS AN ETHICAL SPACE

In writing about ethics of research involving indigenous peoples, Willie Ermine, Raven Sinclair, and others have made many important contributions to understanding relationships. One element includes bringing forward the work of Roger Poole, who first coined the term "ethical space" in his book, *Towards Deep Subjectivity*.[16] The term identifies an abstract space that frames an area of encounter and interaction of two entities with different intentions. Ermine et al. bring this concept into an indigenous relational context. The writers have described the space between indigenous and Western worlds with the difference in world views formed by distinct histories, knowledge traditions, values, interests, and social, economic, and political realities. The idea of two spheres of knowledge, two cultures, each distinct from one another in multiple forms, also inspired an abstract, nebulous space of possibility. The in-between space, relative to cultures, is created by the recognition of the separate realities of histories, knowledge traditions, interests, and social, economic, and political imperatives. The neutral zone is the ethical space where a precarious and fragile window of opportunity exists for "critical conversations about democracy, race, gender, class, nation, freedom and community."[17]

The ethical space provides a paradigm for how people from disparate cultures, world views, and knowledge systems can engage in an ethical or moral manner as we work toward giving substance to what the ethical space entails.[18]

CANADIAN NURSES ASSOCIATION CONTRIBUTIONS

My understanding of cultural competence has been developed through the community of nurses to which I belong. According to the Canadian Nurses Association (CNA), Canadian nurses are expected to learn about cultural diversity, and knowledge, skills, and attitudes about culture. The 1999 CNA publication, *Blueprint for the Registered Nurse Examination*, includes the following competencies: demonstrating consideration of client diversity; providing culturally sensitive care (e.g., openness, sensitivity, recognizing culturally based practices and values); and incorporating cultural practices into health promotion activities.[19] The CNA Code of Ethics for Registered Nurses requires that nurses provide care in response to need, regardless of the culture of the client.

The CNA publication, *Nursing Now: Issues and Trends in Canadian Nursing*, states that "it is a challenge for nurses to understand the way clients of various cultures think, feel and behave when it comes to matters of health." It goes on to quote nursing leader Madeleine Leininger's definition of culture as "learning values, beliefs, norms and way of life that influence an individual's thinking, decisions and actions in certain ways. Culture has been characterized as a way of life, a way of viewing things and how one communicates.... [I]t provides an individual with a way of viewing the world, as a starting point for interacting with others ... all encompassing and reflects the assumptions individuals make in every day life."[20] Each of us has a culture and it is individual, learned, and shared. It varies within populations sharing similar racial background and is dynamic in the way it changes over time. A person's culture is rooted in race and ethnicity but also influenced by age, gender, education, life experience, and sexual orientation. Social and economic status and language also affect culture at an individual and family level.[21]

Nursing Now also identifies factors that inhibit the development of a sensitive and responsive health system. These are lack of experience and lack of knowledge, along with attitudinal factors such as fear, ethnocentrism, cultural blindness, racism, and discrimination. This document states that the term "cultural competence" "describes a process in which health care providers develop cultural awareness, knowledge and skill in encounters with people of other cultures."[22] In addition, the publication identifies four key nursing responsibilities for nurses wishing to provide culturally appropriate care:[23]

1. *Cultural assessment.* This area of responsibility challenges nurses to examine personal attitudes and values about health, illness, and health care. The goal of the assessment is to understand the differences between personal values and beliefs and those of the client, and to appreciate the strength of both in order to develop a mutually respectful and effective plan of care.
2. *Cultural knowledge.* This area of responsibility includes learning about health beliefs and values of the clients and how these influence their response to health care and beliefs about self-care in health and illness, the role of health care providers and hospitalization, birth practices, death and dying, family involvement, spirituality, customs, rituals, food, and alternative or traditional therapies. This openness and willingness to understand encourages respectful and open exploration of client attitudes, beliefs, perceptions, and goals.
3. *Verbal and non-verbal communication.* Unfamiliar modes of communication and language barriers between client and provider can be a barrier to accessibility and appropriateness of services. The use of facial expressions, body language, and norms related to eye contact are examples of non-verbal communication that can express potential differences. Listening, respecting, and being open are essential. Specialized health care inter-preters can be effective in interpreting both words and the meaning of health information in a culturally accurate context.
4. *Partnership.* Developing partnerships among clients, providers, and funding agencies is an area of responsibility that is essential to developing a system that incorporates culturally diverse practices into health care services while optimizing health outcomes for the client. Partners can establish health care needs and mutual goals for individuals and commu-nities, and facilitate client choice.

More recently CNA has released a position statement entitled *Promoting Culturally Competent Care.* Here, CNA defines culture broadly, referring to shared patterns of learned behaviours and values that are transmitted over time, and that distinguish the members of one group from another. In this broad sense, culture can include ethnicity, language, religion and spiritual beliefs, gender, socio-economic class, age, sexual orientation, geographic origin, group history, education, upbringing, and life experiences.[24] Cultural competence is describes as "the application of knowledge, skill, attitudes and personal attributes required by nurses to provide appropriate care and services in relation to cultural characteristics of their clients." Clients, in this context, may be an individual, family, a group, or a population. Cultural competence includes valuing diversity and knowing about and being sensitive to cultural mores and traditions of the populations being served. CNA believes that to provide the best possible patient outcomes, nurses must provide culturally competent care. CNA further believes the responsibility of supporting culturally competent care is shared between individuals, professional associations, regulatory bodies, health-service delivery and accreditation organizations, educational institutions, and governments.

Promoting Culturally Competent Care identifies culture as one of the twelve key determinants of health, which is a "complex set of factors or conditions that determine the level of health of Canadians."[25] Understanding and providing culturally competent care will make a difference to the health outcomes of many cultural groups, including Canada's Aboriginal population, which made up 3.3 percent of the population in 2001 and has higher rates of infant mortality, chronic disease, and suicide than other Canadians.[26]

Nursing authors and organizations throughout Canada and around the world have contributed to the development of broader and deeper understanding of cultural competence and to the development of supports for the enhancement of cultural competence in nursing practice. In the majority of cases, First Nations and other Aboriginal people are considered along with immigrant and other "visible minority" populations. There are significant problems with this approach as indigenous populations that have experienced the effects of colonization have unique aspects that cannot be fully considered within a generic approach to cultural competence.

ORGANIZATIONAL CULTURAL COMPETENCE

The Registered Nurses' Association of Ontario is leading the way in organizational cultural competence with the development and release of a nursing best practice guideline entitled "Embracing Cultural Diversity in Health Care: Developing Cultural Competence." Cultural competence in the workplace can be described as a congruent set of workforce behaviours, management practices, and institutional policies within a practice setting, resulting in an organizational environment that is respectful and inclusive of cultural and other forms of diversity. The guideline provides recommendations that health professionals at every level can use to embed work environments with a culture that moves all team members past knowing about diversity to understanding it, accepting the differences it brings to the work setting, and finally to seeking and embracing it.[27]

The overall goal and objectives of this project are to promote a healthy work environment for nurses by identifying best practices for embracing diversity within health care organizations. The objectives are "identifying culturally competent practices that enhance outcomes for nurses, organizations and systems" and "identifying organizational values, relationships, structures, and processes required for developing and sustaining culturally competent practices."[28]

The best practice guideline was developed by a group that included Lisa Dutcher, former president of Aboriginal Nurses Association of Canada. It is a very important contribution to understanding the optimal organizational context to support cultural competence at the interface between care providers, patients/clients, families, and communities.

FAMILY AND COMMUNITY CULTURAL COMPETENCE

The ideas related to relational cultural competence presented in this chapter have been developed with a focus on the individual and family level. Defining "individual" is easier than defining family. I define family as any group of two or more people that define themselves as family. The first step in establishing a relationship is determining the family membership and developing an understanding of who speaks for the family and which family members hold the decision-making responsibility. Understanding where the family fits on a spectrum of acculturation and the degree to which the effects of colonization, including residential school attendance, has affected intergenerational family dynamics is also part of developing a culturally competent relationship with a family.

The work of my father, Bill Hanson, is a product of what he learned from his mother, Sally, and his community in northern Manitoba, and has been passed on to me, one of four daughters. His model of Aboriginal community dynamics, as communicated in his book, *Dual Realities—Dual Strategies: The Future Paths of Aboriginal Peoples' Development*, provides a construct for viewing communities and assessing the characteristics and interrelationships between families and other sub-components of a community. The multidimensional diversity within communities and sometimes families is well described in the book. Some individuals and families are aligned with a traditional holistic way of life and struggle to keep this alive. Others have adopted a way of life more aligned with the mainstream, market-oriented, industrial economy. Aboriginal people are caught in the push and pull of acculturation. As stated by the Royal Commission on Aboriginal Peoples, Aboriginal people want to retain their identity, language, and culture, and many want to continue living on the land; and Aboriginal people also want to compete within the wage economy and the international economy.[29]

The differences between the change-oriented and subsistence-oriented realities exist on the dimensions of economics, language, organizational forms, technology, culture, spirituality, relationships with Mother Earth, sense of history, position within the broader society, and the purpose and value of socio-cultural networks. Therefore, the capacity for cultural competence at the family and community levels must include the skills, knowledge, and effective mutual communication to support the assessment and appropriate response to the characteristics as they are expressed. Several aspects of family life to be explored and considered in the development of culturally competent relationships include level of formal education; indigenous language skills; planning horizon (daily versus long-term); time away from the community and purpose for extended stay; standard of living; nature of employment and source(s) of income; access to community power bases; spiritual/religious beliefs and affiliation; size and structure of the "family," including transient members; use of traditional foods/medicine (depending on availability); age of first pregnancy and size of family; and expression of a holisitic perspective (spiritual, emotional, physical, intellectual).

Additional relationship building with the family will reveal further information about housing, sources of formal and informal social support; sources and processes for accessing health knowledge and skills; values, beliefs, and traditions concerning family and the traditional land base; family gatherings; access to traditional knowledge; and economic versus socio-cultural primary values. With a focus on family roles and responsibilities, the following also become important: family characteristics related to matriarchal/patriarchal lineage; roles of mother, father, nuclear family, and extended family; roles and responsibilities on the land (hunting, fishing, gathering, etc.); community roles and responsibilities; gender roles; child-care arrangements related to employment; sharing of economic resources and food; and nature of interracial relationships. Family issues and problems such as multiple poverties, challenges to safety and security; addictions and related problems such as disorganization, neglect, and abuse; intergenerational issues related to residential school, colonization, alcohol, violence, or other trauma; and barriers to geographic mobility may add complexity to the culturally competent engagement with the family.

The understanding of the family along these and other dimensions, as developed over time, will provide a context within which culturally competent care can be provided. Family members may express some degree of diversity within the family. This diversity is not necessarily related to the age of the family member, but more related to education level, life experiences, consistent interest in and access to sources of traditional and land-based knowledge, and the adoption of a less acculturated lifestyle.

In the words of Ermine et al., the term "community" refers to a system of relationships within indigenous societies in which the nature of personhood is identified by the system of relationships and not only includes family, but also extends to comprise relationships of human, ecological, and spiritual origins.[30] Cultural competence at a community level requires the understanding of the community roles, responsibilities, and systems: political, social, gender, clan, familial.[31] The understanding and appropriate response to dynamics between families and the group in the exercise of power in various forms requires experience in working with communities, which is greatly assisted by skilled advisors and culture brokers. For an outsider approaching an Aboriginal community for any number of purposes—from providing a service to selling a product or negotiating an agreement—there is a complex set of processes and protocols that, if understood, can assist the development of effective relationships. Not much has been written regarding the structure and dynamics of communities and less has been written to guide the development of cultural competence at the level of community.

CULTURAL COMPETENCE IN RESEARCH AND POLICY DEVELOPMENT

Dr. Brant Castellano has also made important contributions to underlining the importance of indigenous knowledge and unique ethical frameworks for guiding Aboriginal research, which is another form of cultural competence. She writes about a commitment to traditional ways of living: "When Aboriginal Peoples speak about maintaining and revitalizing their cultures, they are not proposing to go back to igloos and teepees and a hunter-gatherer lifestyle. They are talking about restoring order to daily living in conformity with ancient and enduring values that affirm life. The relationship between individual behavior, customs and community protocols, ethics, values and world view rest as a tree on the earth which supports us—the earth is like the unseen world of spirit—vast, mysterious and friendly if we learn how to respect the laws that govern it."[32]

The National Aboriginal Health Organization has laid out five main principles for research activities:

1. research will be focussed on the community priorities and needs;
2. methods will be culturally appropriate and respectful of diversity;
3. the research process will be transparent and inclusive;
4. research designs will be credible and of high quality; and
5. the research will respect the principles of Aboriginal ownership, control, access and possession (OCAP—collective community ownership of the cultural knowledge, data and information; control of research processes; access to data and possession of data).[33]

Cultural competence in policy development is an emerging concept to which Aboriginal women are contributing. They are asserting that traditional principles guide policy making and that a diversity of world views be taken into account in writing culturally competent policy. Janet Smylie writes that "in order for healing to take effect, we must foster the principle of respect. For changes to take place in people's health, they must have respect for themselves and their place in the world. This respect will form the foundation for all interactions and will also direct or guide any attempts to make changes in order to improve or restore health. Again, the methods and means will be as diverse as the cultures that developed them."[34]

In "Aboriginal Women in Canada: Strategic Research Directions for Policy Development," Madeleine Dion Stout and Gregory D. Kipling make a link between research and policy. The authors provide a profile of Aboriginal women and an analysis and synthesis of the literature, with conclusions and recommendations with policy implications. The purpose of the paper is to identify those areas in greatest need of further research and documentation, and to promote the development of an integrated policy agenda in which Aboriginal women's role as key agents of change is highlighted, documented, and supported. The authors suggest using an holistic principle in research to foster the interplay between all relevant policy fields. Consultation mechanisms ensure that priorities of researchers and policy makers reflect those of the Aboriginal women themselves. Research that describes women in the context of their households and communities helps policy makers see them in their socio-economic context. In addition, the elimination of attitudes and conditions that have contributed to marginalization, and a commitment to facilitating and supporting women's integration, contribute to this approach. In this way, decision-making capacity in all relevant political structures can be cultivated. The sum total of these contributions provide an excellent foundation for further developing the concept of culturally competent policy making.[35]

Madeleine Dion Stout presented a paper entitled "Social Determinants of Health across the Life-Span: Research to Policy to Action—A Cree Perspective" at York University on 1 December 2000. She spoke about "the self," including personal agency and connectedness with others. Families, with a view to cultural continuity, mutual duty, and obligation, were a second level in her concept, and communities, with their diversity and unity, were the third. Nations, including cultures, structures, and the world, were a further area of focus.[36] Stout demonstrated how a Cree perspective brings a way of understanding society and responding to the interconnectedness at a number of indivisible levels, which is an important foundational concept for culturally competent policy making in specific circumstances.

GUIDING THE DEVELOPMENT OF CULTURAL COMPETENCE

The National Aboriginal Health Organization has identified priorities for teaching cultural competence within the educational programs of health care providers. Curricula should include history of colonization and effects on Aboriginal people's health; recognition and valuing of traditional healing practices and medicines; and information about health determinants. The development of standards specific to care of Aboriginal people and related accreditation of health care delivery institutions also form part of these recommendations.[37] This is a good beginning and should be further developed and enriched with a relational perspective.

Increasingly, university and college programs in nursing, medicine, and other disciplines have begun to explore ways of teaching cultural competence, not only as it relates to Aboriginal people and visible minority populations, but also as it relates to all individuals, families, and communities. I am not sure that cultural competence can be taught in a classroom, but it can be learned, given the right mix of real-life learning experiences. The informational and skill-building components are important, as are the access to learning experiences with role models, experiential learning, supported practice, and use of multimedia presentations to demonstrate what cultural competence looks like and sounds like in behavioural and communication terms. Optimally, students being prepared for engagement with indigenous people have well-developed knowledge, skills, abilities, and personal attributes that support lifelong learning and development of cultural competence. This will provide a foundation for making effective contributions to cultural continuity and community development.

CONCLUSION

I am hopeful that I have been successful in "walking the talk" of cultural competence in making a contribution to the path many other Aboriginal researchers and writers are walking in their own way. My personal path includes the weaving together of oral tradition, personal experience, and the teachings of others working in the field. Like a braid of sweet grass, the full braid cannot exist without all three strands moving together. Each has to be of similar thickness and length, because in that way each source of knowledge is equally respected as it is brought into the braid. As is my understanding of this tradition, I have been respectful in my analysis of the work of others, acknowledging and sharing knowledge independent of its alignment with the direction of my thoughts.

Cultural competence is the human relational capacity to seek and find compassionate understanding within, between, and among people of differing cultural backgrounds and perspectives. It applies to many fields, including research and policy development. The multi-dimensional nature of relationships between individuals and groups from different cultural backgrounds and perspectives must be applied at intrapersonal, interpersonal, and larger group levels. Research and policy making is also about relationships—learning more about the interrelatedness of "all things," in the case of research, and formalizing relationships within an organization or nation, in the case of policy.

I have made my best attempt at walking the path of a spirit-led scholar. I am grateful for the support and encouragement from my wise and supportive colleagues and the spirit realms that have guided this work. I leave you with the blessing that speaks to the oneness of all things: all my relations.

Notes

1   L. Dutcher, "ANAC's Efforts Relative to Cultural Competency," paper presented at "Building Cultural Competence in Nursing through Traditional Knowledge: Our 30 Year Journey," conference of the Aboriginal Nurses Association of Canada, Vancouver, BC, 2005. Laurie M. Anderson et al. "Culturally competent healthcare systems: A systematic review," *American Journal of Preventive Medicine* 24, suppl. 3 (2003): 68–79.

2   Roberta Stout, *Aboriginal Health Nursing Project: Initiating Dialogue*, Aboriginal Nurses Association of Canada, March 2006, 6.

3   Irahapeti Ramsden, "Kawa Whakaruruhau: Cultural Safety in Nursing Education in Aotearoa," *Nursing Praxis in New Zealand* 8, 3 (1993), as quoted in Stout, *Aboriginal Health*, 6.

4   *Kitimakisowin* is a Cree concept referring to poverty "of all kinds and to the pathologies they bring about if unresolved," quoted in *An Aboriginal Nursing Specialty*, Aboriginal Nurses Association of Canada, May 2001, 5–8, as quoted in Stout, *Aboriginal Health*, 6.

5   Sunita Kosaraju, summer student within the Policy and Research Unit, National Aboriginal Health Organization, as quoted in *The National Aboriginal Health Organization Bulletin* 3, 10 (2004): 4.

6   National Aboriginal Health Organization Fact Sheet on Cultural Safety, http://www.naho.ca/english/documents/Culturalsafetyfactsheet.pdf.

7   Dianne Wepa, *Cultural Safety in Aotearoa New Zealand* (Auckland, New Zealand: Pearson, 2005).

8   Ibid.

9   L.D. Purnell and B.J. Paulanka, *Transcultural Health Care* (Philadelphia: F.A. Davis and Co., 1998).

10 S. Mutha, C. Allen, and M. Welch, "Toward Culturally Competent Care: A toolbox for reaching Communication Strategies" (Regents of the University of California, 2002), 2, as quoted in Stout, *Aboriginal Health*, 18.

11 Laurie Dokis, "Cultural Competence for Registered Nurses," *Canadian Women's Health Network Magazine* 4/5, 4/1 (2001/2002), http://www.cwhn.ca/network-reseau/5-1/5-1pg9.html.

12 Margaret Cargo, "Dr. Cornelia Wieman at the Institute for Community and family Psychiatry: The Mind-Body Connection: Stress, Depression and Diabetes in the Aboriginal Population," *Widening the Circle, Newsletter of the Aboriginal Mental Health Research Team* 4, 2 (2001).

13 Marlene Brant Castellano, Lynn Davis, Louise Lahache, *Aboriginal Education* (Vancouver: University of British Columbia Press, 2000).

14   Janet Smylie, "A Guide for Health Professionals Working with Aboriginal Peoples," Society Obstetricians and of Gynecologists of Canada Policy Statement, No. 100, March 2001.

15   John O'Neil, Judith Bartlett, Janvier Mignone, "Best Practices in Intercultural Health," Manitoba Centre for Aboriginal Health Research, University of Manitoba, June 2005.

16   Roger Poole, *Towards Deep Subjectivity* (New York: Harper and Row, 1972).

17   N. Denzin and Y. Lincoln, *Handbook of Qualitative Research* (London: Sage, 2000), as quoted in W. Ermine, et al., "The Ethics of Research Involving Indigenous Peoples: Report of the Indigenous Peoples Health Research Centre to the Interagency Advisory Panel on Research Ethics" (Regina: Indigenous Peoples Health Research Centre, 2004), 20.

18   W. Ermine, et al., "Ethics of Research," 20.

19   Canadian Nurses Association, *Blueprint for the Registered Nurse Examination*, 1999.

20   Canadian Nurses Association, *Nursing Now: Issues and Trends in Canadian Nursing*, 2000.

21   Canadian Nurses Association, *Nursing Now*, 2000, 2.

22   Ibid., 3.

23   Ibid.

24   Canadian Nurses Association, *Position Statement on Promoting Culturally Competent Care*, 2004, 2.

25   Health Canada, "What determines health?" 2003, http://www.hc-sc.gc.ca/hppb/phdd/determinants/determinants.html (accessed 6 January 2004), as cited in Canadian Nurses Association, Position Statement on Promoting Culturally Competent Care, March 2004, 2.

26   Canadian Nurses Association, Position Statement, 3.

27   Registered Nurses' Association of Ontario Centre for Professional Nursing Excellence, "Embracing Cultural Diversity in Health Care: Developing Cultural Competence," update on draft document under review, http://rnao.org/Page.asp?PageID=122&ContentID=1200&SiteNodelID=241&BL_E (accessed 17 November 2006).

28   Registered Nurses' Association of Ontario, "Embracing Cultural Diversity," 17.

29   B. Hanson, *Dual Realities – Dual Strategies: Future Paths of Aboriginal Peoples' Development* (Saskatoon: self-published, 1985).

30   W. Ermine, et al., "Ethics of Research," 5.

31   B. Downey, "Cultural Safety: Effecting and Supporting Transformative Change and Improving the Health of First Nations, Inuit and Métis People" (presented at "Building Cultural Competence in Nursing through Traditional Knowledge: Our 30 Year Journey," conference of the Aboriginal Nurses Association of Canada, Vancouver, BC, 2005).

32   Marlene Brant Castellano, "Ethics of Aboriginal Research," *Journal of Aboriginal Health* 1, 1 (2004): 98–107.

33   National Aboriginal Health Organization Policy Research Unit, "Ways of Knowing: A Framework for Health Research," National Aboriginal Health Organization, 15 April 2003.

34   Smylie, "Guide for Health Professionals" and Madeleine Dion-Stout, Gregory D. Kipling, and Roberta Stout, *Establishing a Leading Knowledge-Based Organization* (Ottawa: National Aboriginal Health Organization, 2001).

35   Madeleine Dion Stout and Gregory Kipling, "Aboriginal Women in Canada: Strategic Research Directions for Policy Development" (Status of Women in Canada, March 1998), http://www.swc-cfc.gc.ca/pubs/pubspr/0662634314/index_e.html.

36   Madeleine Dion Stout, "Social Determinants of Health across the Life-Span: Research to Policy to Action—A Cree Perspective" (presentation made at York University, 1 December 2000).

37   Downey, "Cultural Safety."

Theme 4: Arts, Culture, and Language

Teresa Marshall, *Mikmaq Worldview*, 2005

A Culture of Art: Profiles of Contemporary First Nations Women Artists

Viviane Gray

THERE IS A SCARCITY of literature on women as visual artists in Canada. In the Canadian publication on female artists, *Female Gazes*, by Elizabeth Martin and Vivian Meyer—that included, among the celebrated women artists from the sixteenth century to the present, Aboriginal artists Daphne Odjig, Rebecca Belmore, and Pitseolak Ashoona—Martin and Meyer remarked, "The task of telling the stories of Canadian women artists is a relatively recent one. This work is now unfolding, but it is difficult to find material on Canadian women artists without sifting through journals, magazines and newspapers" (Martin and Meyer 11).

It is even more difficult to find published literature on Aboriginal women and the arts. Published literature on women as visual artists focuses mainly on non-Aboriginal art, and art historical references are usually European-based. There is also no mention or definition of Aboriginal women's art in contemporary Canadian art history.

Where do we find a definition of Aboriginal art and the view and place of women as visual artists in Aboriginal art? How do we appropriately describe Aboriginal art in Canada when Aboriginal representation is made up of over fifty-six national languages and unique cultures? Does the term "Aboriginal art" fully represent art of the past and the present? An examination of the lives and art of the seven First Nations artists selected for this essay helps provide answers to these questions.

A CULTURE OF ART

In her curatorial essay, "Metamorphosis," for the exhibition catalogue of *Topographies—Aspects of BC Art* in 1996, artist, curator and historian Doreen Jensen (Gitksan) from British Columbia described the place of art in the lives of the First Nations: "In my language, there is no word for art. This is not because we are devoid of art, but because art is so powerfully integrated with all aspects of life, we are replete with it" (Arnold, Gagnon, and Jensen 1996, 120).

This explanation is consistent with other Aboriginal views of art. Métis author, playwright, filmmaker, and academic Maria Campbell says in the introduction to her book, *Achimoona*, that

> in the Plains Cree language, art is part of the mind or *mon tune ay chi kun* which translates to "the sacred place inside each one of us where no one else can go." It is this place that each one of us can dream, fantasize, create and, yes, even talk to the grandfathers and grandmothers.... The thoughts and images that come from this place are called *mom tune ay kuna*, which mean wisdoms, and they can be given to others in stories, songs, dances and art.... Stories are called *achimoona*, songs are *nugamoona*, dances are *neemeetoona* and art is *tatsinaikewin*. They sound almost the same, don't they? That is because all these words describe gifts that come from the sacred place inside [Campbell 1995].

The appreciation of art among Aboriginal people is evident not only in our beautiful cultural objects of the past and present, but in our languages, dances, songs, and storytelling. It is especially through our Aboriginal languages that we see the importance of art in our daily life, for our words describe not only the creative but the emotive images of the spiritual. In this reality, Aboriginal people belong to a culture of art, and the traditions of the culture of art of Canada's First Nations people are most apparent among contemporary First Nations artists.

At a time of heightened globalization in the twenty-first century, it is not surprising to see that the holistic view of Aboriginal life—past and present—is essential to the artistic creations of contemporary Aboriginal artists. Their works capture the knowledge and traditions of their cultural past, as well as their ingenious fusion of the past with the present for the future.

FIRST NATIONS FEMALE ARTISTS

As in other cultures, First Nations women were involved in the creative process as artisans, singers, dancers, musicians, storytellers, and performers. The artists profiled in this essay are only a selection of many women who have made outstanding contributions in Canadian fine arts. These artists were selected not only for being outstanding in their respective arts, but for changing the landscape and view of Aboriginal art in Canada.

The artists featured in this essay represent the culture of art—a trait that best describes one of the many surviving traditions of Aboriginal people in Canada. They include Jane Ash Poitras (Cree Chippewyan), visual artist and educator from Fort Chipewyan, Alberta; Rebecca Belmore (Anishinabe), visual artist and performance artist from Upsala, Ontario; Joane Cardinal-Schubert (Kainai/Blackfoot), mixed-media visual artist, writer, and art activist from Red Deer, Alberta; Shirley Cheechoo (Cree), visual artist, actor, writer, theatre director, and film director and producer from Eastmain, Quebec; Daphne Odjig (Odawa), visual artist from the Wikwemikong Reserve, Manitoulin Island, Ontario; Susan Point (Coast Salish), visual artist from the Musqueam First Nation, British Columbia; and Ann Smith (Tutchone/Tlingit), textile artist and former chief of the Kwanlin Dun First Nations, Yukon.

How do we define women's art for the First Nations when, in the Aboriginal reality, many of our Aboriginal languages are not gender-based? They do not contain the male and female differentiations found in European languages.[1] Our non-gender-based languages must have an effect on our Aboriginal psyche and it obviously played an important part in creating societies and cultures that did not divide men from women, girls from boys, and the female from the male, as in non-Aboriginal cultures. In traditional First Nations' communities, women and men are not relegated to male and female roles based on gender. Perhaps this is why feminism, as a social phenomenon, never took hold in First Nations cultures. Could this be because our non-gender-based languages did not allow us the luxury of separating place and conduct according to gender?

Many examples in First Nations traditions demonstrate how male and female roles are interchangeable. In the seventeenth century, it was reported that among the Mi'kmaq of Nova Scotia, women would train the men as warriors (Lescarbot 308). In the shamanistic society of the Medewewin of the Anishinabe or Ojibwa of northern Ontario, members included and still include today both men and women. Among the Iroquoian people, male sub-chiefs work closely with clan mothers for advice and teachings.

There is also a commonly held belief among the First Nations that we, as human beings, are both male and female. Writer and philosopher Jeannette Armstrong, of the Okanagan First Nation of British Columbia, describes this phenomenon:

> In the Okanagan, as in many Native tribes, the order of life learning is that you are born without sex and as a child, through learning, you move toward full capacity as either male or female. Only when appropriately prepared for the role do you become a man or woman. The natural progression into parenthood provides immense learning from each other, the love, compassion and cooperation necessary to maintain family and community. Finally as an elder you emerge as both male and female, a complete human, with all skills and capacities complete [Young-Ing 1991, 102].

The phenomenon of a non-gender-based society is obvious not only in the way First Nations women artists developed through time, but also through the themes in their artwork, which are not limited to female issues. As well, First Nations female artists are generally given the same level of recognition as their male counterparts in contemporary art today.

However, our basic Aboriginal philosophies are not easily transferable to the gender-based cultures of non-Aboriginal peoples, especially for First Nations women. In fact, present Aboriginal reality reveals that our First Nations traditional views of women are almost forgotten. Today's social issues, such as poverty and violence against women, are serious problems for First Nations women in Canada. In this example, violence against women is often depicted in works by First Nations artists as part of contemporary Aboriginal reality.

ART AND SURVIVAL

Despite all the disruptions brought about by the intrusion of European cultures in the lives of the First Nations, vestiges of our traditions have survived through the centuries and have contributed to our survival. One of the most valuable traditions is our commonly held philosophy of a culture of art. The history of our material culture shows that the First Nations adapted their traditional skills and aesthetics to the needs of the European colonizers by providing the early settlers with products such as baskets, jewellery, clothing, and curios and trinkets. These early trade items were used as early as the seventeenth century on the East Coast in Nova Scotia by Mi'kmaq women who traded baskets fashioned out of birch bark and porcupine quillwork with

Susan Point, *Survivor,* 1992.

COLLECTION OF INDIAN AND NORTHERN AFFAIRS CANADA.
PHOTO BY LAWRENCE COOK. REPRODUCED BY PERMISSION OF SUSAN POINT.

Alice Olsen Williams, *Midewiwin Women's Colours,* 1999.

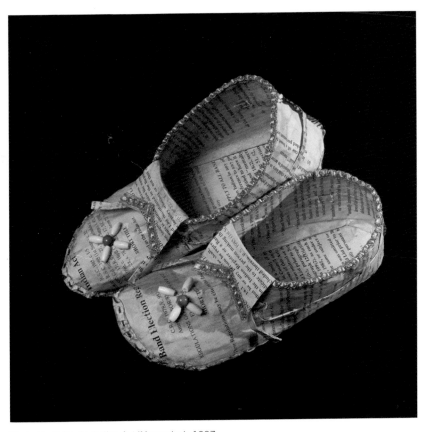

Maria Hupfield, *An Indian Act* (Moccasins), 1997.

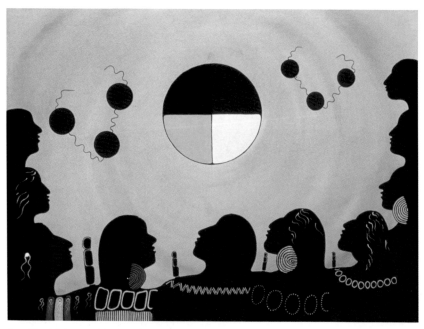

Zoey Wood-Salomon, *Meeting with the Chiefs,* 1993.

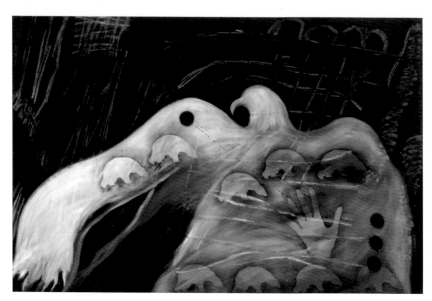

Joane Cardinal-Schubert, *My Mother's Vision,* 1983.

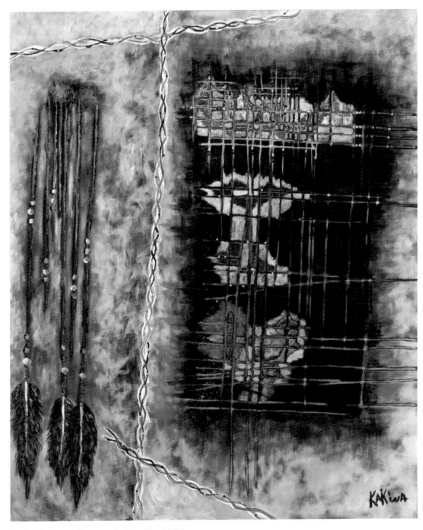

Katia Kurtness, *Fragment of Textile,* 2004.

Teresa Marshall, *Mikmaq Worldview,* 2005.

Katia Kurtness, *Our Language on 3 Lines*, 2004.

Jane Ash Poitras, *Magenta Earth Manitou*, 1986.

Joane Cardinal-Schubert, *In the Garden, My Mother's Vision,* 1987.

"This painting deliberated the state of identity I was feeling at the time. It might be best described as a self-portrait of a person caught between the worlds of traditional and contemporary. The screaming mouth is hidden by the eagle bringing a message, the arms welcoming and supportive, framed by the lodge poles and the sun dance structure, with the echo of the sweat lodge dome creating a microcosm of birth, spiritual belief and memory, self-determination, place, and responsibility of place rising out of the abyss of the times. It is a statement about Mother Earth's protection and the protection that must be returned by us all. It is the respectful acknowledgment and received directive of my *Kaniaii*, Great Grandmother Rose.

"Bobtail Chief, a caller of the sun dance, whose effort to be recorded on the band list as Mrs. Lee under the heading Indian women married to white men, pointed out her vision to me—of her concern for the future of her children and their children. I am my mother and my father and my sister and my brothers, I am my grandfather and my grandmother.... and I am an Indian."—Joane Cardinal-Schubert, 2000

Still from *Bearwalker*.

Photo courtesy of Sophie Geraud. © *Girls from the Backroads*, 2000.

Left to right: Greta Cheechoo, Renai Morrisseau, and Shirley Cheechoo. The film is set on a fictional reserve in Canada in 1976. This dark drama explores racism and abuse that explode into the lives of four sisters and the forces that lead to a fateful conclusion.

Daphne Odjig, *In the Bosom of the Earth*, 1969.

Susan Point, *Flight*, 1994.

COMMISSIONED BY THE VANCOUVER INTERNATIONAL AIRPORT AUTHORITY.
PHOTO COURTESY OF SUSAN POINT.

Ann Smith displaying her traditional Ravenstail woven dance robe with leggings and apron.

French sailors for bread and clothing. Indian "finery," as it was then called, was an important part of our economy throughout our history with the first Canadians.

Our dependency on our cultural knowledge and appreciation of our art was even more evident in our survival prior to and after World War II. Life was difficult for everyone in Canada in the 1940s, but especially so for the First Nations. Stories abound on how our parents and grandparents survived by selling their crafted products door-to-door or trading for food or clothing. This was common practice for First Nations men and women across Canada from about 1850 to 1950.

The mid-twentieth century was a period of intense changes and challenges for the First Nations in Canada. During this period, provincial and national Aboriginal political organizations were created. There was an increased interest in revitalizing Aboriginal languages and culture among First Nations, and more First Nations people were graduating from high schools, colleges, and universities.

In 1948, Kwakwaka'wakw artist Ellen Neel (1916–1966), one of the first female carvers of Alert Bay, British Columbia, played an active role in the popularization of Native art in British Columbia. Her determination to have First Nations art appear in public places such as Stanley Park and the provincial museum in British Columbia earned her an important place in our cultural history.

The 1960s saw the emergence of a pan-Indian approach to the development and promotion of First Nations art, crafts, and culture. This revival or renaissance of First Nations culture was especially evident through the work of First Nations visual artists, writers, and performing artists. Some of these artists are considered senior master artists today.

In the 1970s, First Nations visual artists emerged as strong voices in the political and social spheres. Expo '67 in Montreal prepared the path for renewed interest in Canadian First Nations art. Ojibwa artist Norval Morrisseau had a sold-out exhibition of his paintings at the Pollock Gallery in Toronto in 1972, and the Royal Ontario Museum showcased "Canadian Indian Art '74" in Toronto.

Today, contemporary Aboriginal artists are creating works of art with different materials from those used by their ancestors. They have adopted new technologies, have a new world view, and speak non-Aboriginal languages. Nevertheless, contemporary Aboriginal artists all share the understanding of *mon tune ay chi kun*, or that sacred place inside each one of us, allowing us to dream and visualize our world and to continue our culture of art. History has shown that gender differences are not a major issue for contemporary First Nations female artists as they continue their path in the traditions and world view of their ancestors. Art by First Nations women artists has always been art of their contemporaries.

JANE ASH POITRAS

Jane Ash Poitras (Cree Chippewyan) from Fort Chipewyan, Alberta, was born in 1951. Jane earned several degrees including two degrees in microbiology and fine arts from the University of Alberta and a master of fine arts degree from Columbia University, New York.

Jane Ash Poitras, 2006
PHOTO COURTESY OF CLINT BUEHLER

As an emerging artist in the early 1980s, Jane Ash Poitras quickly grabbed the attention of art dealers and collectors in Canada and the United States. Her exuberant spirit was apparent in her prints and paintings that displayed bold and colourful imagery. Throughout her career, Jane Ash Poitras has displayed a curiosity about life that is a trademark of her work. Jane is able to incorporate her broad background of American and European art history with the history and current realities of Aboriginal peoples. This is evident in her solo exhibitions, such as *Primordial Memories* (Vincent Gallery, Ottawa, 2005), *Consecrated Medicine* (Thunder Bay Art Gallery, 2004), and *Shamans and Sages* (Russell Gallery, Peterborough, 1998).

Over the past twenty-five years, Jane Ash Poitras has earned an international reputation as one of Canada's important female artists. Her artistic career includes numerous solo and group exhibitions, and her work is included in private, corporate, and public art collections throughout the world. In the 1980s, Jane's unique art style placed her at the forefront of a new generation of First Nations artists. Her style is not easy to categorize as it is a mixture of influences from the American contemporary artists Cy Twombly, Joseph Cornell, Mark Rothko, and Robert Rauschenberg, and her own. Her artwork is a testimony that critical art analysis and the continual development of new and renewed Aboriginal aesthetics as contemporary art is not only possible but important for First Nations art.

In her lifetime, Jane received numerous awards, including becoming a member of the Royal Academy of the Arts and a recipient of the National Aboriginal Achievement Award for Arts and Culture in 2006. She is also known for her social and art activism. In 1990, Jane joined other First Nations Alberta artists Joane Cardinal-Schubert, Faye HeavyShield, and others in a demonstration against the sale of the Alberta Arts and Crafts Collection at a local auction in Edmonton, Alberta. These Alberta artists managed to save the important collection, which was purchased by the Department of Indian and Northern Affairs for a future Aboriginal art gallery or museum in Alberta. In addition, she has been a mentor to many young First Nations artists in Alberta.

Jane has raised a family while working full-time as an artist and teaching at the University of Alberta.

REBECCA BELMORE

> I have with me the influence of my Kukum (grandmother) and my mother. I can see their hands at work. Hands swimming through the water, moving earth and feeling sky: warm hands. I can see their hands touching hide, cloth, and bead creating colour beauty: work hands. I look at my hands and I am aware of their hands. That is how I wish to work.
> — Rebecca Belmore, 1989

Rebecca Belmore was born in 1960 in Upsala, Ontario, and is a member of the Lac Seul First Nations. She is a graduate of the Ontario College of Art. Since the 1990s, she has been at the forefront of artistic multimedia projects that combine the visual arts, film and video, and performance. Rebecca Belmore's unique artistic style and her portrayal of Native women have earned her an international reputation as a socially engaged artist with a focus on the realities of Native women. Rebecca pushes the boundaries of women's art in various art forms by representing social and economic injustice, environmental issues, as well as personal issues of identity, loss, and love.

Belmore displays a unique ability to combine the Aboriginal traditions of natural aesthetics, storytelling, song, and dance into contemporary forms of performance art, installations, multimedia, and visual arts. This has not only produced memorable art, but has provided her with the forum to deliver poignant and unforgettable moments that include poetic imagery and strong political and social statements.

One of Belmore's better known performances was *Exhibit #671B* in 1988. This quasi-sit-in/performance/demonstration/museum installation was held at the Thunder Bay Art Gallery, Thunder Bay, Ontario. The artist represented herself as a living Aboriginal artifact that had been excluded from the exhibition, *The Spirit Sings*, by the Glenbow Museum in Calgary, Alberta. This performance was in support of the land claim by the Lubicon Cree and helped to demonstrate how they were affected by Shell Oil, who had sponsored *The Spirit Sings* exhibition.

Early in her artistic career, one of Rebecca's signature performances was her miniature dioramas, which were displayed on top of large hats. These dioramas were usually worn at art openings and would represent her personal artistic statements or a political statement of the moment.

In 2005, Rebecca Belmore was honoured for her body of work at the fifty-first Venice Biennale, one of the world's most prestigious cultural art events. Rebecca was the first Aboriginal woman to represent Canada there. For the event, she created a part-sculpture, part-video installation entitled *Fountain*. A video captured the artist in a dramatic ritual of retrieving water and throwing it onto the video screen, or the "face of the viewer." The artist recreated the painful and arduous tasks of surviving the perpetual effects of European colonization.

Rebecca Belmore's artistic career spans almost twenty years. This is a feat for any artist, but even more so for a performance artist, whose works defy the need for economic viability and collectors, as they are created for the moment—for the event—for the memory. The lack of permanence in Belmore's choice of art is, paradoxically, permanent in terms of being part of the Aboriginal culture of art. It includes the semblance of the past through language, memory, storytelling, dance, and song, and incorporates the present through her use of ready-made and natural objects such as water, earth, wind, and fire. In this way, her work represents the most permanent and yet impermanent of all creations: memories.

JOANE CARDINAL-SCHUBERT

Joane Cardinal-Schubert (Kainai/Blackfoot) was born in 1942 in Red Deer, Alberta. Joane studied for three years at the Alberta College of Art and obtained a bachelor of fine arts degree, double major in printmaking and painting, from the University of Calgary. She also received an honorary degree from the

University of Calgary in 2003. Joane was elected to the Royal Academy of the Arts in 1986 and received the Commemorative Medal of Canada in 1993 for her contributions to the arts. In 2006, upon its seventy-fifth anniversary celebration, the Alberta College of Art and Design board of governors presented the artist with the Alumni Award of Excellence in recognition of exceptional achievement in art and design. In 2007, Joane received the Arts and Culture Award from the National Aboriginal Achievement Foundation.

Joane was encouraged to study the visual arts early in her life by her father. Her family also includes her brother, the well-known architect, Douglas Cardinal. This artistic family brought a broad scope to the artistic career of Joane Cardinal-Schubert. In her career, Joane has achieved an international reputation as a multimedia visual and installation artist. She is also a writer, lecturer, freelance curator, and director of film and video, as well as an ardent arts advocate, especially for Aboriginal arts and artists.

Cardinal-Schubert's paintings and art installations have been recognized for their strong social commentaries and masterly skill of the art media. Her body of work over the past thirty years has brought her critical acclaim from Canadian and international art circles, and has been included in prestigious publications, art exhibitions in major art galleries, and museums in Canada and abroad.

Joane is known for her artistic work as one of Canada's best contemporary visual artists, but also for her strong social leadership role in helping young, urban Aboriginal artists. Her advocacy for Aboriginal art includes working with the Aboriginal Arts Society in Calgary since 1988 and with the Society of Canadian Artists of Native Ancestry. Her most recent art commission was the creation of a large-scale sculpture, "Drum Dancer—Messenger, AKA Painted Pony," in 2005 at the Calgary International Airport.

Joane Cardinal-Schubert has raised a family while working full-time as an artist. She currently lives and works in Calgary, Alberta.

SHIRLEY CHEECHOO

> A human beomg who has a vision is not able to use the power of it until after they have performed the vision on earth for people to see.
> —Black Elk, Olga Sioux

Shirley Cheechoo (Cree) is from Eastmain, Quebec, and was born in 1952. She is an artist, writer, award-winning actor, and a film director and producer with an international reputation. Among her many accomplishments, Shirley is the founder of the very successful De-ba-jeh-mu-jig Theatre of Manitoulin Island. Shirley Cheechoo is also the first Canadian Aboriginal woman to write, produce, direct, and act in her own feature-length film, *Bearwalker* (2000; formerly known as *Backroads*), which won acclaim from notable film festivals such as the Reel World Film Festival, the San Francisco Film Festival, and the Sundance Film Festival. The film is set on a fictional reserve in Canada in 1976. This dark drama explores racism and abuse that explode into the lives of four sisters and the forces that lead to a fateful conclusion.

Shirley Cheechoo
PHOTO COURTESY OF THE ARTIST.

Shirley Cheechoo's filmography is extensive, including *Johnny Tootall* (2005; writer and director), *Silent Tears* (1998) (director, producer and actor), *In Shadow* (2003; director), and *Pikutiskaau (Mother Earth)* (2003; director and producer). As well, Shirley has acted in films such as *Christmas in the Clouds* (2001), *Johnny Greyeyes* (2000), *Silent Tears* (1998), and *Song of Hiawatha* (1997), and television productions such as *The Rez* (1996), *Medicine River* (1993), and *Spirit Bay* (1984). Shirley Cheechoo's work has given Aboriginal perspective an important place in film and video.

Shirley Cheechoo is married to artist Blake Debassige and lives in M'Chigeeng, Manitoulin Island, Ontario, with her family.

DAPHNE ODJIG

> There's nothing else that I like to do more than creating something out of my mind and heart, nothing else. I live it. I eat it. I breathe it. I once said I was born with a paintbrush in my hand! Really!—Daphne Odjig, 1992

Daphne Odjig (Odawa) was born in 1919 and raised on the Wikwemikong Reserve, Manitoulin Island, Ontario. Daphne is a self-taught artist who began painting at an early age and was encouraged by her parents to pursue her

Daphne Odjig
PHOTO COURTESY OF FRED CATTROLL.

talents. Over the course of an artistic career that spanned forty-five years, Daphne developed a very personal painting style that was partially based on the Woodlands school of art.

From her early realistic drawings of the people of the Wikwemikong and northern Manitoba communities in the 1960s, to the Woodlands-style paintings and drawings of Anishinabe legends and the cubist abstract works of the 1970s, Daphne Odjig's body of works displays a wide range of styles so characteristic of her constant curiosity and creativity. However, it is in the works produced in the 1980s and the 1990s that we see the birth of Daphne Odjig's unique style. The artworks from this period retain some elements of her earlier styles, but her later works explode with new colour and movement. Her later works are more autobiographical, expressing a feminine point of view by a woman who has realized the beauty and strengths of her life as a First Nations woman.

Daphne Odjig is one of the first Aboriginal women artists to exhibit her work in art galleries with other artists of the 1960s, at a time when only a few other Aboriginal artists were part of the Canadian art scene. Over the past forty-five years, she had numerous national and international exhibitions of her work. One of her first major exhibitions was held at the Canadian Pavilion at Expo '70 in Osaka, Japan. One of the most important exhibitions of her career was a retrospective exhibition of her works from 1946 to 1985, organized by the Thunder Bay National Exhibition Centre and Centre for Indian Art in 1985. This exhibition travelled to the McMichael Canadian Art Collection, Kleinberg, Ontario; the Woodland Cultural Centre Museum, Brantford, Ontario; and Laurentian University, Sudbury, Ontario.

Daphne is also a social activist in support of Aboriginal rights, especially for the recognition of Aboriginal art and artists. Some of her accomplishments include her involvement as co-founder of the Indian/First Nations' artist group, the "Indian Group of Seven," in the 1970s, which included artists Norval Morrisseau, Jackson Beardy, Alex Janvier, Carl Ray, Eddy Cobiness, and Joseph Sanchez. All these artists, including Odjig, became notable artists in their own right and affected changes in the Canadian Indian art movement. Morrisseau, Ray, Cobiness, and Beardy are now deceased, but Janvier, Sanchez, and Odjig are still active contemporary artists whose works have influenced generations of First Nations artists.

Daphne Odjig has received numerous honours and awards in recognition of her life accomplishments, including the Governor General's Visual Arts

Award in 2007, the National Aboriginal Achievement Award in 1998, appointment to the Royal Canadian Academy of Arts in 1989, the Order of Canada in 1986, and numerous honorary doctorates from Canadian universities. The most distinctive honour was in 1978 with the presentation of an eagle feather by Chief Wakageshigon on behalf of the Wikwemikong Reserve in recognition of Odjig's artistic accomplishments—an honour previously reserved for men to acknowledge prowess in hunting or war.

Many books and art catalogues discuss the work of Daphne Odjig. In particular, *A Paintbrush in My Hand* by Rosamond Vanderburg and Beth Southcott, published in 1992, is one of the best publications on Daphne Odjig, as it was written in collaboration with the artist and is both an excellent biographical and art historical publication.

Daphne Odjig, artist, mother, and grandmother, is recognized by the First Nations community as a cultural icon. She presently lives in British Columbia with her husband and family.

SUSAN POINT

> The task of my generation is to remember all that was taught, and pass that knowledge and wisdom onto our children.
> —Susan Point

Susan Point (Coast Salish) from the Musqueam First Nation, British Columbia, was born in 1952. She is known as one of the most dynamic creative artists today. Susan has been developing her work as sculptor, jeweller, and mixed media artist for the past twenty-five years, and is one of the few female West Coast First Nations artists to achieve international recognition as a visual artist. Her ability to blend traditional forms and designs of the Coast Salish culture into contemporary works of art has brought her enormous success. Her recent accomplishments include commissions for large-scale sculptures at the

Susan Point
PHOTO COURTESY OF THE ARTIST.

Vancouver International Airport as well as for the new Museum of the American Indian of the Smithsonian Institution in Washington, DC.

Susan studied the traditional art forms and designs of the Coast Salish people. Her use of the traditional Salish object, the spindle whorl (an elaborately carved wooden disk used to spin wool traditionally used by women), has become one of her trademark symbols. Many of her contemporary designs for her silkscreen prints, sculpture, glassware, and jewellery include variations of this circular design. For example, one of her most notable public art commissions, for the Vancouver International Airport terminal in Richmond, British Columbia, in 1994, entitled *Flight,* includes an oversized, carved, red cedar spindle whorl (seventeen feet in diameter) flanked by two cedar Coast Salish welcome figures.

Susan Point was awarded an honorary doctorate in fine arts from the University of Victoria, British Columbia, in 2000; was appointed to the Royal Canadian Academy of the Arts in 2004; received a National Aboriginal Achievement Award for the Visual Arts in 2004; and received the Order of Canada in 2006. Her art is included in numerous private and corporate collections and in major art galleries and museums in Canada and abroad.

Susan Point lives and works in Vancouver, British Columbia.

ANN SMITH

As I weave on these traditional garments, I feel a sense of peace and satisfaction that I am contributing towards a rebirth of our culture.
—Ann Smith, 2004

Ann Smith is a Tutchone/Tlingit artist from the Kwanlin Dun First Nations in the Yukon. She credits her education to her parents, who taught her valuable family traditions as well as the traditional skills of sewing, beading, tanning hides, and making clothing and footwear. Before becoming an artist, Ann Smith was active in politics and was elected chief of the Kwanlin Dun First Nation near Whitehorse, Yukon.

In the early 1990s, Ann Smith studied the lost art of Chilkat and Ravenstail weaving from American weaver Cheryl Samuel. To further her research on the lost art form, Ann also travelled throughout the Yukon and Alaska, learning more of the traditional weaving techniques from Tlingit elders. Over the past two decades, Ann has made several blankets and dance or ceremonial regalia in the Ravenstail and Chilkat weaving styles.

Ravenstail weaving uses an ancient technique also known as the "twining technique." It is noted for its geometric patterns and was usually done mainly in black and white sheep's wool with some yellow wool intertwined throughout the geometric pattern. It is said that Ravenstail weaving originated from south-east Alaska and northern British Columbia.

Chilkat weaving may have originated with the Tsimshian and was adopted by the Chilkat people from the northern Pacific Coast. The Chilkat comprise a family within the Tlingit language group on the Alaskan coast between Cape Fox and Yakutat Bay. More generally, the term, "Chilkat weaving," applies to any garment woven by these peoples. Chilkat weaving has curvilinear forms and is characterized by box-like shapes, faces, and colours. Chilkat blankets will add blue to the usual black, white, and yellow of the northwest coast Ravenstail weaving style.

Ann's intense interest in this tradition has given her and the people of the Yukon renewed pride in the art of Chilkat weaving. In her weaving, Ann uses traditional materials, such as mountain sheep's wool, natural dyes from the Yukon plants and vegetation, cedar bark, and the horns and hoofs of the mountain sheep.

Ann Smith's woven works of art are exhibited in Canada and throughout the world. In 2003, she participated in the art festival and traditional weaving exhibition *Toi Maori—The Eternal Thread* in Porirua, New Zealand with other Aboriginal artists.

One of Ann Smith's woven masterpieces, a fully hand-woven dance regalia, is included in the living collection of the Department of Indian and Northern Affairs. The Indian and Northern Affairs Aboriginal art collection is referred to as a "living collection" because the department allows the artists to present their works in their exhibitions or for ceremonial purposes. Ann's dance regalia includes the dance robe, *Box within a Box* (1993), woven in the Ravenstail technique; the Ravens tail dance apron, *Knowledge from the Stars* (1992); and the Ravenstail leggings, *Shadow from the Trees* (1991). Ann created the whole dance regalia in a three-year period. Another of her most beautiful pieces is titled *Grandmother's Robe*, a hand-woven, full-bodied robe that integrates ancient twining techniques and took eight months to complete.

Ann Smith is a mother and grandmother, and is currently taking care of her grandchildren and weaving a full-size ceremonial Chilkat blanket robe. She also plays an active role as a cultural activist with Yukon artists, and in promoting the idea of an Aboriginal Cultural Centre in Yukon.

CONCLUSION

The artists profiled in this chapter as First Nations women in contemporary life defy the common notions of Western feminism. Their lives and work as artists broadens the definition of First Nations women. They are not only strong. They represent strength, for they have all overcome obstacles in their lives to reach personal and professional success. They are caring and compassionate as women in female roles—as grandmothers, mothers, daughters, aunts, sisters, and friends. They are also innovators in the arts as they have all mastered various mediums of their art forms and have pushed the limits of their individual potentials and creativity. They are also role models for all First Nations people as successful individuals who proudly identify themselves as Aboriginal. Their personal contributions as artists have also reinforced the identity and definition of contemporary Aboriginal art in Canada.

Notes

1   The term "non-gender" as used in linguistics by J.A.A. van Berkum (1996, 4): "there is no gender in the Uralic family, several of the major families of Asia, and most of the languages in America."

Looking for Stories and Unbroken Threads: Museum Artifacts as Women's History and Cultural Legacy

Sherry Farrell Racette

THE RELATIONSHIP BETWEEN First Nations and museums began in the initial years of contact. Museums originated as colonial treasure chests, the material evidence of empire. Explorers, adventurers, and traders acquired "curiosities" for people engaged in collecting a wide array of natural and cultural materials from "new worlds." Consequently, the oldest surviving elements of our collective visual culture often lie in museum collections thousands of kilometres from their communities of origin. The surviving details of their acquisition and origins are usually vague. A hide and quillwork tunic identified as "a Match-coat from Canada" was probably collected from the St. Lawrence River region.[1] It appeared in a 1656 inventory of items acquired by John Tradescant, a noted gardener, world traveller, and collector of "curiosities." A set of quillwork accessories, acquired on an early voyage to Hudson Bay, was presented to John Bargrave, the Canon of Canterbury, some time before 1676 for his private museum.[2] James Isham, a Hudson's Bay Company fur trader posted at York Factory and Churchill from 1732 until his death in 1761, acquired items now in the United College Collection at the Royal Scottish Museum in Edinburgh.[3] Cabinets of "curiosities" were displayed in private homes and occasionally made accessible to the public. European scientists and intellectuals developed increasingly complex systems of classification to organize both their growing knowledge and their expanding collections. This is the persistent colonial legacy of museums, the organization and arrangement of natural and cultural materials that engage the observer in the wonders of the world, while simultaneously constructing a trajectory of development that classifies human societies along a continuum that ranges from the primitive to the civilized.

Over time, the language used to describe objects in museums has shifted from "the curiosity" to "the artifact" and, more recently, "the ethnographic object." A typical definition of the ethnographic object is "an object made, modified or used by man and collected and documented for the interpretation and descriptive study of human culture."[4] The emergence in the twentieth century of the notion of "primitive art" as an area of appreciation and collection further removed some objects from their context, isolating them for aesthetic contemplation and basing their selection on a combination of Western aesthetics, exotic appeal, and perceived symbolic content.[5] The primitive art movement took objects out of museums and into art galleries and collectors' homes to be exhibited in the same manner as, and frequently with, other works of art. Barbara Appelbaum explains how an object can shift from being ethnographic to a work of art: "If the purpose of the object in its setting is to shed light on the culture that made it or the people who used it, then it is an ethnographic object.... If we wish to see the piece as it came from the creator's hands, it becomes a work of art; if we are more interested in how it looked when it was being used, then it is by definition an ethnographic object."[6] The irony for First Nations communities was that much of our rich visual culture was removed from both our physical and intellectual control.

Museum concepts, of course, did not exist in indigenous languages, although new words have been developed to discuss and name these phenomena. In Algonquian languages, objects are animate (containing or embodying a creative life force) or inanimate.[7] The Cree language has two categories of objects: *oseechigun* or *oseetahinu*, that which is created; and *apucheechigun* or *apucheetahinu*, that which is useful.[8] There are also words for things that are beautiful, things that are wonderful, things that are well made, accumulations, and collections. The notion that special objects should be cared for and kept for future generations was also an indigenous concept. Objects of importance, such as wampum belts, pipes, drums, and a range of ceremonial objects, had keepers or caretakers who were entrusted with their care and proper use.

By the 1970s, Canadian museums began to engage and consult First Nations communities, partially in response to increased demands for access to cultural materials, particularly items of a sacred or ceremonial nature. The controversy surrounding the 1988 *Spirit Sings* exhibition and the resulting Task Force on Museums and First Peoples accelerated the process.[9] This was part of a global wave of pressure from indigenous communities to reclaim and re-establish control over how individual items were named, exhibited, and housed. Curators became increasingly aware of the cultural meanings attached to the objects in their care.

In 1989, oblivious to the evolving semiotics within the museum field, I had my first opportunity to sit quietly with some very old things. I was awed by their age, but I was most struck by their familiarity. I recognized the sewing techniques that I had been taught and the careful tiny stitches that marked a well-made garment. I imagined a long invisible thread that stretched across the centuries and connected the thread in my needles to the fine strands of sinew used by the unknown women who lived long ago. It was an opportunity to learn from the masters. Over the years, I have returned to the slides and drawings made during that first research trip, and each time I see something new. They are objects encoded with knowledge, although they are sometimes impenetrable and difficult to understand. Most often sleeping on a shelf in a museum storage room, completely decontextualized from their cultures of origin, they are the raw material of women's history. Through the power of colour and design, the objects in museum collections not only speak a powerful aesthetic, they also reveal critical information about the worlds and circumstances in which they were created. Connecting to archival records, the oral tradition, and embedded knowledge within First Nations languages greatly enriches our capacity to understand the stories these objects tell.

Women's voices are often conspicuously absent from historic documents. Women have left few written records of their lives, and early observers and the anthropologists who followed them often ignored or diminished their activities, primarily being men interested in the doings of other men. However, if we remember that women created most of the material in museum collections, even if much of it was used by men, we can see it as a remarkable intellectual, technical, and artistic legacy. Women's artistic work gives evidence to the critical role they played in integrating new materials and ideas, while simultaneously maintaining a certain stable and continuous core of ancient knowledge. Collectively, the objects tell a story, accumulated as they made their way from their makers' hands to museum shelves. It is a story that recounts the important roles women played in communicating visual information to an audience of humans, animals, and spirits; these women who clothed their families, negotiated change, and contributed to the economic survival of their communities.

SOLICITING LUCK AND HONOURING THE NATURAL WORLD

A major focus of women's energies was the preparation of furs and hides and the construction of clothing for their families. This was not only important in terms of survival and economic pursuits, it was one of several strategies that women employed to maintain balance with the natural world. For the most part, hunting big game was men's work, but once the kill was made, it entered the women's domain, where it was transformed. The hide was taken, the meat carefully cut, and decisions were made regarding preservation for future use, immediate needs, and distribution throughout the community. Stories collected by Naomi Adelson from her Cree research consultants at Whapmagoostui on James Bay speak of a uniquely female relationship between women and the animals upon which they relied.[10] In Cree oral tradition, the spirit of the caribou is female: *pihkutiskwaauu*, the Lady Spirit of the Caribou.[11] In one story, two hunters made a shaking tent where they are told they would soon kill two caribou:

> They were given instructions about how to take care of these caribou. They had to be extra careful ... if [they] did not take care of the caribou well, it would be [their] last time killing anything.... One of the men remembered what they were told and took extra care and handled the caribou with great respect and care.... The one who was very careful had ... instructed his wife to take care of the skin well and to make it very good and beautiful.... When a shaking tent was held for the purpose of asking for caribou.... the spirit of the caribou [asked], "I want to see for myself, to see how you took care of me." The spirit said that, meaning it wanted to see how they had softened and tanned the cariboo skin. The man who had been careful told his wife, "Put the caribou skin that you softened and tanned inside the shaking tent." His wife put the caribou skin inside the shaking tent. The caribou spirit was expressing its happiness and thankfulness about the caribou skin it was seeing.... So as it happened he [the one who was careful].... As soon as he left the family he killed some caribou. As for the other family I guess they perished because they could not survive themselves. The man and his family lived because he had done what he was told to do and he had pleased the pihkutiskwaauu when he showed how well he had taken care of it.[12]

Finely tanned and embellished hides were a means of communicating respect to the all-seeing spirits, and sending a hunter into the bush dressed in fine clothing pleased the animals.[13] The practice of embellishing hunters extended onto the animals on which the hunter depended, the dog and the horse, and his hunting tools, such as shot pouches, game bags, and gun sleeves.

One of the items returned to Canada with the Speyer collection, a painted caribou skin (circa 1740) embellished with porcupine quillwork, brass cones, and animal hair was associated with the *makushan*, a feast held to honour the caribou spirit and seek luck for hunting.[14] The *makushan* is still part of Innu life in Quebec and Labrador. A wide variety of men's hunting coats, carefully painted with similar designs that evoke animals, plant life, and trails, were also collected from northern Cree, Anishinabe, and Innu territory.[15] One such Cree or northern Anishinabe coat in the collection of the Glasgow Museum is painted with a geometric design that appears to symbolize a beaver. A pair of coats, once in the Wellcome Historical Medical Museum and now housed separately at the Pitt Rivers Museum in Oxford and the British Museum in London, are painted with large, stylized shapes resembling humans and horned animals.[16]

Across a wide spectrum of First Nations, luck or good fortune and one's ability to attract good fortune take a tangible, almost personified form. Luck is capricious, easily distracted, and easily offended. The spirits of the natural world, on which survival depended, watched carefully. Those enjoying good fortune needed to be careful, respectful, and humble, lest luck and the animals abandon them. Women were charged with the responsibility of visually communicating that respect and soliciting the approval of the animals. In Anishinabe, the word for hide or leather is *bashkwegin*, an inanimate noun, but nouns identifying specific animal hides such as *amikwayaan* (beaver skin) and *waawaahkeshiwayaan* (deer hide) are animate. *Asekaan*, the word for tanned hide, is also animate.[17] Similarly, in Cree, *uska'kin*, a fresh or green hide, and any words using the stem *pahkekin* are inanimate, but if the stem *wayan* is used in conjunction with the name of an animal, it becomes animate as in *atihko-wayan* (caribou hide) or *apismoswayan* (deer hide).[18] The original media used for embellishment were also animate. *Mekis*, which literally translates as "shell," the Cree word for bead, and *mekwun* (quill) are animate. Similarly, the Anishinabe term for beads, *manidoo minens* (spirit seeds), is also animate. Both *mekis* and *manidoo minens* can be confirmed in the archaeological record as having been the original beads used by the Cree, Anishinabe, and others.[19] Women worked with living media on living surfaces to construct messages for an unseen viewer, actively engaging the spirit world through their artwork. The words, as well as the meanings, attached to the original, natural media were grandmothered onto the trade goods that gradually replaced them, items that have persisted to the present time. The Anishinabe term still in use today for beadwork—*manidoominenskikaan*—is an animate noun.

NEGOTIATING CHANGE: NEWCOMERS AND NEW MARKETS

Some of the material in museums constructs a story, not only of women's artistic lives, but of their roles as producers and marketers in the changing economic lives of their communities. Raw artistic goods, such as indigenous beads, hide, fur, and finely crafted items, had always been an integral part of the indigenous trade networks that criss-crossed the continent. Then, European fur traders, explorers, and adventurers became the stimulus for a shift in artistic production. A significant proportion of the items that found their way into museum collections are clothing and accessories. This speaks to the importance of clothing to both indigenous and non-indigenous consumers. Articles of indigenous dress were often more affordable, readily available, and better suited to the climate and extremes in temperature. This was particularly important during winter and for people whose occupations required travel. The clothing essential for survival was quickly appropriated by newcomers, in both traditional and innovative hybrid forms.

Hudson's Bay Company employees adopted elements of regional Cree dress, and, by 1743, James Isham described "English Dress in these Norther'n parts ... not unbecomming to us in this part of the world,—Which is a Beaver Coate or tockey which Reaches to the Calf of the Leg."[20] The tockey, or "toggey," as it was also called, derived from the Cree *mikota'ki*. A mikota'ki was a long, straight-cut, painted hide coat, often trimmed with fur and elaborate porcupine quillwork.[21] Robert Ballantyne, writing in 1848, described it as "the usual costume of the Cree Indians: a large leathern coat, very much overlapped in front."[22] It became an essential form of winter clothing worn well into the nineteenth century at northern posts.

Women who lived in close proximity to trading posts and other outfitting centres were kept busy dressing men employed in the fur trade, often their own husbands and sons, and a steady stream of other travellers. Moccasins were of particular importance, and a party travelling a long distance might wear out many pairs before their destination was reached. Most expeditions included women hired for the express purpose of making moccasins and repairing clothing. People visiting museums often assume that the clothing and accessories they see was created for indigenous men, but a surprising volume was made for, and worn by, European consumers. The disproportionate number of remarkably similar fire bags found on museum shelves bears witness to the fact that every man who worked or travelled in Canada had to be able to make a fire. When European men returned home, these essential items were no longer required, and they often became children's playthings until they eventually ended up in local museums. Writing in 1934, the donor of a painted hide coat now in the Museum of Anthropology and Archaeology at Cambridge University told a common story. Her grandfather had worked for the Hudson's Bay Company, returning to England in 1831 or 1832. The donor had eventually inherited the coat and other items, which she remembered as the "Indian things in which we had all dressed up as children."[23]

The desire and need for these garments created a vibrant market that was capitalized on by Métis free traders on the western prairies. Women from their own communities created the bulk of the quilled and beaded saddles, jackets, moccasins, and other goods that Métis traders marketed, but quality leather clothing from other communities was also acquired through trade. Moïse Goulet, a Red River trader in the late 1860s, "did a roaring business in buying and selling suits of moose hide and deer."[24] According to his son, "he made five trips to Lac la Biche and two to Lesser Slave Lake" over the course of two seasons. "Each time he came home loaded with outfits made of moose and cariboo hides and with pelts."[25] Norbert Welsh, a Saskatchewan trader, also marketed the work of both Métis and First Nations women. Shortly after the 1885 Northwest Resistance, Welsh bought property and built a store near the File Hills Indian Agency. He wrote,

> I bought all kinds of moccasins from the Indians. They were handsome moccasins, embroidered in all colors, and trimmed with weasel fur— ermine. They were of different styles. Some were made with tops, while others were slippers ... brought to me in big packs of twenty-four or forty-eight pairs lashed together with shaggannappi [rough hide rope]. I paid from fifty cents a pair up for them, according to the quality.

> Those for which I paid fifty cents, I sold for from a dollar and a quarter to a dollar and a half, depending on the style and amount of decoration. The Hudson's Bay Company bought all my moccasins. Some were sold in this country, and some were shipped to England.[26]

Given an initial mark-up of at least 125 percent, and the subsequent one added by the Hudson's Bay Company, female producers received a very low return for their skills, artistic talents, and labour. The profound poverty in both First Nations and Métis communities in the post-resistance years provided the motivation for women to accept low prices.

As the fur trade gave way to settlement, women in some regions continued to produce and market traditional clothing for a different customer, although styles gradually changed. In the north, the police, missionaries, visiting government officials, and the continuing presence of the Hudson's Bay Company created a steady demand for beaded leather jackets, moccasins, mittens, and warm fur hats. In the western plains and mountain regions, the clothing worn by fur traders became the garb of ranchers, guides, and outfitters. Museum collections reflect the manner in which women adjusted their production to capture shifting markets and consumer needs, and form a visual record of both change and continuity.

In addition to clothing and accessories, women also began to develop and produce a range of items that met consumer demand for souvenirs to take or send home.[27] The production of goods solely intended for the souvenir market can be traced, both in historic records and museum collections, to a very early date. If the earliest items in collections were acquired as "curiosities," it did not take long for First Nations women to identify new consumers and develop products that catered to their tastes. Both the originality and longevity of these innovative art forms are remarkable. Among the first women to participate in the emerging souvenir trade were the Huron-Wendat of Lorrette, the Mi'kmaq of the Maritime region, and the Cree of Hudson Bay. Among the earliest items to be adapted for the souvenir trade were containers and baskets made of bark, splint ash, or finely woven grasses. A variety of baskets and containers, based on traditional, functional forms, was developed and marketed by First Nations women from the Atlantic to the Pacific coast. Souvenir items were generally small, easily portable, more heavily embellished, and marketed for uniquely European needs: containers for playing cards, cigars, and cigarettes; dishes for calling cards; and groups of nesting baskets. Women in different regions tended to specialize in particular items.

The Ursuline convent in Montreal had a role in the commodification and possibly the development of souvenir items in the east. There are small, decorative, bark and moose-hair objects attributed to the Ursuline sisters in museum collections.[28] The Ursulines were certainly aware of the desire for "curiosities" and documented Mi'kmaq women producing moccasins for French consumers as early as 1708. The fine moose-hair embroidery produced by Huron-Wendat women appears to have the closest relationship to the work attributed to Ursuline sisters. However, First Nations girls who attended the Ursuline convent were not subjected to the systematic efforts to eradicate culture and language that became the hallmark of residential schools 200 years later.

The objectives of the Ursulines were to francize their young charges, primarily through Catholic conversion and fluency in the French language.[29] In the words of the Ursuline, Marie de l'Incarnation: "We have 'francised' many Huron and Algonquin girls, who we then married to the French to make a good strong mixture."[30] The girls who contributed to this "good strong mixture" were not simply brown French girls. Catherine Annenontak was taken to the Ursuline convent as an infant and raised there until her marriage to Jean Durand in 1662. Yet, when she took her own daughter, Marie Durand, to the convent, the Ursulines recorded that Marie had been raised according to the customs of her mother's nation, was dressed in the Huron style, and spoke the language. Madame Durand had remained sufficiently Huron to raise her children in the traditions of her people and also supplemented her family's income with snowshoes and moccasins. One can speculate that the Ursulines incorporated traditional skills into their curricula or simply didn't interfere when older girls and women engaged in cultural pursuits, as evidenced in their tolerance of dancing "à la mode de leur pays."[31] It is likely that the little moose-hair embroidered objects that reside in museum collections tell the story of hybrid art forms that were the result of a creative dialogue between First Nations and French women that evolved over generations of interaction.

Ruth Holmes Whitehead's comprehensive study of Mi'kmaq quillwork placed the emergence of distinct decorative quilled boxes to sometime before 1750 to 1760.[32] Although their origins are hazy, the forms and designs have maintained remarkable stability and are still created by artists today. A watercolour in the Nova Scotia Museum in Halifax, circa 1791, shows three Mi'kmaq men gathered around a woman working on a small splint ash basket. At her feet sits a bark container with a lid covered with porcupine quillwork.[33] Decorative objects and household furnishings produced for market consumption make up the greatest proportion of Mi'kmaq material in museums and speak to women's energy and innovative practice, and their contribution to the economic lives of their communities. Similarly, Haudenausanee women developed and marketed a variety of items. After the War of 1812, Tuscarora women were given the exclusive right to trade their beadwork on property belonging to the Porter family close to Niagara Falls, already a leading tourist attraction. The development of tourist items for sale at Niagara Falls and other locations became the focus of considerable creative and economic activity.

By the early nineteenth century, women from Akwesasne and Kahnawake were also marketing small beaded bags and decorative objects, baskets, and moccasins. Paintings and, later, photographs document women marketing their work in Halifax, Quebec City, and Montreal.

Many of the abundance of small bags in museum collections came from the bundles and baskets of women who peddled their goods on urban streets. The provenance accompanying a small red bag with floral beadwork in the Perth Museum and Art Gallery, Scotland, stated that a Captain Robertson acquired it in 1844 at Montreal.[34] Between 1847 and 1852, Canadian artist Cornelius Krieghoff painted a series of paintings depicting local Aboriginal people, among them two paintings of a woman from Kahnawake carrying an assortment of small bags and moccasins as she trudges along a snowy road, wrapped in a white Hudson's Bay blanket.[35] These women must have been a common sight. Representations of women selling baskets and moccasins are a theme in early Canadian art, their distinct clothing and appearance emerging as a recurring motif. The paintings show women from Akwesasne, Kahnesatake, and Kahnawake wearing top hats trimmed with feathers and shawls, skirts, and leggings trimmed with fine ribbon and beadwork, or Mi'kmaq women with their distinctive pointed hoods. This probably represents a visual stereotype, and certainly a romantic and generalized image, but women could easily have "dressed up" to go to town, manipulating their appearance to attract interest or provide a visual signal to potential customers. Their continued artistic and economic activity moves into the photographic record by 1860 and continues into the twentieth century.

The economic impact of women's artistic production was considerable and is frequently mentioned in the annual reports of the Department of Indian Affairs. In 1884, it was reported that there was "an extensive business in Indian handicraft [at Kahnawake] and several of them have become well off through the sale of these wares."[36] A photograph from this time period shows two men selling an array of beaded items from a stand.[37] Kahnawake itself had become a tourist destination and was advertised among the attractions for Montreal and area.[38] Abenaki women, on the other hand, were described as travelling long distances to "dispose of ... large quantities of baskets, chip and straw hats, moccasins and other Indian wares."[39] The Indian agent at Becancourt reported that the goods produced by that community were exported to tourist sites in the United States, requiring their absence from the reserve from "June to about the middle of autumn."[40] However, the agent at St. François de Sales wrote the superintendent-general that same year to express his concern that while the Abenaki were "as prosperous as in the past [and the] basket trade still good," the growing scarcity of raw materials would soon "render the business unprofitable."[41] The Abenaki were described as financially independent with their hunting economy supplemented by "the manufacture of moccasins and mittens which they sold, but as colonization has now driven away nearly all the game, skins cannot be procured so easily." The subsequent increase of basket production was now threatening the supply of ash and birch.

The economic importance of women's artistic endeavours was not limited to the eastern regions. The 1904 report from the Department of Indian Affairs' superintendent's office in Victoria, British Columbia, also commented on the economic impact of women's production: "The Indian women, it may be remarked, are also money-earners to no inconsiderable extent; during the canning season and at the hop-fields they find profitable employment; they engage extensively in the manufacture of baskets, which they dispose of profitably to tourists and others; they cure and dress deer and cariboo skins, out of which are made gloves and moccasins; and they frequently find a market for dressed skins intact, they being useful for many purposes; mats from the inner bark of the cedar and of rags are also made, some, of which are of an attractive and superior quality."[42]

For many communities, the success of marketing and maintaining artistic quality were tied to the continuance of natural resources and their ability to participate in independent entrepreneurial ventures. Artists required the freedom to harvest raw materials, travel to their markets, and participate in public exhibitions, performance troupes, and other opportunities that were in vogue at the turn of the century. These freedoms were to be challenged.

TO THE BRINK AND BACK: PERSISTENCE AND SURVIVAL

Despite the Department of Indian Affairs' professed enthusiasm for women's artistic production, late nineteenth-century and early twentieth-century policies relating to education and cultural practice were oppressive, and the department entered the contradictory state of discouraging cultural practice on the one hand, while maintaining a steadfast expectation that communities would sustain a vigorous arts practice. According to the annual reports of the Department of Indian Affairs, girls attending residential school worked and learned in the kitchen, laundry, and sewing room. In addition to the basics of literacy and numeracy, the typical school curricula embraced cooking, cleaning, knitting, sewing, darning, and mending.[43] Every school employed a seamstress, and students negotiated the transition from the sewing traditions in their home communities to the skills and crafts encouraged by the schools. In 1893, St. Paul's Residential School in Cardston, Alberta, hired one of their graduates as a seamstress. Mary Cochrane was described as "an Indian girl, who received her training in this school. She is 23 years old.... a most deserving girl, a diligent worker, self-possessed, has an excellent manner with the younger girls, and ... having a good knowledge of dress-making."[44] Two sisters at the St. Boniface Residential School in Manitoba worked as seamstresses and the girls demonstrated commendable skill. As demonstrated by an 1895 report from an Indian agent, the Department of Indian Affairs was eager to take credit for the artistic abilities of the girls in their care: "I was shown other results of their handiwork in made up clothing, knitting, mending, patching, darning, patchwork quilts, hearthrugs, the carpet before mentioned as being in use in the dormitories, then many articles of fancy work, netting, tatting, crochet work, silk work, bead work, &c., &c. The girls are taught to do home work, cook, bake and be generally useful."[45]

The girls were being trained as domestic labourers, and, in 1893, Father Hugonard at the Qu'Appelle Industrial School reported that he had more applications "for girls for domestic service than he can supply."[46] That year, the Chicago World's Fair provided a global stage for products created by residential school students, and eighty samples from the Qu'Appelle school were included in the exhibition. Girls in residential and industrial schools across the country also participated, with their male classmates, in a wide range of provincial exhibitions and agricultural fairs that celebrated student achievement and proclaimed the success of the colonial project. Both the Royal Regina Museum and the Provincial Museum of Alberta have residential student work in their collections, much of it acquired at these exhibitions.

While residential schools introduced students to new skills and venues for their work, they also removed girls from the teaching circles of older, more experienced artists. Excellence in traditional art forms typically relies on opportunities throughout childhood to observe, play, help, engage in mentoring relationships with experienced artists, and acquire the environmental and technical knowledge needed to secure and prepare raw materials. Many of these activities were seasonal, and students were often away at school when critical events and seasonal harvesting took place. While the department moved forward with its educational agenda, it also took steps to transform the communities to which the girls would return home.

On 19 April 1884, the *Indian Act* was amended to include section 114, a clause that made the celebration of two northwest coast ceremonial events illegal: the potlatch and the *tamanawas* [grass dance].[47] An amendment in 1895 gave Indian agents on the prairies the authority to suppress the grass dance and giveaways. Department officials saw dancing as the heart of an array of interrelated cultural values and practices that were in direct opposition to their planned transformation of First Nations people into a class of skilled servants, labourers, and farmers.

In 1903, the principal at the Qu'Appelle Industrial School complained that "the dancing set" on neighbouring reserves "bitterly oppose all progressive ideas and methods and endeavour by ridicule or cajolery to get [returning residential school graduates] to join their ranks."[48] He identified participation in dance "as the first downward step in the career of ex-pupils ... once they become dancers, progressive ideas and actions are abandoned." In 1914, section 149 was added to the *Indian Act* to give the department even greater control over dance and performance, broadening its policy to suppress all forms of dance. The amendment made it illegal for any First Nations individual to make public appearances and take part in any dance, performance, or stampede "in aboriginal costume" without the permission of the Indian agent.[49] Anything other than government-sanctioned performance was illegal. Participation in such events had, according to the annual report, "a most unsettling effect." Upon conviction, offenders would "be liable to a penalty not exceeding twenty-five dollars or to imprisonment for one month, or to both penalty and imprisonment." In 1933, the phrase "in aboriginal costume" was removed with the purpose of extending "the application of the subsection" to apply "to an Indian whether he was in aboriginal costume or not."[50] Also implemented during the 1930s was an amendment to restrict freedom of assembly (section 185, 1930).[51]

The impact of these oppressive policies on traditional artistic expression was significant. A considerable volume of ceremonial objects related to prayer and dance, often representing the highest artistic standards of a community, were confiscated and removed. Museum collections are now home to much of this material. The celebration of dance and ceremony also provided the purpose for a wide range of artistic expressions. Much of the resentment directed towards dance was due to the time and energy spent in preparation. The Department of Indian Affairs, through the *Indian Act*, repressed artwork associated with any ceremony or dance and encouraged only the production of art they perceived as devoid of cultural meaning or purpose. In 1886, it was reported with satisfaction that northwest coast women had "found a ready market" among their own neighbours at a large gathering held at Quamichan village, organized to return property distributed at the recently banned potlatches. The women had brought a "large quantity of fancy baskets and mats ... to sell."[52] The report also noted that the Indian Industrial Exhibition held at Cowichan had featured high-quality bead and fine needlework, "the judges declaring that they were equal to anything of the kind they had in the exhibitions at Victoria."[53]

Not surprisingly, this time period saw a decline in the production of most traditional media and art forms, and the department began to receive complaints from concerned individuals. Officials were also becoming anxious about the economic impact of a decline in quality arts production. In 1909, the Canadian Handicraft Guild, which took an active role in promoting and marketing traditional arts unique to Canada, began a working relationship with the Department of Indian Affairs. One of their members, Amelia Paget, toured First Nations communities in southern Saskatchewan, meeting artists and promoting traditional arts. She initiated a project in 1913 that involved Melanie Blondeau, a Métis woman from the Qu'Appelle Valley who supported her family with her arts production. She described their meeting in her report:

> I ... made enquiries for the address of a certain French family, by name of Blondeau, whose women were noted years ago for the fancy work they did in quill, silk and beadwork, as well as for moccasin making.... I found that Melanie was the sole support of her family, and that she earned every cent by her excellent work ... Melanie was doing a beautiful piece of quill work (a tea-cozy) on smoked deerskin. As it was an order I could not obtain it for the Shop.... I left some deerskin and beads with her to do some work for the Guild which she was delighted to get.[54]

A quillwork tea cozy associated with Melanie Blondeau is in the collection of the Glenbow-Alberta Institute.[55] Amelia Paget embarked on an energetic campaign to have Melanie hired "on the Staff of the School, to teach the little

Indian girls." She gave her strongest endorsement, urging the Department of Indian Affairs to take "this opportunity of having such a splendid teacher, so competent in every way." The Canadian Handicraft Guild followed up with correspondence urging the department to act. Duncan Campbell Scott replied that "while the school authorities, of course, are not called upon to furnish instruction of this kind ... I think that if the Department could secure the services of this girl at a small wage, say $15.00 or $20.00 a month it would be well to make the appointment in the interests of the children of the school."[56] As a result, the Qu'Appelle Industrial School was the only residential school in Canada with a line budget item for craft instruction in the annual reports of the Department of Indian Affairs. The budget item for "handicraft instructor" appeared continuously in the annual reports from 1914 to 1931—"Salary, Melanie Blondeau, instructor in Indian handicraft."[57] On average, she was paid $225.00 annually for eleven and one-quarter months' work. During her tenure as handicraft instructor, the school was involved with great success in the Regina Exhibition.

In addition to access to skilled teachers, women needed a purpose to excel. As the emerging Indian handicraft movement was to discover, the general public demanded inexpensive goods.[58] The work produced became increasingly generic, and artists gave serious consideration to the financial return on material costs and time. However, there were still places where the purpose of arts production stimulated excellence. The organizers of the Calgary Stampede and the Banff Indian Days were able to convince the Department of Indian Affairs to endorse First Nations participation. Since their role was to provide an "authentic" presence, traditional performance with its accompanying artwork and spirit of lively competition among artists created the stimulus for both the continuation of traditional work and artistic excellence.

The Nakoda of Morley, Alberta, began to participate in the Banff Indian Days in 1889 and continued to for over sixty years.[59] The first Calgary Stampede was held September 1912, and its poster promised "The Last Great West: Expert Riders, Ropers, Cowboys, Indians, Vaqueros, Wild Horses, Wild Cattle, Stage Coach Races and Red River Carts."[60] The "Indian Village" was part of the original stampede format, and when the event became an annual event in 1923, the village's official participants were the Siksika, Nakoda, and Tsuu T'ina. The 1931 poster advertised "Indian Races and Indian Street Parades." These events provided a showcase for artists, and prominent displays of beadwork and traditional dress were an important component. Artists such as Maggie Big Belly (Tsuu T'ina) wore a hide dress with solid-beaded cape and displayed her beadwork inside her tipi.[61] Although performing "Indianness" for consumption by a white audience may seem exploitive and stereotypical from a twenty-first-century vantage point, the Banff Indian Days and Calgary Stampede provided women with a rare artistic and cultural outlet during a particularly oppressive time period in First Nations history.

The Department of Indian Affairs' response to lobbying during the 1930s by individuals such as Saskatchewan author Mary Weekes was a tentative shift in direction.[62] Efforts to revive handicraft production were undertaken in 1937 by the Welfare division. By 1940, the department reported modest returns on a modest investment. The total 1939 budget expenditure of $5895.80 was devoted to promote participation in handicraft and agricultural fairs. Only two exhibitions reported sales with a total of $8000 revenue. The Handicraft and Home Industries section in the 1947 annual report showed a remarkable degree of respect for art forms created by cultures the department had tried so enthusiastically to stamp out:

> Canadian Indians are noted for their ... ability to create useful and beautiful articles from whatever materials are at hand. For instance, in some districts many styles of basketry are made from black ash splints, woven with sweet grass. These baskets range from bushel baskets used for picking potatoes and fruits, to finely made work baskets, thimble holders, and needle books.... heavy birch bark, storage boxes and carrying baskets are made, sewn with strong roots; and in still other areas, thinner birch bark forms the foundation of various useful articles, which are decorated in fine designs with porcupine quills.... The workmanship and design are amazing—fine needlework, using tiny seed beads of many colours, or embroidering the design with silkwork. The preparing of the skins used for this work is an art in itself. Various tribes in British Columbia are noted for the exceptionally high standard of craft work produced: the miniature baskets and boxes made from fine roots and seaweed, with woven designs depicting actual occurrences; the large containers made from heavier roots and embroidered in geometric designs using cedar ... the Cowichan sweaters with designs so unusual they are being copied all over the world; the handwoven Chilcot rugs and blankets—these and many other fine hand arts are part of the heritage of Canadian Indians.[63]

The report indirectly acknowledged the persistence of traditional artists, as they acknowledged that "the Indian goods produced and marketed under the supervision of the Welfare and Training Service form a very small percentage of the goods produced by the Indians throughout the Dominion," but it was believed that the department's involvement stabilized prices and prevented exploitation "by the occasional unscrupulous dealer."

In Manitoba, a loosely organized group of women with close ties to the United Church began a handicraft project in 1958 that would evolve into Indian Handicrafts of Manitoba, Inc.[64] Women's activist and author Nan Shipley was one of the original organizers. The initiative began as an attempt to organize a handicraft display and sale at the annual Indian and Métis conferences held in Winnipeg under the auspices of the Winnipeg Community Welfare and Planning Council. The correspondence Shipley received in response to her call for quality work provides a window into the state of traditional arts production during that time. In some responses, such as the 1959 letter received from a sanatorium in Brandon, the impact of changing tastes and residential school curricula can be seen: "I only have two Indian girls at present that will do beadwork. The Indians we have here do very beautiful embroidery, crocheting and knitting, but the younger generation do not know how to bead ... they tell me their grandmothers can do it, but they themselves do not care to learn."[65] By contrast, in areas where traditional arts thrived, the proposed handicraft initiative had little relevance to most women. In 1960, Rev. Robert Lindsay, the United Church missionary at Cross Lake, reported, "There are quite a few women ... who do excellent bead and silk work. However, the 'export' market means little to them as the production of moccasins, mukluks [etc.] stays well behind the 'home' demand. It's a question of getting moose hide. The wives of those men who are successful hunters seem to have lots of work ahead.... Almost any adult woman in Cross Lake, and quite a number of teenagers, can turn out good beadwork."[66]

In 1961, the women from Island Lake, Manitoba, sent a variety of beadwork and baskets, and were still producing woven rabbit-skin clothing.[67] The same year, the Indian agent at Nelson River Agency reported that while quality beaded clothing was still available, "the greater proportion is utilized by the band members themselves." He cautioned that over-marketing could lead to a footwear shortage, "as there is only a certain surplus available.... Marketing has never been a problem as demand is always greater than the supply."[68]

The well-intentioned, but paternalistic, organizers had the intention of reviving "truly native handicrafts," but their own awareness of what that meant was often lacking and they rejected items that had been "traditional" for decades. They were also unaware of the established tradition of producing goods for a market and the continued community need for traditional clothing. As Lindsay cautioned in his earlier letter, "Generally these ladies do not prepare a lot of things on spec, but prefer to have an order for definite items in definite sizes. They like payment on the spot."[69]

The express goal of the fledgling organization was to obtain "a fair price," but it was continually hampered by the low prices demanded by consumers. A memo sent out to Manitoba chiefs in 1962 expresses these contradictions: "The Tourist or Buyer wants to buy real Indian Handicrafts, the same things Indians made many years ago.... Things priced under $5.00 sell the best."[70] However, the organization forged valuable connections with women, who shared the challenges they faced. Vina Jane Everett, the vice-president of the United Church Women's Auxiliary in Berens River, wrote Nan Shipley: "Sorry we can't make no Birch-bark articles this time of year. The best time of the year to take Birchbark is in the spring in May, but we will make them this coming spring and this month we will send some beadwork. I may go to that conference in Winnipeg if they let me go over ... lots of poor people around here who need help."[71]

Through their relationships with traditional artists, organizers learned about hide shortages and the difficulties in obtaining supplies in remote communities. At the eleventh annual Indian and Metis Conference in 1965, women discussed the difficulties of obtaining hand-tanned hide, expressed their concerns with pricing their work, and identified the high markup on goods sold through the Hudson's Bay Company and Eaton's.[72]

The chronic challenge of the Indian handicrafts movement across the country was a market that expected quality, but resisted paying a fair price for it. The 1961–1962 Indian Handicrafts of Manitoba's standard prices for beaded adult moccasins ranged from five to seven dollars, beaded leather purses were priced at four dollars, and a pair of child's mittens backed with fur sold for one dollar and fifty cents. Artists had responded to the organization's encouragement to create new craft forms. Silk-embroidered leather bookmarks were "priced anywhere from fifty cents to one dollar and fifty cents, depending on the size" and beaded leather pillbox hats with pelican-feather trim sold from eight to ten dollars. Several of these elegant hats have found their way into Manitoba museum collections. Regardless of their limitations, Indian Handicrafts of Manitoba, Inc., and the myriad similar projects that sprang up across the country, played a role in reviving traditional arts. Contemporary Métis beadwork artist Jennine Krauchi, whose mother, Jenny McLeod Myer, was an artist active in Indian Handicrafts of Manitoba, learned to bead at the Winnipeg Friendship Centre. Said Krauchi, "I was about ten when I first started beadwork. Women were teaching beadwork at the Friendship Centre on Donald Street and my mom was involved.... From the time I was quite young I was involved in this type of work."[73]

In other regions, traditional arts related to ceremony were preserved in elders' memories and a few old pieces carefully hidden from the watchful eye of the Indian agent. Significant designs and motifs were reproduced and preserved on the decorative surfaces of baskets, beadwork sweaters, and carvings. The bitter experiences of the Potlatch Law became part of the oral tradition on the northwest coast. Button blankets and other regalia associated with the potlatch had fallen into disuse and were, for the most part, a memory. As Haida elder Florence Davidson recalled:

> Before I was born, they did away with all the totem poles, just one standing by the road, a great big one. I saw a few others, too, but I don't remember where. The minister came around and made everyone cut all the totem poles down and burn them. Some houses had three poles. The minister called it "their gods." But it is not, it's to let the descendants know who they are.... The button blankets have the crests on them too.... My grandmother didn't make button blankets during my time. When they were young they had them. They didn't make them after the minister came around.[74]

Gitksan elder Fanny Smith remembered seeing her grandfather take his button blanket out of a bentwood box: "My grandfather did not really say anything. He would just take the blanket out to check and see if it was still okay. The blanket was navy with red trim and buttons. My grandfather called it gwiss-gan-m'ala."[75] She drew on these memories to create her first button blanket in 1972. While men such as Haida artists Bill Reid and Robert Davidson have been credited with the revitalization of northwest coast arts, women were at the forefront of both its continuation and its rebirth. Ellen Curley, a Nu-cha-nulth basketmaker, and another woman were among the seven artists from Canada's northwest coast who attended the 1893 World's Fair in Chicago. Female elders such as Florence Davidson (Haida), and artists Freida Deising (Haida) and Doreen Jensen (Gitksan), played critical roles in the revitalization of traditional art forms and ceremony. Doreen Jensen was one of the founding members of the 'Ksan Association and, decades later, the Society of Canadian Artists of Native Ancestry. Doreen continues to negotiate the connection between traditional and contemporary arts practice and to break new ground as a senior artist and elder. She comments, "The Kitanmax School of Northwest Coastal Art was started because we needed to reclaim our traditional performance arts for a play we were putting on called *Breath of Our Grandfathers*. Up until 1951 we couldn't practice our arts because of the potlatch ban and the danger of going to jail. Once the potlatch law was lifted, we had to reclaim our arts by relearning them."[76]

In 1951, the *Indian Act* was revised and many of the oppressive sections were repealed. Almost immediately, First Nations people began to dance again, and women across the country picked up their needles.

INNOVATION AND REBIRTH

One of the marks of a vibrant arts tradition is continued innovation and creativity. As traditional arts have been revitalized, they have also been transformed. Motivated by need, competition with other artists, or their own imaginations, women have pushed the boundaries of traditional media and form. Métis artist Madeleine Bouvier Laferte (Lafferty) of Fort Providence developed moose-hair tufting as a creative solution to the shortage of materials experienced during World War I.[77] Unable to obtain a satisfactory supply of silk thread and beads, she developed a new form of artistic expression by applying the wool punchwork techniques taught at the Catholic mission to moose and caribou hair. Celine Laviolette Laferte, Madeleine Bouvier Laferte's daughter-in-law, taught the technique to Sister Beatrice Leduc, who incorporated moose-hair tufting into her arts curriculum at the mission school. Her students carried the art form across the Northwest Territories and beyond.

The 1930s saw the addition of splintwood flowers to the Mi'kmaq basketry repertoire. Madeline Joe Knockwood of Shubenacadie, Nova Scotia, is credited with developing the flowers in 1937.[78] The flowers have individual petals shaped from splint ash and dyed with commercial dyes. However, a photograph taken in 1930 shows an unknown Mi'kmaq woman holding a simple splint flower in her hand, so it is likely that Knockwood perfected and elaborated on an existing tradition, or that several women were engaged in creative experimentation. Since Madeline Knockwood's death in 1945, women in her home community have continued to create what has become a new art form. Annie Paul is one of the notable artists who continue this tradition.

During her life, Cree birchbark artist Angelique Merasty was routinely represented as the last practitioner of birchbark biting, the embodiment of conservatism. However, in the 1950s, when the art form was still practised by a small number of Cree women along the northern border between Saskatchewan and Manitoba, Merasty was known as an innovator. She and her mother, Susan Ballantyne, had begun to sell their work at a summer resort near their home on Beaver Lake. Merasty's work was noted for its versatility and her unique biting technique that produced tiny holes in the birchbark. While other women marked the bark with lines, Angelique had developed a pointillist approach, creating patterns with tiny holes that illuminated the design. She was also a skilled bead artist, and her work in both media was distinguished by the variety and creativity of her designs. In 1956, a reporter for the *Winnipeg Free Press* commented,

> That Mrs. Merasty is versatile is seen in the many designs she has developed ... and remembered when she sits down to bite some bark. Most of her designs come from what she sees around her at her island home at the edge of thick bush land. There are many designs of leaves and flowers, an owl sitting on a stump or tree, her impression of the devil, a little boy, a deer and many other forest and lake scenes. Angelique ... is a master of her native arts. Her beadwork compares with the best ... and she develops new designs from what must be a great imagination.[79]

Other senior artists have had to wait for improved financial security before they could focus on innovation. Mary Kawennatakie Adams of Akwesasne made baskets during her lifetime. For much of that time, basket making was a subsistence activity. She learned to make functional splint ash and sweet grass baskets as a six-year-old, and, by the age of ten, she was making baskets to support herself and her brother.[80] Following her mother's death, Mary would send baskets to a local merchant, who traded them for cigarettes, and then take the cigarettes to another merchant to exchange for cash. She recalled, "Sometimes we would be sitting all night working on the baskets to get done, so we would get the money to buy groceries. That is the way we were, I don't know how many years."[81] It wasn't until Mary Adams reached her early fifties that she was able to shift from market production to emerge as an influential and important basket artist who pushed traditional forms to express her own ideas. One of her most significant artistic achievements was a special basket conceived and executed in honour of Kateri Tekawitha and presented by the artist to Pope John Paul II at the beatification ceremony in 1980.[82] In 1999, at the age of eighty-two, her work was included in the exhibition *Crossing the Threshold* at the University Art Museum, Albany, New York, which celebrated the work of thirty-two female artists between the ages of seventy and ninety-two.

More recently, women such as Dorothy Grant (Haida) and Tammy Beauvais (Mohawk) have created contemporary fashion that draws upon the skills and imagery of their artistic heritages. Dorothy Grant's "Feastwear," in particular, has been embraced as fine art. Her work has been discussed in art magazines and exhibited in museum and art gallery venues.[83] The institutional acquisitions of Grant's work are an indicator of the shifting boundaries and dissolving categories between art and ethnographic objects. Her button blankets have been acquired by the National Gallery of Canada and her high-fashion clothing has been purchased by the University of British Columbia's Museum of Anthropology. The Canadian Museum of Civilization has collected examples of both her traditional and contemporary work. Tammy Beauvais, of Tammy Beauvais Designs in Kahnawake, also draws on her Mohawk visual traditions to create fashions that have been acquired by the Heard Museum in Phoenix, Arizona, and the McCord Museum in Montreal.

RECONNECTING: MUSEUM OBJECTS AND CONTEMPORARY ARTISTS

Many artists have used museum collections as a means to reconnect with their artistic legacy, and there they find objects that have preserved artistic principles, aesthetic standards, and techniques. These objects also tell stories. A pair of eighteenth-century Cree dolls in the Horniman Museum, London, is one such record of artistic virtuosity and women's history. Collected from "Hudson's Bay," they were most probably created, not as a plaything for a Cree girl, but as a "curiosity" to be sent home to England.[84] They are hybrid objects, primarily made of indigenous materials, but incorporating bits of cloth and a few beads. The doll heads are European imports, the bodies and limbs roughly carved of wood. They speak to a particular moment in Cree history when James Bay was on the initial line of contact and women formed economic and personal relationships with incoming traders. But they are much more than that.

The tiny hide garments form an extraordinary artistic record of media and technique. The scale of the work reflects the skill of the artist. She executed four different quillwork techniques: wrapping, folding, netting, and loomwork. There is incised and painted decoration, similar to that found on painted hide coats. The dolls are also a record of indigenous clothing worn by Cree women, and, unlike documentary art, we do not have to look at them through the filter of biases and omissions of the male observer. They tell us a number of important things. They tell us that there was individuality in Cree dress, that all women did not dress alike. Each doll's clothing, while similar, has different elements. They allow us, under close scrutiny, to explore the techniques: the cut of the clothing, the seams, the placement of motifs. One doll wears a side-fold dress, another a strap dress; each has a pair of detachable sleeves with a highly decorated yoke holding them together. One wears a pointed hood and a painted robe, while the other has elaborate quillwork hair ties and holds a tiny bag. They each wear a pair of painted moccasins and leggings with a tiny quill-wrapped fringe along the outside seam. While there are a few surviving Cree women's garments scattered in museum collections in Europe and North America, these dolls provide the only record of complete ensembles and reflect the variations within a particular clothing tradition.

Many artists and museum curators have negotiated the continuing tensions between the larger museum community and First Nations to form productive relationships. For artists of the northwest coast, whose communities were so fiercely oppressed by section 114 of the *Indian Act*, museum collections have held particular importance. According to Wendy Grant, the Salish weavers at Sardis and Musqueam "taught themselves, studying examples of old weaving and questioning elders to learn whatever they remembered of the art."[85] Relationships developed among the curators, the blankets, and the women who came to see them. According to Elizabeth Johnson, the curator who worked with the women of Musqueam, "On the day the Weavers came, the blankets began to take on life again."[86]

Jennine Krauchi and her mother, Jenny McLeod Myer, have created reproductions of museum objects for Parks Canada and the Manitoba Museum. They also create contemporary traditional clothing, specializing in beaded vests and hide jackets. Krauchi says their relationship with the Manitoba Museum has helped them regain the aesthetic standards of the past: "I get a lot of inspiration from the collection.... When I was doing some of these pieces I was running back and forth to the museum.... I'd just have a good look—how did they do that piece, how did that get put in there? I'd come back and I'd work, then I'd have to go back and have another look. Then you really have a chance to see the workmanship, the detail. The tiny little stitches putting in the lining of some little bag. Who cares what the lining looks like, but they cared."[87]

UNBROKEN THREADS AND NEW STORIES

If we deconstruct the stories that museum exhibitions tell and reposition the objects along the continuum of First Nations women's history, they become the voice of women across generations, unfolding over centuries. A chronological view reveals obvious changes in style and media, but a closer examination reveals a remarkable continuity in technique, aesthetic principles, and function. These objects also tell the story of women who preserved traditional values and struggled to create beauty in a world that changed at an alarming rate. Perhaps, like Mary Adams, who said, "Making baskets is my medicine. I'll die if I don't keep making baskets," they too experienced the healing power of their work.[88] The extraordinary beauty of much of the material, often created during times of great duress and change, reflects the power of the creative process to provide respite in times of trouble and the enduring ability of women to create sacred moments through artistic expression.

The work created by historic artists sets the highest standards of craftsmanship and continues to inspire generations of contemporary artists. Traditional artists and their practice have received growing recognition from the arts funding bodies from which they had been previously excluded. The First Peoples Heritage, Language and Culture Program in British Columbia was launched in 1990 and included Aboriginal arts development awards. Several provinces have funding programs targeted at indigenous artists and include traditional arts within a general visual arts category. The Canada Council for the Arts' Aboriginal Traditional Art Forms Program includes a grant category specifically for the creation of new work in traditional visual arts, as does the Saskatchewan Arts Board's Indigenous Traditional Arts Grant Program. Women continue to wrap their families in finely crafted clothing, create ceremonial regalia, and push the boundaries of form and function. Recently, the innovative beaded hide footwear created by Dene artists Caroline and Virginia Montgrand of Turnor Lake in northern Saskatchewan has found its way into the Pitt Rivers Museum in Oxford, joining the work of their ancestors, adding a new chapter to the story.[89]

Notes

1   Hide tunic, collected before 1656, Tradescant Coll. Museum ID No. 1656, p. 47, "A Match-coat from Canada," Ashmoleon Museum, Oxford, England. Also author's research notes, 11 April 1989, Oxford.

2 Cree belt, neck ornament, and garters, Access. No. B58, collected by Tymothy Conley at Hudson Bay before 1676, John Bargrave Collection, Dean and Chapter of Canterbury Cathedral, Canterbury, England. Also author's research notes, 31 March 1989, Canterbury Cathedral.

3 James Isham was an early donor to the collection, but it is not known what specific items can be attributed to him.

4 Agreement Between the Inuit of the Nunavut Settlement Area and Her Majesty the Queen in right of Canada, 25 May 1993, Section 34.1.1, Article 1: Definitions, p. 1.

5 See Franz Boas, *Primitive Art* (Dover Publications, 1955) and Sally Price, *Primitive Art in Civilized Places* (University of Chicago Press, 1989) as works that span the development and contemporary critique of the primitive art movement.

6 Barbara Appelbaum, "Criteria for the Treatment of Collections Housed in Historic Structures," *Journal of the American Institute for Conservation* 33, 2 (1994): 185.

7 Many thanks to Keith Goulet, Cumberland House Cree Métis, for his patient assistance in helping me glean the knowledge embedded within his much beloved Cree language. Keith Goulet, personal communication, Regina, Saskatchewan, July 2005.

8 Keith Goulet, personal communication.

9 *The Spirit Sings: Artistic Traditions of Canada's First Peoples* organized by the Glenbow Museum for the 1988 Winter Olympics held in Calgary, Alberta, became a lightning rod for the growing tensions between First Nations communities and museums. The resulting controversies and protests triggered a major shift in Canadian museum practice, and a task force was established to examine policies and protocols.

10 Naomi Adelson, *Being Alive and Well: Health and the Politics of Cree Well-Being* (Toronto: University of Toronto Press, 2000), 59–68.

11 Ibid., 69.

12 Ibid., 72–73.

13 These beliefs have been widely documented by scholars working with the James Bay Cree, but material evidence in museum collections and continued practice indicates this was a widespread phenomena. See Cath Oberholtzer, "Cree Leggings as a Form of Communication," in William Cowan, ed., *actes du Vingt-Cinquieme Congres des Algonquinistes* (Ottawa: Carleton University, 1994) and Adrian Tanner, *Bringing Home Animals: Religious Ideology and Mode of Production of the Mistassini Cree Hunters* (St. John's, Newfoundland: Institute of Social and Economic Research, Memorial University of Newfoundland, 1979).

14 Access. No. 25, Speyer Collection, Naskapi painted caribou mat, Canadian Museum of Civilization. See T. J. Brasser, "News Release: The Speyer Collection; Retrieving a Piece of Canada," p. 3, Search File: Natives-Art, Hudson's Bay Company Archives, Winnipeg, Manitoba.

15 See Dorothy K. Burnham, *To Please the Caribou: Painted Caribou-Skin Coats Worn by the Naskapi, Montagnais and Cree Hunters of he Quebec-Labrador Peninsula* (Toronto: Royal Ontario Museum, 1992).

16 Painted hide coats, Access. No. ETH/NN/564, Glasgow Museums, Glasgow, Scotland, Access. No. 1951.2.19, Wellcome Historical Museum, Pitt Rivers Museum, Oxford, England, Access. No. 1954 WAM 5965, British Museum, London, England.

17 Anishinabe terms come from the work done by Anishinabe elder-artist Maude Kegg and John Nichols. See John D. Nichols and Earl Nyholm, *A Concise Dictionary of Minnesota Ojibwe* (Minneapolis: University of Minnesota Press, 1995).

18 Cree terms come from Reverend Richard Faries, ed., *A Dictionary of the Cree Language as Spoken in the Provinces of Quebec, Ontario, Manitoba, Saskatchewan and Alberta* (Toronto: Church of England in Canada, 1938) and Arok Wolvengrey, *Nehiyawewin: itwewina: Cree: words, Vol. 1 and 2* (Regina: Canadian Plains Research Center, University of Regina, 2001).

19 For a description of shell beads from a woman's hood see James A. Tuck, *Ancient People of Port au Choix: the Excavation of an Archaic Indian Cemetery in Newfoundland.* (St. John's: Memorial University of Newfoundland, 1989); Cath Oberholtzer, "Together We Survive: East Cree Material Culture" (PhD. dissertation, McMaster University, 1994), 124–126. An outline of a woman's hood in a Manitoba burial site was formed by 1641 pin cherry seed beads. Kevin Brownlee and E. Leigh Syms, *Kayasoch Kikawenow: Our Mother from Long Ago, an Early Cree Woman and Her Personal Belongings from Nagami Bay, Southern Indian Lake* (Winnipeg: Manitoba Museum of Man and Nature, 1999), 16.

20 E.E. Rich, ed., *James Isham's Observations on Hudson's Bay, 1743 and Notes and Observations on a Book Entitled a Voyage to Hudson's Bay in the Dobbs Galley, 1749* (London: Hudson's Bay Record Society, 1949), 117.

21 James Isham's Cree vocabulary listed "muska togy" in "Of Cloaths and Things Carried Abt. One &C," *Observations on Hudson's Bay*, 14. I am using the spelling given by Richard Faries, Edward Ahenakew, and John McKay, collaborators in Faries, ed., *Dictionary of the Cree Language*, 42.

22 Robert M. Ballantyne, *Hudson's Bay, or, Everyday life in the wilds of North America* (London: W. Blackwood, 1848), 59.

23 The coat itself was never worn and appears to have been acquired as a memento of William Cobbold Woodthorpe's time in North America, Access. No. 1934.151, Donor letter, 1934 Letter Box, Paper Archives, Museum of Anthropology and Archaeology, University of Cambridge.

24 Guillaume Charette, *Vanishing Spaces: Memoirs of Louis Goulet* (Winnipeg: Editions Bois Brulés, 1980), 67.

25 Ibid., 68.

26 Norbert Welsh, *The Last Buffalo Hunter* (New York: Thomas Nelson and Sons, 1939), 291–292.

27 For discussions of the development and history of indigenous "tourist art" see Ruth B. Phillips, *Trading Identities: The Souvenir in Native North American Art from the Northeast, 1700–1900* (Montreal: McGill-Queen's University Press, 1998) and Ruth B. Phillips and Christopher B. Steiner eds., *Unpacking Culture: Art and Commodity in Colonial and Postcolonial Worlds* (Berkeley: University of California Press, 1999).

28 The sisters themselves produced and marketed bark embroidery in the early decades of the eighteenth century. Ruth B. Phillips, "Nuns, Ladies and the "Queen of the Huron," in Phillips and Steiner, *Unpacking Culture*, 35–36.

29 Thierry Berthet, "La Francisation des Amerindiens en Nouvelle France: Politiques et enjeux-Frenchifing the Natives in New France: Policies and Aims," *Canadian Studies* 34 (1993): 79-89. See also Olive Dickason for a description of early French/First Nations interaction and intermarriage. Olive Dickason, "From 'One Nation' in the Northeast to 'New Nation' in the Northwest: A look at the emergence of the metis," in Jacqueline Peterson and Jennifer Brown, eds., *The New Peoples: Being and Becoming Métis in North America* (Winnipeg: University of Manitoba Press, 1985), 19-36.

30 Joseph and Vinteur Durand, *Jean Durand et sa Posterité* (Sillery, QC: L'Association des Families Durand, 1991), 82.

31 "La plus grande récréation des jeunes filles est de danser à la mode de leur pays; ces petites pensionnaires ne se livrent pas néanmoins à cet amusement sans en avoir démandé de la permission." (The greatest recreation of the young girls is to dance in the style of their country; however, these little students never begin this amusement without having asked for permission). *Les Ursulines de Quebec*, as cited in J. and V. Durand, *Jean Durand*, 114.

32 Ruth Holmes Whitehead, *Micmac Quillwork* (Halifax: The Nova Scotia Museum, 1982), 28–29.

33 Hibbert Newton Binney (1766–1842), *Mi'kmaq family group; woman making a splint basket*, watercolour, pencil and ink, P113/79.146/N-8419, Micmac Portraits Collection, Nova Scotia Museum, Halifax.

34 Beaded red bag, Access. No. 1978.438, Perth Museum and Art Gallery, Perth, Scotland.

35 *Indian Woman with Moccasins* (1848–1850), Cornelius Krieghoff, Accession No. 1989-505-2 and *Caughnawaga Indian (Quebec)* (circa 1850), Cornelius Krieghoff, Accession No. 1937-79, Library and Archives Canada. See also *Indian Moccasin Seller (Quebec) (lithograph circa 1860)*, Cornelius Krieghoff, Accession No. 1970-188-2260 (Coverdale Collection of Canadiana), Library and Archives Canada.

36 *Annual Report of Indian Affairs*, 1884, xxiv.

37 Kahnawake Men Selling Beaded Crafts, circa 1890, Neg. No. 370, Kanien'kehake Raotitiohkwa Cultural Center, Kahnawake.

38 Guide to Montreal and Environs, Illustrated with Over 30 Engravings, 1897. RB-1420, McCord Museum.

39 *Annual Report of Indian Affairs*, 1884, xxiv.

40 P.E. Robbillard, Indian Agent to The Superintendent-General of Indian Affairs, Becancourt, Quebec, 20 August 1891, *Annual Report of Indian Affairs*, 1891, 32.

41 W.H. Lomas, Indian Agent to The Superintendent-General of Indian Affairs, St. François de Sales, Quebec, 2 October, 1886. *Annual Report of Indian Affairs*, 1886, 93.

42 *Annual Report of Indian Affairs*, 1904, 290.

43 *Annual Report of Indian Affairs*, 1893, 178.

44 *Annual Report of Indian Affairs*, 1895, 114.

45 *Annual Report of Indian Affairs*, 1895, 112.

46 *Annual Report of Indian Affairs*, 1893, 178.

47 Katherine Pettipas, *Severing the Ties that Bind: Government Repression of Indigenous Religious Ceremonies on the Prairies* (Winnipeg: University of Manitoba Press, 1994), 92–93.

48 *Annual Report of Indian Affairs*, 1903, 398.

49 *Annual Report of Indian Affairs*, 1914, xxv.

50 *Annual Report of Indian Affairs*, 1933, 11.

51 Pettipas, *Severing the Ties*, 165.

52 *Annual Report of Indian Affairs*, 1886, 93.

53 *Annual Report of Indian Affairs*, 1886, 99.

54 Amelia M. Paget (1913), "Report on the Qu'Appelle Agencies," file 40,000-9, vol. 7908, Department of Indian Affairs, Record Group 10, Government of Canada Files, Library and Archives Canada.

55 Quill worked tea cozy, AR 12, Glenbow-Alberta Institute.

56 D.C. Scott to Mr. Pedley. Ottawa, 27 February 1913, Ottawa, file 41,000-9, vol. 7908, RG 10, Library and Archives Canada.

57 Qu'Appelle Industrial School, *Annual Reports of the Department of Indian Affairs*, 1914–1931.

58 For a discussion of the struggles of "Indian craft" producers, see Gerald R. McMaster, "Tenuous Lines of Descent: Indian Arts and Crafts of the Reservation Period," *The Canadian Journal of Native Studies* 9, 2 (1989): 205–236.

59 McMaster, "Tenuous Lines," 217.

60 Calgary Stampede Posters 1912 (CES 1912) and 1931 (CES 1931), Calgary Exhibition and Stampede Historical Committee Archives, Calgary, Alberta.

61 Maggie was married to an Englishman, Arnold Lupson, who took many photographs of their family and friends, Arnold Lupson Fonds, Glenbow Archives, Calgary, Alberta.

62 McMaster, "Tenuous Lines," 220.

63 *Annual Report of Indian Affairs*, 1947, 216–217.

64 Indian Handicrafts of Manitoba, Inc., was initially a loosely organized group with close ties to the Winnipeg Community Welfare and Planning Council, the United Church, and the Department of Indian Affairs. They had an annual sale and exhibition at the Indian and Metis Conference and by 1960 had a handicraft room at the newly opened Indian Friendship Centre. They were incorporated in 1963 and were closely affiliated with the Friendship Centre. Minutes, 16 November 1968, p. 1, File 1968, Box 1, Indian Handicrafts of Manitoba, Inc. (1959–1974) Collection, MG10 C49, Archives of Manitoba.

65 Vera M. Davidson to Nan Shipley, Assiniboine Hospital, Brandon, Manitoba, 8 December 1959, File 1959, Box 1, IHM Coll.

66 Rev. Robert Lindsay to Nan Shipley, United Church Mission, Cross Lake, Manitoba, 14 January 1960. File 1960, Box 1, IHM Coll.

67 C.S. Middleton, Indian Agent to Nan Shipley, 6 February 1961, Berens River, Manitoba, File 1961, Box 1, IHM Coll.

68 J.H. Sheane, Superintendent, Nelson River Indian Agency to Mrs. M. Laing, 16 June 1961, Ilford, Manitoba, File 1961, Box 1, IHM Coll.

69 Rev. Robert Lindsay to Nan Shipley, United Church Mission, Cross Lake, Manitoba, 14 January 1960. File 1960, Box 1, IHM Coll.

70 Marie Laing, Chairman for Indian and Metis Handicrafts to the Chiefs, Indian Reservations, Manitoba, August, 1962, Winnipeg, Manitoba. IHM Coll.

71 Mrs. Vina Jane Everett to Nan Shipley.

72 Minutes of the Women's Meeting, Indian and Metis 11th Annual Conference, Royal Alexandra Hotel, Winnipeg, Manitoba, February 8, 1965, File 1965, Box 1, IHM Coll.

73 Jennine Krauchi, interview with the author, Winnipeg, Manitoba. 1 August 2002.

74 Doreen Jensen and Polly Sargent, *Robes of Power: Totem Poles on Cloth* (Vancouver: The University of British Columbia Press and Kianmax Northwest Cost Indian Arts Society, 1986), 52.

75 Idid., 17.

76 http://www.abcbookworld.com/view_author.php?id=3702.

77 For a discussion of the development and diffusion of moose hair tufting see Barbara A. Hail and Kate C. Duncan, *Out of the North: The Subarctic Collection of the Haffenreffer Museum of Anthropology* (Providence, RI: Haffenreffer Museum of Anthropology, Brown University, 1989), 251–253. Madeleine Bouvier was born in 1862, the daughter of Joseph Bouvier and Catherine Beaulieu. She married Boniface Laferte or Lafferty in 1879 at Fort Providence. Madeleine Laferte claim 198, vol. 1353, series D-11-8-c, RG 15.

78 "Madeline Joe Knockwood Making Splint Flowers circa 1945," P113/N19, 341, MP 0908, Mi'kmaq Portrait Collection, Nova Scotia Museum, Halifax. "Bear River Mi'kmaq woman Holding a Splint Flower, 1930," P113/2000.4.38/N18,106, Evangeline F. Pictou and Irene Sexton Collection, MP 1167, Mi'kmaq Portrait Collection, Nova Scotia Museum, Halifax.

79 Tom Dobson, "Ancient Cree Art Goes Commercial," *Winnipeg Free Press*, 3 November 1956, p. 28.

80 Olivia Thornburn, "Mary Kawennatakie Adams: Mohawk Basket Maker and Artist, *American Art* 15, 2 (2001): 90–95. See also *Mary Adams: An Exhibition of her Work, October 5–December 14, 1997* (Howes Cave, NY: Iroquois Indian Museum, 1997); Carol White, *Teionkwahontasen: Sweetgrass is Around Us: Basketmakers of Akwesasne* (Hogansburg, NY: Akwesasne Cultural Centre, 1996).

81 Thornburn, "Mary Kawennatakie Adams."

82 Kateri Tekawitha was a devout Mohawk-Algonquin woman who died at Kahnawake in 1680. She was venerated by the Catholic Church in 1943, beatified in 1980. For a discussion of Mary Adams devotion to Kateri Tekawitha see Thornburn, "Mary Kawennatakie Adams," 92.

83   Publications and exhbitions include Margaret Blackman, "Feastwear: Haida Art Goes Couture," *American Indian Art Magazine* 17, 4 (1992) and *Feastwear: Haida Culture/The Fabric Art of Dorothy Grant*, Seattle Art Museum, Seattle, Washington, 2005.

84   Dolls dressed in Cree clothing, circa 1790, Access. No. 1976.459-460, Horniman Museum, London, England.

85   Wendy Grant (founder of the Musqueam Weavers), "Salish Weaving: An Art Nearly Lost," in Elizabeth Lominska Johnson and Kathryn Bernick, eds., *Hands of Our Ancestors: the Revival of Salish Weaving at Musqueam*, Museum Note No. 16 (Vancouver: Museum of Anthropology, University of British Columbia, 1986), 2.

86   Johnson and Bernick, *Hands of Our Ancestors*, 1.

87   The artists have worked with curator Katherine Pettipas at the Manitoba Museum for several years. Jennine Krauchi, interview with the author, Winnipeg, Manitoba, 1 August 2002.

88   Mary Kawennatakie Adams, Artist Statement, *Crossing the Threshold*, University Art Museum, University of Albany at State University of New York, 26 January–28 February 1999.

89   Indigenous Traditional Arts Grant Program, Saskatchewan Arts Board, http://www.artsboard.sk.ca/Grants/grants.shtml#latest, and Laura Peers, curator and keeper of the North American Collections, Pitt Rivers Museum, Oxford, England, personal communication, 7 May 2005, Oxford, England.

The Role of First Nations Women in Language Continuity and Transition

Mary Jane Norris[1]

FIRST NATIONS WOMEN'S contributions to community development and cultural continuity hold a personal meaning for me as well as a professional interest. Through my mother, who was reinstated as a Registered Indian under the 1985 amendments to the *Indian Act* (Bill C-31), I am personally aware of both the challenges First Nations women face and their contributions. When my grandmother "married out," she lost her Registered Indian status and left her reserve community. Although my mother did not learn her mother's Algonquin language, she did gain a strong awareness and knowledge of her culture and heritage, which she transmitted to her own children. I was also fortunate to know my great-aunt—my grandmother's sister, Sarah Lavalley, who was a mentor throughout her life to her reserve community, the Algonquins of Pikwákanagán (Golden Lake). She contributed to community development and cultural continuity in many ways: serving as a midwife and an educator in the community; providing support to those in hospitals and prisons; and teaching the Algonquin language and customs until her death at the age of ninety-five in 1991. She received many honours for her outstanding contributions, including the Order of Canada in 1981.[2]

This chapter explores the role of First Nations women in Aboriginal language continuity and transition in Canada, the challenges they face, and the contributions they make to keeping their languages and cultures alive for future generations. It considers the conflicting pressures confronting First Nations women as they strive to maintain cultural continuity, on the one hand, and ensure success in education and work, on the other. It also considers their efforts to achieve both goals of cultural continuity and community development in tandem.

Perhaps not so obvious but nevertheless significant is the impact of the *Indian Act*, particularly in relation to the pre-1985 provisions regarding "legislative" intermarriage (also known as out-marriage) of a Registered Indian person to a partner without Registered Indian status (non-status). Through these provisions (and some would argue even those of Bill C-31), the *Indian Act* has had and continues to have significant intergenerational impacts on women's roles in cultural and linguistic continuity, particularly in relation to identity, family, and community. This situation is further complicated by the factor of linguistic intermarriage, wherein a First Nations person with an Aboriginal mother tongue marries a partner who has a non-Aboriginal mother tongue, usually being one of the dominant languages of English or French.

In addressing the current linguistic situation of First Nations women, it is necessary to understand their roles with respect to the intergenerational transmission of culture through the language outcomes of their children. Using census data, a number of language outcomes are examined for both children and adults based on measures related to mother tongue, home language, and language knowledge or ability. Patterns of language transmission and acquisition can be derived from an analysis of these different measures.

The analysis is provided in two parts. The first part looks at the linguistic outcomes of those children whose mothers have an Aboriginal mother tongue by family type and by place of residence. The second part explores mother-child transmission in relation to the viability of the many different First Nations languages. The analysis demonstrates the significance of First Nations women's linguistic marriage/parenting patterns and their residence within reserve communities in their roles in language continuity and transition.

This chapter concludes with a discussion on the outlook for First Nations women in language revitalization and maintenance by addressing their challenges, contributions, and the recognition of their roles. It considers the many challenges of language continuity confronting First Nations women today—challenges exacerbated by both legislative and linguistic intermarriage, marital and family dissolution, migration from communities, and urbanization—as well as challenges more common to women and minority languages in general, such as globalization and the significant demands of balancing conflicting pressures of cultural and linguistic continuity against increasing mainstream forces. At the same time, the chapter highlights the contributions of women within families and communities in a number of roles: as parents (in the transmission of First Nations languages to their children), community leaders, entrepreneurs, and language practitioners and teachers. Finally, it underlines two aspects of recognition and support critical to First Nations women in balancing traditional and mainstream pressures; first, in relation to the importance of women's roles in maintaining linguistic continuity within their families and communities; and second, in relation to the importance of incorporating traditional values of language and culture in education, community well-being, and economic development.

OVERALL STATE OF ABORIGINAL LANGUAGES IN CANADA

Language transmission from one generation to another is the major factor in Aboriginal language survival and maintenance. Like other minority languages, the continual exposure to the more dominant languages, with the necessity for their use in everyday life, is a powerful catalyst for the decline of Aboriginal languages. Many of Canada's Aboriginal languages are endangered and have already suffered great losses due to the forces of colonization, their outlawing in residential schools, the influence of dominant languages, and possibly the fact that many Aboriginal languages are predominantly oral.

The variety in Aboriginal culture and identity is reflected in Canada's Aboriginal languages, which are many and diverse. Today, some fifty individual languages belong to eleven Aboriginal language families or isolates (languages that cannot be related to any of the major families): ten First Nations and Inuktitut. Most language families consist of separate but related member languages (e.g., the Algonquian language family consists of individual languages such as Cree, Blackfoot, and Algonquian, among others), as well as separate dialects. These languages reflect a diversity of distinctive histories, cultures, and identities linked to family, community, the land, and traditional knowledge. Indeed, for many First Nations, Inuit, and Métis people, these languages are at the very core of their Aboriginal identity.[3]

Aboriginal people, though, are confronted with the fact that many of their languages are disappearing, an issue that may have profound implications for

Aboriginal culture in Canada. Over the past 100 years or more, at least ten once-flourishing languages have become extinct. Currently, only a minority of the Aboriginal population in Canada is able to speak or understand an Aboriginal language. According to 2001 census data, the most recent data available at the time of this analysis, among the 976,300 people who self-identified as Aboriginal, 235,000, or 24 percent, reported they were able to conduct a conversation in an Aboriginal language. This represents a sharp drop from 29 percent in 1996[4] and confirms a substantial erosion in the use of Aboriginal languages in recent decades. Another definite indicator of the erosion is the declining percentage of the Aboriginal population whose mother tongue is Aboriginal. In 2001, just 21 percent of Aboriginal people in Canada had an Aboriginal mother tongue, down from 26 percent in 1996. For the first time since 1981, the population with an Aboriginal mother tongue declined from 1996 to 2001, a reversal of past trends due to the overall long-term decline in transmission of an Aboriginal mother tongue from parent to child. However, the loss of mother-tongue speakers is counterbalanced to some degree by the number of people learning an Aboriginal language as their second language. According to the 2001 census, 20 percent of all Aboriginal language speakers— over 47,100 people—had learned it as a second language.

It appears that this is especially the case for younger generations learning endangered languages and, as well, in urban areas (Norris and Jantzen 2003). Second-language speakers tend to be considerably younger than mother-tongue speakers: about 45 percent of second-language speakers were less than twenty-five years old, compared with 38 percent of mother-tongue speakers. Learning an Aboriginal language as a second language cannot be considered a substitute for learning it as a mother tongue. Nevertheless, increasing the number of second-language speakers is part of the process of language revitalization and may go some way towards preventing, or at least slowing, the rapid erosion and possible extinction of endangered languages. Indeed, the acquisition of an Aboriginal language as a second language may be the only option available to many Aboriginal communities if language transmission from parent to child is no longer viable.

Trends in the acquisition of Aboriginal languages as second languages attest to the fact that learning an Aboriginal language is considered important by Aboriginal people of all ages, for youth, their parents, and adults in general, within and outside Aboriginal communities. For example, according to the 2001 Aboriginal Peoples Survey, parents of 60 percent of Aboriginal children in non-reserve areas believed it was very important or somewhat important for their children to speak and understand an Aboriginal language. The ability of young Aboriginal people to speak the traditional language of their parents or grandparents may go some way towards fostering family ties and preserving their cultures. The process itself of learning an Aboriginal language may contribute to increased self-esteem and community well-being, as well as cultural continuity.

With respect to gender, the literature suggests that men and women differ in their patterns of language maintenance, shift, and revitalization. For at least the past twenty-five years (since 1981), women have seemed to experience less language maintenance or continuity in speaking their mother tongue than men. This pattern was noted by Burnaby and Beaujot even in 1986. This lower continuity may be associated with higher rates for women of out-marriage and out-migration from communities or reserves. Findings from an analysis of language continuity (1981 to 1996) also show that it was women during the child-bearing years who experienced the greatest decline in language continuity over the fifteen-year period (Norris 2003).

Research demonstrates the importance of Aboriginal communities, like First Nations reserves, as enclaves in supporting language transmission. Furthermore, both family and community together play critical roles in the transmission of language from parent to child. On their own, neither family capacity nor community support is sufficient to ensure the adequate transmission of an Aboriginal language as a population's mother tongue from one generation to the next. Intergenerational transmission is maximized in Aboriginal communities among families where both parents have an Aboriginal mother tongue. Outside Aboriginal communities, particularly within large cities, transmission and continuity are significantly reduced, even under ideal conditions of linguistically endogamous families (i.e., in which both parents speak an Aboriginal mother tongue). For exogamous families (i.e., in which only one of the parents speaks an Aboriginal mother tongue and the other parent speaks a non-Aboriginal mother tongue), it appears that community effect, while positive, is nevertheless limited in offsetting their lower rate of mother-tongue transmission.

IMPORTANCE OF WOMEN'S PARTICIPATION AND CONTRIBUTIONS TO CULTURAL CONTINUITY AND COMMUNITY DEVELOPMENT

In general, women are key players in the development and transmission of their languages and cultures, and this is particularly true for Aboriginal women. Cora Voyageur's research on Aboriginal women and communities attests to the significant roles of Aboriginal women. She writes, "Aboriginal women are playing a greater part in the education of their children, and in promoting health, training, and recreational programs in their communities. They are concerned about the loss of cultural identity and the decrease in language retention in the youth because of pressures from the dominant society" (Voyageur 2000, 100).

Much of the literature on women and language stresses the critical role women play in language maintenance and language loss. For Aboriginal women, that role can be linked to issues ranging from gender equality to community economic development. Findlay and Wuttunee write that "Aboriginal women remain important stewards of the world's linguistic and biological diversity (Lertzman and Vredenburg 2005), active promoters of social change and vital economic players where gender equality is promoted (Jones, Snelgrove, and Muckosy 2006)" (Findlay and Wuttunee 2007, 5), adding, "the women's stories make clear that culture is a prerequisite to economic success" (19).

However, the relationship between language and community well-being is complex. In her research on community well-being in First Nations, Susan Wingert observed that communities where respondents were much more likely to have learned an Aboriginal language as their first language were below average in terms of their community well-being (CWB), whereas respondents were more likely to have learned English or French in those communities with average or above average CWB. She suggests that the positive effects of culture may be offset by the negative effects of socio-economic deprivation in some communities: "With respect to first language, we may be seeing a spurious relationship because Cree, one of the most prevalent Aboriginal languages, is concentrated across the prairie provinces, which also have a disproportionate number of below average CWB communities.... However, there may indeed be a relationship between first language and economic integration, which means those without proficiency in English or French may be more likely to experience economic disadvantage" (Wingert 2007, 14).

The relationship between language and economic-related well-being is also important in language choice in terms of continuity, use, and intergenerational transmission, and germane to the discussion here, for women and their children. To take this further, it is also the case that the impact and demands of globalization cannot be ignored in today's world and that women have often made linguistic choices for themselves and their children, their families, and even their communities in consideration of their prospects for success in education and work. Ultimately, then, the women's roles in language continuity and transition have a bearing not only on cultural continuity but also on community development and well-being.

WOMEN'S ROLES IN LANGUAGE MAINTENANCE AND REVITALIZATION

According to the literature, the role of women can basically be viewed from two different perspectives. One view is that women hold a "traditional" role as the "keepers" or transmitters of their languages and cultures. The other view is that women are at the forefront of linguistic change. Women can play key roles not only in language maintenance, but also in language shift, language loss, and language revitalization. Thus, women's impacts on cultural continuity, through their traditional role or at the forefront of linguistic change, are best understood in relation to their impact on the type and extent of language transmission and change within communities and families, and on the language outcomes of children.

Women have generally been viewed as the traditional keepers of their languages and cultures, customs, and indigenous knowledge. This is not surprising, since in general women's language roles tend to be defined in relation to their gender role—raising children in the home, where early language education is generally undertaken by mothers. In "The Role of Women in Language Maintenance and Shift," Dipika Mukherjee (2003) references a Peruvian study that reinforces the truism that women's language roles are often still defined by their gender role: "As Quencha speakers and as women, they are the guardians of the indigenous cultures.... It is by raising children and by interacting effectively in kinship networks, however wide, that women both value themselves and are valued" (Harvey 1994, 55).

And, closer to home, in his study of Aboriginal women in Canada, Jeremy Hull notes that marriage and family tend to be largely the domain of women. Hull writes, "Marriage and family life are important social institutions that have historically been seen as more the domain of women than of men. Families are the primary vehicle for child rearing, socialization and transmission of culture, and also have important educational and economic dimensions" (Hull 2006, 30).

Throughout the world, women also play a significant role in the evolution of their languages, cultures, and identities from one generation to the next. Because women are often at the forefront of linguistic change, they affect the processes of language loss, language maintenance, and revitalization. The interplay of various factors, such as marriage residence, community, and identity, can affect women's language outcomes and those of their families and communities. For example, linguistic intermarriage—marriage to someone with a different mother tongue (also referred to as "out-marriage" or "exogamy")—can have implications for language use not only between husband and wife, but also for their children. Similarly, women's choices between traditional or dominant language use and the places or domains where they use their languages (at home, in the community, schools, or the workplace) extend beyond themselves. These choices can be individual, sometimes affecting the group or community as much as the group affects the individual. As well, choices and identities of individuals are also shaped by the effects of community, historical, socio-economic, political, and legal considerations.

Some interesting examples of women being actively responsible for language loss as well as language maintenance have been documented. Mukherjee notes a study in Austria by Susan Gal that showed that "women could and did change the language of an entire community from Hungarian to German because of greater social mobility possible with the German language" (Gal 1979). In Mukherjee's own study on the role of Bengali women in language maintenance and language shift within their own community in Malaysia, she writes that "the Malaysian-Bengali women leave the community through exogamous marriages, leading to language loss. At the same time the Bengali brides from India ensure the continuity of the group through the marriage of their sons…. The Malaysian-Bengali women constantly make choices about which group to belong to and ensure the continuity of the group through the marriage of their sons" (Mukherjee 2003, 105).

As parents, women do make linguistic choices for their children with regard to their children's prospects for "success," particularly in relation to their knowledge and use of the mainstream language in education and work. In his article, "Language, Education and Ethnicity: Whose Rights Will Prevail in an Age of Globalisation?" Keith Watson suggests that, in spite of the increased awareness of the importance of language survival and rights, globalization may indeed prevail to the point where "many linguistic and ethnic groups are in danger of being further marginalized" (Watson 2007). He continues,

> Unfortunately, in today's globalised world, governments and minorities are faced with conflicting pressures: on the one hand, for the development and use of education in a global/international language; on the other for the use and development of mother tongue, local or indigenous languages in education....While there is now greater recognition of the importance of language both for economic and educational development, as well as for human rights, the forces of globalisation are leading towards uniformity in the languages used, in culture and even in education. They are working against the development of language rights for smaller groups.

The challenge of linguistic continuity of Aboriginal traditional languages in the context of globalization means that, unlike older generations, Aboriginal youth today have to contend with the prevailing influence of English and French through mass media, popular culture, and other aspects of their daily lives such as education and work. At the same time, their traditional language can serve a different role than that of mainstream languages. According to David Crystal, it can be a means to "express the identity of the speakers of a community ... fostering family ties, maintaining social relationships, preserving historical links...." (Crystal 2000, 81).

The challenges of language maintenance and intergenerational transmission are exacerbated particularly for First Nations women. Unlike their male counterparts, First Nations women have faced long-term problems specific to their gender in relation to their identity and roles as First Nations women; equality; residency; and matrimonial property rights within their communities. These problems have undermined their traditional roles as keepers of their languages and cultures and in many ways have pushed them into the forefront of linguistic change.

WOMEN AND LANGUAGE IN THE FIRST NATIONS CONTEXT

Given that there is no single Aboriginal nation, there are many complexities and diversities regarding the traditional roles of women. However, the literature is fairly consistent regarding the impact of colonialism, Western-imposed patriarchal systems, and gender inequality in the lives of Aboriginal women, families, and communities. In many pre-colonial Aboriginal societies, women traditionally had greater influence in their communities than in the postcolonial era: women had equality and shared power with men; leaders were often accountable to women in the community; matriarchal systems were characteristic of many Aboriginal societies; and the roles and contributions of Aboriginal women to their communities were recognized and valued. Today, Aboriginal women struggle to fulfill these roles (Kenny 2002; RCAP 1996; Voyageur 2000).

Some observers believe the goal of gender equality is not necessarily appropriate within the context of Aboriginal societies. As Kenny writes, "The goal of equality with White men creates a concept of gender equality that denies Aboriginal experiences and is conceptually and culturally inappropriate for First Nations women. [Turpel-Lafond] notes that in the Cree community, women are at the centre and men traditionally have a responsibility to be women's helpers. Responsibility to the people is the central organizing principle of the community, not equality" (Kenny 2002, citing Turpel-Lafond 1997).

However, colonialism has undermined women's traditional roles with respect to culture: as women's contributions became undervalued, so did the need to carry out traditional practices (Nahanee 1990, from Kenny 2002). The breakdown of women's traditional roles directly affected the education of children, and the impact of Western economies, education, and religion also further created alienation of First Nations women from their cultures and traditional work (Kenny 2002).

Two very clear examples of the historical and generational impact of colonialism reside with the effects of the residential school system and the *Indian Act*. Fiske and George (2006) refer to Yellow Horse Brave Heart's definition of "historic trauma" as "collective and compounding emotional and psychic wounding over time…. multi-generational and is not limited to [an individual's] life span." Historic trauma is "experienced across wide networks of people and is transferred through generations as lived experiences of descendants of the original trauma victims are shaped by the past" (6). They cite residential schools and the *Indian Act* as examples of historic trauma that continue today to affect the identities, languages, cultures, and social practices of First Nations, including the devaluing and denigration of women's traditional roles. Residential schools in particular had a devastating impact on Aboriginal women and communities. They undermined and displaced the traditional roles of First Nations mothers, thereby affecting the education of their children and those traditional practices and family structures that contributed to the intergenerational transmission of languages.

Many First Nations women also view the imposition of the *Indian Act* over the last 120 years as immensely destructive (RCAP 1996, vol. 4); that it "intended and did alter the lives of Indian women by destroying their roles within Indian society," and that the "onslaught" continues today (McIvor 1994). As already stated by others in this book, the *Indian Act* had a significant impact on many aspects of the lives of First Nations women, particularly in relation to past discriminations of the Act (before the 1985 amendments). Most notable are the provisions regarding intermarriage and their implications for transmission of language and culture, and other areas such as self-governance and matrimonial property rights. According to Nahanee (1992), "the *Indian Act* imposed a system of patriarchal customs and laws on First Nations communities that has become so ingrained among First Nations peoples that it stripped women of gender equality and created male privilege as the norm on reserve lands" (Kenny 2002, citing Nahanee 1992).

The enactment of intermarriage provisions in the *Indian Act* had a profound impact on the role of First Nations women as keepers of their languages and cultures. "From 1869 until 1985 the determination of Indian status," writes Silman,

> was determined by a patrilineal system; that is, by a person's relationship to a male person who is a direct descendent in the male line of a male person.... When she married a non-status man, an Indian woman born with status lost it, unable to gain it even if she subsequently was divorced or widowed. Along with her status, the woman lost her band membership and with it, her property, inheritance, residency, burial, medical, educational and voting rights on the reserve. In direct contrast, an Indian man bestowed his status upon his white wife and their children, and could bestow it by adoption upon any other children. Consequently every Indian woman was dependent upon a man—first her father and then her husband—for her identity, rights and status under the *Indian Act* [Silman 1987].

In order to fully understand the implications of the *Indian Act* on the relationship between legislative intermarriage and language maintenance, it is necessary to look at the Act's provisions both pre-1985 and post-1985, given their different consequences for intermarriage. Prior to 1985, Registered Indian status could be lost or gained through the process of intermarriage, whereas, following Bill C-31 in 1985, status could no longer be lost through intermarriage but rather through inheritance, according to the degree of out-marriage, such that after two successive generations of out-marriage, Registered Indian descendants are not eligible to inherit status.[5]

The pre-1985 provisions of the *Indian Act* concerning intermarriage would have had a significantly greater dampening effect on women's role in language maintenance than the current post-1985 (Bill C-31) provisions of the Act. Prior to 1985, in a legislative intermarriage, women had to leave their reserve communities and were not allowed to move back, even in the event of divorce or widowhood. After 1985, although status could no longer be lost or gained through intermarriage, and women and their children could live on reserve communities, the *Indian Act* still had consequences for First Nations women in terms of identity and cultural continuity because of the second-generation cut-off rule. Fiske and George assert that "the social and psychological consequences for First Nations individuals whose identity has been subject to either reinstatement to the Indian Register and band membership or classification under [section] 6(2) doubly constitute historic trauma. Bill C-31 emerges from colonial distortion of identity and belonging, and exists within current cultural disruption that denies individuals access to a coherent culture from which the wisdom and skills necessary for community survival are drawn" (Fiske and George 2006, 40).

The cultural impacts of the marriage patterns of First Nations women exist not only with respect to legislative intermarriage and the pre- and post-1985 *Indian Act* provisions, but also persist with respect to linguistic intermarriage. It is clear that the pressures and preferences confronting women in their marriage choices concerning language and intermarriage can place them at the forefront of linguistic change. Women's patterns of linguistic intermarriage can directly affect language outcomes of both women and their children—affecting parent-child transmission and often leading to language loss and little intergenerational transmission with respect to their Native tongues. In cases of legislative intermarriage prior to 1985, women who had "married out" effectively lost the support of their community so essential to intergenerational language transmission. In the second case of linguistic intermarriage, where an Aboriginal first-language speaker marries a person whose mother tongue is not Aboriginal (most likely being one of the dominant languages of English or French), the impact is more direct, occurring within the family where parent-child transmission is affected by husband/wife dynamics. Both types of intermarriage present challenges to women's role in language continuity as they try to balance the demands of culture, community, and the larger society.

Exploring the factors that underlie the causes and patterns of intermarriage, in general, is key to examining the marriage patterns of First Nations women. The literature cites a complex set of factors—be it racial, ethnic, religious, or linguistic—that can involve cultural preferences, demographic pressures, place of residence, and generational impacts of intermarriage. From the viewpoint of effects of intermarriage over the generations, certainly the pre-1985 provisions of the *Indian Act* for women increased the chances of both legislative and linguistic intermarriage with each successive generation of Registered Indian out-marriage, since women who out-married were obliged to leave their reserve community. Once the women were outside their community, the odds of "marrying out" increased significantly for their own children. Distance and location in relation to one's community can also affect the chances of intermarriage in general. However, demographic pressures can also come from the reserve community itself, particularly small ones where the number of prospective mates is not large. As Fiske and George note, such pressures underlie concerns about the impact of the *Indian Act* and implications for the family, matrilineal descent, and community:

> A number of participants spoke of the conflict between Bill C-31 and local patterns of marriage in remote communities where most residents are related. Generations have been taught that out-marriage is necessary to avoid violating social rules governing incest within clans and marriage to close relatives. In consequence, women were often encouraged to marry non-Indians in customary marriages. Communities were unaware of the implications of the *Indian Act* for matrilineal First Nations. As long as the married couple maintained harmonious relations with the community and the Indian agent failed to intervene, children were registered and integrated fully in their natal community. In some cases, the children were raised by a non-biological father from the community, a practice that placed them beyond intervention by the Indian agent. With this practice, matrilineal descent remained undisrupted and children's birthright in the community unquestioned. In small communities, this is extraordinarily significant. Out-marrying is necessary to avoid marrying kin relations or clan members. As Clatworthy (2001) and others indicated, out-marriage and potential loss of future members is highest in communities under 100 members [Fiske and George 2006, 43].

On many reserves, women were not always aware of the far-reaching implications of "marrying out" until they later sought to move back to the reserve, such as in the case of women who were either divorced or widowed from white husbands (Silman 1987). The loss of not only status, but also residency rights for themselves and their descendants, had a significant impact on those women who "married out" and had to leave their reserve, especially with respect to their ability to maintain their original languages and to be able to transmit their languages and cultures to their children.

In her article, "Identity and Equality: Language, Culture and Gender Rights," Sharon McIvor (2002) argues that the pre-1985 version of the *Indian Act* was a genocidal law because it was designed to separate Indian women from their communities upon marriage to non-Indian men, while admitting non-Indian women who married Indian men into the community. She says the deleterious effect of the Act on linguistic and cultural maintenance within communities is two-fold: one, through the removal of First Nations women from their communities; and, two, with the admission of non-Indian women into communities: "It is women who pass on culture and language ... Indian communities suffered cultural loss when women were removed, and cultural dilution when non-Indian women were admitted" (McIvor 2002).

And, with respect to the impact of the Bill C-31 amendments ending this practice of separating First Nations women from their communities upon marriage to non-registered Indians, McIvor comments that she "can only hope that with the return of women to the Aboriginal community under the revised *Indian Act*, the languages and cultures will experience a rebirth" (McIvor 2002, from INAC 2005, 118).

The sentiment that the return to the reserve of women who had "married out" legislatively prior to 1985 would help strengthen language and culture of the community is also echoed in response to the argument used by some leaders against reinstatement of women because it would "dilute Indian culture." "How could it?" asks Silman. "I teach my children my Indian culture; the white women teach their kids their white culture, because the men are out working. It's mostly the mothers that teach the kids. My children are surrounded by my culture, my language, so how can we dilute it? I think Indian women coming back will improve it" (Silman 1987, 240).

The challenges posed by intermarriage in maintaining languages and cultures are recognized in the following interview with Skonaganleh:rá (Sylvia Maracle) concerning women's perspectives: "Woman has had a traditional role as Centre, maintaining the fire—the fire which is at the centre of our beliefs. She is the Keeper of the Culture. She has been able to play that role even in a home divided.... She has maintained her role despite intermarriage which caused her to be cut off from her roots, both legislatively and sometimes physically.... Her home is divided as a result of.... I don't know how many more ways you can divide her house and she'll continue to maintain that fire—but she will!" (RCAP, vol. 4). Since reserves serve as important enclaves in the maintenance and survival of First Nations languages (Norris 1998), for those First Nations women living outside their reserve communities, especially in urban areas, the impact on their ability as mothers to transmit their languages and cultures to their children is profound.

It is also important to recognize that the place of residence of First Nations women and their children can be affected not only by their patterns of marriage, but also by their patterns of marital disruption. Many of the issues associated with matrimonial property rights of First Nations women on reserve can also be linked to effects on women and children in terms of language and culture as documented in a 2007 report by Wendy Grant-John. This report addresses the lack of matrimonial real property protections on-reserve in the event of marital and family breakdown. Grant-John argues that these protections are especially relevant for women and children in a number of areas, such as housing and residency on-reserve, that could arise out of property issues: "Rates of marital breakdown for both married and common law couples on reserve are comparable to the off-reserve population. The impacts of the lack of matrimonial real property protections have been greater for First Nations women overall than for First Nations men due to current social roles and ongoing impacts from past discriminatory provisions of the *Indian Act* that excluded First Nations women from governance and property" (Grant-John 2007, 1).

Impacts of marital dissolution on reserve extend beyond basic property rights, and include effects on language and culture as described in the report's results of consultations on issues and recommendations. For example, Grant-John notes that one of the recommendations of the Native Women's Association of Canada concerned the intergenerational impacts of colonization: "A mechanism is developed to implement compensation for the lack of protection for women and their descendants including disenfranchisement from First Nations communities and loss of languages, cultures and identities as a result of Matrimonial Real Property" (Grant-John 2007, 50). Similarly, the importance of residency within communities for the children of women so affected by matrimonial real property was also addressed in the Assembly of First Nations (AFN) publication, "Final Reports: Our Lands, Our Families, Our Solutions," as follows: "To preserve our cultures and strengthen First

Nations families, it is essential that solutions enable First Nations children to remain in their communities, live among their extended family, and be taught their language and culture" (Grant-John 2007, Appendix B, 13). Thus, patterns of both marriage and marital dissolution among First Nations women can have profound implications for the transmission of languages and cultures to their children.

VALUES, PRESSURES, AND CHOICES

Many First Nations women face conflicting choices and pressures in trying to ensure that their cultural values are in harmony with achieving success within the larger mainstream realms of education and work. A common perception is that achieving one comes at the expense of the other, especially in the face of globalization, increasing mobility, and urbanization.

In the past, choosing to use the dominant language over the traditional language may have been seen as a way of improving status, but today, while language status is not as major an issue, it is the case that there are nevertheless pressures for Aboriginal people to know the mainstream language as well as the original language in the areas of education and work. Yet, often these pressures can mean a shift away from use of the traditional language, as can be the situation for youth who are bilingual in both their traditional and mainstream languages. Furthermore, the impact of mainstream language pressures is evident in the shift away from the use of traditional languages in the home. This language shift and loss within the home are most liable to occur during the transition from youth into the labour force, and over the family-formation years.

Schools can play a significant role in language revitalization in teaching First Nations languages. However, despite the growing evidence that immersion in traditional languages during the elementary school years provides the · best chances of learning the language, many parents are reluctant to enroll their children due to concerns that their children will not get enough instruction in other courses, like maths and the sciences. In her article, "North American Indian, Métis and Inuit Women Speak about Culture, Education and Work," Carolyn Kenny captures this dilemma confronting Aboriginal women between cultural/linguistic continuity and work success:

> Generalizing Aboriginal women's experiences with respect to education and work does not accurately reflect the diversity and uniqueness of their experiences; thus, it is difficult to clearly pinpoint markers of "successful" Aboriginal women in the work world, in categorical terms. Caroline

> Anawak, a northern politician, was asked specifically about the qualities of successful northern Aboriginal women. Her response was that successful women are those who step out of traditional women's roles; they either marry outside their Aboriginal culture, or separate from their husbands to obtain a living (Illnik 1990). For Aboriginal women of other nations, success may be understood and defined differently [Kenny 2002, 5].

This response exemplifies the types of pressures that can underlie women's roles in language transition.

On the other hand, Kenny also emphasizes the importance that Aboriginal women of all ages and educational backgrounds attribute to cultural values over "getting ahead" in the work world. "So many of the women in this study," she writes,

> reported that when forced to make a choice between these cultural values, which represented the soul or spirit of their people, and work offered by colonizing authorities including band councils, they would choose values and culture over the education and work. This is the strength of Aboriginal women. Yet, it is also the benchmark in the conflict between retaining their most important support, spiritually, and "getting ahead" in the modern world.... Indeed, one has to question the loss of Aboriginal women's traditional roles in the society as the keepers of the moral character of the community, as one of the indicators for Aboriginal women's difficult choices when it comes to culture, education and work. When in a position of choosing, culture and family must come first [Kenny 66].

Bea Medicine, an anthropologist and member of the Lakota Sioux tribe in South Dakota, in her study, "The Role of American Indian Women in Cultural Continuity and Transition," examines the impact of white culture and language on American Indian women (Medicine 1987). According to Medicine, in terms of their community's relation to mainstream society, one role that women have played and continue to play in many American Indian cultures is that of mediator between their own community and mainstream society. In addition, women were often recruited to work in the houses of missionaries and other agents of change. In order to interact on this level, women learned the English language as a means of survival in a rapidly changing situation. Women also taught the children that interaction in two different worlds required entirely different languages and subsumed a new behavioural pattern. Interestingly, as women began to incorporate English into their communities, Medicine notes, males often criticized women for "learning the English tongue too well" since getting too close to the white society is taken as a sign of assimilation and consequent rejection of one's own cultural values.

Women have often made deliberate choices to incorporate English, as well as ancestral languages, into the lives of their children to ensure their success in schools, with an emphasis on bilingualism and biculturalism. Medicine writes that, even as agents of change, women achieved both goals of cultural continuity and educational success: "before the days of relevant Indian curricula, many of the mothers encouraged the use of oral history, legends, and native materials to write histories of the various villages or towns on the reservation as a means of interesting students in improving writing competency in English" (Medicine 1987, 164). Women in American Indian communities hold attitudes toward language use ranging from very traditional ones, in which ancestral language and values are used in the home, even though English is also used, to a more assimilationist one in which children are not spoken to in their ancestral language. Some families may try to maintain a bilingual home, while others may use just the ancestral language at home, while children learn English at school, and others might follow a bilingual school model. The choices women make for their families and children at home and school will affect how a child will learn his ancestral language (Medicine 1987, 164).

PATTERNS OF MOTHER-CHILD LANGUAGE TRANSMISSION

The impacts of mother-child transmission are demonstrated by contrasting children's language outcomes between those with First Nations mothers and fathers, including female versus male lone parents, and exogamous female parent (father speaks non-Aboriginal mother tongue) versus exogamous male parent (mother speaks non-Aboriginal mother tongue). Using 1996 census data, this analysis looks at the language outcomes of some 50,000 First Nations children aged five to fourteen living in a census family who have at least one parent with an Aboriginal or First Nations mother tongue.

Table 1: Five Comparative Groups of Family Types

Comparative groups /Family Types	Description
Endogamous [Endo]	Husband-wife family where both parents have an Aboriginal mother tongue.
Exogamous Mother [Exo Mother]	Husband-wife family where only the mother has an Aboriginal mother tongue.
Exogamous Father [Exo Father]	Husband-wife family where only the father has an Aboriginal mother tongue.
Lone Parent Mother [LP Mother]	Single-mother family where the mother has an Aboriginal mother tongue
Lone Parent Father [LP Father]	Single-father family where the father has an Aboriginal mother tongue.

Table 1 shows the five comparative groups of different family types that will be analyzed. Endogamous families are those in which both the husband and wife have an Aboriginal mother tongue. When a man or woman with an Aboriginal mother tongue linguistically "marries out," or marries a person who does not have an Aboriginal mother tongue, they create an exogamous family. There can be two types of linguistically exogamous families; where only the mother has an Aboriginal mother tongue, or alternatively where only the father has an Aboriginal mother tongue. A lone-parent family is a family headed by only one parent who has an Aboriginal mother tongue. The two types of lone-parent families are lone-parent mother (with an Aboriginal mother tongue) and lone-parent father (with an Aboriginal mother tongue).

As discussed earlier, the effects of the *Indian Act* provisions regarding out-marriage of Registered Indians to persons without Registered Indian status, particularly in relation to women having to leave their reserves, could adversely affect language continuity. In this chapter, it is not possible to directly assess the impact of the pre-1985 *Indian Act* provisions. However, it is reasonable to expect that the effects of the *Indian Act* could underlie patterns of language transmission, since children in this study, aged five to fourteen in 1996, were born between the years 1982 and 1991, under both pre-1985 and 1985 inter-marriage provisions of the *Indian Act*. This implies that some of these children, as descendants of First Nations women and men with an Aboriginal mother tongue—specifically older children born before 1985 (aged eleven to fourteen in 1996)—could have been affected along with their mothers by pre-1985 provisions. Apart from the effects of linguistic intermarriage of their mothers, the language continuity of these older children could also have been dimin-ished had their mothers been one of the many Registered Indian women who married out and parented with a man who did not have registered status.

Close to half (48 percent of the 50,000 children of parents) with a First Nations mother tongue are in endogamous husband-wife families. Children of First Nations mothers are much more likely to be in linguistically exoga-mous or lone-parent family situations compared to those of First Nations fathers. Nearly a third (31 percent) of children raised by First Nations mothers who had an Aboriginal mother tongue were in families where only the mother had the Aboriginal mother tongue, either in husband-wife families where the father had a non-Aboriginal mother tongue (12 percent) or in lone-parent families (19 percent). In sharp contrast, only 18 percent of children raised by First Nations fathers were in families where only the father had an Aboriginal mother tongue, with 16 percent in husband-wife families and just 3 percent in lone-parent families.[6]

Figure 1: Children of Parent(s) with First Nation Mother Tongue: % Children On- and Off-Reserve by Family Type, Canada, 1996

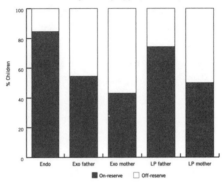

Source: Statistics Canada, 1996 Census of Canada, custom tabulation.

Overall, two out of three children in this study reside on-reserve, while the remaining third are more or less evenly distributed across rural areas (12 percent), small urban areas or towns (census agglomerations or CAS; 11 percent), and large urban areas or cities (census metropolitan areas or CMAS; 10 percent). Children in endogamous families, where both parents have a First Nations mother tongue, form the highest share (85 percent) of children residing on-reserve (Figure 1). The largest number of children in these comparative groups is found in the family/residence category of children in endogamous families residing on reserves, accounting for 41 percent of all children. The next six largest family/residence groupings of children are lone-parent female families on reserve (10 percent); exogamous husband families on reserve (8 percent); exogamous wife families on reserve (6 percent); endogamous families in rural areas (5 percent); and lone-parent females at 4 percent each in non-CMA urban and CMA urban areas.

First Nations mothers not only are more likely to linguistically intermarry or be lone parents than First Nations fathers, they are also more likely in these parenting patterns to reside outside reserve communities. As shown in Figure 1, over half (57 percent) of children with First Nations mothers in exogamous marriages reside off-reserve, compared to 45 percent of children with fathers in exogamous marriages. The contrast in community residency is even more pronounced in the case of lone parents. Only one out of four (26 percent) children raised by single fathers live off-reserve, while half (50 percent) of the children raised by single mothers live off-reserve.

As parents whose mother tongue is a First Nations language, First Nations women are much more likely than First Nations men to be living outside reserve communities and to be either married/parenting with a spouse whose mother tongue is not Aboriginal, or to be a lone-parent. These patterns have significant implications for the challenges First Nations mothers face in transmitting their languages to their children, given that continuity is best supported within a First Nations community and ideally within a linguistically endogamous family, conditions that children of First Nations fathers are more likely to experience.

The language outcomes of children are examined, within the context of this analysis, from the perspective of women's marriage and residency patterns on the one hand, and from the perspective of viability of First Nations languages on the other hand. While the first part of this analysis examines children's language outcomes by marriage and family type in relation to their residency on- or off-reserve (including rural and urban areas), the second part considers children's outcomes within families in relation to the viability and endangerment of their traditional languages. Five measures are used for this analysis:

1. Mother tongue: acquisition of their parents' Aboriginal language as a mother tongue.
2. Home language: use of their parents' Aboriginal language as the major language at home.
3. Continuity (maintenance): for those children who have an Aboriginal mother tongue, extent to which their Aboriginal language is spoken as their major language at home.
4. Knowledge: ability to speak their parents' Aboriginal language.
5. Second-language acquisition: for those who can speak an Aboriginal language, extent to which it was learned as a second language.

PART 1: IMPACT OF MARRIAGE AND RESIDENCY PATTERNS ON LANGUAGE OUTCOMES OF CHILDREN

First Nations children are most likely to acquire their mother's Aboriginal mother tongue in husband-wife families where the husband also has an Aboriginal mother tongue and the family resides within a First Nations reserve community.[7] Sixty-eight percent of children living in these learning conditions have a First Nations mother tongue. However, even for children in linguistically endogamous husband-wife families, but living outside First Nations communities, the percentage with an Aboriginal mother tongue declines to 55 percent in rural areas, 21 percent in small urban areas, and 42 percent in large urban centres (Figure 2).

Figure 2: Children of Parent(s) with First Nation Mother Tongue: % with Mother Tongue by Family Type and Residence, Canada, 1996

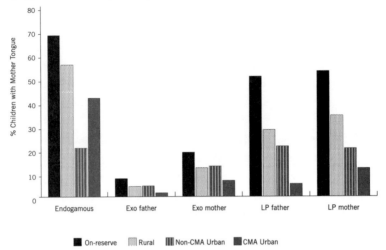

Source: Statistics Canada, 1996 Census of Canada, custom tabulation.

First Nations children are not very likely to acquire their mother's Aboriginal mother tongue in husband-wife families where the father's mother tongue is non-Aboriginal, even if they are living in a First Nations reserve community. On-reserve, only 19 percent of children in exogamous mother families have an Aboriginal mother tongue. Off-reserve, these children's chances are even lower, with only 7 percent of children in large cities having an Aboriginal mother tongue. In the situation of First Nations men marrying and raising children in a husband-wife family where the mother does not have an Aboriginal mother tongue, prospects for children are even lower: only 8 percent of children on-reserve and less than 2 percent in large cities acquire an Aboriginal mother tongue (Figure 2).

First Nations children raised by a single mother on reserve have a relatively good chance of acquiring their mother's Aboriginal language as a mother tongue: just over half (53 percent) of children residing in female lone-parent families acquired an Aboriginal mother tongue. But, without the support of a community, chances are significantly diminished, with about a third (34 percent) of children in female lone-parent families in rural areas having an Aboriginal mother tongue, declining further to 20 percent in small urban areas, and to 12 percent in larger cities. In the case of male lone parents, the situation is very similar. The prospects of First Nations children acquiring their father's mother tongue are best if they live within a community (50 percent), but are similarly diminished outside communities (Figure 2).

First Nations children are most likely (57 percent) to speak an Aboriginal language at home if they are raised in linguistically endogamous families on-reserve. However, without the support of the community, the chances of children speaking an Aboriginal language at home are considerably diminished, even with both parents having an Aboriginal mother tongue: 44 percent in rural areas, 27 percent in large cities, and only 8 percent in small cities (Figure 3).

First Nations children whose fathers do not have an Aboriginal mother tongue are not very likely to speak their mother's Aboriginal language at home, regardless of their place of residence. On-reserve, 10 percent of these children speak their mother's Aboriginal language most often at home, compared to 5 percent and 6 percent, respectively, in rural and small urban areas. Most notably, none in large cities speak an Aboriginal language. Residential patterns are similar in the situation of First Nations men raising children in a husband-wife family where the mother does not have an Aboriginal mother tongue, although the prospects for children using their father's Aboriginal language are even lower (Figure 3).

Figure 3: Children of Parent(s) with First Nation Mother Tongue: % with Home Language by Family Type and Residence, Canada, 1996

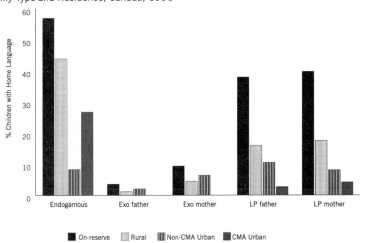

Source: Statistics Canada, 1996 Census of Canada, custom tabulation.

First Nations children raised by a single mother on-reserve have a relatively good chance (40 percent) of speaking their mother's Aboriginal language at home. Without the support of a reserve community, chances of home use are significantly diminished, with about one-fifth (18 percent) of children in female lone-parent families in rural areas speaking an Aboriginal language at home, which declines further to about 8 percent in small urban areas and to just 4 percent in larger cities. In the case of male lone parents, the situation is very similar: First Nations children are most likely to speak their father's Aboriginal language at home if they live within a reserve community (38 percent), but are similarly diminished outside communities. (Figure 3).

The third measure in this analysis refers to language continuity, which compares language behaviour—that is, speaking an Aboriginal language at home—to the language characteristic of Aboriginal mother tongue. It is reasonable to expect that since children learn their mother tongue at home, continuity levels—that is, speaking their Aboriginal mother tongue languages at home—should remain relatively high throughout childhood years. However, maintenance of their mother-tongue languages as major home languages is not as high among children in linguistically mixed husband-wife families.

First Nations children are most likely to continue speaking their Aboriginal mother tongue at home if they are raised in linguistically endogamous families on reserve: for every 100 children with an Aboriginal mother tongue, eighty-four continue to speak it as the major language at home (Figure 4). The use of children's Aboriginal mother tongues at home also remains strong in rural areas outside reserves with a continuity index of seventy-nine. However, as to be expected, it declines in large cities (sixty-five).

Figure 4: Children of Parent(s) with First Nation Mother Tongue: Continuity Index by Family Type and Residence, Canada, 1996

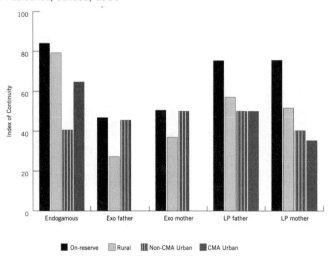

Source: Statistics Canada, 1996 Census of Canada, custom tabulation.

First Nations children whose fathers do not have an Aboriginal mother tongue are less likely to speak their mother's Aboriginal language at home, especially if they live outside reserve communities. Even so, on-reserve or in small cities, the prospects of maintaining children's Aboriginal mother tongues as major languages in the home are about the same for linguistically mixed families, with continuity indexes of about fifty. In rural areas, the continuity index is somewhat lower (forty). These patterns are also very similar for children with Aboriginal mother tongues in linguistically mixed families where only the father has an Aboriginal mother tongue.

First Nations children raised by a single mother on-reserve have a relatively good chance of continuing to speak their Aboriginal mother tongue as their major language at home (seventy-six), almost to the same extent as children in reserve families where both parents have an Aboriginal mother tongue. Prospects of continued home language use in lone-parent families is clearly diminished outside reserves, with lowered continuity indexes of fifty-two in rural areas, forty in small cities, and thirty-five in large cities. For male lone parents, the situation is very similar, although continuity is somewhat higher than that of female lone parents, perhaps a reflection of differences in previous marital status. For example, Aboriginal women (with higher rates of intermarriage and community out-migration) would probably be more likely than men to have been in exogamous marriage/parenting arrangements prior to being lone parents, such that their children would be more likely to also speak a mainstream language.

Figure 5: Children of Parent(s) with First Nation Mother Tongue: % with Knowledge by Family Type and Residence, Canada, 1996

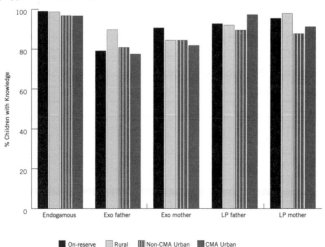

Source: Statistics Canada, 1996 Census of Canada, custom tabulation.

The fourth measure refers to the knowledge of, or ability to speak, their parents' Aboriginal language regardless of how they learned the language, whether as a mother tongue or as a second language. Children's ability to speak their parents' Aboriginal language is considerably less affected by the marriage, parenting, and residence patterns of their parents than are their chances of acquiring an Aboriginal mother tongue and maintaining an Aboriginal home language. In fact, regardless of marriage, parenting, family type, and residence, at least 80 percent of children whose parent(s) have an Aboriginal mother tongue can speak an Aboriginal language. Almost all children who have both parents with an Aboriginal mother tongue can speak their parents' Aboriginal language (99 percent of children in communities and rural areas, and 97 percent in urban areas). These patterns, particularly for linguistically mixed husband-wife families where only one parent has an Aboriginal mother tongue and children are not likely to acquire an Aboriginal mother tongue, suggest that many of these children must be learning their parents' Aboriginal languages as a second language (Figure 5).

The fifth measure builds upon the two previous sections in looking at how children who can speak their parents' Aboriginal language actually learned their traditional language; the measure compares children's ability to speak an Aboriginal language in relation to their having an Aboriginal or non-Aboriginal mother tongue. Children of First Nations women who are in husband-wife exogamous families where the father does not have an Aboriginal mother tongue are much more likely to learn their mother's First Nations language as a second language, rather than as a mother tongue. On-reserve, only 19 percent of children of First Nations women in linguistically mixed families have an Aboriginal mother tongue, yet 91 percent of them have the ability to speak their mother's Aboriginal language. This means there are 480 speakers for every 100 children with an Aboriginal mother tongue (Figure 6). Outside First Nations reserve communities, second-language acquisition is even higher, especially in large cities.

Figure 6: Children of Parent(s) with First Nation Mother Tongue: Ability Index by Family Type and Residence, Canada, 1996

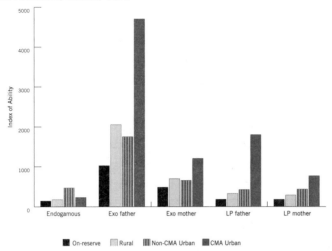

On-reserve   Rural   Non-CMA Urban   CMA Urban

Source: Statistics Canada, 1996 Census of Canada, custom tabulation.

Prospects of children learning their First Nations language as a second language instead of as a mother tongue are indeed high within linguistically mixed families, especially when it is the father, rather than the mother, who has a First Nations mother tongue. In families where only one of the parents has a First Nations mother tongue, children with mothers who have a non-Aboriginal mother tongue are at least twice as likely to learn their Aboriginal language as a second rather than as a first language, compared to those children whose mothers have an Aboriginal mother tongue. In linguistically mixed families living in large cities, children with fathers (and not mothers) who have a First Nations mother tongue are almost four times more likely to learn their Aboriginal language as a second language compared to those whose mothers have a First Nations mother tongue.

In sharp contrast, children of First Nations single mothers in lone-parent families are less likely to learn their Aboriginal language as a second language, but more likely than children in families where both parents have an Aboriginal mother tongue. Off-reserve, particularly in large cities, children of single fathers are more likely to learn their Aboriginal language as a second language, compared to children of single mothers.

To conclude this portion of the analysis, the best prospects for intergenerational transmission and continuity of First Nations languages occur within reserve communities, in families where either both parents or the lone parent (female or male) has a First Nations mother tongue. Children fare worse in linguistically mixed husband-wife families, especially those in which only the father has an Aboriginal mother tongue, and outside First Nations reserve communities, particularly within large cities, where language continuity and home use is practically nil. With respect to parent-child language transmission, First Nations women are particularly disadvantaged compared to First Nations men due to a number of factors, such as their higher rates of linguistic intermarriage and, as single parents or in mixed marriages, the likelihood they are not living in within a First Nation community. Yet, as the analysis demonstrated, when these differences in marriage and residency patterns are controlled for between men and women, we see that within linguistically mixed families, children are more likely to acquire a First Nations mother tongue and speak it at home if it is the mother as opposed to the father who has a First Nations mother tongue. As lone parents, First Nations women and men tend to fare similarly in the transmission and home use of their First Nations languages, such that reserves provide the best support for their children's language outcomes. However, it must be remembered that either as parents in linguistically mixed marriages or as lone parents, the majority of First Nations women, unlike First Nations men, do not live on reserve, meaning that they do not have the same access to community supports in passing their languages on to their children.

PART II: LANGUAGE TRANSMISSION FOR VIABLE AND ENDANGERED LANGUAGES

Children's language outcomes are analyzed here in relation to the viability of their ancestral First Nations languages (for a discussion on viable and endangered Aboriginal languages in Canada see Kinkade 1991 and Norris 1998). The viability of languages is also a major consideration, since for many first-language speakers of the smaller First Nations languages, intermarriage is increasingly the only option, due to demographic and geographic pressures. Most of the children in this study, 96 percent, have parents whose Aboriginal mother tongue is one of the viable languages: while the remaining 4 percent are children of parents speaking one of the endangered languages. Yet, the share of children whose parents speak one of the endangered languages does vary by family type, being disproportionately highest in linguistically mixed families. Not surprisingly, the propensity to linguistic out-marriage is greater among speakers of endangered languages due to small numbers (Norris 2003), with the effect that the proportion of children whose parents speak one of the endangered languages is highest among linguistically mixed families, at 10 percent, where the father is the parent with the endangered language, followed by 7 percent, where the mother is the endangered-language speaker. In contrast, the lowest proportion of children of endangered-language speakers, at 2 percent, is found in endogamous families where both parents have a First Nations mother tongue. In lone-parent families, the corresponding proportions of children of endangered language speakers are 6 percent in single-father and 4 percent in single-mother families (Figure 7).

Figure 7: Children of Parent(s) with a First Nation Mother Tongue: Proportion with Parents Speaking an Endangered Language, by Family Type

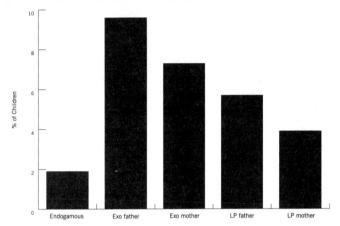

Source: Statistics Canada, 1996 Census of Canada, custom tabulation.

Figure 8: Children of Parent(s) with First Nation Mother Tongue: % with Mother Tongue by Family Type and Language Status, Canada, 1996

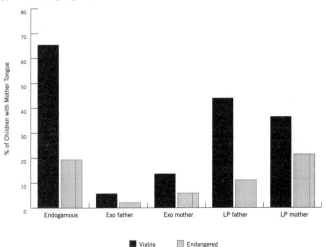

Source: Statistics Canada, 1996 Census of Canada, custom tabulation.

As expected, children of parents whose mother tongues are endangered are significantly worse off in their language outcomes as compared to children of viable language speakers. Among children in families with both parents speaking an endangered language, 19 percent have acquired their parents' language as their mother tongue; compared to only 3 percent of children in linguistically mixed families. In the case of lone-parent families of endangered-language heritage, prospects for intergenerational transmission are higher in those headed by a single mother rather than a single father: 22 percent of children had acquired their mother's endangered language as their mother tongue, while half as many (11 percent) children in male lone-parent families had learned their father's endangered language as a mother tongue. (Figure 8.)

First Nations women contribute to the transmission of endangered languages to their children to a greater extent than First Nations men. Overall, about 11 percent of children had learned their parent's endangered language as a mother tongue, and at least three out of four of these children had acquired their Aboriginal mother tongue either in families where both the mother and father are first-language speakers, or in female lone-parent families with the mother speaking the endangered language.

In the case of viable languages, somewhat similar variations in children's language outcomes occur across marriage and family types, although the degree of transmission is significantly higher than that for endangered languages. For example, 65 percent of children with both parents speaking one of the viable First Nations languages have a First Nations mother tongue, compared to significantly lower shares of children—less than 15 percent—in linguistically mixed families.

Figure 9: Children of Parent(s) with First Nation Mother Tongue: % with Home Language by Family Type and Language Status, Canada, 1996

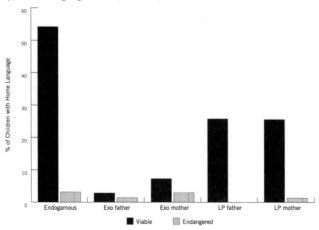

Source: Statistics Canada, 1996 Census of Canada, custom tabulation.

In the case of home language use (Figure 9), prospects for children of endangered-language speakers are extremely low, with only 2 percent of these children overall speaking their parents' language at home, in contrast to some 40 percent of children of viable-language speakers. Even in the case of linguistically endogamous families, home use of an endangered language is still very low at only 3 percent of children, compared to 60 percent of children with both parents speaking a viable language. Similarly, in lone-parent families about a third of children of viable language speakers use their language at home, compared to just 1 percent of children of endangered-language speakers. In linguistically mixed families, home language use drops for viable languages, faring only slightly better for children where it is the mother who has a First Nations language.

First Nations children of parents who speak a viable language are most likely to continue speaking their mother tongue as their home language, either in families where both parents are First Nations speakers or in female lone-parent families, with continuity indexes of about eighty-five and seventy respectively (Figure 10). First Nations children of parents who speak an endangered language are not very likely to continue speaking their mother tongue as their home language, even in families where both parents have the endangered mother tongue, with a continuity index of only seventeen. As a consequence of almost no home use, the outlook for continuity of endangered languages is practically nil with few if any children speaking these languages at home.

For both endangered and viable languages, children's ability to speak their parents' First Nations language is less affected by parenting and family patterns as compared to their learning the language as a mother tongue or speaking it at home (Figure 11). Overall, almost three-quarters (73 percent) of children of endangered-language speakers had the knowledge of and ability to speak their parents' language; compared to nearly all (94 percent) children of viable-language speakers. Also, while clearly the chances of children being able to speak a First Nations language are higher if their parents speak a viable language as opposed to an endangered one, the differences between viable and endangered languages are less pronounced on this measure as compared to mother-tongue acquisition or home language use.

Figure 10: Children of Parent(s) with First Nation Mother Tongue: Continuity Index by Family Type and Language Status, Canada, 1996

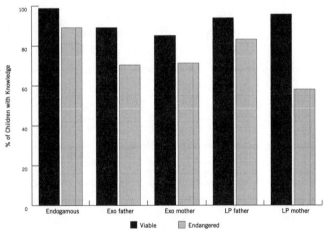

Source: Statistics Canada, 1996 Census of Canada, custom tabulation.

Figure 11: Children of Parent(s) with First Nation Mother Tongue: % with Knowledge by Family Type and Language Status, Canada, 1996

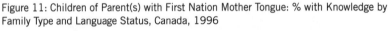

Source: Statistics Canada, 1996 Census of Canada, custom tabulation.

For both viable and endangered languages, the chances that children can speak their parents' mother tongue are greatest within endogamous families, with 90 percent of children of endangered-language speakers and 99 percent of children of viable-language speakers able to speak their parents' first language. Children tend to be least likely to speak their parents' language, whether viable or endangered, in linguistically mixed marriages; still, a good majority of these children know their parents' First Nations language. One exception to this pattern appears among children of female lone parents speaking an endangered language, with the lowest proportion of children speakers at 60 percent compared to those in male lone-parent and linguistically exogamous families, perhaps reflecting that, overall, the proportion of lone-parent females living on-reserve is lower than that of lone-parent males.

For both viable and endangered language speakers, second-language acquisition is highest among children within linguistically mixed families, especially when it is the father and not mother who has an Aboriginal mother tongue. The tendency towards second-language acquisition is notably greater among endangered languages for all family types, but is most pronounced among children who are in linguistically mixed families, especially children whose fathers, but not their mothers, have an endangered language as a mother tongue (Figure 12).

Figure 12: Children of Parent(s) with First Nation Mother Tongue: Ability Index by Family Type and Language Status, Canada, 1996

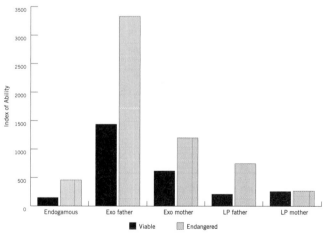

Source: Statistics Canada, 1996 Census of Canada, custom tabulation.

Second-language acquisition appears to be an important dimension among First Nations youth in learning their endangered languages. Young people make up a substantial share of Aboriginal second-language speakers among endangered languages. In 2001, among children under age fifteen who could speak an endangered language, 71 percent learned it as a second language (Norris 2007, 22).

OUTLOOK FOR FIRST NATIONS WOMEN IN THE REVITALIZATION AND MAINTENANCE OF THEIR TRADITIONAL LANGUAGES

Challenges

There can be no doubt that many challenges confront First Nations women in the revitalization and maintenance of their languages. Some of these challenges are unique to First Nations women alone, while others are common to women and minority languages in general. Challenges specific to First Nations women that have arisen and intensified over time are embedded in many aspects of First Nations history associated with colonization, patriarchy, residential schools and legislative factors, such as the *Indian Act* and issues of matrimonial real property on-reserve. These various factors effectively contributed to an erosion and devaluing of the role of women within their own communities as keepers of their traditional cultures and contributed to various issues, such as gender inequality, residency in a First Nations reserve community, and matrimonial property rights. And while legislative changes, such as the Bill C-31 revisions to the *Indian Act* in 1985, have attempted to rectify issues of gender inequality regarding provisions concerning intermarriage and status inheritance, there still remain issues of inequality, identity, and community belonging. Many of these challenges confronting First Nations women and communities today in the maintenance and survival of their traditional languages are exacerbated by linguistic intermarriage, family dissolution, migration from reserves, and urbanization.

As well, in ensuring the survival of their traditional languages, First Nations women have to contend with broader challenges shared by indigenous women and minority-language speakers around the world. The forces of globalization are threatening the diversity of the world's languages, as many linguistic groups become increasingly marginalized and endangered. Today, the continual exposure to the more dominant languages through mass media, popular culture, and many aspects of everyday life, such as education and work, is a powerful catalyst for the decline of First Nations and other minority languages. First Nations women, like their indigenous sisters throughout the world, are faced with making linguistic choices for themselves, their children, families, and communities in relation to the prospects for success in a global world. And, definitely, this will be one of the greatest challenges for First Nations women: the demands of balancing conflicting pressures of cultural and linguistic continuity, in their traditional role as "keepers" of their languages, against the pressures of an increasingly competitive world for their children, as well as for themselves. By facing these challenges, First Nations women take their place at the forefront of language transition, as agents of change.

Yet, as experiences of First Nations women demonstrate, both goals of cultural continuity and educational/work success are critical to community well-being and economic development. In this context, Findlay and Wuttunee stress the acceptance and recognition of the value of culture in economic development: "Aboriginal women entrepreneurs tell us of the ways that they resist those who fear their strength and draw on their rich heritage in pursuing innovation and enterprise in the name of community success… It means stretching the terms and categories to make space for their own visions. It means educating those in administrative silos about the value of cultural knowledge and the importance of culture in socio-economic development" (Findlay and Wuttunee 2007, 12).

And surely, community well-being and development can occur in tandem with linguistic and cultural continuity. This is perhaps consistent with the view that traditional languages can coexist with and serve a different role than mainstream languages in fostering family and community ties (Norris 2007, 26).

Contributions

While there can be no doubt that First Nations women face considerable challenges in the continuity and revitalization of their languages, it is also certainly the case that they have made significant contributions within families and communities as parents, community leaders, entrepreneurs, language practitioners, and teachers in building the desire and ability in learning First Nations languages today and for future generations.

As mothers, First Nations women play a major role in the transmission of traditional languages to their children, one best supported within reserve communities. The analysis of children's language outcomes demonstrates the importance of both family and community support. For both mothers and fathers, the prospects of their children having a First Nations mother tongue are greatest in reserve communities *and* in families where either both parents are first-language speakers, while lowest outside reserve communities, especially within linguistically mixed families. These findings support the view that intergenerational transmission of a mother tongue relies heavily on daily expo-sure both within family and community. In this respect, First Nations mothers are significantly disadvantaged as compared to First Nations fathers: not only are their children more likely to be living in lone-parent and linguistically mixed families, the majority in such families are also more likely to be living outside reserve communities.

How children learn their language, whether as a mother tongue or as a second language, is also critical to the long-term health of a language. Although it is encouraging that a language, especially an endangered one, is learned as a second language, there is generally no equivalent to learning a language as a mother tongue. To survive, a language must be passed on from one generation to the next (Norris 1998). In this respect, within lone-parent families, First Nations single mothers are more likely than First Nations single fathers to pass their endangered Aboriginal language on to their children as a mother tongue. In the case of linguistic intermarriage, children of First Nations fathers are much more likely to learn their language as a second language compared to children of First Nations mothers.

Beyond the domain of the family, First Nations women have particularly influenced the state of their traditional languages within their communities. While it is true that in general women have over the long term been character-ized by lower levels of language maintenance than men, they nevertheless have made significant contributions to language revitalization within their commu-nities. In her 1997 discussion on indigenous-language needs and the impor-tance of leadership and vision in communities, Burnaby reflects on the fact that most community leaders in language maintenance and revitalization in Canada have been women:

> The single most important factor I have seen in the development of successful indigenous language stabilization activities in Canada in the past thirty years has been the presence of leadership. Each exceptional program or movement has been started by a community member who had a vision of what could be done. This person was able not only to dream but also to inspire others to share in this dream. For a reason I do not understand, most of these leaders have been women ... I think of Roseanne Houle, Ida McLeod, Ida Wasacase, Verna Kirkness, Emma Jane Crate, Lena White, Mary Lou Fox, Greg Spence, Reg Henry, Dorothy Lazore, Sr. Catherine Tekakwitha, Luci Salt, Annie Whiskeychan, Mildred Millea, Bernie Francis, Beatrice Watt, and many others [Burnaby 1997, 292–300].

The contributions of women as community leaders are certainly pertinent to the need for language planning at the community and local level, given the diversity of language situations across communities and the need to "develop the right strategies for different size language communities … to pay attention to the amount and variety of language use actually going on in communities" and to respect local priorities and foster local leadership (Burnaby 1997, 292). This need for a community-driven revitalization strategy was also echoed in a June 2005 report from the Canadian government's Task Force on Aboriginal Languages and Cultures. This report emphasized that language planning and revitalization must reflect community-level language states, issues, and objectives (e.g., where languages have a large number of speakers the focus may be on maintenance, while in other communities, with only a few elderly speakers remaining, preservation efforts might be considered more appropriate) (Canadian Heritage 2005, 63–64). Census-based classifications of several hundred Aboriginal communities attest to the need for community-level approaches, given the diversity and range in the state of languages across communities: from flourishing large young mother-tongue populations (in about 16 percent of communities) to declining populations of learners, with few or no speakers remaining (comprising about half of communities). In between these two extremes, about a third of communities are undergoing a transition in language learning, moving from mother-tongue transmission to second-language acquisition.

Finally, women's contributions are increasingly needed at the local and community level, not only as community leaders, but also as language practitioners and teachers. Although it is beyond the scope of this chapter to document ongoing efforts in the teaching of Aboriginal languages, the Canadian Indigenous Languages and Literacy Development Institute (CILLDI), established in 1999, is one example of an institution that was established and developed with significant input from First Nations women (such as Cree scholars and language specialists, Freda Ahenakew and Verna Kirkness) to address "the shortage of teachers, curriculum developers, researchers, and community linguists prepared to work in Indigenous language education" (Settee 2008, 4). Participants who take the range of CILLDI courses include undergraduate and graduate students interested in learning an indigenous language or gaining expertise in the areas of linguistics, language and literacy, curriculum development, and second-language teaching and research. In discussing her paper at the United Nations International Expert Group meeting in January 2008,

Priscilla Settee, herself a Cree scholar and professor in Native studies at the University of Saskatchewan, noted that most of the course participants are women and stressed the importance of women's indigenous knowledge and participation in traditional activities to language revitalization.

Recognition and Support

Two aspects of recognition and support are most critical to the outlook for First Nations women and their languages. First, there is a need for the recognition and support of women's roles in families, communities, and organizations as parents, leaders, educators, planners, and decision makers. Second, it is increasingly vital to recognize the value of language and culture in education, community well-being, and economic development, particularly as it affects the conflicting pressures First Nations women face in balancing values of cultural and linguistic continuity with those of the mainstream.

On many fronts today, there is increasing understanding, recognition, and support of the critical roles First Nations women play in language continuity and revitalization in communities. As part of the National Aboriginal Women's Summit in June 2007, policy recommendations presented by the Assembly of First Nations (AFN) addressed the need for this recognition and support. AFN recommendations dealt with issues such as past failures to adequately recognize the role of First Nations women in their communities as "bearers of language and tradition" and the need to support the unique roles of women that in the past had made for strong and dynamic First Nations communities. In recognizing that "women are fundamental to the revitalization of culture and languages, not only because of their role in sustaining culture, but also because of their role in educating children" recommendations stressed the need for greater recognition and investment in supporting women to carry out "linguistic and cultural teaching, inside and outside the home." Other summit recommendations included strategies to help Aboriginal women reclaim and pass on their traditional roles and knowledge, and to revitalize their culture and communities. In terms of outcomes, the AFN discussion acknowledged that recognition will also "allow First Nations women to act with strength, to find the balance between their own aspirations and their roles within their own communities and in the broader environment" (Assembly of First Nations 2007, 10).

In *Strong Women Stories: Native Vision and Community Survival*, edited by Kim Anderson and Bonita Lawrence, discussions of traditions, cultures, and languages address issues of gender inequality and the need for recognition, more participation, and decision making of women within their Aboriginal communities. Carl Fernández's chapter on gender equity in Aboriginal communities argues that the contributions of women as community leaders in protecting the future by transmitting language and culture to their children are often not recognized. He suggests that the current state of communities is one of imbalance and uncertainty—and that a return to traditions marked by gender balance will serve to strengthen Aboriginal communities, noting that "the traditional balance between the roles of men and women kept our communities healthy" (Fernández 2003, 242, 244, and 252)

On the international front, the United Nations Economic and Social Council report from the international expert group meeting on indigenous languages, held in January 2008, recommended the recognition and empowerment of indigenous women in their roles as keepers of traditional languages and cultures. In addressing indigenous peoples' efforts to stabilize their languages and keep them alive, the report recommended that "indigenous peoples, mindful of the important role of men, should recognize that indigenous women are often the primary transmitters of indigenous languages to future generations and empower them for a greater participation in decision-making and language revitalization" (United Nations Economic and Social Council 2008, Recommendation 68).

With respect to the value of language and culture, there is also growing recognition of the importance of culture and language continuity in education, and that achieving one does not necessarily come at the expense of the other. In some communities, other priorities may outweigh language and cultural issues, such that the "pressure to meet ... mainstream requirements ... may not leave room for a focus on indigenous languages, with parents reluctant to enroll children in immersion programs, wanting their children to be educated so that they can compete in the wider society" (Burnaby 1997). However, there is growing evidence of successful immersion programs that are seeing First Nations children graduate with a strong education well prepared for the mainstream world but still with their traditional linguistic and cultural traditions well intact (Society for the Advancement of Excellence in Education 2007). On many education and policy fronts, success in Aboriginal education is being redefined and expanded with the increasing recognition of the need for an education that recognizes the importance of language and cultures (such as in the 2007 report of the Canadian Council on Learning) and that supports the strengthening of Aboriginal peoples' identity, "emphasizing language, cultural and traditional knowledge, and the effective reincorporation of elders and women in educating younger generations" (National Association of Friendship Centres 2007, 12).

On an international scale, these very same issues are also reflected in the United Nations Recommendations on Indigenous Languages. The recommendations recognize the importance of supporting culturally relevant curriculums and mother-tongue education for indigenous children, and quality indigenous education policies that provide indigenous children with the capacities to become productive members of national societies. A further recommendation calls for the creation of indigenous universities and language departments to promote indigenous languages (United Nations Economic and Social Council 2008, Recommendations 35, 47, and 48).

Thus, while First Nations women face many challenges in the revitalization and maintenance of their traditional languages, their contributions and roles are nevertheless significant. And, the outlook is encouraging from the perspective that women are receiving increasing recognition and support for their work in linguistic and cultural continuity, along with the growing realization that language and culture do have a place in education, community well-being, and economic development. These developments will aid First Nations women in achieving and maintaining a balance in many areas of their lives, including the conflicting pressures between traditional values and mainstream demands. In this respect, Johnathan Lear's book, *Radical Hope: Ethics in the Face of Cultural Devastation*, offers inspiration about the wisdom and leadership of Chief Plenty Coups of the Crow Nation, who in the face of cultural collapse incurred by the arrival of Europeans and the disappearance of the buffalo displayed courage and creative adaptation. He offered a "radical hope"—that is, that somehow the Crow way of life would continue but in a different and unknown context. Indeed, they did hold onto their precious land, and onto the possibility of transmitting their values and memories of their traditions to another generation that would see "the future flourishing of traditional tribal values, customs and memories in a new context" (Lear 2006, 144–145).

Notes

1   The author acknowledges with thanks research and editorial assistance provided by Marianne Snider of the Strategic Research and Analysis Directorate. The views expressed are those of the author and do not necessarily represent the views of Indian and Northern Affairs.

2   For more information on the late Sarah Lavalley of the Algonquins of Pikwákanagán (Golden Lake) in the Ottawa Valley, see Mary Cook, "Lady Sarah," *Ottawa Today's Seniors*, January 1997, p. 32, and Mary Hawkins, *Here to Stay* (Ottawa: Native Council of Canada, 1983), 9. See also http://www.gg.ca/honours/search-recherche/honours-desc. asp?lang=e&TypeID=orc&id=959.

3   For discussions on size, diversity, and viability of Canada's Aboriginal languages, see M.D. Kinkade, "The Decline of Native Languages in Canada," in R.H. Robins and E.M. Uhlenbeck, eds., *Endangered Languages* (Oxford: Berg Publishers Limited, 1991), and M. J. Norris, "Canada's Aboriginal Languages," *Canadian Social Trends* 51 (1998): 8–16. Catalogue no. 11-008-XPE (Ottawa: Statistics Canada, 1998), http://www.statcan.ca/ english/freepub/11-008-XIE/1998003/articles/4003.pdf. See also M.J. Norris, "The Diversity and State of Aboriginal Languages in Canada," in *Canadian and French Perspectives on Diversity*, conference proceedings, 6 October 2003 (Ottawa: Canadian Heritage, 2005), http://www.pch.gc.ca/pc-ch/pubs/diversity2003/norris_e.cfm.

4   Part of this decrease in the proportion of Aboriginal people able to speak an Aboriginal language over the 1996–2001 period is also attributable to the significant growth in the Aboriginal population itself, which has been affected by the increased tendency of people to identify themselves in the census as Aboriginal, especially Métis—among whom only a small proportion report the ability to speak an Aboriginal language. See Statistics Canada, "Aboriginal peoples of Canada: A demographic profile," *2001 Census: Analysis Series*, Catalogue no. 96 F00030XIE2001007 (Ottawa: Statistics Canada, 2003).

5   For an in-depth discussion of this issue, see Stewart Clatworthy, "Impacts of the 1985 Amendments to the Indian Act on First Nations Populations," in J.P. White, P.S. Maxim, and D. Beavon, eds., *Aboriginal Conditions: Research as a foundation for public policy* (Vancouver: University of British Columbia Press, 2003).

6   With respect to lone-parent families, the previous marital/parenting status of the mother is not known, whether the child was originally in a husband-wife family prior to female lone parent; or whether marriage/parenting was linguistically endogamous (father with Aboriginal mother tongue) or exogamous (father non-Aboriginal mother tongue).

7   In the discussion on language outcomes for children the analysis here refers to residence of the child at the time of enumeration, and is to some extent limited since it is not known where the child actually acquired their mother tongue in the event of migration.

Bibliography

Aboriginal Family Healing Joint Steering Committee. *For Generations to Come: The Time is Now.* Final report of the Aboriginal Family Healing Joint Steering Committee. Toronto: Aboriginal Family Healing Joint Steering Committee, 1993.

Aboriginal Healing Foundation. *A Healing Journey, Reclaiming Wellness.* Ottawa: Aboriginal Healing Foundation, 2006.

Aboriginal Justice Implementation Commission. *Final Report.* Winnipeg: Government of Manitoba, 2001.

Aboriginal Justice Inquiry of Manitoba. *The Deaths of Helen Betty Osborne and John Joseph Harper.* Volume 2 of *Report of the Aboriginal Justice Inquiry of Manitoba.* Winnipeg: Aboriginal Justice Inquiry of Manitoba, 1991.

Aboriginal Nurses Association of Canada. *Finding Our Way: A Sexual and Reproductive Health Sourcebook for Aboriginal Communities.* Ottawa: Aboriginal Nurses Association of Canada, 2002. http://www.anac.on.ca/sourcebook/toc.htm.

Acoose, Janice. *Iskwewak: Kah' Ki Yaw Niwahkomakanak.* Toronto: Women's Press, 1995.

Adair, James. *Adair's History of the American Indians.* Edited by Samuel Cole Williams. Ann Arbor: Argonaut Press, 1966.

Adelson, Naomi. "Reducing Health Disparities And Promoting Equity For Vulnerable Populations." Paper presented at Reducing Health Disparities and Promoting Equity for Vulnerable Populations, International Think Tank, Ottawa, ON, September 2003.

———. *Being Alive and Well: Health and the Politics of Cree Well-Being.* Toronto: University of Toronto Press, 2000.

Akiwenzie-Damm, Kateri. *My Heart Is a Stray Bullet.* Cape Croker, ON: Kegedonce Press, 1993.

——. *Without Reservation: Indigenous Erotica.* Wiarton, ON: Kegedonce Press, 2003.

Alba, R. *Ethnic Identity: The Transformation of White America.* New Haven: Yale University Press, 1990.

Alfred, Taiaiake, and Corntassel, Jeff. "Being Indigenous: Resurgences Against Contemporary Colonialism." *Government and Opposition* 40 (2005). http://www.wasase.org/pdfs/goop_166.pdf (accessed 5 March 2006).

Allen, Paula Gunn. *The Sacred Hoop: Recovering the Feminine in American Indian Traditions.* Boston: Beacon Press, 1986.

Amnesty International (Canada). *Stolen Sisters: A Human Rights Response to Discrimination and Violence Against Aboriginal Women in Canada.* Ottawa: Amnesty International (Canada), 2004.

Anderson, Kim. *A Recognition of Being: Reconstructing Native Womanhood.* Toronto: Sumach Press, 2000.

Appelbaum, Barbara. "Criteria for the Treatment of Collections Housed in Historic Structures." *Journal of the American Institute for Conservation* 33, 2 (1994): 185–191.

Armstrong, Jeannette. *Whispering in Shadows.* Penticton, BC: Theytus Books, 2000.

——. "Invocation: The Real Power of Aboriginal Women." In Christine Miller and Patricia Chuchryk, eds., *Women of the First Nations: Power, Wisdom, and Strength.* Winnipeg: University of Manitoba Press, 1996.

——. *Looking at the Words of Our People: First Nations Analysis of Literature.* Penticton, BC: Theytus Books, 1993.

——. *Breath Tracks.* Toronto: Williams-Wallace Publishers, 1991.

——. *Slash.* Penticton, BC: Theytus Books, 1985.

Armstrong, Jeannette, and Lally Grauer, eds. *Native Poetry in Canada: A Contemporary Anthology.* Peterborough: Broadview Press, 2001.

Arnold, Grant, Monika Kin Gagnon, and Doreen Jensen, eds. *Topographies—Aspects of Recent BC Art.* Vancouver: Douglas and McIntyre, 1996.

Arnott, Joanne. *Steepy Mountain Love Poetry.* Cape Croker, ON: Kegedonce Press, 2004.

——. *Wiles of Girlhood.* Vancouver: Press Gang, 1991.

Assembly of First Nations. Policy recommendations. Presented at the National Aboriginal Women's Summit, June 2007.

Assembly of First Nations. *Residential School Update.* Ottawa: Assembly of First Nations, 1998.

Attwood, B. *The Making of the Aborigines.* Sydney: Allen and Unwin, 1989.

Backhouse, C. "Nineteenth Century Prostitution Law: Reflection of a Discriminatory Society." *Social History/Histoire Sociale* 8, 35 (1985): 387.

Bailey, Alfred G. *The Conflict of European and Eastern Algonkian Cultures, 1504–1700: A Study in Canadian Civilization.* Toronto: University of Toronto Press, 1969.

Baker, Marie Annharte. *Exercises in Lip Pointing*. Vancouver: New Sky Books, 2003.

———. *Coyote Columbus Café*. Winnipeg: Moonprint, 1994

———. *Being on the Moon*. Winlaw, BC: Polestar Press, 1990.

Ballantyne, Robert M. *Hudson's Bay, or, Everyday life in the wilds of North America*. London: W. Blackwood, 1848.

Barman, Jean. "Taming Aboriginal Sexuality: Gender, Power, and Race in British Columbia, 1850–1900." *BC Studies* 115–116 (1997): 237–266.

Barth, F. *Ethnic Groups and Boundaries: The Social Organization of Cultural Difference*. Boston: Little Brown, 1969.

Bastien, Betty. "Voices Through Time." In Christine Miller and Patricia Chuchryk, eds., *Women of the First Nations: Power, Wisdom, and Strength*. Winnipeg: University of Manitoba Press, 1996.

Beaty Chiste, Katherine. "Aboriginal Women and Self-Government: Challenging Leviathan." *American Indian Culture and Research Journal* 18, 3/4 (1994).

Beavon, D., and M. Cooke. "An Application of the United States Human Development Index to Registered Indians in Canada, 1996." In J. White, P. Maxim, and D. Beavon, eds., *Aboriginal Conditions: Research Foundations for Public Policy*. Vancouver: University of British Columbia Press, 2003.

Bédard, Catherine. ed. *Osopikahikiwak: Jane Ash Poitras/Rick Rivet*. Paris: Services culturel de l'Ambassade du Canada, 1999.

Belfrage, Jane. "The Great Australian Silence: Inside Acoustic Space." The Australian Sound Design Project, 1994. http://www.sounddesign.unimelb.edu.au/site/papers.html (accessed 31 May 2005).

Berlo, Janet C., and Ruth B. Phillips. *Native North American Art: Oxford History of Art*. New York: Oxford University Press, 1998.

Bernard, Bonnie. "Turning the Corner: From Risk to Resiliency, A Compilation of Articles from the *Western Center News*." Portland, OR: Western Regional Center for Drug-Free Schools and Communities, 1993.

Berndt, C.H. "Digging Sticks and Spears, or the Two-Sex Model." In F. Gale, ed., *Woman's Role in Aboriginal Society*. Canberra: Australian Institute of Aboriginal Studies, 1970.

Berthet, Thierry. "La Francisation des Amerindiens en Nouvelle France: Politiques et enjeux / Frenchifing the Natives in New France: Policies and Aims." *Canadian Studies* 34 (1993): 79–89.

Blackman, Margaret. "Feastwear: Haida Art Goes Couture." *American Indian Art Magazine* 17, 4 (1992).

Blaney, Fay. "Aboriginal Women's Action Network." In Kim Anderson and Bonita Lawrence, eds., *Strong Women Stories: Native Vision and Community Survival*. Toronto: Sumach Press, 2003.

Blaut, J.M. *The Colonizer's Model of the World: Geographical Diffusionism and Eurocentric History*. New York: The Guilford Press, 1993.

Boas, Franz. *Primitive Art*. New York: Dover Publications, 1955.

Bobet, E. "Teenage Pregnancy. Literature Review and Scan for Programs in First Nation Communities." Report prepared for the Public Health Department, James Bay Cree Board of Health and Social Services, 2005.

Boyer, Bob, and Carol Podedworny. *Odjig: The Art of Daphne Odjig 1960–2000*. Toronto: Key Porter Books, 2001.

Boyer, Y. "First Nation Métis and Inuit Health Care: The Crown's Fiduciary Obligation." In Discussion Paper Series in Aboriginal Health, No. 2. Ottawa: National Aboriginal Health Organization and the Native Law Centre, 2004.

———. "The International Right to Health for Indigenous Peoples in Canada." In Discussion Paper Series in Aboriginal Health, No. 3. Ottawa: National Aboriginal Health Organization and the Native Law Centre of Canada, 2004.

Brant Castellano, Marlene. "Ethics of Aboriginal Research." *Journal of Aboriginal Health* 1, 1 (2004): 98–107.

———. "Native Women—Past." In *Portraits: Peterborough Area Women Past and Present*. Peterborough, ON: Portraits Group, 1975. Reprinted in part as "Women in Huron and Ojibwa Societies." In Nuzhat Amin, et al., eds., *Canadian Woman Studies: An Introductory Reader*. Toronto: Inanna Publications and Education Inc., 1999.

———. "Canadian Case Study—The Role of Adult Education Promoting Community Involvement in Primary Health Care." *Saskatchewan Indian Federated College Journal* 4, 1 (1988): 23–54.

Brant Castellano, Marlene. "Updating Aboriginal Traditions of Knowledge." In George Sefa Dei, Budd Hall, and Dorothy Rosenberg, eds., *Indigenous Knowledges in Global Contexts: Multiple Readings of Our World*. Toronto: University of Toronto Press, 2000.

Brant Castellano, Marlene, Lynn Davis, and Louise Lahache. *Aboriginal Education: Fulfilling the Promise*. Vancouver: University of British Columbia Press, 2001 on p. 252.

Brant Castellano, Marlene, and Janice Hill. "First Nations Women: Reclaiming Our Responsibilities." In Joy Parr, ed., *A Diversity of Women, Ontario, 1945–1980*. Toronto: University of Toronto Press, 1995.

Brant, Beth, ed. *A Gathering of Spirit: Writing and Art of North American Indian Women*. Toronto: The Women's Press, 1988.

———. *Mohawk Trail*. Ithaca, NY: Firebrand Books, 1985.

Brant, Beth, and Sandra Laronde, eds. *Sweetgrass Grows All Around Her*. Toronto: Native Women in the Arts, 1996.

Brown, D., and J. Kulig. "The Concept of Resilience: Theoretical Lessons from Community Research." *Health and Canadian Society* 4, 1 (1996): 29–50.

Brownlee, Kevin, and E. Leigh Syms. *Kayasoch Kikawenow: Our Mother from Long Ago, an Early Cree Woman and Her Personal Belongings from Nagami Bay, Southern Indian Lake*. Winnipeg: Manitoba Museum of Man and Nature, 1999.

Bryce, P.H. *The Story of a National Crime—Being a Record of the Health Conditions of the Indians of Canada from 1904–1921*. Ottawa: James Hope and Sons, 1922.

Burnaby, B. "Personal thoughts on Indigenous language stabilization." In J. Reyhner, ed., *Teaching Indigenous Languages*. Flagstaff: Northern Arizona University, 1997. http://jan.ucc. nau.edu/~jar/TIL_24.html (accessed 19 October 2007).

Burnaby, B., and Beaujot, R. *The Use of Aboriginal Languages in Canada: An Analysis of 1981 Census Data*. Ottawa: Social Trends Analysis Directorate and Native Citizens Directorate, Department of the Secretary of State, 1986.

Campbell, Maria. *Achimoona*. Saskatoon: Fifth House, 2005. First published 1985.

———. *Stories of the Road Allowance People*. Penticton, BC: Theytus Books, 1995.

———. *Halfbreed*. Toronto: McClelland and Stewart, 1973.

Canada, Department of Foreign Affairs and International Trade. "Canada's International Human Rights Policy." Ottawa: Department of Foreign Affairs and International Trade, 2004.

Canada, Secretary of State. *Speaking Together: Canada's Native Women*. Ottawa: Department of the Secretary of State, 1975.

Canadian Broadcasting Corporation. "Women in First Nations Politics." 22 November 2005. http://www.cbc.ca/news/background/aboriginals/roleofwomen.html.

———. "Sterilized Woman Sues Stanton Hospital." 2 August 2004. http://north.cbc.ca/ regional/servlet/View?filename=aug02stantonsuit02082004 (accessed 5 March 2006).

———. "Family Wants Answers after Fetus Returned in Cardboard Box." 21 May 2004. http:// www.cbc.ca/canada/story/2004/05/19/unbornchild040519.html (accessed 5 March 2006).

———. "Alberta Apologizes for Forced Sterilization." 9 November 1999. http://www.cbc.ca/ canada/story/1999/11/02/sterilize991102.html (accessed 5 March 2006).

———. "We are Deeply Sorry." 7 January 1998. http://archives.cbc.ca/IDC-1-70-692-4011/ disasters_tragedies/residential_schools/clip9 (accessed 5 March 2006).

———. "Abuse Affects the Next Generation." 2 April 1993. http://archives.cbc.ca/society/ education/topics/692-4008/ (accessed 5 March 2006).

Canadian Council on Learning. *State of Learning in Canada: No Time for Complacency*. Ottawa: Canadian Council on Learning, 2007. http://www.ccl-cca.ca/CCL/Reports/ StateofLearning/StateofLearning2007.htm.

Canadian Heritage. *Towards a New Beginning: A Foundation Report for a Strategy to Revitalize First Nation, Inuit and Métis Languages and Cultures*. Report to the Minister of Canadian Heritage by the Task Force on Aboriginal Languages and Cultures. Catalogue No. CH4-96/2005. Ottawa: Canadian Heritage, 2005.

Cannon, Martin. "The Regulation of First Nations Sexuality." *Canadian Journal of Native Studies* 18, 1 (1998): 1–18.

Cardinal, H., and W. Hildebrandt. *Treaty Elders of Saskatchewan*. Calgary: University of Calgary Press, 2001.

Carter, Sarah. "Categories and Terrains of Exclusion: Constructing the 'Indian Woman' in the Early Settlement Era in Western Canada." In Catherine Cavanaugh and Randi Warne, ed., *Telling Tales*. Vancouver: University of British Columbia Press, 2000.

Cattell, J.P., R.A. MacKinnon, and E. Forster. "Limited Goal Therapy in a Psychiatric Clinic." *American Journal of Psychiatry* 120 (1963): 255–260.

Chametzky, Jules. "Public Intellectuals—Now and Then." *Melus* 29 (2004). Cook-Lynn, Elizabeth. "American Indian Intellectualism and the New Indian Story." *American Indian Quarterly* 20 (1996): 214.

Charbonneau, H. "Trois siècles de dépopulation amérindienne." In L. Normandeau and V. Piché, eds., *Les populations amérindiennes et inuit du Canada*. Montreal: University of Montreal Press, 1984.

Charette, Guillaume. *Vanishing Spaces: Memoirs of Louis Goulet*. Winnipeg: Editions Bois Brulés, 1980.

Clatworthy, Stewart. "Aboriginal Population Projections for Canada, Provinces and Regions: 2001–2026." Report prepared for the Strategic Research and Analysis Directorate at Indian and Northern Affairs Canada, Ottawa, 2006.

———. "Impacts of the 1985 Amendments to the Indian Act on First Nations Populations." In J. White, P. Maxim and D. Beavon, eds., *Aboriginal Conditions: Research Foundations for Public Policy*. Vancouver: University of British Columbia Press, 2003a.

———. "Factors Contributing to Unstated Paternity." Report prepared for the Strategic Research and Analysis Directorate at Indian and Northern Affairs Canada, Ottawa, 2003b. http://dsp-psd.pwgsc.gc.ca/Collection/R2-255-2003E.pdf.

———. *Re-assessing the Population Impacts of Bill C-31*. Report prepared for the Strategic Research and Analysis Directorate at Indian and Northern Affairs Canada, Ottawa, 2001. http://dsp-psd.pwgsc.gc.ca/Collection/R2-363-2004E.pdf.

Clegg, Jennifer. "Death, Disability, and Dogma." *Philosophy, Psychiatry, and Psychology* 10, 1 (March 2003): 67–79.

Cook, Mary. "Lady Sarah." *Ottawa Today's Seniors*, January 1997, p. 32.

Cook, Noble David. *Born to Die: Disease and New World Conquest, 1492–1650*. London: Cambridge University Press, 1998.

Cook, Sherburne F. "The Significance of Disease in the Extinction of the New England Indians." *Human Biology* 45, 3 (1973): 485–508.

Cooke, M. "Using UNDP Indices to Examine Gender Equality and Well-being." In J. White, D. Beavon, and N. Spence, eds., *Aboriginal Well-Being: Canada's Continuing Challenge*. Toronto: Thompson Educational Publishing, 2007.

Cooke, M., and D. Beavon. 2007. "The Registered Indian Human Development Index, 1981-2001." In J. White, D. Beavon, and N. Spence, eds., *Aboriginal Well-Being: Canada's Continuing Challenge*. Toronto: Thompson Educational Publishing, 2007.

Cooke, M., D. Beavon, and M. McHardy. *Measuring the Well-Being of Aboriginal People: An Application of the United Nations' Human Development Index to Registered Indians in Canada, 1981–2001*. Ottawa: Indian and Northern Affairs Canada, 2004. http://www.ainc-inac.gc.ca/ai/rs/pubs/re/mwb/mwb-eng.asp.

Cooke, M., and E. Guimond. *Gender Equality and Well-Being*. Ottawa: Indian and Northern Affairs Canada, 2006. http://www.ainc-inac.gc.ca/ai/rs/pubs/re/gewb/gewb-eng.pdf.

Cooper, James Fenimore. *The Last of the Mohicans*. Albany: State University of New York Press, 1983.

Cornet, Wendy. "First Nations Governance, the Indian Act and Women's Equality Rights." In *First Nations Women, Governance and the Indian Act: A Collection of Policy Research Reports*. Ottawa: Status of Women Canada, 2001.

Crate, Joan. *Foreign Homes*. London, ON: Brick Books, 2002.

———. *Pale As Real Ladies: Poems for Pauline Johnson*. London, ON: Brick Books, 1991.

Crégheur, A. *Assessment of Data on Aboriginal Identity. 1986 Census of Canada*. Ottawa: Statistics Canada, Housing, Family and Social Statistics Division, 1988.

Crystal, David. *Language Death*. London: Cambridge University Press, 2000.

Culleton, Beatrice. *Spirit of the White Bison*. Winnipeg: Pemmican Publications, 1985.

———. *In Search of April Raintree*. Winnipeg: Pemmican Publications, 1983.

Currie, Noel Elizabeth. "Jeannette Armstrong, The Colonial Legacy." In W.H. New, ed., *Native Writers and Canadian Writing*. Vancouver: University of British Columbia Press, 1990.

Cuthand, Beth. *Voices in the Waterfall*. Vancouver: Lazara Press, 1989.

Denevan, William M., ed. *The Native Population of the Americas in 1492*. Madison: University of Wisconsin Press, 1976.

Dickason, Olive P. *Canada's First Nations : A History of Founding Peoples from Earliest Times*. Toronto: McClelland and Stewart, 1992.

———. "The Many Faces of Canada's History as it Relates to Aboriginal People." In Ute Lischke and David T. McNab, eds., *Walking a Tightrope: Aboriginal Peoples and their Representations*. Waterloo: Wilfrid Laurier University Press, 2005.

———. *Canada's First Nations: A History of Founding Peoples from Earliest Times*. Toronto: Oxford University Press, 1992.

———. "From 'One Nation' in the Northeast to 'New Nation' in the Northwest: A look at the emergence of the metis." In Jacqueline Peterson and Jennifer Brown, eds., *The New Peoples: Being and Becoming Métis in North America*. Winnipeg: University of Manitoba Press, 1985.

———. *The Myth of the Savage and the Beginnings of French Colonization in the Americas*. Edmonton: University of Alberta Press, 1984.

Dobson, Tom. "Ancient Cree Art Goes Commercial." *Winnipeg Free Press*, 3 November 1956, p. 28.

Dobyns, Henry F. *Their Number Become Thinned: Native American Population Dynamics in Eastern North America*. Knoxville, TN: University of Tennessee Press, 1983.

Dokis, Laurie. "Cultural Competence for Registered Nurses." *Canadian Women's Health Network Magazine* 4/5 (2001–2002). http://www.cwhn.ca/network-reseau/5-1/5-1pg9.html.

Downey, B., "Cultural Safety: Effecting and Supporting Transformative Change and Improving the Health of First Nations, Inuit and Métis People." Presented at Building Cultural Competence in Nursing through Traditional Knowledge: Our 30 Year Journey, conference of the Aboriginal Nurses Association of Canada, Vancouver, BC, 2005.

Doxtator, Deborah. *Fluffs and Feathers: An Exhibit on the Symbols of Indianness*. Brantford: Woodland Cultural Centre, 1992.

Dudziak, Suzanne. "The Politics and Process of Partnership: A Case Study of the Aboriginal Healing and Wellness Strategy." PhD thesis, University of Toronto, 2000.

Dumont. Marilyn. *Green Girl Dreams Mountains*. Lantville, BC: Ooolichan Books, 2001.

———. *A Really Good Brown Girl*. London, ON: Brick Books, 1996.

Duran, Eduardo, and Bonnie Duran. *Native American Postcolonial Psychology*. Albany: State University of New York Press, 1995.

Durand, Joseph and Vinteur Durand. *Jean Durand et sa Posterité*. Sillery, QC: L'Association des Famillies Durand, 1991.

Durie, Mason. "Indigenous Resilience: from disease to disadvantage to the realization of potential." Paper presented at the Pacific Region Indigenous Doctors Congress, Rotorua, New Zealand, 7 December 2006.

Dutcher, L. "A.N.A.C.'s Efforts Relative to Cultural Competency." Presented at Building Cultural Competence in Nursing through Traditional Knowledge: Our 30 Year Journey, conference of the Aboriginal Nurses Association of Canada, Vancouver, BC, 2005.

Eigenbrod, Renate. *Travelling Knowledges: Positioning The Im/Migrant Reader of Aboriginal Literature in Canada*. Winnipeg: University of Manitoba Press, 2005.

Emberly, Julia V. *Thresholds of Difference: Feminist Critique, Native Women's Writings, Postcolonial Theory*. Toronto: University of Toronto Press, 1993.

Ermine, W., R. Sinclair, B. Jeffery. "The Ethics of Research Involving Indigenous Peoples: Report of the Indigenous Peoples Health Research Centre to the Interagency Advisory Panel on Research Ethics." Regina: Indigenous Peoples Health Research Centre, 2004. http://www.iphrc.ca/Upload/ethics_review_iphrc.pdf.

Faries, Rev. Richard, ed. *A Dictionary of the Cree Language as Spoken in the Provinces of Quebec, Ontario, Manitoba, Saskatchewan and Alberta*. Toronto: Church of England in Canada, 1938.

Farley, Melissa, Jacqueline Lynne, and Ann J. Cotton. "Prostitution in Vancouver: Violence and the Colonization of First Nations Women." *Transcultural Psychiatry* 42, 2 (2005): 242–271.

Fee, Margery. "Upsetting Fake Ideas: Jeannette Armstrong's *Slash* and Beatrice Culleton's *April Raintree*." In W.H. New, ed., *Native Writers and Canadian Writing*. Vancouver: University of British Columbia Press, 1990.

Ferguson, R.G. *Studies in Tuberculosis*. Toronto: University of Toronto Press, 1955.

Fernandez, C. "Coming full circle: A young man's perspective on building gender equity in Aboriginal communities." In K. Anderson and B. Lawrence, eds., *Strong Women Stories: Native Vision and Community Survival*. Toronto: Sumach Press, 2003.

Fife, Connie, ed. *The Colour of Resistance: A Contemporary Collection of Writing by Aboriginal Women*. Toronto: Sister Vision Press. 1993.

Findlay, I.M., and W. Wuttunee. "Aboriginal women's community economic development: Measuring and promoting success." *Institute for Research on Public Policy Choices* 13, 4 (2007).

Fiske, Jo-Anne. "Political Status of Native Indian Women: Contradictory Implications of Canadian State Policy." *American Indian Culture and Research Journal* 19, 1/2 (1995): 1–30.

———. "Child of the State, Mother of the Nation: Aboriginal Women and the Ideology of Motherhood." *Culture* 12, 1 (1993): 17–35.

———. "Carrier Women and the Politics of Mothering." In Gillian Creese and Veronica Strong-Boag, eds., *BC Reconsidered: Essays on Women*. Vancouver: Press Gang, 1992.

———. "Native Women in Reserve Politics: Strategies and Struggles." *Journal of Legal Pluralism and Unofficial Law* 30 (1991): 121–137.

Fiske, Jo-Anne, and E. George. *Seeking Alternatives to Bill C-31: From Cultural Trauma to Cultural Revitalization through Customary Law*. Ottawa: Status of Women Canada, 2006.

Fiske, Jo-Anne, Melonie Newell, and Evelyn George. "First Nations Women and Governance: A Study of Custom and Innovation among Lake Babine Nation Women." In *First Nations Women, Governance and the Indian Act: A Collection of Policy Research Reports*. Ottawa: Status of Women Canada, 2001.

Francis, Daniel. *The Imaginary Indian: The Image of the Indian in Canadian Culture*. Vancouver: Arsenal Pulp Press, 1992.

Fulford, G., with J.M. Daigle, B. Stevenson, C. Tolley, and T. Wade. *Sharing our Success: More Case Studies in Aboriginal Schooling*. Kelowna, BC: Society for the Advancement of Excellence in Education, 2007.

Furst, Sidney S., ed. *Psychic Trauma*. New York: Basic Books, 1967.

Gal, Susan. *Language Shift: Social Determinants of Linguistic Change in Bilingual Austria*. New York: Academic Press, 1979.

Godard, Barbara. "The Politics of Representation: Some Native Canadian Women Writers." In W.H. New, ed., *Native Writers and Canadian Writing*. Vancouver: University of British Columbia Press, 1990.

Goldmann, G. *The Aboriginal Population and the Census. 120 Years of Information—1871 to 1991*. Paper presented at the Conference of the International Union for the Scientific Study of Population, Montreal, 1993.

Gorman, Brian. "Late Starter." *Canadian Geographic* 124, 5 (Sep/Oct 2004).

Graham-Cumming, G. "Health of the Original Canadians, 1867–1967." *Medical Services Journal Canada* 23 (1967).

Gramsci, A. *Selections from the Prison Notebooks*. London: Lawrence and Wishart, 1971.

Grant, Agnes, ed. *Our Bit of Truth: An Anthology of Canadian Native Literature*. Winnipeg: Pemmican Publications, 1990.

Grant, Wendy. "Salish Weaving: An Art Nearly Lost." In Elizabeth Lominska Johnson and Kathryn Bernick, eds., *Hands of Our Ancestors: the Revival of Salish Weaving at Musqueam*. Museum Note No. 16. Vancouver: Museum of Anthropology, University of British Columbia, 1986.

Grant-John, W. *Report of the Ministerial Representative Matrimonial Real Property Issues on Reserves*. 2007. http://www.ainc-inac.gc.ca/br/mrp/pubs/rmr/rmr-eng.asp.

Graves, Theodore D. "Urban Indian Personality and the 'Culture of Poverty.'" *American Ethnologist* 1, 1 (1974): 65–86.

Green, Joyce. "Transforming at the Margins of the Academy" In I. Oakes, R. Riewe., M. Bennet, and B. Chisholm, eds. *Pushing the Margins: Native and Northern Studies*. Winnipeg: Native Studies Press, University of Manitoba, 2001.

———. "Constitutionalizing the Patriarchy: Aboriginal Women and Aboriginal Government." *Constitutional Forum* 4, 4 (1993).

Grekul, Jana, et al. "Sterilizing the 'Feeble-minded': Eugenics in Alberta, Canada, 1929–1972," *Journal of Historical Sociology* 17, 4 (2004): 359.

Greschner, Donna. "Aboriginal Women, the Constitution and Criminal Justice." *University of British Columbia Law Review*, Special edition (1992): 338.

Guimond, Eric. "L'explosion démographique des populations autochtones du Canada de 1986 à 2001." PhD thesis, University of Montreal, 2009.

———. *First Nations Community Well-Being and Teen Fertility*. Ottawa: Indian and Northern Affairs Canada, Strategic Research and Analysis Directorate, 2008.

———. *Aboriginal Demographics: Population Size, Growth and Well-Being*. Presentation to the Standing Committee on Aboriginal Affairs and Northern Development, Ottawa, 2006.

———. *Measuring the Well-Being of Registered Indian Men and Women*. Presentation made at the Social Cohesion Workshop organized by the Policy Research Initiative, Government of Canada, 2004.

———. "Changing Ethnicity: The Concept of Ethnic Drifters." In J. White, P. Maxim, and D. Beavon, eds., *Aboriginal Conditions: Research Foundations for Public Policy*. Vancouver: University of British Columbia Press, 2003.

———. "Ethnic Mobility and the Demographic Growth of Canada's Aboriginal Populations from 1986 to 1996." In A. Bélanger, ed., *Report on the Demographic Situation in Canada, 1998–1999*. Ottawa: Statistics Canada, 1999. Catalogue #91-209-XIE: 187–200.

Guimond, E., and M. Cooke. "The Current Well-Being of Registered Indians Youth: Concerns for the Future?" *Horizons* 10, 1 (2008): 26–30.

Guimond, E., N. Robitaille, and S. Senécal. 2007. *Fuzzy Definitions and Demographic Explosion of Aboriginal Populations in Canada, from 1986 to 2001*. Paper presented at the Conférence internationale Statistiques sociales et diversité ethnique: doit-on compter, comment et à quelles fins? co-organized by Centre interuniversitaire québécois de statistiques sociales (Canada) and Institut national d'études démographiques (France), 2007.

Gunn Allen, Paula. *The Sacred Hoop: Recovering the Feminine in American Indian Traditions*. Boston: Beacon Press, 1986.

Hager, Barbara. "Verna Kirkness: Lady of the Longhouse." In *Honour Song: A Tribute*. Vancouver: Raincoast Books, 1996.

Hail, Barbara A., and Kate C. Duncan. *Out of the North: The Subarctic Collection of the Haffenreffer Museum of Anthropology*. Providence, RI: Haffenreffer Museum of Anthropology, Brown University, 1989.

Halfe, Louise. *Blue Marrow*. Regina: Coteau Books, 2004. First published 1998 by McClelland and Stewart.

———. *Bear Bones and Feathers*. Regina: Coteau Books, 1994.

Hallowell, Alfred Irving. "Ojibwa Personality and Acculturation." In P. Bohannan and F. Plog, eds., *Beyond the Frontier: Social Process and Cultural Change*. New York: Natural History Press, 1967.

Hampton, Eber. "Towards a Redefinition of Indian Education." In Marie Battiste, Marie and Jean Barman, eds., *First Nations Education in Canada: The Circle Unfolds*. Vancouver: University of British Columbia Press, 1995.

Hanson, B. *Dual Realities – Dual Strategies: Future Paths of Aboriginal Peoples' Development*. Saskatoon, SK: self-published, 1985.

Hartley, G. "The Search for Consensus: A Legislative History of Bill C-31, 1969–1985." In J.P. White, E. Anderson, W. Cornet, and D. Beavon, eds., *Aboriginal Policy Research: Moving Forward, Making a Difference*. Toronto: Thompson Educational Publishing, 2007.

Harvey, Penelope. "The presence and absence of speech in the communication of gender." In Pauline Burton, Ketaki Kushari Dyson, and Shirley Ardener, eds., *Bilingual Women: Anthropological Approaches to Second language Use*. Providence, RI: Berg, 1994.

Hawkins, Mary. *Here to Stay*. Ottawa: Native Council of Canada, 1983.

Hawthorn, Harry B. *A Survey of the Contemporary Indians of Canada: Economic, Political, Educational Needs and Policies*. Ottawa: Indian Affairs Branch, 1967.

Health Canada. *Diabetes among Aboriginal People (First Nations, Inuit and Métis) in Canada: The Evidence*. Ottawa: Health Canada, First Nations and Inuit Health Branch, 2000.

———. *Indian Health Policy 1979*. Ottawa: Health Canada, 1979.

———. *A New Perspective on the Health of Canadians*. Ottawa: Health Canada, 1974.

Henderson, J. Sákéj. "Postcolonial Ghost Dancing: Diagnosing European Colonialism." In Marie Battiste, ed., *Reclaiming Indigenous Voice and Vision*. Vancouver: University of British Columbia Press, 2000.

Henry, L. *Dictionnaire démographique multilingue*. Liège, Belgium: Ordina Éditions, International Union for the Scientific Study in Population, 1981.

Herman, Judith. *Trauma and Recovery: The Aftermath of Violence, from Domestic Abuse to Political Terror*. New York: Basic Books, 1997.

Hilbert, Vi. *Lady Louse Lived There*. Seattle: Lushootseed Press, 1996.

Hill, B.H. *Shaking the Rattle: Healing the Trauma of Colonization*. Penticton, BC: Theytus Books, 1995.

Hobcraft, J. "Towards a Conceptual Framework on Population, Reproductive Health, Gender and Poverty Reduction." In *Population and Poverty: Achieving Equity, Equality and Sustainability*. Population and Development Strategies Series 8. New York: United Nations Population Fund, 2003.

Hodgson, Heather, ed. *Seventh Generation: Contemporary Native Writing*. Penticton, BC: Theytus Books, 1989.

Hoff, Joan. *Law, Gender and Injustice: A Legal History of U.S. Women*. New York: New York University Press, 1991.

Hogg, P.W. *Constitutional Law of Canada*. Fourth edition. Scarborough: Carswell, 2002.

Holmes, Leilani. "Heart Knowledge, Blood Memory, and the Voice of the Land: Implications of Research among Hawaiian Elders." In George J. Sefa Dei, Budd L. Hall, and Dorothy Goldin Rosenberg, eds., *Indigenous Knowledges in Global Contexts: Multiple Readings of Our World*. Toronto: University of Toronto Press. 2000.

Holmes Whitehead, Ruth. *Micmac Quillwork*. Halifax: The Nova Scotia Museum, 1982.

Horner, James. "The Sterilization of Leilani Muir." http://www.canadiancontent.ca/issues/0299sterilization.html (accessed 5 March 2006).

Horn-Miller, Kahente. "Otiyaner: The 'Women's Path' Through Colonialism." *Atlantis* 29, 2 (2005).

Hoy, Helen. *How Should I Read These? Native Women Writers in Canada*. Toronto: University of Toronto Press. 2001.

Hulan, Rene, ed. *Native North America: Critical and Cultural Perspectives*. Toronto: ECW Press, 1999.

Hull, J. *Aboriginal Women: A Profile from the 2001 Census*. 2006. http://www.ainc-inac.gc.ca/ai/rs/pubs/re/abw/abw-eng.pdf (accessed 13 June 2007).

Hunter, Lynette. *Outsider Notes: Feminist Approaches to Nation State Ideology: Writers/Readers and Publishing*. Vancouver: Talon Books. 1996.

Illnick, Karen. "Women in Politics in the North: An interview with Caroline Anawak." In Mary Crnkovich, ed., *Gossip: A Spoken History of Women in the North* (Ottawa: Canadian Arctic Resources Committee Publishing Program, 1990).

Indian and Northern Affairs Canada. *Aboriginal Demography: Population, Household and Family Projections, 2001–2026*. Ottawa: Indian and Northern Affairs Canada, 2008. http://www.ainc-inac.gc.ca/ai/rs/pubs/re/abd/abd-eng.asp.

———. *Basic Departmental Data 2004*. Ottawa: Indian and Northern Affairs Canada, First Nations and Northern Statistics Section, 2005.

———. *Words First An Evolving Terminology Relating to Aboriginal Peoples in Canada*. Ottawa: Indian and Northern Affairs Canada, 2004. http://www.ainc-inac.gc.ca/pr/pub/wf/index_e.html.

———. "Aboriginal Women: A Demographic, Social and Economic Profile." http://www.hc-sc.gc.ca/hl-vs/pubs/women-femmes/aborauto_e.html (accessed 5 March 2006).

———. "Aboriginal Women: Meeting the Challenges." http://www.ainc-inac.gc.ca/ai/ss/pubs/wnm/wnm-eng.asp (accessed 5 March 2006).

———. "Gender Equality Analysis Policy" http://www.ainc-inac.gc.ca/pr/pub/eql/eql_e.html (accessed 21 September 2006).

Jaimes, M. Annette, and Theresa Halsey. "American Indian Women at the Center of Indigenous Resistance in Contemporary North America." In M. Annette Jaimes, ed., *The State of Native America: Genocide: Colonization and Resistance*. Boston: South End Press, 1992.

Jaine, Linda, and Drew Hayden Taylor, eds. *Voices: Being Native in Canada*. Saskatoon: University of Saskatchewan, Extension Division, 1992.

Jeanings, Francis. *The Invasion of America: Indians, Colonialism and the Cant of Conquest*. Chapel Hill: University of North Carolina Press, 1976.

Jeffries, Theresa M. "Sechelt Women and Self-Government." In Gillian Creese and Veronica Strong-Boag, eds., *BC Reconsidered: Essays on Women*. Vancouver: Press Gang, 1992.

Jensen, Doreen, and Polly Sargent. *Robes of Power: Totem Poles on Cloth*. Vancouver: University of British Columbia Press and Kianmax Northwest Cost Indian Arts Society, 1986.

Joe, Rita. *Song of Rita Joe: Autobiography of a Mi'kmaq Poet*. Charlottetown: Ragweed Press, 1996.

———. *The Song of Eskasoni: More Poems of Rita Joe*. Charlottetown: Ragweed Press, 1988.

———. *Poems of Rita Joe*. Halifax: Abenaki Press, 1978.

Johnson, Pauline E. *Flint and Feather*. 1917. Toronto: Paperjacks Ltd., 1987.

Jones, Linda, Alexandra Snelgrove, and Pamela Muckosy, "The Double-X Factor: Harnessing Female Human Capital for Economic Growth," International Journal of Emerging Markets. Emerald Insight Publishing, 1, 4 (2006).

Kane, Margo. "Moonlodge." In Daniel David Moses and Terry Goldie, eds., *Anthology of Canadian Native Literature in English*. 3rd ed. Toronto: Oxford University Press, 2005.

Kane, Marlyn, and Sylvia Maracle. "Our World According to Osennontion and Skonaganleh:ra." *Canadian Woman Studies* 10 2/3 (1989): 7–19.

Keeshig-Tobias, Lenore. *Into the Moon: Heart, Mind, Body, Soul*. Toronto: Sister Vision Press, 1996.

Keeshig-Tobias, Lenore. "Trickster Beyond 1992: Our Relationship." In Gerald McMaster and Lee-Ann Martin, eds., *Indigena*. Vancouver: Douglas and McIntyre, 1992.

Keeshig-Tobias, Lenore, ed. *Into The Moon*. Toronto: Sisters Vision, 1996.

Kehoe, Alice Beck. "Transcribing Insima, a Blackfoot 'Old Lady.'" In Jennifer S.H. Brown and Elizabeth Vibert, eds., *Reading Beyond Words: Contexts for Native History*. Ontario: Broadview Press, 1996.

Kenny, C. *North American Indian, Métis and Inuit Women Speak about Culture, Education and Work*. Ottawa: Status of Women Canada, 2002.

Kindred, H., et al. *International Law, Chiefly as Interpreted and Applied in Canada*. Fourth edition. Toronto: Emond Montgomery Publications, 1987.

King, Thomas, ed. *All My Relations*. Toronto: McClelland and Stewart, 1990.

King, Thomas, Cheryle Calver, and Helen Hoy, eds. *The Native in Literature*. Oakville: ECW Press, 1987.

Kinkade, M.D. "The Decline of Native Languages in Canada." In R.H. Robins and E.M. Uhlenbeck, eds., *Endangered Languages*. Oxford: Berg Publishers Limited, 1991.

Kirkness, Verna J. "Aboriginal Education in Canada: A Retrospective and a Prospective." *Journal of American Indian Education* 39, 1, Special Issue–Part 2 (1999): 14–30.

Kirkness, Verna J. "Keynote: October 1, 1992." In Jo-ann Archibald, ed., Selected Papers from the 1992 Mokakit Conference: Giving Voice to our Ancestors. Vancouver: University of British Columbia, 1993.

Kirkness, Verna J. *Khot-La-Cha: The Autobiography of Chief Simon Baker*. Vancouver: Douglas and McIntyre, 1994.

Kirkness, Verna J., and Jo-ann Archibald. *The First Nations Longhouse: Our Home Away from Home*. Vancouver: First Nations House of Learning, 2001.

Kirkness, Verna J., and Ray Barnhardt. "First Nations and Higher Education: The Four R's: Respect, Relevance, Reciprocity, and Responsibility." *Journal of American Indian Education* 30, 3 (1991).

Kirkpatrick, D., A. Amick, and H. Resnick. *The Impact of Homicide on Surviving Family Members. Final Report.* National Institute of Justice, Grant #87-IJ-CX-0017. Washington, DC: National Institute of Justice, 1990.

Klein, Laura F., and Lillian A. Ackerman, eds. *Women and Power in Native North America*. Norman: University of Oklahoma Press, 1995.

Krosenbrink-Gelissen, Liliane Ernestine. *Sexual Equality as an Aboriginal Right: The Native Women's Association of Canada and the Constitutional Process on Aboriginal Matters 1982–1987*. Saarbrücken: Verlag Breitenbach, 1991.

Lambert, John. "An Indian and His Squaw." Early Canadiana On-line. http://www.canadiana.org/citm/imagepopups/c014488_e.html (accessed 5 March 2006).

LaRocque, Emma. "From the Land to the Classroom: Broadening Epistemology." In Jill Oakes, R. Riewe, M. Bennet, and B. Chisholm, eds., *Pushing The Margins: Native and Northern Studies*. Winnipeg: Native Studies Press, University of Manitoba, 2001.

———. "When the Wild West Is Me: Re-Viewing Cowboys and Indians." In Lorry Felske and B. Rasporich, eds., *Challenging Frontiers: The Canadian West*. Calgary: University of Calgary Press. 2004.

———. "Native Identity and the Metis: Otehpayimsuak Peoples." In David Taras and B. Rasporich, eds., *A Passion for Identity: Canadian Studies for the 21ˢᵗ Century*. Scarborough: Nelson Thomson Learning, 2001.

———. "Native Writers Resisting Colonizing Practices in Canadian Historiography and Literature." PhD dissertation, University of Manitoba, 1999.

———. *Violence in Aboriginal Communities*. Ottawa: National Clearinghouse on Family Violence, Health Canada, 1994.

———. "Tides, Towns and Trains." Joan Turner, ed. *Living the Changes*. Winnipeg: University of Manitoba Press, 1990.

———. *Defeathering the Indian*. Agincourt: The Book Society of Canada, 1975.

LaRoque, Lorie-Ann. "Citizen of the year: An inspiration to all." *Saskatchewan Indian*, May 1992.

Larsen, Clark S., and George R. Milner. *In the Wake of Contact: Biological Responses to Conquest*. New York: John Wiley and Sons Inc., 1994.

Latulippe-Sakamoto, C. *Estimation de la mortalité des Indiens du Canada, 1900–1968*. University of Ottawa, Department of Sociology, 1971.

Lear, J. *Radical Hope: Ethics in the Face of Cultural Devastation*. Cambridge, MA: Harvard University Press, 2006.

Lee, T. *Definitions of Indigeneous Peoples in Selected Countries*. Quantitative Analysis and Socio-demographic Research, Working Paper Series 90-4. Ottawa: Indian and Northern Affairs Canada, 1990.

Leipert, Beverly D., and Linda Reutter. "Developing Resilience: How Women Maintain Their Health in Northern Geographically Isolated Settings." *Qualitative Health Research* 15, 1 (2005): 49–65.

Lertzman, D.A., and Vredenburg, H. "Indigenous peoples, resource extraction and sustainable development: An ethical approach." *Journal of Business Ethics* 56 (2005): 239–254.

Lescarbot, Marc. *Nova Francia, A Description of Acadia, 1606*. 1609. Trans. P. Erondelle. New York: Harper and Brothers, 1928.

Loh, S., R. Verma, E. Ng, M.J. Norris, M. George, and J. Perreault. *Population Projections of Registered Indians, 1996–2021*. Prepared by the Population Projections Section, Demography Division, Statistics Canada. Ottawa: Indian Affairs and Northern Development, 1998.

Loo, Tina. "Dan Cranmer's Potlatch: Law as Coercion, Symbol, and Rhetoric in British Columbia, 1884-1951." *Canadian Historical Review* 73, 2 (1992): 125–165.

Lorde, Andre. "The Master's Tools Will Never Dismantle the Master's House." In C. Moraga and G. Anzaldua, eds., *This Bridge Called My Back: Writings by Radical Women of Color*. New York: Kitchen Table: Women of Color Press, 1981.

Lutz, Hartmut. "Contemporary Native Literature in Canada." In Jorn Carlsen, ed., *O Canada: Essays on Canadian Native Literature and Culture*. Aarhus, Denmark: Aarhus University Press, 1995.

———. "The Voice of the Mother." In Jorn Carlsen, ed., *O Canada: Essays on Canadian Native Literature and Culture*. Aarhus, Denmark: Aarhus University Press, 1995.

Lux, M. *Medicine That Walks: Disease, Medicine, and Canadian Plains Native Peoples: 1880–1940*. Toronto: University of Toronto Press, 2001.

MacIvor, Sharon D. "The Indian Act as Patriarchal Control of Women." *Aboriginal Women's Law Journal* 41, 1 (1994): 41.

MacLeish, William H. *The Day Before America*. Boston: Houghton Mifflin Company, 1994.

Malloch, Lesley. "Indian Medicine, Indian Health: Study Between Red and White Medicine." *Canadian Woman Studies* 10, 2/3 (1989): 105–112.

Manitoba, Aboriginal Justice Implementation Commission. *The Aboriginal Justice Implementation Commission Final Report*. Winnipeg: Government of Manitoba, 2001. http://www.ajic.mb.ca/reports/final_toc.html (accessed 5 March 2006).

Mann, Barbara A. *Iroquoian Women: The Gantowisas*. New York: Peter Lang, 2000.

Maracle, Lee. *Daughters Are Forever*. Vancouver: Polestar, 2002.

Maracle, Lee, and Sandra Laronde, eds. *My Home as I Remember*. Toronto: Natural Heritage Books, 2000.

———. *Bent Box*. Penticton, BC: Theytus Books, 2000.

———. *Ravensong*. Vancouver: Press Gang Publishers, 1993.

———. *Sundogs*. Penticton, BC: Theytus Books, 1992.

———. *I Am Woman*. Vancouver: Write-On Press, 1988.

——— [Bobbi Lee, pseud.]. *Bobbi Lee: Indian Rebel*. Richmond: Liberation Support Movement Information Center, 1975. Reprint, Toronto: Women's Press, 1980.

Maracle, Sylvia. "The Eagle Has Landed: Native Women, Leadership and Community Development." In Kim Anderson and Bonita Lawrence, eds., *Strong Women Stories: Native Vision and Community Survival*. Toronto: Sumach Press, 2003.

Martin, Calvin L., ed. *The American Indian and the Problem of History*. New York: Oxford University Press, 1987.

Martin, Elizabeth, and Vivian Meyer. *Female Gazes—Seventy-five Women Artists*. Toronto: Second Story Press, 1997.

Mawani, Renisa. "The 'Savage Indian' and the 'Foreign Plague': Mapping Racial Categories and Legal Geographies of Race in British Columbia, 1871–1925." PhD thesis, University of Toronto, 2001. http://www.collectionscanada.ca/obj/s4/f2/dsk3/ftp04/NQ58938.pdf (accessed 5 March 2006).

Maynard, R. 1996. "The Study, the Context, and the Findings in Brief." In R. Maynard, ed., *Kids Having Kids: Economic Costs and Social Consequences of Teen Pregnancy*. Washington, DC: Urban Institute Press, 1996.

McClintock, Anne, Aamir Mufti, and Ella Shohat, eds. *Dangerous Liaisons: Gender, Nation, and Postcolonial Perspectives*. Minneapolis: University of Minnesota Press, 1997.

McIvor, Sharon Donna. "Identity and Equality: Language, Culture and Gender Rights." Symposium to Commemorate the 20th Anniversary of the Canadian Charter of Rights and Freedoms. Canada: Nicola Valley Institute of Technology, 2002.

———. "The Indian Act as Patriarchal Control of Women." *Aboriginal Women's Law Journal* 41, 1 (1994): 41–52.

McMaster, Gerald R. "Tenuous Lines of Descent: Indian Arts and Crafts of the Reservation Period." *Canadian Journal of Native Studies* 9, 2 (1989): 205–236.

McMaster, Gerald, and Lee-Ann Martin, eds. *Indigena: Contemporary Native Perspectives*. Vancouver: Douglas and McIntyre, 1992.

Medicine, B. "The role of American Indian women in cultural continuity and transition." In J. Penfield, ed., *Women and language in transition*. Albany: State University of New York Press, 1987.

Mihesuah, Devon. "Colonialism and Disempowerment." In Devon Mihesuah, ed., *Indigenous American Women: Decolonization, Empowerment, Activism*. Lincoln: University of Nebraska Press, 2003.

Miller, Christine, and P. Chuchryk, eds. *Women of the First Nations: Power, Wisdom and Strength.* Winnipeg: University of Manitoba Press, 1997.

Mills, Heather. *The Visual Arts—Primary Documents of 20ᵗʰ Century Canada.* Oakville, ON: Rubicon Publishing, 2003.

Montour, Martha. "Iroquois Women's Rights with Respect to Matrimonial Property on Indian Reserves." *Canadian Native Law Reporter* 4 (1987): 1.

Monture-Angus, Patricia. "The Lived Experience of Discrimination: Aboriginal Women Who Are Federally Sentenced and The Law: Duties and Rights." 2002. http://www.elizabethfry. ca/submissn/aborigin/1.htm (accessed 5 March 2006).

———. *Thunder in My Soul: A Mohawk Woman Speaks.* Halifax: Fernwood, 1995.

Monture-Okanee, P.A., and M.E. Turpel. "Aboriginal Peoples and Canadian Criminal Law: Rethinking Justice." *University of British Columbia Law Review*, special edition (1992): 239.

Morrison, R.B., and C.R. Wilson, eds. *Native Peoples: The Canadian Experience.* 3rd ed. Oxford: Oxford University Press, 2004.

Moses, Daniel David, and Terry Goldie, eds. *An Anthology of Canadian Native Literature.* Toronto: Oxford University Press, 1992.

Mukherjee, D. "Role of women in language maintenance and language shift: focus on the Bengali community in Malaysia." *International Journal of the Sociology of Language* 161 (2003): 103–120.

Muldoon, James. *The Americas in the Spanish World Order, The Justification for Conquest in the Seventeenth Century.* Philadelphia: University of Pennsylvania Press, 1994.

———. *Popes, Lawyers, and Infidels: The Church and the Non-Christian World 1250–1550.* Philadelphia: University of Pennsylvania Press, 1979.

National Aboriginal Health Organization Policy Research Unit. "Ways of Knowing: A Framework for Health Research." Ottawa: National Aboriginal Health Organization, 2003.

National Association of Friendship Centres. *Urban Aboriginal Women: Social Determinants of Health and Well-Being.* Ottawa: National Association of Friendship Centres, 2007. http:// www.naws-sfna.ca/pdf/NAFC-UrbanAboriginalWomen.pdf (accessed 7 February 2008).

National Indian Brotherhood. *Indian Control of Indian Education.* Ottawa: National Indian Brotherhood, 1972.

Native Women's Association of Canada. *Aboriginal Women and Health Care in Canada.* Submission to the Commission on the Future of Health Care in Canada, May 2002.

———. *Matriarchy and the Canadian Charter: A Discussion Paper.* Ottawa: Native Women's Association of Canada, 1991.

Nault, F., J. Chen, M.V. George, and M.J. Norris. *Population projections of registered Indians, 1991–2015.* Report prepared for Indian and Northern Affairs Canada by the Population Projections Section, Demography Division, Statistics Canada, 1993.

Neal, Arthur G. *National Trauma and Collective Memory: Major Events in the American Century.* New York: M.E. Sharpe Publishing, 1998.

Nemiroff, Diana, Robert Houle, and Charlotte Townsend-Gault. *Land Spirit Power—First Nations at the National Gallery of Canada.* Ottawa: National Gallery of Canada, 1992.

New, W.H., ed. *Native Writers and Canadian Writing: Canadian Literature Special Issue*. Vancouver: University of British Columbia Press, 1990.

Newhouse, David, Don McCaskill, and John Milloy. "Culture, Tradition, and Evolution: The Department of Native Studies at Trent University." In Duane Champagne and Jay Stauss, eds., *Native American Studies in Higher Education: Models for Collaboration between Universities and Indigenous Nations*. New York: Altamira Press, 2002.

Newhouse, D. "Magic and Joy: Traditional Aboriginal Views of Human Sexuality." Sex Information and Education Council of Canada newsletter in *Canadian Journal of Human Sexuality* 7, 2 (1998): 183–187.

Newlands, Anne. *Canadian Art—From its Beginnings to 2000*. Richmond Hill, ON: Firefly Books, 2000.

Newman, Peter C. *Caesars of the Wilderness*. Markham: Viking, 1987.

Nichols, John D., and Earl Nyholm. *A Concise Dictionary of Minnesota Ojibwe*. Minneapolis: University of Minnesota Press, 1995.

Norris, Mary Jane. "Aboriginal languages in Canada: Emerging trends and perspectives on second language acquisition." *Canadian Social Trends, 83* (2007): 19–27. Catalogue no. 11-008. Ottawa: Statistics Canada, 2007.

———. "Aboriginal languages in Canada: Trends and perspectives on maintenance and revitalization." In J.P. White, S. Wingert, D. Beavon, and P.Maxim, eds., *Aboriginal Policy Research Volume III: Moving Forward, Making a Difference*. Toronto: Thompson Educational Publishing, 2006.

———. "From generation to generation: Survival and maintenance of Canada's Aboriginal languages within families, communities and cities." In J. Blythe and R. McKenna Brown, eds., *Maintaining the Links Language, Identity and the Lands*. Proceedings of the 7th Conference of the Foundation for Endangered Languages, Broome, Western Australia, 22–24 September 2003.

———. "The Diversity and State of Aboriginal Languages in Canada." In *Canadian and French Perspectives on Diversity*, conference proceedings, 6 October 2003. Ottawa: Canadian Heritage, 2005.

———. "Canada's Aboriginal Languages." *Canadian Social Trends* 51 (1998): 8–16. Catalogue no. 11-008-XPE. Ottawa: Statistics Canada, 1998. http://www.statcan.ca/english/freepub/11-008-XIE/1998003/articles/4003.pdf.

Norris, Mary Jane, and L. Jantzen. "Aboriginal languages in Canada's urban areas: Characteristics, considerations and implications." In D. Newhouse and E. Peters, eds., *Not Strangers in these Parts: Urban Aboriginal Peoples*. Ottawa: Policy Research Initiative, 2003. http://recherchepolitique.gc.ca/doclib/AboriginalBook_e.pdf.

Norris, Mary Jane, D. Kerr and, F. Nault. *Projections of the Population with Aboriginal Identity in Canada, 1991–2016*. Prepared for the Royal Commission on Aboriginal Peoples. Ottawa: Statistics Canada, Demography division, 1995.

Norris, Mary Jane, and K. MacCon. "Aboriginal language transmission and maintenance in families: Results of an intergenerational and gender-based analysis for Canada, 1996." In J.P. White, P.S. Maxim, and D. Beavon, eds., *Aboriginal Conditions: Research as a Foundation for Public Policy*. Vancouver: University of British Columbia Press, 2003.

Nowak, Peter. "A Spiritual View of Indian History." *Globe and Mail*, 21 May 2003, p. R4.

Oberholtzer, Cath. "Cree Leggings as a Form of Communication." In William Cowan, ed., *actes du Vingt-Cinquieme Congres des Algonquinistes*. Ottawa: Carleton University, 1994.

O'Neil, John, Judith Bartlett, Janvier Mignone. "Best Practices in Intercultural Health." Manitoba Centre for Aboriginal Health Research, University of Manitoba, June 2005.

———. "Together We Survive: East Cree Material Culture." PhD dissertation, McMaster University, 1994.

Ontario Federation of Friendship Centres. *Tenuous Connections. Urban Aboriginal Youth Sexual Health and Pregnancy*. Report prepared by the Write Circle (Kim Anderson, principal researcher). Toronto: Ontario Federation of Friendship Centres, 2002.

O'Sullivan, E., and M. McHardy. "The Community Well-being Index (CWB): Well-being in First Nations Communities, Present, Past, and Future." In J. White, D. Beavon and N. Spence, eds., *Aboriginal Well-Being: Canada's Continuing Challenge*. Toronto: Thompson Educational Publishing, 2007.

Palys, T.S. "Prospects for Aboriginal Justice in Canada." Draft paper, Simon Fraser University, 1993.

Pearce, Roy Harvey. *Savagism and Civilization*. Baltimore: Johns Hopkins University Press, 1967.

Peers, Laura. "The Guardian of All: Jesuit Missionary and Salish Perceptions of the Virgin Mary." In Jennifer S.H. Brown and Elizabeth Vibert, eds., *Reading Beyond Words: Contexts for Native History*. Ontario: Broadview Press, 1996.

Perreault, Jeanne, and Sylvia Vance, eds. *Writing The Circle: Native Women of Western Canada*. Edmonton; NeWest Publishers, 1990.

Peterson, Jacqueline, and Jennifer Brown, eds. *The New Peoples: Being and Becoming Métis in North America*. Winnipeg: University of Manitoba Press, 1985.

Petone, Penny. *Native Literature in Canada: From the Oral Tradition to the Present*. Toronto: Oxford University Press, 1990.

Pettipas, Katherine. *Severing the Ties that Bind: Government Repression of Indigenous Religious Ceremonies on the Prairies*. Winnipeg: University of Manitoba Press, 1994.

Phillips, Ruth B. *Trading Identities: The Souvenir in Native North American Art from the Northeast, 1700–1900*. Montreal: McGill-Queen's University Press, 1998.

Phillips, Ruth B., and Christopher B. Steiner, eds. *Unpacking Culture: Art and Commodity in Colonial and Postcolonial Worlds*. Berkeley: University of California Press, 1999.

Piché, V., and M.V. George. "Estimates of Vital Rates for the Canadian Indians, 1960–1970." *Demography* 10, 3 (1973): 367–382.

Porter, Tom. "Traditions of the Constitution of the Six Nations." In Leroy Little Bear, Menno Boldt, J. Anthony Long, eds., *Pathways to Self-Determination*. Toronto: University of Toronto Press, 1984.

Pressat, R. *Dictionnaire de démographie*. Paris: Presses Universitaires de France, 1979.

Price, Sally. *Primitive Art in Civilized Places*. Chicago: University of Chicago Press, 1989.

Priest, Lisa. *Conspiracy of Silence*. Toronto: McClelland and Stewart, 1989.

Proulx-Turner, Sharron. *What The Auntys Say*. Toronto: McGilligan Books, 2002.

Ramsden, Irahapeti. "Kawa Whakaruruhau: Cultural Safety in Nursing Education in Aotearoa." *Nursing Praxis in New Zealand* 8, 3 (1993).

Rasporich, Beverly. "Native Women Writing: Tracing The Patterns." *Canadian Ethnic Studies* 28, 1 (1996).

Registered Nurses' Association of Ontario, Centre for Professional Nursing Excellence. "Embracing Cultural Diversity in Health Care: Developing Cultural Competence." http://rnao.org/Page.asp?PageID=122&ContentID=1200&SiteNodeID=241&BL_E (accessed 17 November 2006).

Rich, E.E., ed. *James Isham's Observations on Hudson's Bay, 1743 and Notes and Observations on a Book Entitled a Voyage to Hudson's Bay in the Dobbs Galley, 1749*. London: Hudson's Bay Record Society, 1949.

Robertson, Sheila. "Sexual and Racial Politics Underpin Collection of Indian, Cowgirl Images." *Saskatoon Star-Phoenix*, 12 August 2000, p. E17.

Robinson, Eden. *Monkey Beach*. Toronto: Alfred A. Knopf, 2000.

Robitaille, N., and R. Choinière. "L'accroissement démographique des groupes autochtones du Canada au XXe siècle." *Cahiers Québécois de démographie* 16, 1 (1987): 3–35.

Robitaille, N., and E. Guimond. "La reproduction des populations autochtones du Canada: exogamie, fécondité et mobilité ethnique." *Cahiers québécois de démographie* 32, 2 (2003): 295–314.

Rogers, C.R. *On Becoming a Person*. Boston: Houghton Mifflin, 1961.

Romaniuc, A. "Increase in Natural Fertility During the Early Stages of Modernization: Canadian Indians Case Study." *Demography* 18, 2 (1981): 157–172.

Romaniuc, A., and V. Piché. "Natality Estimates for the Canadian Indians by Stable Population Models, 1900–1969." *Canadian Review of Sociology and Anthropology* 9, 1 (1972): 1–20.

Royal Commission on Aboriginal Peoples. *For Seven Generations: Report of the Royal Commission on Aboriginal Peoples*. Ottawa: Minister of Supply and Services Canada, 1996. CD-ROM.

Royal Commission on Aboriginal Peoples. *Report of the Royal Commission on Aboriginal Peoples*. Ottawa: Canada Communications Group, 1996. http://www.ainc-inac.gc.ca/ap/pubs/sg/sg-eng.asp.

Rutter, M. "Psychosocial Adversity: Risk, Resilience and Recovery." In J. Richmond and M. Fraser, eds., *The Context of Youth Violence: Resilience, Risk, and Protection*. Westport, CT: Praeger Publishers, 2001.

Ryan, Allan, J. *The Trickster Shift—Humour and Irony in Contemporary Native Art*. Vancouver: University of British Columbia Press, 1999.

Said, E.W. *Culture And Imperialism*. New York: Vintage Books, 1994.

Savard, R., and J.R. Proulx. *Canada. Derrière l'épopée, les autochtones*. Montreal: l'Hexagone, 1982.

Sayers, Judith F., and Kelly A. MacDonald. "A Strong and Meaningful Role for First Nations Women in Governance." In *First Nations Women, Governance and the Indian Act: A Collection of Policy Research Reports*. Ottawa: Status of Women Canada, 2001.

Settee, P. "Native Languages Supporting Indigenous Knowledge." Presented at the United Nations International Expert Group Meeting on Indigenous Languages, New York, 8–10 January 2008. http://www.un.org/esa/socdev/unpfii/en/EGM_IL.html.

Shapiro, Ester R. "Family Bereavement and Cultural Diversity: A Social Developmental Perspective." *Family Process* 35, 3 (1996): 313–332.

Shoemaker, N., ed. *Negotiators of Change: Historical Perspectives on Native American Women*. New York: Routledge, 1995.

Siggner, A.J. *An Overview of Demographic, Social and Economic Conditions of Canada's Registered Indian Population*. Ottawa: Indian and Northern Affairs Canada, 1979.

Silman, J., ed. *Enough is Enough: Aboriginal Women Speak out*. Toronto: The Women's Press, 1987.

Simpson, Audra. "To the Reserve and Back Again: Kahnawake Mohawk Narratives of Self, Home and Nation." PhD thesis, McGill University, 2003.

Sinclair, A.M. *Introduction to Real Property Law*. 3rd ed. Toronto: Butterworths, 1987.

Sinclair, M. "Foreword." In Anne McGillivray and Brenda Comaskey, *Black Eyes All of the Time*. Toronto: University of Toronto Press, 1999.

Slipperjack, Ruby. *Weesquachak and the Lost Ones*. Penticton, BC: Theytus Books Ltd., 2000.

———. *Silent Words*. Saskatoon: Fifth House Publishers, 1992.

———. *Honour The Sun*. Winnipeg: Pemmican Publications, 1987.

Smith, D. *The Seventh Fire: The Struggle for Aboriginal Government*. Toronto: Key Porter Books, 1993.

Smith, Erica. "'Gentlemen, This is no Ordinary Trial': Sexual Narratives in the Trial of the Reverend Corbett, Red River, 1863." In Jennifer S.H. Brown and Elizabeth Vibert, eds., *Reading Beyond Words: Contexts for Native History*. Ontario: Broadview Press, 1996.

Smith, Graham Hingangaroa. "Transformative Praxis: Indigenous Reclaiming of the Academy and Higher Education." Paper delivered at the Canadian Indigenous and Native Studies Association annual conference, 9 July 2005.

Smolewski, Magdalena. "Learning from the Known: Historical and Cultural Factors Influencing the Position of Women in Two Australian Aboriginal Societies." PhD dissertation, University of Toronto, 2004.

Smylie, Janet. "A Guide for Health Professionals Working with Aboriginal Peoples." Society of Obstetricians and Gynecologists of Canada Policy Statement, No. 100, March 2001.

Society for the Advancement of Excellence in Education. *Sharing our Success: Promising Practices in Aboriginal Education*. Proceedings of the conference, Winnipeg, MB, 23–24 November 2007. http://www.saee.ca/successconference.

Sotomayor, Marta. "Language, Culture and Ethnicity in Developing Self-Concept." In M. Bloom, ed., *Life Span Development: Bases for Preventive and Interventive Helping*. New York: Macmillan, 1980.

Spikes, J. "Grief, Death and Dying." In E.W. Busse and D.G. Blazer, eds., *Handbook of Geriatric Psychiatry*. New York: Van Nostrand Reinhold Company, 1980.

Statistics Canada. *2006 Census Dictionary*. Catalogue No. 92-566-XWE. Ottawa: Department of Industry, 2008. http://www12.statcan.ca/english/census06/reference/dictionary/index.cfm.

———. "Aboriginal Women in Canada." In *Women in Canada 2005*. Catalogue no. 89-503-XIE. Ottawa: Statistics Canada, 2005.

———. *Aboriginal Peoples Survey 2001—Initial Findings: Well-being of the non-reserve Aboriginal Population*. Ottawa: Statistics Canada, 2003. http://www.statcan.ca/english/freepub/89-589-XIE/free.htm.

———. *2001 Census Dictionary*. Catalogue No. 92-378-XIE. Ottawa: Department of Industry, 2003.

———. "Aboriginal peoples of Canada: A demographic profile." *2001 Census: Analysis Series*. Catalogue no. 96 F00030XIE2001007. Ottawa: Statistics Canada, 2003.

———. *2001 Census. Analysis Series Aboriginal Peoples of Canada: A Demographic Profile*. Ottawa: Statistics Canada, 2001.

———. *General review of the 1986 Census*. Catalogue 99-137E. Ottawa: Supply and Services Canada, 1989.

Status of Women Canada. "Traditional Roles of First Nations Women." In First Nations Women, Governance and the *Indian Act*: A Collection of Policy Research Reports. Ottawa: Status of Women Canada. http://www.swc-cfc.gc.ca/pubs/pubspr/066231140X/200111_066231140X_8_e.html.

Sterling, Shirley. *My Name Is Seepeetza*. Toronto: Douglas and McIntyre, 1992.

Stevens, G., M.E.M. McKillip, and H. Ishizawa. "Intermarriage in the second generation: Choosing between newcomers and natives." *Migration Information Source*, October 2006. http://www.migrationinformation.org/Feature/display.cfm?id=444.

Stoler, Ann Laura. "Making Empires Respectable: The Politics of Race and Sexual Morality in Twentieth-Century Colonial Cultures." In Anne McClintock, Aarnir Mufti, and Ella Shohat, eds., *Dangerous Liaisons: Gender, Nation, and Postcolonial Perspectives*. Minneapolis: University of Minnesota Press, 1997.

Stout, Madeleine Dion. "Social Determinants of Health across the Life-Span: Research to Policy to Action—A Cree Perspective." Presented at York University, 1 December 2000.

Stout, Madeleine Dion, and Gregory Kipling. "Aboriginal Women in Canada: Strategic Research Directions for Policy Development." Ottawa: Status of Women Canada, 1998. http://www.swc-cfc.gc.ca/pubs/pubspr/0662634314/index_e.html.

Stout, Madeleine Dion, Gregory Kipling, and Roberta Stout. *Aboriginal Women's Health Research Synthesis Project: Final Report*. Winnipeg: Centres of Excellence for Women's Health, 2001.

Strange, Carolyn, and Tina Loo. *Making Good: Law and Moral Regulation in Canada, 1867–1939*. Toronto: University of Toronto Press, 1997.

Tanner, Adrian. *Bringing Home Animals: Religious Ideology and Mode of Production of the Mistassini Cree Hunters*. St. John's, NL: Institute of Social and Economic Research, Memorial Univesity of Newfoundland, 1979.

Tapinos, G. *Éléments de démographie. Analyse, déterminants socioéconomiques et histoire des populations*. Paris: Armand Colin, 1985.

Thomas, Isaac, and Mary Sue Maloughney. "Dually Disadvantaged and Historically Forgotten? Aboriginal Women and the Inherent Right to Self-Government." *Manitoba Law Journal* 21, 2 (1992).

Thomas, Jacob E. *Teachings from the Longhouse*. Don Mills, ON: Stoddart, 1994.

Thompson, Martie P., and Paula J. Vardaman. "The Role of Religion in Coping with the Loss of a Family Member to Homicide." *Journal for the Scientific Study of Religion* 36, 1 (1997): 44–51.

Thornburn, Olivia. "Mary Kawennatakie Adams: Mohawk Basket Maker and Artist." *American Art* 15, 2 (2001): 90–95.

Thornton, Russell. *American Indian Holocaust and Survival: A Population History Since 1492*. Norman, OK: University of Oklahoma Press, 1987.

Todd, Douglas. "The Best B.C. Thinkers." *Vancouver Sun*, 25 August 2000, p. A12.

Treaties and Historical Research Centre. *The Historical Development of the Indian Act*. 2nd ed. Ottawa: Department of Indian and Northern Affairs, 1978.

Trigger, Bruce G. *Natives and Newcomers: Canada's "Heroic Age" Reconsidered*. Kingston and Montreal: McGill-Queen's University Press, 1985.

Tuck, James A. *Ancient People of Port au Choix: The Excavation of an Archaic Indian Cemetary in Newfoundland*. St. John's: Memorial University of Newfoundland, 1989.

Turpel-Lafond, Mary-Ellen. "Patriarchy and Paternalism: The Legacy of the Canadian State for First Nations Women." Caroline Andrew and Sandra Rodgers, eds., *Women and the Canadian State*. Kingston and Montreal: McGill-Queen's University Press, 1997.

———. "Patriarchy and Paternalism: The Legacy of the Canadian State for First Nations Women." *Canadian Journal of Women and the Law* 6 (1993): 174–192.

Ubelaker, Douglas. "North American Indian Population Size, A.D. 1500 to 1985." *American Journal of Physical Anthropology* 77 (1988): 289–294.

United Nations Economic and Social Council. Report of the international expert group meeting on indigenous languages, New York, 8–10 January 2008. http://www.un.org/esa/socdev/unpfii/en/EGM_IL.html.

United Nations Secretariat of the Permanent Forum on Indigenous Issues. *Study of the Problem of Discrimination Against Indigenous Populations*. http://www.un.org/esa/socdev/unpfii/en/spdaip.html.

United Nations. *Demographic Yearbook 1995*. New York: United Nations, 1997.

Ursmiant, Renate, ed. *Kelusultiek: Original Women's Voices of Atlantic Canada*. Halifax: Institute for the Study of Women, Mount St. Vincent University, 1994.

Vaillant, George. *The Wisdom of the Ego*. Cambridge, MA: Harvard University Press, 1993.

Valaskakis, Gail Guthrie. *Indian Country: Essays on Contemporary Native Culture*. Waterloo: Wilfrid Laurier University Press, 2005.

Van Berkum, Dr. J.J.A. *The psycholinguistics of grammatical gender: Studies in language comprehension and production*. Nijmegen, Netherlands: Nigmegen University Press, 1996.

Van Kirk, Sylvia. *Many Tender Ties: Women in Fur-Trade Society, 1670–1870.* Winnipeg: Watson and Dwyer Publishing Ltd., 1980.

Vanderburg, R.M., and M.E. Southcott. *A Paintbrush in my Hand—Daphne Odjig.* Toronto: Natural Heritage, National History Inc., 1992.

Vecsey, Christopher. *On the Padres Trail. American Indian Catholics.* Volume 1. Indiana: University of Notre Dame Press, 1996.

———. *Imagine Ourselves Richly: Mythic Narratives of North American Indians.* New York: Crossroad/Herder and Herder, 1988.

Verma, R., M. Michalowski, and P.R. Gauvin. "Abridged Life Tables for Registered Indians in Canada, 1976–1980 to 1996–2000." *Canadian Studies in Population* 31, 2 (2004): 197–235.

Vermaeten, Annette, Mary Jane Norris, and Marion Buchmeier. "Educational Outcomes of Students Funded by the Department of Indian and Northern Affairs Canada: Illustration of a Longitudinal Assessment with Potential Application to Policy Research." In Jerry White, Paul Maxim, and Dan Beavon, eds., *Aboriginal Policy Research: Setting the Agenda for Change.* Toronto: Thompson Educational Publishing, 2004.

Voyageur, Cora J. *Firekeepers of the Twenty-First Century.* Montreal: McGill-Queen's University Press, 2008.

Voyageur, Cora J. "The Community Owns You: Experiences of Female Chiefs in Canada." In Andrea Martinez and Meryn Stuart, eds., *Out of the Ivory Tower: Feminist Research for Social Change.* Toronto: Sumach Press, 2003.

———. "Keeping All the Balls in the Air: The Experiences of Canada's Women Chiefs." In Audrey MacNevin et al., eds., *Women and Leadership.* Ottawa: Canadian Institute for the Advancement of Women, 2002.

———. "Contemporary Aboriginal Women in Canada." In David Long and Olive Patricia Dickason, eds., *Visions of the Heart: Canadian Aboriginal Issues.* 2nd ed. Toronto: Harcourt Canada, 2000.

Warren, K.B., ed. *The Violence Within: Cultural and Political Opposition in Divided Nations.* Boulder: Westview Press, 1993.

Watson, K. "Language, education and ethnicity: Whose rights will prevail in an age of globalization?" *International Journal of Educational Development* 27, 3 (2007): 252–265.

Weatherford, Jack. *How The Indians Enriched America.* New York: Fawcett Books, 1991.

———. *Native Roots: How the Indians Enriched America.* New York: Fawcett Columbine, 1991.

———. *Indian Givers: How the Indians of the Americas Transformed the World.* New York: Fawcett Books, 1988.

Welsh, Norbert. *The Last Buffalo Hunter.* New York: Thomas Nelson and Sons, 1939.

Wesley-Esquimaux, Cynthia C., and Magdalena Smolewski. *Historic Trauma and Aboriginal Healing.* Ottawa: Aboriginal Healing Foundation, 2004.

West, Jim. "Aboriginal Women at a Crossroads." *First Nations Drum,* Fall 2002. http://www.firstnationsdrum.com/Fall2002/PolWomen.htm (accessed 5 March 2006).

White, Carol. *Teionkwahontasen: Sweetgrass is Around Us: Basketmakers of Akwesasne.* Hogansburg, NY: Akwesasne Cultural Centre, 1996.

White, G.M. 2000. "Afterword: Lives and Histories." In P.J. Stewart and A. Strathern, eds., *Identity Work: Constructing Pacific Lives.* Pittsburgh: University of Pittsburgh Press, 2000.

Williams, Robert A. "Columbus's Legacy: Law as an Instrument of Racial Discrimination against Indigenous peoples' Right to Self-Determination." *Arizona Journal of International and Comparative Law* 8 (1991).

———. "Gendered Checks and Balances: Understanding the Legacy of White Patriarchy in an American Indian Cultural Context." *Georgia Law Review* 4 (1990).

Willis, Jane. *Geneish: An Indian Girlhood.* Toronto: New Press. 1973.

Wingert, S. "Well-being in First Nations communities: A comparison of objective and subjective dimensions." In J. White, D. Beavon, and N. Spence, eds. *Aboriginal Well-being: Canada's Continuing Challenge.* Toronto: Thompson Educational Publishing, 2007.

Wissler, Clark. *Red Man Reservations.* New York: Collier, New York. 1971. Originally published as *Indian Cavalcade or Life on the Old-Time Indian Reservations* (New York: Sheridan House, 1938).

Wolvengrey, Arok. *Nehiyawewin: itwewina: Cree: words, Vol. 1 and 2.* Regina: Canadian Plains Research Center, 2001.

Woods, Clyde M. *Culture Change.* Dubuque, IA: W.C. Brown Co., 1975.

Wyatt, Gary R. *Mythic Beings—Spirit Art of the Northwest Coast.* Vancouver: Douglas & McIntyre, 1999.

Yellow Horse Brave Heart, Maria. "Oyate Ptayela: Rebuilding the Lakota Nation through Addressing Historical Trauma among Lakota Parents." *Journal of Human Behavior and the Social Environment* 2, 1/2 (1999): 109–126.

Young Man, Alfred. *North American Indian Art: It's a Question of Integrity.* Kamloops, BC: Kamloops Art Gallery, 1998.

Young, Alan. *The Harmony of Illusions: Inventing Post-Traumatic Stress Disorder.* New Jersey: Princeton University Press, 1995.

Young-Ing, Greg, ed. *The Native Creative Process—A Collaborative Discourse between Douglas Cardinal and Jeannette Armstrong, With Photographs by Greg Younging.* Penticton, BC: Theytus Books, 1991.

Zaher, Claudia. "When a Woman's Marital Status Determined Her Legal Status: A Research Guide on the Common Law Doctrine of Coverture." *Law Library Journal* 94, 3 (2002): 460.